Real World OCaml

Yaron Minsky, Anil Madhavapeddy, and Jason Hickey

Beijing · Cambridge · Farnham · Köln · Sebastopol · Tokyo

Real World OCaml

by Yaron Minsky, Anil Madhavapeddy, and Jason Hickey

Printed in the United States of America.

Published by O'Reilly Media, Inc., 1005 Gravenstein Highway North, Sebastopol, CA 95472.

O'Reilly books may be purchased for educational, business, or sales promotional use. Online editions are also available for most titles (*http://my.safaribooksonline.com*). For more information, contact our corporate/institutional sales department: 800-998-9938 or *corporate@oreilly.com*.

Editors: Mike Loukides and Andy Oram	**Indexer:** Judith McConville
Production Editor: Christopher Hearse	**Cover Designer:** Randy Comer
Copyeditor: Amanda Kersey	**Interior Designer:** David Futato
Proofreader: Becca Freed	**Illustrator:** Rebecca Demarest

November 2013:   First Edition

Revision History for the First Edition:

2013-10-31:   First release

See *http://oreilly.com/catalog/errata.csp?isbn=9781449323912* for release details.

Nutshell Handbook, the Nutshell Handbook logo, and the O'Reilly logo are registered trademarks of O'Reilly Media, Inc. *Real World OCaml*, the image of a Bactrian camel, and related trade dress are trademarks of O'Reilly Media, Inc.

Many of the designations used by manufacturers and sellers to distinguish their products are claimed as trademarks. Where those designations appear in this book, and O'Reilly Media, Inc., was aware of a trademark claim, the designations have been printed in caps or initial caps.

While every precaution has been taken in the preparation of this book, the publisher and authors assume no responsibility for errors or omissions, or for damages resulting from the use of the information contained herein.

ISBN: 978-1-449-32391-2

[LSI]

For Lisa, a believer in the power of words, who helps me find mine. —Yaron

For Mum and Dad, who took me to the library and unlocked my imagination. —Anil

For Nobu, who takes me on a new journey every day. —Jason

Table of Contents

Part II. Tools and Techniques

Part III.   The Runtime System

Prologue

Why OCaml?

Programming languages matter. They affect the reliability, security, and efficiency of the code you write, as well as how easy it is to read, refactor, and extend. The languages you know can also change how you think, influencing the way you design software even when you're not using them.

We wrote this book because we believe in the importance of programming languages, and that OCaml in particular is an important language to learn. The three of us have been using OCaml in our academic and professional lives for over 15 years, and in that time we've come to see it as a secret weapon for building complex software systems. This book aims to make this secret weapon available to a wider audience, by providing a clear guide to what you need to know to use OCaml effectively in the real world.

What makes OCaml special is that it occupies a sweet spot in the space of programming language designs. It provides a combination of efficiency, expressiveness and practicality that is matched by no other language. That is in large part because OCaml is an elegant combination of a few key language features that have been developed over the last 40 years. These include:

- *Garbage collection* for automatic memory management, now a feature of almost every modern, high-level language.
- *First-class functions* that can be passed around like ordinary values, as seen in Java-Script, Common Lisp, and C#.
- *Static type-checking* to increase performance and reduce the number of runtime errors, as found in Java and C#.
- *Parametric polymorphism*, which enables the construction of abstractions that work across different data types, similar to generics in Java and C# and templates in C++.

- Good support for *immutable programming*, i.e., programming without making destructive updates to data structures. This is present in traditional functional languages like Scheme, and is also found in distributed, big-data frameworks like Hadoop.

- *Automatic type inference* to avoid having to laboriously define the type of every single variable in a program and instead have them inferred based on how a value is used. Available in a limited form in C# with implicitly typed local variables, and in C++11 with its auto keyword.

- *Algebraic data types* and *pattern matching* to define and manipulate complex data structures. Available in Scala and F#.

Some of you will know and love all of these features, and for others they will be largely new, but most of you will have seen *some* of them in other languages that you've used. As we'll demonstrate over the course of this book, there is something transformative about having them all together and able to interact in a single language. Despite their importance, these ideas have made only limited inroads into mainstream languages, and when they do arrive there, like first-class functions in C# or parametric polymorphism in Java, it's typically in a limited and awkward form. The only languages that completely embody these ideas are *statically typed, functional programming languages* like OCaml, F#, Haskell, Scala, and Standard ML.

Among this worthy set of languages, OCaml stands apart because it manages to provide a great deal of power while remaining highly pragmatic. The compiler has a straightforward compilation strategy that produces performant code without requiring heavy optimization and without the complexities of dynamic just-in-time (JIT) compilation. This, along with OCaml's strict evaluation model, makes runtime behavior easy to predict. The garbage collector is *incremental*, letting you avoid large garbage collection (GC)-related pauses, and *precise*, meaning it will collect all unreferenced data (unlike many reference-counting collectors), and the runtime is simple and highly portable.

All of this makes OCaml a great choice for programmers who want to step up to a better programming language, and at the same time get practical work done.

A Brief History

OCaml was written in 1996 by Xavier Leroy, Jérôme Vouillon, Damien Doligez, and Didier Rémy at INRIA in France. It was inspired by a long line of research into ML starting in the 1960s, and continues to have deep links to the academic community.

ML was originally the *meta language* of the LCF (Logic for Computable Functions) proof assistant released by Robin Milner in 1972 (at Stanford, and later at Cambridge). ML was turned into a compiler in order to make it easier to use LCF on different machines, and it was gradually turned into a full-fledged system of its own by the 1980s.

The first implementation of Caml appeared in 1987. It was created by Ascánder Suárez and later continued by Pierre Weis and Michel Mauny. In 1990, Xavier Leroy and Damien Doligez built a new implementation called Caml Light that was based on a bytecode interpreter with a fast, sequential garbage collector. Over the next few years useful libraries appeared, such as Michel Mauny's syntax manipulation tools, and this helped promote the use of Caml in education and research teams.

Xavier Leroy continued extending Caml Light with new features, which resulted in the 1995 release of Caml Special Light. This improved the executable efficiency significantly by adding a fast native code compiler that made Caml's performance competitive with mainstream languages such as C++. A module system inspired by Standard ML also provided powerful facilities for abstraction and made larger-scale programs easier to construct.

The modern OCaml emerged in 1996, when a powerful and elegant object system was implemented by Didier Rémy and Jérôme Vouillon. This object system was notable for supporting many common object-oriented idioms in a statically type-safe way, whereas the same idioms required runtime checks in languages such as C++ or Java. In 2000, Jacques Garrigue extended OCaml with several new features such as polymorphic methods, variants, and labeled and optional arguments.

The last decade has seen OCaml attract a significant user base, and language improvements have been steadily added to support the growing commercial and academic codebases. First-class modules, Generalized Algebraic Data Types (GADTs), and dynamic linking have improved the flexibility of the language. There is also fast native code support for x86_64, ARM, PowerPC, and Sparc, making OCaml a good choice for systems where resource usage, predictability, and performance all matter.

The Core Standard Library

A language on its own isn't enough. You also need a rich set of libraries to base your applications on. A common source of frustration for those learning OCaml is that the standard library that ships with the compiler is limited, covering only a small subset of the functionality you would expect from a general-purpose standard library. That's because the standard library isn't a general-purpose tool; it was developed for use in bootstrapping the compiler and is purposefully kept small and simple.

Happily, in the world of open source software, nothing stops alternative libraries from being written to supplement the compiler-supplied standard library, and this is exactly what the Core distribution is.

Jane Street, a company that has been using OCaml for more than a decade, developed Core for its own internal use, but designed it from the start with an eye toward being a general-purpose standard library. Like the OCaml language itself, Core is engineered with correctness, reliability, and performance in mind.

Core is distributed with syntax extensions that provide useful new functionality to OCaml, and there are additional libraries such as the Async network communications library that extend the reach of Core into building complex distributed systems. All of these libraries are distributed under a liberal Apache 2 license to permit free use in hobby, academic, and commercial settings.

The OCaml Platform

Core is a comprehensive and effective standard library, but there's much more OCaml software out there. A large community of programmers has been using OCaml since its first release in 1996, and has generated many useful libraries and tools. We'll introduce some of these libraries in the course of the examples presented in the book.

The installation and management of these third-party libraries is made much easier via a package management tool known as OPAM (*http://opam.ocaml.org/*). We'll explain more about OPAM as the book unfolds, but it forms the basis of the Platform, which is a set of tools and libraries that, along with the OCaml compiler, lets you build real-world applications quickly and effectively.

We'll also use OPAM for installing the *utop* command-line interface. This is a modern interactive tool that supports command history, macro expansion, module completion, and other niceties that make it much more pleasant to work with the language. We'll be using *utop* throughout the book to let you step through the examples interactively.

About This Book

Real World OCaml is aimed at programmers who have some experience with conventional programming languages, but not specifically with statically typed functional programming. Depending on your background, many of the concepts we cover will be new, including traditional functional-programming techniques like higher-order functions and immutable data types, as well as aspects of OCaml's powerful type and module systems.

If you already know OCaml, this book may surprise you. Core redefines most of the standard namespace to make better use of the OCaml module system and expose a number of powerful, reusable data structures by default. Older OCaml code will still interoperate with Core, but you may need to adapt it for maximal benefit. All the new code that we write uses Core, and we believe the Core model is worth learning; it's been successfully used on large, multimillion-line codebases and removes a big barrier to building sophisticated applications in OCaml.

Code that uses only the traditional compiler standard library will always exist, but there are other online resources for learning how that works. *Real World OCaml* focuses on the techniques the authors have used in their personal experience to construct scalable, robust software systems.

What to Expect

Real World OCaml is split into three parts:

- Part I covers the language itself, opening with a guided tour designed to provide a quick sketch of the language. Don't expect to understand everything in the tour; it's meant to give you a taste of many different aspects of the language, but the ideas covered there will be explained in more depth in the chapters that follow.

  After covering the core language, Part I then moves onto more advanced features like modules, functors, and objects, which may take some time to digest. Understanding these concepts is important, though. These ideas will put you in good stead even beyond OCaml when switching to other modern languages, many of which have drawn inspiration from ML.

- Part II builds on the basics by working through useful tools and techniques for addressing common practical applications, from command-line parsing to asynchronous network programming. Along the way, you'll see how some of the concepts from Part I are glued together into real libraries and tools that combine different features of the language to good effect.

- Part III discusses OCaml's runtime system and compiler toolchain. It is remarkably simple when compared to some other language implementations (such as Java's or .NET's CLR). Reading this part will enable you to build very-high-performance systems, or to interface with C libraries. This is also where we talk about profiling and debugging techniques using tools such as GNU *gdb*.

Installation Instructions

Real World OCaml uses some tools that we've developed while writing this book. Some of these resulted in improvements to the OCaml compiler, which means that you will need to ensure that you have an up-to-date development environment (using the 4.01 version of the compiler). The installation process is largely automated through the OPAM package manager. Instructions on how to it set up and what packages to install can be found at this Real World OCaml page (*http://realworldocaml.org/install*).

As of publication time, the Windows operating system is unsupported by Core, and so only Mac OS X, Linux, FreeBSD, and OpenBSD can be expected to work reliably. Please check the online installation instructions for updates regarding Windows, or install a Linux virtual machine to work through the book as it stands.

This book is not intended as a reference manual. We aim to teach you about the language and about libraries tools and techniques that will help you be a more effective OCaml programmer. But it's no replacement for API documentation or the OCaml manual and man pages. You can find documentation for all of the libraries and tools referenced in the book online (*https://realworldocaml.org/doc*).

Code Examples

All of the code examples in this book are available freely online under a public-domain-like license. You are most welcome to copy and use any of the snippets as you see fit in your own code, without any attribution or other restrictions on their use.

The code repository is available online at *https://github.com/realworldocaml/examples*. Every code snippet in the book has a clickable header that tells you the filename in that repository to find the source code, shell script, or ancillary data file that the snippet was sourced from.

If you feel your use of code examples falls outside fair use or the permission given above, feel free to contact us at *permissions@oreilly.com*.

Safari® Books Online

 Safari Books Online (*www.safaribooksonline.com*) is an on-demand digital library that delivers expert content in both book and video form from the world's leading authors in technology and business. Technology professionals, software developers, web designers, and business and creative professionals use Safari Books Online as their primary resource for research, problem solving, learning, and certification training.

Safari Books Online offers a range of product mixes and pricing programs for organizations, government agencies, and individuals. Subscribers have access to thousands of books, training videos, and prepublication manuscripts in one fully searchable database from publishers like O'Reilly Media, Prentice Hall Professional, Addison-Wesley Professional, Microsoft Press, Sams, Que, Peachpit Press, Focal Press, Cisco Press, John Wiley & Sons, Syngress, Morgan Kaufmann, IBM Redbooks, Packt, Adobe Press, FT Press, Apress, Manning, New Riders, McGraw-Hill, Jones & Bartlett, Course Technology, and dozens more. For more information about Safari Books Online, please visit us online.

How to Contact Us

Please address comments and questions concerning this book to the publisher:

O'Reilly Media, Inc.
1005 Gravenstein Highway North
Sebastopol, CA 95472
800-998-9938 (in the United States or Canada)
707-829-0515 (international or local)
707-829-0104 (fax)

We have a web page for this book, where we list errata, examples, and any additional information. You can access this page at:

http://oreil.ly/realworldOCaml

To comment or ask technical questions about this book, send email to:

bookquestions@oreilly.com

For more information about our books, courses, conferences, and news, see our website at *http://www.oreilly.com*.

Find us on Facebook: *http://facebook.com/oreilly*

Follow us on Twitter: *http://twitter.com/oreillymedia*

Watch us on YouTube: *http://www.youtube.com/oreillymedia*

Contributors

We would especially like to thank the following individuals for improving *Real World OCaml*:

- Leo White contributed greatly to the content and examples in Chapter 11 and Chapter 12.
- Jeremy Yallop authored and documented the Ctypes library described in Chapter 19.
- Stephen Weeks is responsible for much of the modular architecture behind Core, and his extensive notes formed the basis of Chapter 20 and Chapter 21.
- Jeremie Dimino, the author of *utop*, the interactive command-line interface that is used throughout this book. We're particularly grateful for the changes that he pushed through to make *utop* work better in the context of the book.

- The many people who collectively submitted over 2400 comments to online drafts of this book, through whose efforts countless errors were found and fixed.

Language Concepts

Part I covers the basic language concepts you'll need to know when building OCaml programs. It opens up with a guided tour to give you a quick overview of the language using an interactive command-line interface. The subsequent chapters cover the material that is touched upon by the tour in much more detail, including detailed coverage of OCaml's approach to imperative programming.

The last few chapters introduce OCaml's powerful abstraction facilities. We start by using functors to build a library for programming with intervals, and then use first-class modules to build a type-safe plugin system. OCaml also supports object-oriented programming, and we close Part I with two chapters that cover the object system; the first showing how to use OCaml's objects directly, and the second showing how to use the class system to add more advanced features like inheritance. This description comes together in the design of a simple object-oriented graphics library.

## CHAPTER 1

A Guided Tour

This chapter gives an overview of OCaml by walking through a series of small examples that cover most of the major features of the language. This should provide a sense of what OCaml can do, without getting too deep into any one topic.

Throughout the book we're going to use Core, a more full-featured and capable replacement for OCaml's standard library. We'll also use *utop*, a shell that lets you type in expressions and evaluate them interactively. *utop* is an easier-to-use version of OCaml's standard toplevel (which you can start by typing *ocaml* at the command line). These instructions will assume you're using *utop* specifically.

Before getting started, make sure you have a working OCaml installation so you can try out the examples as you read through the chapter.

OCaml as a Calculator

The first thing you need to do when using Core is to open `Core.Std`:

OCaml utop

```
$ utop
```

```
# open Core.Std;;
```

This makes the definitions in Core available and is required for many of the examples in the tour and in the remainder of the book.

Now let's try a few simple numerical calculations:

OCaml utop (part 1)

```
# 3 + 4;;
- : int = 7
# 8 / 3;;
- : int = 2
# 3.5 +. 6.;;
```

```
- : float = 9.5
# 30_000_000 / 300_000;;
- : int = 100
# sqrt 9.;;
- : float = 3.
```

By and large, this is pretty similar to what you'd find in any programming language, but a few things jump right out at you:

- We needed to type ;; in order to tell the toplevel that it should evaluate an expression. This is a peculiarity of the toplevel that is not required in standalone programs (though it is sometimes helpful to include ;; to improve OCaml's error reporting, by making it more explicit where a given top-level declaration was intended to end).

- After evaluating an expression, the toplevel first prints the type of the result, and then prints the result itself.

- Function arguments are separated by spaces instead of by parentheses and commas, which is more like the UNIX shell than it is like traditional programming languages such as C or Java.

- OCaml allows you to place underscores in the middle of numeric literals to improve readability. Note that underscores can be placed anywhere within a number, not just every three digits.

- OCaml carefully distinguishes between float, the type for floating-point numbers, and int, the type for integers. The types have different literals (6. instead of 6) and different infix operators (+. instead of +), and OCaml doesn't automatically cast between these types. This can be a bit of a nuisance, but it has its benefits, since it prevents some kinds of bugs that arise in other languages due to unexpected differences between the behavior of int and float. For example, in many languages, 1 / 3 is zero, but 1 / 3.0 is a third. OCaml requires you to be explicit about which operation you're doing.

We can also create a variable to name the value of a given expression, using the let keyword. This is known as a *let binding*:

OCaml utop (part 2)

```
# let x = 3 + 4;;
val x : int = 7
# let y = x + x;;
val y : int = 14
```

After a new variable is created, the toplevel tells us the name of the variable (x or y), in addition to its type (int) and value (7 or 14).

Note that there are some constraints on what identifiers can be used for variable names. Punctuation is excluded, except for _ and ', and variables must start with a lowercase letter or an underscore. Thus, these are legal:

```
# let x7 = 3 + 4;;
val x7 : int = 7
# let x_plus_y = x + y;;
val x_plus_y : int = 21
# let x' = x + 1;;
val x' : int = 8
# let _x' = x' + x';;
# _x';;
- : int = 16
```

Note that by default, *utop* doesn't bother to print out variables starting with an underscore.

The following examples, however, are not legal:

```
# let Seven = 3 + 4;;
Characters 4-9:
Error: Unbound constructor Seven
# let 7x = 7;;
Characters 5-10:
Error: This expression should not be a function, the expected type is
int
# let x-plus-y = x + y;;
Characters 4-5:
Error: Parse error: [fun_binding] expected after [ipatt] (in [let_binding])
```

The error messages here are a little confusing, but they'll make more sense as you learn more about the language.

Functions and Type Inference

The let syntax can also be used to define a function:

```
# let square x = x * x ;;
val square : int -> int = <fun>
# square 2;;
- : int = 4
# square (square 2);;
- : int = 16
```

Functions in OCaml are values like any other, which is why we use the let keyword to bind a function to a variable name, just as we use let to bind a simple value like an integer to a variable name. When using let to define a function, the first identifier after the let is the function name, and each subsequent identifier is a different argument to the function. Thus, square is a function with a single argument.

Now that we're creating more interesting values like functions, the types have gotten more interesting too. int -> int is a function type, in this case indicating a function that takes an int and returns an int. We can also write functions that take multiple arguments. (Note that the following example will not work if you haven't opened Core.Std as was suggested earlier.)

OCaml utop (part 6)

```
# let ratio x y =
    Float.of_int x /. Float.of_int y
  ;;
val ratio : int -> int -> float = <fun>
# ratio 4 7;;
- : float = 0.571428571429
```

The preceding example also happens to be our first use of modules. Here, Float.of_int refers to the of_int function contained in the Float module. This is different from what you might expect from an object-oriented language, where dot-notation is typically used for accessing a method of an object. Note that module names always start with a capital letter.

The notation for the type-signature of a multiargument function may be a little surprising at first, but we'll explain where it comes from when we get to function currying in "Multiargument functions" on page 33. For the moment, think of the arrows as separating different arguments of the function, with the type after the final arrow being the return value. Thus, int -> int -> float describes a function that takes two int arguments and returns a float.

We can also write functions that take other functions as arguments. Here's an example of a function that takes three arguments: a test function and two integer arguments. The function returns the sum of the integers that pass the test:

OCaml utop (part 7)

```
# let sum_if_true test first second =
    (if test first then first else 0)
    + (if test second then second else 0)
  ;;
val sum_if_true : (int -> bool) -> int -> int -> int = <fun>
```

If we look at the inferred type signature in detail, we see that the first argument is a function that takes an integer and returns a boolean, and that the remaining two arguments are integers. Here's an example of this function in action:

OCaml utop (part 8)

```
# let even x =
    x mod 2 = 0 ;;
val even : int -> bool = <fun>
# sum_if_true even 3 4;;
- : int = 4
# sum_if_true even 2 4;;
- : int = 6
```

Note that in the definition of even, we used = in two different ways: once as the part of the let binding that separates the thing being defined from its definition; and once as an equality test, when comparing x mod 2 to 0. These are very different operations despite the fact that they share some syntax.

Type Inference

As the types we encounter get more complicated, you might ask yourself how OCaml is able to figure them out, given that we didn't write down any explicit type information.

OCaml determines the type of an expression using a technique called *type inference*, by which the type of an expression is inferred from the available type information about the components of that expression.

As an example, let's walk through the process of inferring the type of sum_if_true:

1. OCaml requires that both branches of an if statement have the same type, so the expression if test first then first else 0 requires that first must be the same type as 0, and so first must be of type int. Similarly, from if test second then second else 0 we can infer that second has type int.

2. test is passed first as an argument. Since first has type int, the input type of test must be int.

3. test first is used as the condition in an if statement, so the return type of test must be bool.

4. The fact that + returns int implies that the return value of sum_if_true must be int.

Together, that nails down the types of all the variables, which determines the overall type of sum_if_true.

Over time, you'll build a rough intuition for how the OCaml inference engine works, which makes it easier to reason through your programs. You can make it easier to understand the types of a given expression by adding explicit type annotations. These annotations don't change the behavior of an OCaml program, but they can serve as useful documentation, as well as catch unintended type changes. They can also be helpful in figuring out why a given piece of code fails to compile.

Here's an annotated version of sum_if_true:

OCaml utop (part 9)

```
# let sum_if_true (test : int -> bool) (x : int) (y : int) : int =
    (if test x then x else 0)
    + (if test y then y else 0)
  ;;
val sum_if_true : (int -> bool) -> int -> int -> int = <fun>
```

In the above, we've marked every argument to the function with its type, with the final annotation indicating the type of the return value. Such type annotations can be placed on any expression in an OCaml program:

Inferring Generic Types

Sometimes, there isn't enough information to fully determine the concrete type of a given value. Consider this function.

OCaml utop (part 10)

```
# let first_if_true test x y =
    if test x then x else y
  ;;
val first_if_true : ('a -> bool) -> 'a -> 'a -> 'a = <fun>
```

first_if_true takes as its arguments a function test, and two values, x and y, where x is to be returned if test x evaluates to true, and y otherwise. So what's the type of first_if_true? There are no obvious clues such as arithmetic operators or literals to tell you what the type of x and y are. That makes it seem like one could use first_if_true on values of any type.

Indeed, if we look at the type returned by the toplevel, we see that rather than choose a single concrete type, OCaml has introduced a *type variable* 'a to express that the type is generic. (You can tell it's a type variable by the leading single quote mark.) In particular, the type of the test argument is ('a -> bool), which means that test is a one-argument function whose return value is bool and whose argument could be of any type 'a. But, whatever type 'a is, it has to be the same as the type of the other two arguments, x and y, and of the return value of first_if_true. This kind of genericity is called *parametric polymorphism* because it works by parameterizing the type in question with a type variable. It is very similar to generics in C# and Java.

The generic type of first_if_true allows us to write this:

OCaml utop (part 11)

```
# let long_string s = String.length s > 6;;
val long_string : string -> bool = <fun>
# first_if_true long_string "short" "loooooong";;
- : string = "loooooong"
```

As well as this:

OCaml utop (part 12)

```
# let big_number x = x > 3;;
val big_number : int -> bool = <fun>
# first_if_true big_number 4 3;;
- : int = 4
```

Both long_string and big_number are functions, and each is passed to first_if_true with two other arguments of the appropriate type (strings in the first example, and integers in the second). But we can't mix and match two different concrete types for 'a in the same use of first_if_true:

OCaml utop (part 13)

```
# first_if_true big_number "short" "loooooong";;
Characters 25-32:
Error: This expression has type string but an expression was expected of type
       int
```

In this example, big_number requires that 'a be instantiated as int, whereas "short" and "loooooong" require that 'a be instantiated as string, and they can't both be right at the same time.

Type Errors Versus Exceptions

There's a big difference in OCaml (and really in any compiled language) between errors that are caught at compile time and those that are caught at runtime. It's better to catch errors as early as possible in the development process, and compilation time is best of all.

Working in the toplevel somewhat obscures the difference between runtime and compile-time errors, but that difference is still there. Generally, type errors like this one:

OCaml utop (part 14)

```
# let add_potato x =
    x + "potato";;
Characters 28-36:
Error: This expression has type string but an expression was expected of type
       int
```

are compile-time errors (because + requires that both its arguments be of type int), whereas errors that can't be caught by the type system, like division by zero, lead to runtime exceptions:

OCaml utop (part 15)

```
# let is_a_multiple x y =
    x mod y = 0 ;;
val is_a_multiple : int -> int -> bool = <fun>
# is_a_multiple 8 2;;
- : bool = true
# is_a_multiple 8 0;;
Exception: Division_by_zero.
```

The distinction here is that type errors will stop you whether or not the offending code is ever actually executed. Merely defining add_potato is an error, whereas is_a_multiple only fails when it's called, and then, only when it's called with an input that triggers the exception.

Tuples, Lists, Options, and Pattern Matching

Tuples

So far we've encountered a handful of basic types like `int`, `float`, and `string`, as well as function types like `string -> int`. But we haven't yet talked about any data structures. We'll start by looking at a particularly simple data structure, the tuple. A tuple is an ordered collection of values that can each be of a different type. You can create a tuple by joining values together with a comma:

OCaml utop (part 16)

```
# let a_tuple = (3,"three");;
val a_tuple : int * string = (3, "three")
# let another_tuple = (3,"four",5.);;
val another_tuple : int * string * float = (3, "four", 5.)
```

(For the mathematically inclined, the `*` character is used because the set of all pairs of type `t * s` corresponds to the Cartesian product of the set of elements of type `t` and the set of elements of type `s`.)

You can extract the components of a tuple using OCaml's pattern-matching syntax, as shown below:

OCaml utop (part 17)

```
# let (x,y) = a_tuple;;
val x : int = 3
val y : string = "three"
```

Here, the `(x,y)` on the lefthand side of the `let` binding is the pattern. This pattern lets us mint the new variables `x` and `y`, each bound to different components of the value being matched. These can now be used in subsequent expressions:

OCaml utop (part 18)

```
# x + String.length y;;
- : int = 8
```

Note that the same syntax is used both for constructing and for pattern matching on tuples.

Pattern matching can also show up in function arguments. Here's a function for computing the distance between two points on the plane, where each point is represented as a pair of `float`s. The pattern-matching syntax lets us get at the values we need with a minimum of fuss:

OCaml utop (part 19)

```
# let distance (x1,y1) (x2,y2) =
    sqrt ((x1 -. x2) ** 2. +. (y1 -. y2) ** 2.)
  ;;
val distance : float * float -> float * float -> float = <fun>
```

The `**` operator used above is for raising a floating-point number to a power.

This is just a first taste of pattern matching. Pattern matching is a pervasive tool in OCaml, and as you'll see, it has surprising power.

Lists

Where tuples let you combine a fixed number of items, potentially of different types, lists let you hold any number of items of the same type. Consider the following example:

OCaml utop (part 20)

```
# let languages = ["OCaml";"Perl";"C"];;
val languages : string list = ["OCaml"; "Perl"; "C"]
```

Note that you can't mix elements of different types in the same list, unlike tuples:

OCaml utop (part 21)

```
# let numbers = [3;"four";5];;
Characters 17-23:
Error: This expression has type string but an expression was expected of type
        int
```

The List module

Core comes with a List module that has a rich collection of functions for working with lists. We can access values from within a module by using dot notation. For example, this is how we compute the length of a list:

OCaml utop (part 22)

```
# List.length languages;;
- : int = 3
```

Here's something a little more complicated. We can compute the list of the lengths of each language as follows:

OCaml utop (part 23)

```
# List.map languages ~f:String.length;;
- : int list = [5; 4; 1]
```

List.map takes two arguments: a list and a function for transforming the elements of that list. It returns a new list with the transformed elements and does not modify the original list.

Notably, the function passed to List.map is passed under a *labeled argument* ~f. Labeled arguments are specified by name rather than by position, and thus allow you to change the order in which arguments are presented to a function without changing its behavior, as you can see here:

OCaml utop (part 24)

```
# List.map ~f:String.length languages;;
- : int list = [5; 4; 1]
```

We'll learn more about labeled arguments and why they're important in Chapter 2.

Constructing lists with ::

In addition to constructing lists using brackets, we can use the operator :: for adding elements to the front of a list:

OCaml utop (part 25)

```
# "French" :: "Spanish" :: languages;;
- : string list = ["French"; "Spanish"; "OCaml"; "Perl"; "C"]
```

Here, we're creating a new and extended list, not changing the list we started with, as you can see below:

OCaml utop (part 26)

```
# languages;;
- : string list = ["OCaml"; "Perl"; "C"]
```

Semicolons Versus Commas

Unlike many other languages, OCaml uses semicolons to separate list elements in lists rather than commas. Commas, instead, are used for separating elements in a tuple. If you try to use commas in a list, you'll see that your code compiles but doesn't do quite what you might expect:

OCaml utop (part 27)

```
# ["OCaml", "Perl", "C"];;
- : (string * string * string) list = [("OCaml", "Perl", "C")]
```

In particular, rather than a list of three strings, what we have is a singleton list containing a three-tuple of strings.

This example uncovers the fact that commas create a tuple, even if there are no surrounding parens. So, we can write:

OCaml utop (part 28)

```
# 1,2,3;;
- : int * int * int = (1, 2, 3)
```

to allocate a tuple of integers. This is generally considered poor style and should be avoided.

The bracket notation for lists is really just syntactic sugar for ::. Thus, the following declarations are all equivalent. Note that [] is used to represent the empty list and that :: is right-associative:

OCaml utop (part 29)

```
# [1; 2; 3];;
- : int list = [1; 2; 3]
# 1 :: (2 :: (3 :: []));;
- : int list = [1; 2; 3]
# 1 :: 2 :: 3 :: [];;
- : int list = [1; 2; 3]
```

The :: operator can only be used for adding one element to the front of the list, with the list terminating at [], the empty list. There's also a list concatenation operator, @, which can concatenate two lists:

OCaml utop (part 30)

```
# [1;2;3] @ [4;5;6];;
- : int list = [1; 2; 3; 4; 5; 6]
```

It's important to remember that, unlike ::, this is not a constant-time operation. Concatenating two lists takes time proportional to the length of the first list.

List patterns using match

The elements of a list can be accessed through pattern matching. List patterns are based on the two list constructors, [] and ::. Here's a simple example:

OCaml utop (part 31)

```
# let my_favorite_language (my_favorite :: the_rest) =
    my_favorite
  ;;
Characters 25-69:
Warning 8: this pattern-matching is not exhaustive.
Here is an example of a value that is not matched:
[]
val my_favorite_language : 'a list -> 'a = <fun>
```

By pattern matching using ::, we've isolated and named the first element of the list (my_favorite) and the remainder of the list (the_rest). If you know Lisp or Scheme, what we've done is the equivalent of using the functions car and cdr to isolate the first element of a list and the remainder of that list.

As you can see, however, the toplevel did not like this definition and spit out a warning indicating that the pattern is not exhaustive. This means that there are values of the type in question that won't be captured by the pattern. The warning even gives an example of a value that doesn't match the provided pattern, in particular, [], the empty list. If we try to run my_favorite_language, we'll see that it works on nonempty list and fails on empty ones:

OCaml utop (part 32)

```
# my_favorite_language ["English";"Spanish";"French"];;
- : string = "English"
# my_favorite_language [];;
Exception: (Match_failure //toplevel// 0 25).
```

You can avoid these warnings, and more importantly make sure that your code actually handles all of the possible cases, by using a match statement instead.

A match statement is a kind of juiced-up version of the switch statement found in C and Java. It essentially lets you list a sequence of patterns, separated by pipe characters (|). (The one before the first case is optional.) The compiler then dispatches to the code following the first matching pattern. As we've already seen, the pattern can mint new variables that correspond to substructures of the value being matched.

Here's a new version of my_favorite_language that uses match and doesn't trigger a compiler warning:

OCaml utop (part 33)

```
# let my_favorite_language languages =
    match languages with
    | first :: the_rest -> first
    | [] -> "OCaml" (* A good default! *)
  ;;
val my_favorite_language : string list -> string = <fun>
# my_favorite_language ["English";"Spanish";"French"];;
- : string = "English"
# my_favorite_language [];;
- : string = "OCaml"
```

The preceding code also includes our first comment. OCaml comments are bounded by (* and *) and can be nested arbitrarily and cover multiple lines. There's no equivalent of C++-style single-line comments that are prefixed by //.

The first pattern, first :: the_rest, covers the case where languages has at least one element, since every list except for the empty list can be written down with one or more ::'s. The second pattern, [], matches only the empty list. These cases are exhaustive, since every list is either empty or has at least one element, a fact that is verified by the compiler.

Recursive list functions

Recursive functions, or functions that call themselves, are an important technique in OCaml and in any functional language. The typical approach to designing a recursive function is to separate the logic into a set of *base cases* that can be solved directly and a set of *inductive cases*, where the function breaks the problem down into smaller pieces and then calls itself to solve those smaller problems.

When writing recursive list functions, this separation between the base cases and the inductive cases is often done using pattern matching. Here's a simple example of a function that sums the elements of a list:

OCaml utop (part 34)

```
# let rec sum l =
    match l with
    | [] -> 0                 (* base case *)
    | hd :: tl -> hd + sum tl  (* inductive case *)
  ;;
val sum : int list -> int = <fun>
# sum [1;2;3];;
- : int = 6
```

Following the common OCaml idiom, we use `hd` to refer to the head of the list and `tl` to refer to the tail. Note that we had to use the `rec` keyword to allow `sum` to refer to itself. As you might imagine, the base case and inductive case are different arms of the match.

Logically, you can think of the evaluation of a simple recursive function like `sum` almost as if it were a mathematical equation whose meaning you were unfolding step by step:

OCaml: guided-tour/recursion.ml

```
sum [1;2;3]
= 1 + sum [2;3]
= 1 + (2 + sum [3])
= 1 + (2 + (3 + sum []))
= 1 + (2 + (3 + 0))
= 1 + (2 + 3)
= 1 + 5
= 6
```

This suggests a reasonable mental model for what OCaml is actually doing to evaluate a recursive function.

We can introduce more complicated list patterns as well. Here's a function for removing sequential duplicates:

OCaml utop (part 35)

```
# let rec destutter list =
    match list with
    | [] -> []
    | hd1 :: hd2 :: tl ->
      if hd1 = hd2 then destutter (hd2 :: tl)
      else hd1 :: destutter (hd2 :: tl)
  ;;
Characters 29-171:
Warning 8: this pattern-matching is not exhaustive.
Here is an example of a value that is not matched:
_::[]
val destutter : 'a list -> 'a list = <fun>
```

Again, the first arm of the match is the base case, and the second is the inductive. Unfortunately, this code has a problem, as is indicated by the warning message. In particular, we don't handle one-element lists. We can fix this warning by adding another case to the match:

OCaml utop (part 36)

```
# let rec destutter list =
    match list with
    | [] -> []
    | [hd] -> [hd]
    | hd1 :: hd2 :: tl ->
      if hd1 = hd2 then destutter (hd2 :: tl)
      else hd1 :: destutter (hd2 :: tl)
  ;;
val destutter : 'a list -> 'a list = <fun>
```

```
# destutter ["hey";"hey";"hey";"man!"];;
- : string list = ["hey"; "man!"]
```

Note that this code used another variant of the list pattern, [hd], to match a list with a single element. We can do this to match a list with any fixed number of elements; for example, [x;y;z] will match any list with exactly three elements and will bind those elements to the variables x, y, and z.

In the last few examples, our list processing code involved a lot of recursive functions. In practice, this isn't usually necessary. Most of the time, you'll find yourself happy to use the iteration functions found in the List module. But it's good to know how to use recursion when you need to do something new.

Options

Another common data structure in OCaml is the option. An option is used to express that a value might or might not be present. For example:

OCaml utop (part 37)

```
# let divide x y =
    if y = 0 then None else Some (x/y) ;;
val divide : int -> int -> int option = <fun>
```

The function divide either returns None if the divisor is zero, or Some of the result of the division otherwise. Some and None are constructors that let you build optional values, just as :: and [] let you build lists. You can think of an option as a specialized list that can only have zero or one elements.

To examine the contents of an option, we use pattern matching, as we did with tuples and lists. Consider the following function for creating a log entry string given an optional time and a message. If no time is provided (i.e., if the time is None), the current time is computed and used in its place:

OCaml utop (part 38)

```
# let log_entry maybe_time message =
    let time =
      match maybe_time with
      | Some x -> x
      | None -> Time.now ()
    in
    Time.to_sec_string time ^ " -- " ^ message
  ;;
val log_entry : Time.t option -> string -> string = <fun>
# log_entry (Some Time.epoch) "A long long time ago";;
- : string = "1970-01-01 01:00:00 -- A long long time ago"
# log_entry None "Up to the minute";;
- : string = "2013-08-18 14:48:08 -- Up to the minute"
```

This example uses Core's `Time` module for dealing with time, as well as the ^ operator for concatenating strings. The concatenation operator is provided as part of the `Perva` `sives` module, which is automatically opened in every OCaml program.

Nesting lets with let and in

`log_entry` was our first use of `let` to define a new variable within the body of a function. A `let` paired with an `in` can be used to introduce a new binding within any local scope, including a function body. The `in` marks the beginning of the scope within which the new variable can be used. Thus, we could write:

OCaml utop

```
# let x = 7 in
  x + x
  ;;
- : int = 14
```

Note that the scope of the `let` binding is terminated by the double-semicolon, so the value of x is no longer available:

OCaml utop (part 1)

```
# x;;
Characters -1-1:
Error: Unbound value x
```

We can also have multiple `let` statements in a row, each one adding a new variable binding to what came before:

OCaml utop (part 2)

```
# let x = 7 in
  let y = x * x in
  x + y
  ;;
- : int = 56
```

This kind of nested `let` binding is a common way of building up a complex expression, with each `let` naming some component, before combining them in one final expression.

Options are important because they are the standard way in OCaml to encode a value that might not be there; there's no such thing as a `NullPointerException` in OCaml. This is different from most other languages, including Java and C#, where most if not all data types are *nullable*, meaning that, whatever their type is, any given value also contains the possibility of being a null value. In such languages, null is lurking everywhere.

In OCaml, however, missing values are explicit. A value of type `string * string` always contains two well-defined values of type `string`. If you want to allow, say, the first of those to be absent, then you need to change the type to `string option * string`. As we'll see in Chapter 7, this explicitness allows the compiler to provide a great deal of help in making sure you're correctly handling the possibility of missing data.

Records and Variants

So far, we've only looked at data structures that were predefined in the language, like lists and tuples. But OCaml also allows us to define new data types. Here's a toy example of a data type representing a point in two-dimensional space:

OCaml utop (part 41)

```
# type point2d = { x : float; y : float };;
type point2d = { x : float; y : float; }
```

point2d is a *record* type, which you can think of as a tuple where the individual fields are named, rather than being defined positionally. Record types are easy enough to construct:

OCaml utop (part 42)

```
# let p = { x = 3.; y = -4. };;
val p : point2d = {x = 3.; y = -4.}
```

And we can get access to the contents of these types using pattern matching:

OCaml utop (part 43)

```
# let magnitude { x = x_pos; y = y_pos } =
    sqrt (x_pos ** 2. +. y_pos ** 2.);;
val magnitude : point2d -> float = <fun>
```

The pattern match here binds the variable x_pos to the value contained in the x field, and the variable y_pos to the value in the y field.

We can write this more tersely using what's called *field punning*. In particular, when the name of the field and the name of the variable it is bound to coincide, we don't have to write them both down. Using this, our magnitude function can be rewritten as follows:

OCaml utop (part 44)

```
# let magnitude { x; y } = sqrt (x ** 2. +. y ** 2.);;
val magnitude : point2d -> float = <fun>
```

Alternatively, we can use dot notation for accessing record fields:

OCaml utop (part 45)

```
# let distance v1 v2 =
    magnitude { x = v1.x -. v2.x; y = v1.y -. v2.y };;
val distance : point2d -> point2d -> float = <fun>
```

And we can of course include our newly defined types as components in larger types. Here, for example, are some types for modeling different geometric objects that contain values of type point2d:

```
# type circle_desc  = { center: point2d; radius: float }
  type rect_desc    = { lower_left: point2d; width: float; height: float }
  type segment_desc = { endpoint1: point2d; endpoint2: point2d } ;;
type circle_desc = { center : point2d; radius : float; }
type rect_desc = { lower_left : point2d; width : float; height : float; }
type segment_desc = { endpoint1 : point2d; endpoint2 : point2d; }
```

Now, imagine that you want to combine multiple objects of these types together as a description of a multiobject scene. You need some unified way of representing these objects together in a single type. One way of doing this is using a *variant* type:

```
# type scene_element =
    | Circle  of circle_desc
    | Rect    of rect_desc
    | Segment of segment_desc
  ;;
type scene_element =
    Circle of circle_desc
  | Rect of rect_desc
  | Segment of segment_desc
```

The | character separates the different cases of the variant (the first | is optional), and each case has a capitalized tag, like Circle, Rect or Segment, to distinguish that case from the others.

Here's how we might write a function for testing whether a point is in the interior of some element of a list of scene_elements:

```
# let is_inside_scene_element point scene_element =
    match scene_element with
    | Circle { center; radius } ->
      distance center point < radius
    | Rect { lower_left; width; height } ->
      point.x    > lower_left.x && point.x < lower_left.x +. width
      && point.y > lower_left.y && point.y < lower_left.y +. height
    | Segment { endpoint1; endpoint2 } -> false
  ;;
val is_inside_scene_element : point2d -> scene_element -> bool = <fun>
# let is_inside_scene point scene =
    List.exists scene
      ~f:(fun el -> is_inside_scene_element point el)
  ;;
val is_inside_scene : point2d -> scene_element list -> bool = <fun>
# is_inside_scene {x=3.;y=7.}
    [ Circle {center = {x=4.;y= 4.}; radius = 0.5 } ];;
- : bool = false
# is_inside_scene {x=3.;y=7.}
    [ Circle {center = {x=4.;y= 4.}; radius = 5.0 } ];;
- : bool = true
```

You might at this point notice that the use of match here is reminiscent of how we used match with option and list. This is no accident: option and list are really just examples of variant types that happen to be important enough to be defined in the standard library (and in the case of lists, to have some special syntax).

We also made our first use of an *anonymous function* in the call to List.exists. Anonymous functions are declared using the fun keyword, and don't need to be explicitly named. Such functions are common in OCaml, particularly when using iteration functions like List.exists.

The purpose of List.exists is to check if there are any elements of the list in question on which the provided function evaluates to true. In this case, we're using List.exists to check if there is a scene element within which our point resides.

Imperative Programming

The code we've written so far has been almost entirely *pure* or *functional*, which roughly speaking means that the code in question doesn't modify variables or values as part of its execution. Indeed, almost all of the data structures we've encountered are *immutable*, meaning there's no way in the language to modify them at all. This is a quite different style from *imperative* programming, where computations are structured as sequences of instructions that operate by making modifications to the state of the program.

Functional code is the default in OCaml, with variable bindings and most data structures being immutable. But OCaml also has excellent support for imperative programming, including mutable data structures like arrays and hash tables, and control-flow constructs like for and while loops.

Arrays

Perhaps the simplest mutable data structure in OCaml is the array. Arrays in OCaml are very similar to arrays in other languages like C: indexing starts at 0, and accessing or modifying an array element is a constant-time operation. Arrays are more compact in terms of memory utilization than most other data structures in OCaml, including lists. Here's an example:

OCaml utop (part 49)

```
# let numbers = [| 1; 2; 3; 4 |];;
val numbers : int array = [|1; 2; 3; 4|]
# numbers.(2) <- 4;;
- : unit = ()
# numbers;;
- : int array = [|1; 2; 4; 4|]
```

The .(i) syntax is used to refer to an element of an array, and the <- syntax is for modification. Because the elements of the array are counted starting at zero, element .(2) is the third element.

The `unit` type that we see in the preceding code is interesting in that it has only one possible value, written `()`. This means that a value of type `unit` doesn't convey any information, and so is generally used as a placeholder. Thus, we use `unit` for the return value of an operation like setting a mutable field that communicates by side effect rather than by returning a value. It's also used as the argument to functions that don't require an input value. This is similar to the role that `void` plays in languages like C and Java.

Mutable Record Fields

The array is an important mutable data structure, but it's not the only one. Records, which are immutable by default, can have some of their fields explicitly declared as mutable. Here's a small example of a data structure for storing a running statistical summary of a collection of numbers.

OCaml utop (part 50)

```
# type running_sum =
  { mutable sum: float;
    mutable sum_sq: float; (* sum of squares *)
    mutable samples: int;
  }
;;
type running_sum = {
  mutable sum : float;
  mutable sum_sq : float;
  mutable samples : int;
}
```

The fields in `running_sum` are designed to be easy to extend incrementally, and sufficient to compute means and standard deviations, as shown in the following example. Note that there are two `let` bindings in a row without a double semicolon between them. That's because the double semicolon is required only to tell *utop* to process the input, not to separate two declarations:

OCaml utop (part 51)

```
# let mean rsum = rsum.sum /. float rsum.samples
  let stdev rsum =
    sqrt (rsum.sum_sq /. float rsum.samples
          -. (rsum.sum /. float rsum.samples) ** 2.) ;;
val mean : running_sum -> float = <fun>
val stdev : running_sum -> float = <fun>
```

We use the function `float` above, which is a convenient equivalent of `Float.of_int` provided by the `Pervasives` library.

We also need functions to create and update `running_sum`s:

OCaml utop (part 52)

```
# let create () = { sum = 0.; sum_sq = 0.; samples = 0 }
  let update rsum x =
    rsum.samples <- rsum.samples + 1;
```

```
      rsum.sum     <- rsum.sum     +. x;
      rsum.sum_sq  <- rsum.sum_sq  +. x *. x
  ;;
val create : unit -> running_sum = <fun>
val update : running_sum -> float -> unit = <fun>
```

create returns a running_sum corresponding to the empty set, and update rsum x changes rsum to reflect the addition of x to its set of samples by updating the number of samples, the sum, and the sum of squares.

Note the use of single semicolons to sequence operations. When we were working purely functionally, this wasn't necessary, but you start needing it when you're writing imperative code.

Here's an example of create and update in action. Note that this code uses List.iter, which calls the function ~f on each element of the provided list:

OCaml utop (part 53)

```
# let rsum = create ();;
val rsum : running_sum = {sum = 0.; sum_sq = 0.; samples = 0}
# List.iter [1.;3.;2.;-7.;4.;5.] ~f:(fun x -> update rsum x);;
- : unit = ()
# mean rsum;;
- : float = 1.33333333333
# stdev rsum;;
- : float = 3.94405318873
```

It's worth noting that the preceding algorithm is numerically naive and has poor precision in the presence of cancellation. You can look at this Wikipedia article on algorithms for calculating variance (*http://en.wikipedia.org/wiki/Algorithms_for_calculating_variance*) for more details, paying particular attention to the weighted incremental and parallel algorithms.

Refs

We can create a single mutable value by using a ref. The ref type comes predefined in the standard library, but there's nothing really special about it. It's just a record type with a single mutable field called contents:

OCaml utop (part 54)

```
# let x = { contents = 0 };;
val x : int ref = {contents = 0}
# x.contents <- x.contents + 1;;
- : unit = ()
# x;;
- : int ref = {contents = 1}
```

There are a handful of useful functions and operators defined for refs to make them more convenient to work with:

```
# let x = ref 0   (* create a ref, i.e., { contents = 0 } *) ;;
val x : int ref = {contents = 0}
# !x                (* get the contents of a ref, i.e., x.contents *) ;;
- : int = 0
# x := !x + 1      (* assignment, i.e., x.contents <- ... *) ;;
- : unit = ()
# !x ;;
- : int = 1
```

There's nothing magical with these operators either. You can completely reimplement the ref type and all of these operators in just a few lines of code:

```
# type 'a ref = { mutable contents : 'a }

  let ref x = { contents = x }
  let (!) r = r.contents
  let (:=) r x = r.contents <- x
  ;;
type 'a ref = { mutable contents : 'a; }
val ref : 'a -> 'a ref = <fun>
val ( ! ) : 'a ref -> 'a = <fun>
val ( := ) : 'a ref -> 'a -> unit = <fun>
```

The 'a before the ref indicates that the ref type is polymorphic, in the same way that lists are polymorphic, meaning it can contain values of any type. The parentheses around ! and := are needed because these are operators, rather than ordinary functions.

Even though a ref is just another record type, it's important because it is the standard way of simulating the traditional mutable variables you'll find in most languages. For example, we can sum over the elements of a list imperatively by calling List.iter to call a simple function on every element of a list, using a ref to accumulate the results:

```
# let sum list =
    let sum = ref 0 in
    List.iter list ~f:(fun x -> sum := !sum + x);
    !sum
  ;;
val sum : int list -> int = <fun>
```

This isn't the most idiomatic way to sum up a list, but it shows how you can use a ref in place of a mutable variable.

For and While Loops

OCaml also supports traditional imperative control-flow constructs like for and while loops. Here, for example, is some code for permuting an array that uses a for loop. We use the Random module as our source of randomness. Random starts with a default seed, but you can call Random.self_init to choose a new seed at random:

```
# let permute array =
    let length = Array.length array in
    for i = 0 to length - 2 do
      (* pick a j to swap with *)
      let j = i + Random.int (length - i) in
      (* Swap i and j *)
      let tmp = array.(i) in
      array.(i) <- array.(j);
      array.(j) <- tmp
    done
  ;;
val permute : 'a array -> unit = <fun>
```

From a syntactic perspective, you should note the keywords that distinguish a for loop: for, to, do, and done.

Here's an example run of this code:

```
# let ar = Array.init 20 ~f:(fun i -> i);;
val ar : int array =
  [|0; 1; 2; 3; 4; 5; 6; 7; 8; 9; 10; 11; 12; 13; 14; 15; 16; 17; 18; 19|]
# permute ar;;
- : unit = ()
# ar;;
- : int array =
[|1; 2; 4; 6; 11; 7; 14; 9; 10; 0; 13; 16; 19; 12; 17; 5; 3; 18; 8; 15|]
```

OCaml also supports while loops, as shown in the following function for finding the position of the first negative entry in an array. Note that while (like for) is also a keyword:

```
# let find_first_negative_entry array =
    let pos = ref 0 in
    while !pos < Array.length array && array.(!pos) >= 0 do
      pos := !pos + 1
    done;
    if !pos = Array.length array then None else Some !pos
  ;;
val find_first_negative_entry : int array -> int option = <fun>
# find_first_negative_entry [|1;2;0;3|];;
- : int option = None
# find_first_negative_entry [|1;-2;0;3|];;
- : int option = Some 1
```

As a side note, the preceding code takes advantage of the fact that &&, OCaml's And operator, short-circuits. In particular, in an expression of the form *expr1* && *expr2*, *expr2* will only be evaluated if *expr1* evaluated to true. Were it not for that, then the preceding function would result in an out-of-bounds error. Indeed, we can trigger that out-of-bounds error by rewriting the function to avoid the short-circuiting:

```
# let find_first_negative_entry array =
    let pos = ref 0 in
    while
      let pos_is_good = !pos < Array.length array in
      let element_is_non_negative = array.(!pos) >= 0 in
      pos_is_good && element_is_non_negative
    do
      pos := !pos + 1
    done;
    if !pos = Array.length array then None else Some !pos
  ;;
val find_first_negative_entry : int array -> int option = <fun>
# find_first_negative_entry [|1;2;0;3|];;
Exception: (Invalid_argument "index out of bounds").
```

The Or operator, ||, short-circuits in a similar way to &&.

A Complete Program

So far, we've played with the basic features of the language via *utop*. Now we'll show how to create a simple standalone program. In particular, we'll create a program that sums up a list of numbers read in from the standard input.

Here's the code, which you can save in a file called *sum.ml*. Note that we don't terminate expressions with ;; here, since it's not required outside the toplevel:

```
open Core.Std

let rec read_and_accumulate accum =
  let line = In_channel.input_line In_channel.stdin in
  match line with
  | None -> accum
  | Some x -> read_and_accumulate (accum +. Float.of_string x)

let () =
  printf "Total: %F\n" (read_and_accumulate 0.)
```

This is our first use of OCaml's input and output routines. The function read_and_ac cumulate is a recursive function that uses In_channel.input_line to read in lines one by one from the standard input, invoking itself at each iteration with its updated accumulated sum. Note that input_line returns an optional value, with None indicating the end of the input stream.

After read_and_accumulate returns, the total needs to be printed. This is done using the printf command, which provides support for type-safe format strings, similar to what you'll find in a variety of languages. The format string is parsed by the compiler and used to determine the number and type of the remaining arguments that are required. In this case, there is a single formatting directive, %F, so `printf` expects one additional argument of type `float`.

Compiling and Running

We'll compile our program using *corebuild*, a small wrapper on top of *ocamlbuild*, a build tool that ships with the OCaml compiler. The *corebuild* script is installed along with Core, and its purpose is to pass in the flags required for building a program with Core.

Terminal

```
$ corebuild sum.native
```

The `.native` suffix indicates that we're building a native-code executable, which we'll discuss more in Chapter 4. Once the build completes, we can use the resulting program like any command-line utility. We can feed input to `sum.native` by typing in a sequence of numbers, one per line, hitting **Ctrl-D** when we're done:

Terminal

```
$ ./sum.native
1
2
3
94.5
Total: 100.5
```

More work is needed to make a really usable command-line program, including a proper command-line parsing interface and better error handling, all of which is covered in Chapter 14.

Where to Go from Here

That's it for the guided tour! There are plenty of features left and lots of details to explain, but we hope that you now have a sense of what to expect from OCaml, and that you'll be more comfortable reading the rest of the book as a result.

## CHAPTER 2

Variables and Functions

Variables and functions are fundamental ideas that show up in virtually all programming languages. OCaml has a different take on these concepts than most languages you're likely to have encountered, so this chapter will cover OCaml's approach to variables and functions in some detail, starting with the basics of how to define a variable, and ending with the intricacies of functions with labeled and optional arguments.

Don't be discouraged if you find yourself overwhelmed by some of the details, especially toward the end of the chapter. The concepts here are important, but if they don't connect for you on your first read, you should return to this chapter after you've gotten a better sense for the rest of the language.

Variables

At its simplest, a variable is an identifier whose meaning is bound to a particular value. In OCaml these bindings are often introduced using the `let` keyword. We can type a so-called *top-level* `let` binding with the following syntax. Note that variable names must start with a lowercase letter or an underscore:

Syntax

```
let <variable> = <expr>
```

As we'll see when we get to the module system in Chapter 4, this same syntax is used for `let` bindings at the top level of a module.

Every variable binding has a *scope*, which is the portion of the code that can refer to that binding. When using *utop*, the scope of a top-level `let` binding is everything that follows it in the session. When it shows up in a module, the scope is the remainder of that module.

Here's a simple example:

```
# let x = 3;;
val x : int = 3
# let y = 4;;
val y : int = 4
# let z = x + y;;
val z : int = 7
```

let can also be used to create a variable binding whose scope is limited to a particular expression, using the following syntax:

```
let <variable> = <expr1> in <expr2>
```

This first evaluates *expr1* and then evaluates *expr2* with *variable* bound to whatever value was produced by the evaluation of *expr1*. Here's how it looks in practice:

```
# let languages = "OCaml,Perl,C++,C";;
val languages : string = "OCaml,Perl,C++,C"
# let dashed_languages =
    let language_list = String.split languages ~on:',' in
    String.concat ~sep:"-" language_list
  ;;
val dashed_languages : string = "OCaml-Perl-C++-C"
```

Note that the scope of language_list is just the expression String.concat ~sep:"-" language_list and is not available at the toplevel, as we can see if we try to access it now:

```
# language_list;;
Characters -1-13:
Error: Unbound value language_list
```

A let binding in an inner scope can *shadow*, or hide, the definition from an outer scope. So, for example, we could have written the dashed_languages example as follows:

```
# let languages = "OCaml,Perl,C++,C";;
val languages : string = "OCaml,Perl,C++,C"
# let dashed_languages =
    let languages = String.split languages ~on:',' in
    String.concat ~sep:"-" languages
  ;;
val dashed_languages : string = "OCaml-Perl-C++-C"
```

This time, in the inner scope we called the list of strings languages instead of language_list, thus hiding the original definition of languages. But once the definition of dashed_languages is complete, the inner scope has closed and the original definition of languages reappears:

```
# languages;;
- : string = "OCaml,Perl,C++,C"
```

One common idiom is to use a series of nested let/in expressions to build up the components of a larger computation. Thus, we might write:

```
# let area_of_ring inner_radius outer_radius =
    let pi = acos (-1.) in
    let area_of_circle r = pi *. r *. r in
    area_of_circle outer_radius -. area_of_circle inner_radius
  ;;
val area_of_ring : float -> float -> float = <fun>
# area_of_ring 1. 3.;;
- : float = 25.1327412287
```

It's important not to confuse a sequence of let bindings with the modification of a mutable variable. For example, consider how area_of_ring would work if we had instead written this purposefully confusing bit of code:

```
# let area_of_ring inner_radius outer_radius =
    let pi = acos (-1.) in
    let area_of_circle r = pi *. r *. r in
    let pi = 0. in
    area_of_circle outer_radius -. area_of_circle inner_radius
  ;;
Characters 126-128:
Warning 26: unused variable pi.
val area_of_ring : float -> float -> float = <fun>
```

Here, we redefined pi to be zero after the definition of area_of_circle. You might think that this would mean that the result of the computation would now be zero, but in fact, the behavior of the function is unchanged. That's because the original definition of pi wasn't changed; it was just shadowed, which means that any subsequent reference to pi would see the new definition of pi as 0, but earlier references would be unchanged. But there is no later use of pi, so the binding of pi to 0. made no difference. This explains the warning produced by the toplevel telling us that there is an unused definition of pi.

In OCaml, let bindings are immutable. There are many kinds of mutable values in OCaml, which we'll discuss in Chapter 8, but there are no mutable variables.

Why Don't Variables Vary?

One source of confusion for people new to OCaml is the fact that variables are immutable. This seems pretty surprising even on linguistic terms. Isn't the whole point of a variable that it can vary?

The answer to this is that variables in OCaml (and generally in functional languages) are really more like variables in an equation than a variable in an imperative language. If you think about the mathematical identity $x(y + z) = xy + xz$, there's no notion of mutating the variables x, y, and z. They vary in the sense that you can instantiate this equation with different numbers for those variables, and it still holds.

The same is true in a functional language. A function can be applied to different inputs, and thus its variables will take on different values, even without mutation.

Pattern Matching and let

Another useful feature of `let` bindings is that they support the use of *patterns* on the lefthand side. Consider the following code, which uses `List.unzip`, a function for converting a list of pairs into a pair of lists:

OCaml utop (part 7)

```
# let (ints,strings) = List.unzip [(1,"one"); (2,"two"); (3,"three")];;
val ints : int list = [1; 2; 3]
val strings : string list = ["one"; "two"; "three"]
```

Here, `(ints,strings)` is a pattern, and the `let` binding assigns values to both of the identifiers that show up in that pattern. A pattern is essentially a description of the shape of a data structure, where some components are identifiers to be bound. As we saw in "Tuples, Lists, Options, and Pattern Matching" on page 10, OCaml has patterns for a variety of different data types.

Using a pattern in a `let` binding makes the most sense for a pattern that is *irrefutable*, *i.e.*, where any value of the type in question is guaranteed to match the pattern. Tuple and record patterns are irrefutable, but list patterns are not. Consider the following code that implements a function for upper casing the first element of a comma-separated list:

OCaml utop (part 8)

```
# let upcase_first_entry line =
    let (first :: rest) = String.split ~on:',' line in
    String.concat ~sep:"," (String.uppercase first :: rest)
  ;;
Characters 40-53:
Warning 8: this pattern-matching is not exhaustive.
Here is an example of a value that is not matched:
[]
val upcase_first_entry : string -> string = <fun>
```

This case can't really come up in practice, because `String.split` always returns a list with at least one element. But the compiler doesn't know this, and so it emits the warning. It's generally better to use a `match` statement to handle such cases explicitly:

OCaml utop (part 9)

```
# let upcase_first_entry line =
    match String.split ~on:',' line with
    | [] -> assert false (* String.split returns at least one element *)
    | first :: rest -> String.concat ~sep:"," (String.uppercase first :: rest)
  ;;
val upcase_first_entry : string -> string = <fun>
```

Note that this is our first use of `assert`, which is useful for marking cases that should be impossible. We'll discuss `assert` in more detail in Chapter 7.

Functions

Given that OCaml is a functional language, it's no surprise that functions are important and pervasive. Indeed, functions have come up in almost every example we've done so far. This section will go into more depth, explaining the details of how OCaml's functions work. As you'll see, functions in OCaml differ in a variety of ways from what you'll find in most mainstream languages.

Anonymous Functions

We'll start by looking at the most basic style of function declaration in OCaml: the *anonymous function*. An anonymous function is a function that is declared without being named. These can be declared using the `fun` keyword, as shown here:

OCaml utop (part 10)

```
# (fun x -> x + 1);;
- : int -> int = <fun>
```

Anonymous functions operate in much the same way as named functions. For example, we can apply an anonymous function to an argument:

OCaml utop (part 11)

```
# (fun x -> x + 1) 7;;
- : int = 8
```

Or pass it to another function. Passing functions to iteration functions like `List.map` is probably the most common use case for anonymous functions:

OCaml utop (part 12)

```
# List.map ~f:(fun x -> x + 1) [1;2;3];;
- : int list = [2; 3; 4]
```

You can even stuff them into a data structure:

```
# let increments = [ (fun x -> x + 1); (fun x -> x + 2) ] ;;
val increments : (int -> int) list = [<fun>; <fun>]
# List.map ~f:(fun g -> g 5) increments;;
- : int list = [6; 7]
```

It's worth stopping for a moment to puzzle this example out, since this kind of higher-order use of functions can be a bit obscure at first. Notice that `(fun g -> g 5)` is a function that takes a function as an argument, and then applies that function to the number 5. The invocation of `List.map` applies `(fun g -> g 5)` to the elements of the `increments` list (which are themselves functions) and returns the list containing the results of these function applications.

The key thing to understand is that functions are ordinary values in OCaml, and you can do everything with them that you'd do with an ordinary value, including passing them to and returning them from other functions and storing them in data structures. We even name functions in the same way that we name other values, by using a `let` binding:

```
# let plusone = (fun x -> x + 1);;
val plusone : int -> int = <fun>
# plusone 3;;
- : int = 4
```

Defining named functions is so common that there is some syntactic sugar for it. Thus, the following definition of `plusone` is equivalent to the previous definition:

```
# let plusone x = x + 1;;
val plusone : int -> int = <fun>
```

This is the most common and convenient way to declare a function, but syntactic niceties aside, the two styles of function definition are equivalent.

let and fun

Functions and `let` bindings have a lot to do with each other. In some sense, you can think of the parameter of a function as a variable being bound to the value passed by the caller. Indeed, the following two expressions are nearly equivalent:

```
# (fun x -> x + 1) 7;;
- : int = 8
# let x = 7 in x + 1;;
- : int = 8
```

This connection is important, and will come up more when programming in a monadic style, as we'll see in Chapter 18.

Multiargument functions

OCaml of course also supports multiargument functions, such as:

OCaml utop (part 17)

```
# let abs_diff x y = abs (x - y);;
val abs_diff : int -> int -> int = <fun>
# abs_diff 3 4;;
- : int = 1
```

You may find the type signature of abs_diff with all of its arrows a little hard to parse. To understand what's going on, let's rewrite abs_diff in an equivalent form, using the fun keyword:

OCaml utop (part 18)

```
# let abs_diff =
    (fun x -> (fun y -> abs (x - y)));;
val abs_diff : int -> int -> int = <fun>
```

This rewrite makes it explicit that abs_diff is actually a function of one argument that returns another function of one argument, which itself returns the final result. Because the functions are nested, the inner expression abs (x - y) has access to both x, which was bound by the outer function application, and y, which was bound by the inner one.

This style of function is called a *curried* function. (Currying is named after Haskell Curry, a logician who had a significant impact on the design and theory of programming languages.) The key to interpreting the type signature of a curried function is the observation that -> is right-associative. The type signature of abs_diff can therefore be parenthesized as follows:

OCaml: variables-and-functions/abs_diff.mli

```
val abs_diff : int -> (int -> int)
```

The parentheses don't change the meaning of the signature, but they make it easier to see the currying.

Currying is more than just a theoretical curiosity. You can make use of currying to specialize a function by feeding in some of the arguments. Here's an example where we create a specialized version of abs_diff that measures the distance of a given number from 3:

OCaml utop (part 19)

```
# let dist_from_3 = abs_diff 3;;
val dist_from_3 : int -> int = <fun>
# dist_from_3 8;;
- : int = 5
# dist_from_3 (-1);;
- : int = 4
```

The practice of applying some of the arguments of a curried function to get a new function is called *partial application*.

Note that the fun keyword supports its own syntax for currying, so the following definition of `abs_diff` is equivalent to the previous one.

OCaml utop (part 20)

```
# let abs_diff = (fun x y -> abs (x - y));;
val abs_diff : int -> int -> int = <fun>
```

You might worry that curried functions are terribly expensive, but this is not the case. In OCaml, there is no penalty for calling a curried function with all of its arguments. (Partial application, unsurprisingly, does have a small extra cost.)

Currying is not the only way of writing a multiargument function in OCaml. It's also possible to use the different parts of a tuple as different arguments. So, we could write:

OCaml utop (part 21)

```
# let abs_diff (x,y) = abs (x - y);;
val abs_diff : int * int -> int = <fun>
# abs_diff (3,4);;
- : int = 1
```

OCaml handles this calling convention efficiently as well. In particular it does not generally have to allocate a tuple just for the purpose of sending arguments to a tuple-style function. You can't, however, use partial application for this style of function.

There are small trade-offs between these two approaches, but most of the time, one should stick to currying, since it's the default style in the OCaml world.

Recursive Functions

A function is *recursive* if it refers to itself in its definition. Recursion is important in any programming language, but is particularly important in functional languages, because it is the way that you build looping constructs. (As will be discussed in more detail in Chapter 8, OCaml also supports imperative looping constructs like for and while, but these are only useful when using OCaml's imperative features.)

In order to define a recursive function, you need to mark the let binding as recursive with the rec keyword, as shown in this function for finding the first sequentially repeated element in a list:

OCaml utop (part 22)

```
# let rec find_first_stutter list =
    match list with
    | [] | [_] ->
      (* only zero or one elements, so no repeats *)
      None
    | x :: y :: tl ->
      if x = y then Some x else find_first_stutter (y::tl)
  ;;
val find_first_stutter : 'a list -> 'a option = <fun>
```

Note that in the code, the pattern | [] | [_] is what's called an *or-pattern*, which is a disjunction of two patterns, meaning that it will be considered a match if either pattern matches. In this case, [] matches the empty list, and [_] matches any single element list. The _ is there so we don't have to put an explicit name on that single element.

We can also define multiple mutually recursive values by using let rec combined with the and keyword. Here's a (gratuitously inefficient) example:

```
# let rec is_even x =
    if x = 0 then true else is_odd (x - 1)
  and is_odd x =
    if x = 0 then false else is_even (x - 1)
 ;;
val is_even : int -> bool = <fun>
val is_odd : int -> bool = <fun>
# List.map ~f:is_even [0;1;2;3;4;5];;
- : bool list = [true; false; true; false; true; false]
# List.map ~f:is_odd [0;1;2;3;4;5];;
- : bool list = [false; true; false; true; false; true]
```

OCaml distinguishes between nonrecursive definitions (using let) and recursive definitions (using let rec) largely for technical reasons: the type-inference algorithm needs to know when a set of function definitions are mutually recursive, and for reasons that don't apply to a pure language like Haskell, these have to be marked explicitly by the programmer.

But this decision has some good effects. For one thing, recursive (and especially mutually recursive) definitions are harder to reason about than nonrecursive ones. It's therefore useful that, in the absence of an explicit rec, you can assume that a let binding is nonrecursive, and so can only build upon previous bindings.

In addition, having a nonrecursive form makes it easier to create a new definition that extends and supersedes an existing one by shadowing it.

Prefix and Infix Operators

So far, we've seen examples of functions used in both prefix and infix style:

```
# Int.max 3 4  (* prefix *);;
- : int = 4
# 3 + 4        (* infix  *);;
- : int = 7
```

You might not have thought of the second example as an ordinary function, but it very much is. Infix operators like + really only differ syntactically from other functions. In fact, if we put parentheses around an infix operator, you can use it as an ordinary prefix function:

```
# (+) 3 4;;
- : int = 7
# List.map ~f:((+) 3) [4;5;6];;
- : int list = [7; 8; 9]
```

In the second expression, we've partially applied (+) to create a function that increments its single argument by 3.

A function is treated syntactically as an operator if the name of that function is chosen from one of a specialized set of identifiers. This set includes identifiers that are sequences of characters from the following set:

```
! $ % & * + - . / : < = > ? @ ^ | ~
```

or is one of a handful of predetermined strings, including mod, the modulus operator, and lsl, for "logical shift left," a bit-shifting operation.

We can define (or redefine) the meaning of an operator. Here's an example of a simple vector-addition operator on int pairs:

```
# let (+!) (x1,y1) (x2,y2) = (x1 + x2, y1 + y2);;
val ( +! ) : int * int -> int * int -> int * int = <fun>
# (3,2) +! (-2,4);;
- : int * int = (1, 6)
```

Note that you have to be careful when dealing with operators containing *. Consider the following example:

```
# let (***) x y = (x ** y) ** y;;
Characters 17-18:
Error: This expression has type int but an expression was expected of type
            float
```

What's going on is that (***) isn't interpreted as an operator at all; it's read as a comment! To get this to work properly, we need to put spaces around any operator that begins or ends with *:

```
# let ( *** ) x y = (x ** y) ** y;;
val ( *** ) : float -> float -> float = <fun>
```

The syntactic role of an operator is typically determined by its first character or two, though there are a few exceptions. Table 2-1 breaks the different operators and other syntactic forms into groups from highest to lowest precedence, explaining how each behaves syntactically. We write !... to indicate the class of operators beginning with !.

Table 2-1. Precedence and associativity

Operator prefix	Associativity
! ..., ? ..., ~ ...	Prefix
. , . (, . [	-
function application, constructor, `assert`, `lazy`	Left associative
- , - .	Prefix
** ..., `lsl`, `lsr`, `asr`	Right associative
* ..., / ..., % ..., `mod`, `land`, `lor`, `lxor`	Left associative
+ ..., - ...	Left associative
: :	Right associative
@ ..., ^ ...	Right associative
= ..., < ..., > ..., | ..., & ..., $ ...	Left associative
& , &&	Right associative
`or`, | |	Right associative
,	-
<- , :=	Right associative
`if`	-
;	Right associative

There's one important special case: - and - ., which are the integer and floating-point subtraction operators, and can act as both prefix operators (for negation) and infix operators (for subtraction). So, both -x and x - y are meaningful expressions. Another thing to remember about negation is that it has lower precedence than function application, which means that if you want to pass a negative value, you need to wrap it in parentheses, as you can see in this code:

OCaml utop (part 29)

```
# Int.max 3 (-4);;
- : int = 3
# Int.max 3 -4;;
Characters -1-9:
Error: This expression has type int -> int
       but an expression was expected of type int
```

Here, OCaml is interpreting the second expression as equivalent to:

OCaml utop (part 30)

```
# (Int.max 3) - 4;;
Characters 1-10:
Error: This expression has type int -> int
       but an expression was expected of type int
```

which obviously doesn't make sense.

Here's an example of a very useful operator from the standard library whose behavior depends critically on the precedence rules described previously:

OCaml utop (part 31)

```
# let (|>) x f = f x ;;
val ( |> ) : 'a -> ('a -> 'b) -> 'b = <fun>
```

It's not quite obvious at first what the purpose of this operator is: it just takes a value and a function and applies the function to the value. Despite that bland-sounding description, it has the useful role of a sequencing operator, similar in spirit to using the pipe character in the UNIX shell. Consider, for example, the following code for printing out the unique elements of your PATH. Note that List.dedup that follows removes duplicates from a list by sorting the list using the provided comparison function:

OCaml utop (part 32)

```
# let path = "/usr/bin:/usr/local/bin:/bin:/sbin";;
val path : string = "/usr/bin:/usr/local/bin:/bin:/sbin"
# String.split ~on:':' path
  |> List.dedup ~compare:String.compare
  |> List.iter ~f:print_endline
  ;;
/bin
/sbin
/usr/bin
/usr/local/bin
- : unit = ()
```

Note that we can do this without |>, but the result is a bit more verbose:

OCaml utop (part 33)

```
# let split_path = String.split ~on:':' path in
  let deduped_path = List.dedup ~compare:String.compare split_path in
  List.iter ~f:print_endline deduped_path
  ;;
/bin
/sbin
/usr/bin
/usr/local/bin
- : unit = ()
```

An important part of what's happening here is partial application. For example, List.iter normally takes two arguments: a function to be called on each element of the list, and the list to iterate over. We can call List.iter with all its arguments:

OCaml utop (part 34)

```
# List.iter ~f:print_endline ["Two"; "lines"];;
Two
lines
- : unit = ()
```

Or, we can pass it just the function argument, leaving us with a function for printing out a list of strings:

```
# List.iter ~f:print_endline;;
- : string list -> unit = <fun>
```

It is this later form that we're using in the preceding |> pipeline.

But |> only works in the intended way because it is left-associative. Let's see what happens if we try using a right-associative operator, like (^>):

```
# let (^>) x f = f x;;
val ( ^> ) : 'a -> ('a -> 'b) -> 'b = <fun>
# Sys.getenv_exn "PATH"
  ^> String.split ~on:':' path
  ^> List.dedup ~compare:String.compare
  ^> List.iter ~f:print_endline
  ;;
Characters 98-124:
Error: This expression has type string list -> unit
       but an expression was expected of type
         (string list -> string list) -> 'a
       Type string list is not compatible with type
         string list -> string list
```

The type error is a little bewildering at first glance. What's going on is that, because ^> is right associative, the operator is trying to feed the value List.dedup ~compare:String.compare to the function List.iter ~f:print_endline. But List.iter ~f:print_endline expects a list of strings as its input, not a function.

The type error aside, this example highlights the importance of choosing the operator you use with care, particularly with respect to associativity.

Declaring Functions with Function

Another way to define a function is using the function keyword. Instead of having syntactic support for declaring multiargument (curried) functions, function has built-in pattern matching. Here's an example:

```
# let some_or_zero = function
    | Some x -> x
    | None -> 0
  ;;
val some_or_zero : int option -> int = <fun>
# List.map ~f:some_or_zero [Some 3; None; Some 4];;
- : int list = [3; 0; 4]
```

This is equivalent to combining an ordinary function definition with a match:

```
# let some_or_zero num_opt =
    match num_opt with
```

```
    | Some x -> x
    | None -> 0
  ;;
val some_or_zero : int option -> int = <fun>
```

We can also combine the different styles of function declaration together, as in the following example, where we declare a two-argument (curried) function with a pattern match on the second argument:

OCaml utop (part 39)

```
# let some_or_default default = function
    | Some x -> x
    | None -> default
  ;;
val some_or_default : 'a -> 'a option -> 'a = <fun>
# some_or_default 3 (Some 5);;
- : int = 5
# List.map ~f:(some_or_default 100) [Some 3; None; Some 4];;
- : int list = [3; 100; 4]
```

Also, note the use of partial application to generate the function passed to List.map. In other words, some_or_default 100 is a function that was created by feeding just the first argument to some_or_default.

Labeled Arguments

Up until now, the functions we've defined have specified their arguments positionally, *i.e.*, by the order in which the arguments are passed to the function. OCaml also supports labeled arguments, which let you identify a function argument by name. Indeed, we've already encountered functions from Core like List.map that use labeled arguments. Labeled arguments are marked by a leading tilde, and a label (followed by a colon) is put in front of the variable to be labeled. Here's an example:

OCaml utop (part 40)

```
# let ratio ~num ~denom = float num /. float denom;;
val ratio : num:int -> denom:int -> float = <fun>
```

We can then provide a labeled argument using a similar convention. As you can see, the arguments can be provided in any order:

OCaml utop (part 41)

```
# ratio ~num:3 ~denom:10;;
- : float = 0.3
# ratio ~denom:10 ~num:3;;
- : float = 0.3
```

OCaml also supports *label punning*, meaning that you get to drop the text after the : if the name of the label and the name of the variable being used are the same. We were actually already using label punning when defining ratio. The following shows how punning can be used when invoking a function:

```
# let num = 3 in
  let denom = 4 in
  ratio ~num ~denom;;
- : float = 0.75
```

Labeled arguments are useful in a few different cases:

- When defining a function with lots of arguments. Beyond a certain number, arguments are easier to remember by name than by position.

- When the meaning of a particular argument is unclear from the type alone. Consider a function for creating a hash table whose first argument is the initial size of the array backing the hash table, and the second is a Boolean flag, which indicates whether that array will ever shrink when elements are removed:

  OCaml
  ```
  val create_hashtable : int -> bool -> ('a,'b) Hashtable.t
  ```

  The signature makes it hard to divine the meaning of those two arguments. but with labeled arguments, we can make the intent immediately clear:

  OCaml
  ```
  val create_hashtable :
    init_size:int -> allow_shrinking:bool -> ('a,'b) Hashtable.t
  ```

  Choosing label names well is especially important for Boolean values, since it's often easy to get confused about whether a value being true is meant to enable or disable a given feature.

- When defining functions that have multiple arguments that might get confused with each other. This is most at issue when the arguments are of the same type. For example, consider this signature for a function that extracts a substring:

  OCaml
  ```
  val substring: string -> int -> int -> string
  ```

  Here, the two `int`s are the starting position and length of the substring to extract, respectively. We can make this fact more obvious from the signature by adding labeled:

  OCaml
  ```
  val substring: string -> pos:int -> len:int -> string
  ```

  This improves the readability of both the signature and of client code that makes use of `substring` and makes it harder to accidentally swap the position and the length.

- When you want flexibility on the order in which arguments are passed. Consider a function like `List.iter`, which takes two arguments: a function and a list of elements to call that function on. A common pattern is to partially apply `List.iter` by giving it just the function, as in the following example from earlier in the chapter:

```
# String.split ~on:':' path
  |> List.dedup ~compare:String.compare
  |> List.iter ~f:print_endline
  ;;
/bin
/sbin
/usr/bin
/usr/local/bin
- : unit = ()
```

This requires that we put the function argument first. In other cases, you want to put the function argument second. One common reason is readability. In particular, a multiline function passed as an argument to another function is easiest to read when it is the final argument to that function.

Higher-order functions and labels

One surprising gotcha with labeled arguments is that while order doesn't matter when calling a function with labeled arguments, it does matter in a higher-order context, *e.g.*, when passing a function with labeled arguments to another function. Here's an example:

```
# let apply_to_tuple f (first,second) = f ~first ~second;;
val apply_to_tuple : (first:'a -> second:'b -> 'c) -> 'a * 'b -> 'c = <fun>
```

Here, the definition of `apply_to_tuple` sets up the expectation that its first argument is a function with two labeled arguments, `first` and `second`, listed in that order. We could have defined `apply_to_tuple` differently to change the order in which the labeled arguments were listed:

```
# let apply_to_tuple_2 f (first,second) = f ~second ~first;;
val apply_to_tuple_2 : (second:'a -> first:'b -> 'c) -> 'b * 'a -> 'c = <fun>
```

It turns out this order matters. In particular, if we define a function that has a different order

```
# let divide ~first ~second = first / second;;
val divide : first:int -> second:int -> int = <fun>
```

we'll find that it can't be passed in to `apply_to_tuple_2`.

```
# apply_to_tuple_2 divide (3,4);;
Characters 17-23:
Error: This expression has type first:int -> second:int -> int
       but an expression was expected of type second:'a -> first:'b -> 'c
```

But, it works smoothly with the original `apply_to_tuple`:

```
# let apply_to_tuple f (first,second) = f ~first ~second;;
val apply_to_tuple : (first:'a -> second:'b -> 'c) -> 'a * 'b -> 'c = <fun>
# apply_to_tuple divide (3,4);;
- : int = 0
```

As a result, when passing labeled functions as arguments, you need to take care to be consistent in your ordering of labeled arguments.

Optional Arguments

An optional argument is like a labeled argument that the caller can choose whether or not to provide. Optional arguments are passed in using the same syntax as labeled arguments, and, like labeled arguments, can be provided in any order.

Here's an example of a string concatenation function with an optional separator. This function uses the ^ operator for pairwise string concatenation:

```
# let concat ?sep x y =
    let sep = match sep with None -> "" | Some x -> x in
    x ^ sep ^ y
  ;;
val concat : ?sep:string -> string -> string -> string = <fun>
# concat "foo" "bar"              (* without the optional argument *);;
- : string = "foobar"
# concat ~sep:":" "foo" "bar"     (* with the optional argument    *);;
- : string = "foo:bar"
```

Here, ? is used in the definition of the function to mark sep as optional. And while the caller can pass a value of type string for sep, internally to the function, sep is seen as a string option, with None appearing when sep is not provided by the caller.

The preceding example needed a bit of boilerplate to choose a default separator when none was provided. This is a common enough pattern that there's an explicit syntax for providing a default value, which allows us to write concat more concisely:

```
# let concat ?(sep="") x y = x ^ sep ^ y ;;
val concat : ?sep:string -> string -> string -> string = <fun>
```

Optional arguments are very useful, but they're also easy to abuse. The key advantage of optional arguments is that they let you write functions with multiple arguments that users can ignore most of the time, only worrying about them when they specifically want to invoke those options. They also allow you to extend an API with new functionality without changing existing code.

The downside is that the caller may be unaware that there is a choice to be made, and so may unknowingly (and wrongly) pick the default behavior. Optional arguments really only make sense when the extra concision of omitting the argument outweighs the corresponding loss of explicitness.

This means that rarely used functions should not have optional arguments. A good rule of thumb is to avoid optional arguments for functions internal to a module, *i.e.*, functions that are not included in the module's interface, or `mli` file. We'll learn more about `mli`s in Chapter 4.

Explicit passing of an optional argument

Under the covers, a function with an optional argument receives `None` when the caller doesn't provide the argument, and `Some` when it does. But the `Some` and `None` are normally not explicitly passed in by the caller.

But sometimes, passing in `Some` or `None` explicitly is exactly what you want. OCaml lets you do this by using ? instead of ~ to mark the argument. Thus, the following two lines are equivalent ways of specifying the `sep` argument to `concat`:

OCaml utop (part 51)

```
# concat ~sep:":" "foo" "bar" (* provide the optional argument *);;
- : string = "foo:bar"
# concat ?sep:(Some ":") "foo" "bar" (* pass an explicit [Some] *);;
- : string = "foo:bar"
```

And the following two lines are equivalent ways of calling `concat` without specifying `sep`:

OCaml utop (part 52)

```
# concat "foo" "bar" (* don't provide the optional argument *);;
- : string = "foobar"
# concat ?sep:None "foo" "bar" (* explicitly pass `None` *);;
- : string = "foobar"
```

One use case for this is when you want to define a wrapper function that mimics the optional arguments of the function it's wrapping. For example, imagine we wanted to create a function called `uppercase_concat`, which is the same as `concat` except that it converts the first string that it's passed to uppercase. We could write the function as follows:

OCaml utop (part 53)

```
# let uppercase_concat ?(sep="") a b = concat ~sep (String.uppercase a) b ;;
val uppercase_concat : ?sep:string -> string -> string -> string = <fun>
# uppercase_concat "foo" "bar";;
- : string = "FOObar"
# uppercase_concat "foo" "bar" ~sep:":";;
- : string = "FOO:bar"
```

In the way we've written it, we've been forced to separately make the decision as to what the default separator is. Thus, if we later change `concat`'s default behavior, we'll need to remember to change `uppercase_concat` to match it.

Instead, we can have `uppercase_concat` simply pass through the optional argument to concat using the ? syntax:

OCaml utop (part 54)

```
# let uppercase_concat ?sep a b = concat ?sep (String.uppercase a) b ;;
val uppercase_concat : ?sep:string -> string -> string -> string = <fun>
```

Now, if someone calls `uppercase_concat` without an argument, an explicit None will be passed to concat, leaving concat to decide what the default behavior should be.

Inference of labeled and optional arguments

One subtle aspect of labeled and optional arguments is how they are inferred by the type system. Consider the following example for computing numerical derivatives of a function of two real variables. The function takes an argument `delta`, which determines the scale at which to compute the derivative; values x and y, which determine at which point to compute the derivative; and the function f, whose derivative is being computed. The function f itself takes two labeled arguments, x and y. Note that you can use an apostrophe as part of a variable name, so x' and y' are just ordinary variables:

OCaml utop (part 55)

```
# let numeric_deriv ~delta ~x ~y ~f =
    let x' = x +. delta in
    let y' = y +. delta in
    let base = f ~x ~y in
    let dx = (f ~x:x' ~y -. base) /. delta in
    let dy = (f ~x ~y:y' -. base) /. delta in
    (dx,dy)
  ;;
val numeric_deriv :
  delta:float ->
  x:float -> y:float -> f:(x:float -> y:float -> float) -> float * float =
  <fun>
```

In principle, it's not obvious how the order of the arguments to f should be chosen. Since labeled arguments can be passed in arbitrary order, it seems like it could as well be `y:float -> x:float -> float` as it is `x:float -> y:float -> float`.

Even worse, it would be perfectly consistent for f to take an optional argument instead of a labeled one, which could lead to this type signature for `numeric_deriv`:

OCaml

```
val numeric_deriv :
  delta:float ->
  x:float -> y:float -> f:(?x:float -> y:float -> float) -> float * float
```

Since there are multiple plausible types to choose from, OCaml needs some heuristic for choosing between them. The heuristic the compiler uses is to prefer labels to options and to choose the order of arguments that shows up in the source code.

Note that these heuristics might at different points in the source suggest different types. Here's a version of `numeric_deriv` where different invocations of f list the arguments in different orders:

OCaml utop (part 56)

```
# let numeric_deriv ~delta ~x ~y ~f =
    let x' = x +. delta in
    let y' = y +. delta in
    let base = f ~x ~y in
    let dx = (f ~y ~x:x' -. base) /. delta in
    let dy = (f ~x ~y:y' -. base) /. delta in
    (dx,dy)
  ;;
Characters 130-131:
Error: This function is applied to arguments
in an order different from other calls.
This is only allowed when the real type is known.
```

As suggested by the error message, we can get OCaml to accept the fact that f is used with different argument orders if we provide explicit type information. Thus, the following code compiles without error, due to the type annotation on f:

OCaml utop (part 57)

```
# let numeric_deriv ~delta ~x ~y ~(f: x:float -> y:float -> float) =
    let x' = x +. delta in
    let y' = y +. delta in
    let base = f ~x ~y in
    let dx = (f ~y ~x:x' -. base) /. delta in
    let dy = (f ~x ~y:y' -. base) /. delta in
    (dx,dy)
  ;;
val numeric_deriv :
  delta:float ->
  x:float -> y:float -> f:(x:float -> y:float -> float) -> float * float =
  <fun>
```

Optional arguments and partial application

Optional arguments can be tricky to think about in the presence of partial application. We can of course partially apply the optional argument itself:

OCaml utop (part 58)

```
# let colon_concat = concat ~sep:":";;
val colon_concat : string -> string -> string = <fun>
# colon_concat "a" "b";;
- : string = "a:b"
```

But what happens if we partially apply just the first argument?

OCaml utop (part 59)

```
# let prepend_pound = concat "# ";;
val prepend_pound : string -> string = <fun>
# prepend_pound "a BASH comment";;
- : string = "# a BASH comment"
```

The optional argument `?sep` has now disappeared, or been *erased*. Indeed, if we try to pass in that optional argument now, it will be rejected:

OCaml utop (part 60)

```
# prepend_pound "a BASH comment" ~sep:":";;
Characters -1-13:
Error: This function has type string -> string
       It is applied to too many arguments; maybe you forgot a `;'.
```

So when does OCaml decide to erase an optional argument?

The rule is: an optional argument is erased as soon as the first positional (i.e., neither labeled nor optional) argument defined *after* the optional argument is passed in. That explains the behavior of `prepend_pound`. But if we had instead defined `concat` with the optional argument in the second position:

OCaml utop (part 61)

```
# let concat x ?(sep="") y = x ^ sep ^ y ;;
val concat : string -> ?sep:string -> string -> string = <fun>
```

then application of the first argument would not cause the optional argument to be erased.

OCaml utop (part 62)

```
# let prepend_pound = concat "# ";;
val prepend_pound : ?sep:string -> string -> string = <fun>
# prepend_pound "a BASH comment";;
- : string = "# a BASH comment"
# prepend_pound "a BASH comment" ~sep:"--- ";;
- : string = "# --- a BASH comment"
```

However, if all arguments to a function are presented at once, then erasure of optional arguments isn't applied until all of the arguments are passed in. This preserves our ability to pass in optional arguments anywhere on the argument list. Thus, we can write:

OCaml utop (part 63)

```
# concat "a" "b" ~sep:"=";;
- : string = "a=b"
```

An optional argument that doesn't have any following positional arguments can't be erased at all, which leads to a compiler warning:

OCaml utop (part 64)

```
# let concat x y ?(sep="") = x ^ sep ^ y ;;
Characters 15-38:
Warning 16: this optional argument cannot be erased.
val concat : string -> string -> ?sep:string -> string = <fun>
```

And indeed, when we provide the two positional arguments, the `sep` argument is not erased, instead returning a function that expects the `sep` argument to be provided:

OCaml utop (part 65)

```
# concat "a" "b";;
- : ?sep:string -> string = <fun>
```

As you can see, OCaml's support for labeled and optional arguments is not without its complexities. But don't let these complexities obscure the usefulness of these features. Labels and optional arguments are very effective tools for making your APIs both more convenient and safer, and it's worth the effort of learning how to use them effectively.

Lists and Patterns

This chapter will focus on two common elements of programming in OCaml: lists and pattern matching. Both of these were discussed in Chapter 1, but we'll go into more depth here, presenting the two topics together and using one to help illustrate the other.

List Basics

An OCaml list is an immutable, finite sequence of elements of the same type. As we've seen, OCaml lists can be generated using a bracket-and-semicolon notation:

OCaml utop

```
# [1;2;3];;
- : int list = [1; 2; 3]
```

And they can also be generated using the equivalent :: notation:

OCaml utop (part 1)

```
# 1 :: (2 :: (3 :: [])) ;;
- : int list = [1; 2; 3]
# 1 :: 2 :: 3 :: [] ;;
- : int list = [1; 2; 3]
```

As you can see, the :: operator is right-associative, which means that we can build up lists without parentheses. The empty list [] is used to terminate a list. Note that the empty list is polymorphic, meaning it can be used with elements of any type, as you can see here:

OCaml utop (part 2)

```
# let empty = [];;
val empty : 'a list = []
# 3 :: empty;;
- : int list = [3]
# "three" :: empty;;
- : string list = ["three"]
```

The way in which the :: operator attaches elements to the front of a list reflects the fact that OCaml's lists are in fact singly linked lists. The figure below is a rough graphical representation of how the list 1 :: 2 :: 3 :: [] is laid out as a data structure. The final arrow (from the box containing 3) points to the empty list.

Diagram

Each :: essentially adds a new block to the proceding picture. Such a block contains two things: a reference to the data in that list element, and a reference to the remainder of the list. This is why :: can extend a list without modifying it; extension allocates a new list element but change any of the existing ones, as you can see:

OCaml utop (part 3)

```
# let l = 1 :: 2 :: 3 :: [];;
val l : int list = [1; 2; 3]
# let m = 0 :: l;;
val m : int list = [0; 1; 2; 3]
# l;;
- : int list = [1; 2; 3]
```

Using Patterns to Extract Data from a List

We can read data out of a list using a match statement. Here's a simple example of a recursive function that computes the sum of all elements of a list:

OCaml utop (part 4)

```
# let rec sum l =
    match l with
    | [] -> 0
    | hd :: tl -> hd + sum tl
  ;;
val sum : int list -> int = <fun>
# sum [1;2;3];;
- : int = 6
# sum [];;
- : int = 0
```

This code follows the convention of using hd to represent the first element (or head) of the list, and tl to represent the remainder (or tail).

The match statement in sum is really doing two things: first, it's acting as a case-analysis tool, breaking down the possibilities into a pattern-indexed list of cases. Second, it lets you name substructures within the data structure being matched. In this case, the variables hd and tl are bound by the pattern that defines the second case of the match statement. Variables that are bound in this way can be used in the expression to the right of the arrow for the pattern in question.

The fact that `match` statements can be used to bind new variables can be a source of confusion. To see how, imagine we wanted to write a function that filtered out from a list all elements equal to a particular value. You might be tempted to write that code as follows, but when you do, the compiler will immediately warn you that something is wrong:

OCaml utop (part 5)

```
# let rec drop_value l to_drop =
    match l with
    | [] -> []
    | to_drop :: tl -> drop_value tl to_drop
    | hd :: tl -> hd :: drop_value tl to_drop
  ;;
Characters 114-122:
Warning 11: this match case is unused.
val drop_value : 'a list -> 'a -> 'a list = <fun>
```

Moreover, the function clearly does the wrong thing, filtering out all elements of the list rather than just those equal to the provided value, as you can see here:

OCaml utop (part 6)

```
# drop_value [1;2;3] 2;;
- : int list = []
```

So, what's going on?

The key observation is that the appearance of `to_drop` in the second case doesn't imply a check that the first element is equal to the value `to_drop` passed in as an argument to `drop_value`. Instead, it just causes a new variable `to_drop` to be bound to whatever happens to be in the first element of the list, shadowing the earlier definition of `to_drop`. The third case is unused because it is essentially the same pattern as we had in the second case.

A better way to write this code is not to use pattern matching for determining whether the first element is equal to `to_drop`, but to instead use an ordinary `if` statement:

OCaml utop (part 7)

```
# let rec drop_value l to_drop =
    match l with
    | [] -> []
    | hd :: tl ->
      let new_tl = drop_value tl to_drop in
      if hd = to_drop then new_tl else hd :: new_tl
  ;;
val drop_value : 'a list -> 'a -> 'a list = <fun>
# drop_value [1;2;3] 2;;
- : int list = [1; 3]
```

Note that if we wanted to drop a particular literal value (rather than a value that was passed in), we could do this using something like our original implementation of `drop_value`:

```
# let rec drop_zero l =
    match l with
    | [] -> []
    | 0  :: tl -> drop_zero tl
    | hd :: tl -> hd :: drop_zero tl
  ;;
val drop_zero : int list -> int list = <fun>
# drop_zero [1;2;0;3];;
- : int list = [1; 2; 3]
```

Limitations (and Blessings) of Pattern Matching

The preceding example highlights an important fact about patterns, which is that they can't be used to express arbitrary conditions. Patterns can characterize the layout of a data structure and can even include literals, as in the drop_zero example, but that's where they stop. A pattern can check if a list has two elements, but it can't check if the first two elements are equal to each other.

You can think of patterns as a specialized sublanguage that can express a limited (though still quite rich) set of conditions. The fact that the pattern language is limited turns out to be a very good thing, making it possible to build better support for patterns in the compiler. In particular, both the efficiency of match statements and the ability of the compiler to detect errors in matches depend on the constrained nature of patterns.

Performance

Naively, you might think that it would be necessary to check each case in a match in sequence to figure out which one fires. If the cases of a match were guarded by arbitrary code, that would be the case. But OCaml is often able to generate machine code that jumps directly to the matched case based on an efficiently chosen set of runtime checks.

As an example, consider the following rather silly functions for incrementing an integer by one. The first is implemented with a match statement, and the second with a sequence of if statements:

```
# let plus_one_match x =
    match x with
    | 0 -> 1
    | 1 -> 2
    | 2 -> 3
    | _ -> x + 1

  let plus_one_if x =
    if      x = 0 then 1
    else if x = 1 then 2
    else if x = 2 then 3
    else x + 1
```

```
;;
val plus_one_match : int -> int = <fun>
val plus_one_if : int -> int = <fun>
```

Note the use of _ in the above match. This is a wildcard pattern that matches any value, but without binding a variable name to the value in question.

If you benchmark these functions, you'll see that plus_one_if is considerably slower than plus_one_match, and the advantage gets larger as the number of cases increases. Here, we'll benchmark these functions using the core_bench library, which can be installed by running opam install core_bench from the command line:

OCaml utop (part 10)

```
# #require "core_bench";;
# open Core_bench.Std;;
# let run_bench tests =
  Bench.bench
    ~ascii_table:true
    ~display:Textutils.Ascii_table.Display.column_titles
    tests
;;
val run_bench : Bench.Test.t list -> unit = <fun>
# [ Bench.Test.create ~name:"plus_one_match" (fun () ->
      ignore (plus_one_match 10))
  ; Bench.Test.create ~name:"plus_one_if" (fun () ->
      ignore (plus_one_if 10)) ]
  |> run_bench
  ;;
Estimated testing time 20s (change using -quota SECS).

  Name                Time (ns)   % of max
  ---------------- ----------- ----------
  plus_one_match       46.81      68.21
  plus_one_if          68.63     100.00

- : unit = ()
```

Here's another, less artificial example. We can rewrite the sum function we described earlier in the chapter using an if statement rather than a match. We can then use the functions is_empty, hd_exn, and tl_exn from the List module to deconstruct the list, allowing us to implement the entire function without pattern matching:

OCaml utop (part 11)

```
# let rec sum_if l =
    if List.is_empty l then 0
    else List.hd_exn l + sum_if (List.tl_exn l)
  ;;
val sum_if : int list -> int = <fun>
```

Again, we can benchmark these to see the difference:

```
# let numbers = List.range 0 1000 in
  [ Bench.Test.create ~name:"sum_if" (fun () -> ignore (sum_if numbers))
  ; Bench.Test.create ~name:"sum"    (fun () -> ignore (sum numbers)) ]
  |> run_bench
  ;;
Estimated testing time 20s (change using -quota SECS).

  Name      Time (ns)   % of max
  --------  ----------  ----------
  sum_if      110_535      100.00
  sum          22_361       20.23

- : unit = ()
```

In this case, the `match`-based implementation is many times faster than the `if`-based implementation. The difference comes because we need to effectively do the same work multiple times, since each function we call has to reexamine the first element of the list to determine whether or not it's the empty cell. With a `match` statement, this work happens exactly once per list element.

Generally, pattern matching is more efficient than the alternatives you might code by hand. One notable exception is matches over strings, which are in fact tested sequentially, so matches containing a long sequence of strings can be outperformed by a hash table. But most of the time, pattern matching is a clear performance win.

Detecting Errors

The error-detecting capabilities of `match` statements are if anything more important than their performance. We've already seen one example of OCaml's ability to find problems in a pattern match: in our broken implementation of `drop_value`, OCaml warned us that the final case was redundant. There are no algorithms for determining if a predicate written in a general-purpose language is redundant, but it can be solved reliably in the context of patterns.

OCaml also checks `match` statements for exhaustiveness. Consider what happens if we modify `drop_zero` by deleting the handler for one of the cases. As you can see, the compiler will produce a warning that we've missed a case, along with an example of an unmatched pattern:

```
# let rec drop_zero l =
    match l with
    | [] -> []
    | 0  :: tl -> drop_zero tl
  ;;
Characters 26-84:
Warning 8: this pattern-matching is not exhaustive.
Here is an example of a value that is not matched:
```

```
1::_
val drop_zero : int list -> 'a list = <fun>
```

Even for simple examples like this, exhaustiveness checks are pretty useful. But as we'll see in Chapter 6, they become yet more valuable as you get to more complicated examples, especially those involving user-defined types. In addition to catching outright errors, they act as a sort of refactoring tool, guiding you to the locations where you need to adapt your code to deal with changing types.

Using the List Module Effectively

We've so far written a fair amount of list-munging code using pattern matching and recursive functions. But in real life, you're usually better off using the List module, which is full of reusable functions that abstract out common patterns for computing with lists.

Let's work through a concrete example to see this in action. We'll write a function render_table that, given a list of column headers and a list of rows, prints them out in a well-formatted text table, as follows:

OCaml utop (part 69)

```
# printf "%s\n"
    (render_table
      ["language";"architect";"first release"]
      [ ["Lisp" ;"John McCarthy" ;"1958"] ;
        ["C"    ;"Dennis Ritchie";"1969"] ;
        ["ML"   ;"Robin Milner"  ;"1973"] ;
        ["OCaml";"Xavier Leroy"  ;"1996"] ;
      ]);;
| language | architect      | first release |
|----------+----------------+---------------|
| Lisp     | John McCarthy  | 1958          |
| C        | Dennis Ritchie | 1969          |
| ML       | Robin Milner   | 1973          |
| OCaml    | Xavier Leroy   | 1996          |
- : unit = ()
```

The first step is to write a function to compute the maximum width of each column of data. We can do this by converting the header and each row into a list of integer lengths, and then taking the element-wise max of those lists of lengths. Writing the code for all of this directly would be a bit of a chore, but we can do it quite concisely by making use of three functions from the List module: map, map2_exn, and fold.

List.map is the simplest to explain. It takes a list and a function for transforming elements of that list, and returns a new list with the transformed elements. Thus, we can write:

```
# List.map ~f:String.length ["Hello"; "World!"];;
- : int list = [5; 6]
```

List.map2_exn is similar to List.map, except that it takes two lists and a function for combining them. Thus, we might write:

```
# List.map2_exn ~f:Int.max [1;2;3] [3;2;1];;
- : int list = [3; 2; 3]
```

The _exn is there because the function throws an exception if the lists are of mismatched length:

```
# List.map2_exn ~f:Int.max [1;2;3] [3;2;1;0];;
Exception: (Invalid_argument "length mismatch in rev_map2_exn: 3 <> 4 ").
```

List.fold is the most complicated of the three, taking three arguments: a list to process, an initial accumulator value, and a function for updating the accumulator. List.fold walks over the list from left to right, updating the accumulator at each step and returning the final value of the accumulator when it's done. You can see some of this by looking at the type-signature for fold:

```
# List.fold;;
- : 'a list -> init:'accum -> f:('accum -> 'a -> 'accum) -> 'accum = <fun>
```

We can use List.fold for something as simple as summing up a list:

```
# List.fold ~init:0 ~f:(+) [1;2;3;4];;
- : int = 10
```

This example is particularly simple because the accumulator and the list elements are of the same type. But fold is not limited to such cases. We can for example use fold to reverse a list, in which case the accumulator is itself a list:

```
# List.fold ~init:[] ~f:(fun list x -> x :: list) [1;2;3;4];;
- : int list = [4; 3; 2; 1]
```

Let's bring our three functions together to compute the maximum column widths:

```
# let max_widths header rows =
    let lengths l = List.map ~f:String.length l in
    List.fold rows
      ~init:(lengths header)
      ~f:(fun acc row ->
        List.map2_exn ~f:Int.max acc (lengths row))
  ;;
val max_widths : string list -> string list list -> int list = <fun>
```

Using `List.map` we define the function `lengths`, which converts a list of strings to a list of integer lengths. `List.fold` is then used to iterate over the rows, using `map2_exn` to take the max of the accumulator with the lengths of the strings in each row of the table, with the accumulator initialized to the lengths of the header row.

Now that we know how to compute column widths, we can write the code to generate the line that separates the header from the rest of the text table. We'll do this in part by mapping `String.make` over the lengths of the columns to generate a string of dashes of the appropriate length. We'll then join these sequences of dashes together using `String.concat`, which concatenates a list of strings with an optional separator string, and `^`, which is a pairwise string concatenation function, to add the delimiters on the outside:

OCaml utop (part 21)

```
# let render_separator widths =
    let pieces = List.map widths
      ~f:(fun w -> String.make (w + 2) '-')
    in
    "|" ^ String.concat ~sep:"+" pieces ^ "|"
  ;;
val render_separator : int list -> string = <fun>
# render_separator [3;6;2];;
- : string = "|-----+--------+----|"
```

Note that we make the line of dashes two larger than the provided width to provide some whitespace around each entry in the table.

Performance of String.concat and ^

In the preceding code we've concatenated strings two different ways: `String.concat`, which operates on lists of strings; and `^`, which is a pairwise operator. You should avoid `^` for joining long numbers of strings, since it allocates a new string every time it runs. Thus, the following code

OCaml utop (part 22)

```
# let s = "." ^ "." ^ "." ^ "." ^ "." ^ "." ^ ".";;
val s : string = "......."
```

will allocate strings of length 2, 3, 4, 5, 6 and 7, whereas this code

OCaml utop (part 23)

```
# let s = String.concat [".";".";".";".";".";".";"."];;
val s : string = "......."
```

allocates one string of size 7, as well as a list of length 7. At these small sizes, the differences don't amount to much, but for assembling large strings, it can be a serious performance issue.

Now we need code for rendering a row with data in it. We'll first write a function called pad, for padding out a string to a specified length plus one blank space on both sides:

OCaml utop (part 24)

```
# let pad s length =
    " " ^ s ^ String.make (length - String.length s + 1) ' '
  ;;
val pad : string -> int -> string = <fun>
# pad "hello" 10;;
- : string = " hello      "
```

We can render a row of data by merging together the padded strings. Again, we'll use List.map2_exn for combining the list of data in the row with the list of widths:

OCaml utop (part 25)

```
# let render_row row widths =
    let padded = List.map2_exn row widths ~f:pad in
    "|" ^ String.concat ~sep:"|" padded ^ "|"
  ;;
val render_row : string list -> int list -> string = <fun>
# render_row ["Hello";"World"] [10;15];;
- : string = "| Hello      | World          |"
```

Now we can bring this all together in a single function that renders the table:

OCaml utop (part 26)

```
# let render_table header rows =
    let widths = max_widths header rows in
    String.concat ~sep:"\n"
      (render_row header widths
       :: render_separator widths
       :: List.map rows ~f:(fun row -> render_row row widths)
      )
  ;;
val render_table : string list -> string list list -> string = <fun>
```

More Useful List Functions

The previous example we worked through touched on only three of the functions in List. We won't cover the entire interface (for that you should look at the online docs (*http://realworldocaml.org/doc*)), but a few more functions are useful enough to mention here.

Combining list elements with List.reduce

List.fold, which we described earlier, is a very general and powerful function. Sometimes, however, you want something simpler and easier to use. One such function is List.reduce, which is essentially a specialized version of List.fold that doesn't require an explicit starting value, and whose accumulator has to consume and produce values of the same type as the elements of the list it applies to.

Here's the type signature:

```
# List.reduce;;
- : 'a list -> f:('a -> 'a -> 'a) -> 'a option = <fun>
```

reduce returns an optional result, returning None when the input list is empty.

Now we can see reduce in action:

```
# List.reduce ~f:(+) [1;2;3;4;5];;
- : int option = Some 15
# List.reduce ~f:(+) [];;
- : int option = None
```

Filtering with List.filter and List.filter_map

Very often when processing lists, you wants to restrict your attention to a subset of the values on your list. The List.filter function is one way of doing that:

```
# List.filter ~f:(fun x -> x mod 2 = 0) [1;2;3;4;5];;
- : int list = [2; 4]
```

Note that the mod used above is an infix operator, as described in Chapter 2.

Sometimes, you want to both transform and filter as part of the same computation. In that case, List.filter_map is what you need. The function passed to List.filter_map returns an optional value, and List.filter_map drops all elements for which None is returned.

Here's an example. The following expression computes the list of file extensions in the current directory, piping the results through List.dedup to remove duplicates. Note that this example also uses some functions from other modules, including Sys.ls_dir to get a directory listing, and String.rsplit2 to split a string on the rightmost appearance of a given character:

```
# List.filter_map (Sys.ls_dir ".") ~f:(fun fname ->
    match String.rsplit2 ~on:'.' fname with
    | None   | Some ("",_) -> None
    | Some (_,ext) ->
      Some ext)
  |> List.dedup
  ;;
- : string list = ["ascii"; "ml"; "mli"; "topscript"]
```

The preceding code is also an example of an Or pattern, which allows you to have multiple subpatterns within a larger pattern. In this case, None | Some ("",_) is an Or pattern. As we'll see later, Or patterns can be nested anywhere within larger patterns.

Partitioning with List.partition_tf

Another useful operation that's closely related to filtering is partitioning. The function `List.partition_tf` takes a list and a function for computing a Boolean condition on the list elements, and returns two lists. The `tf` in the name is a mnemonic to remind the user that `true` elements go to the first list and `false` ones go to the second. Here's an example:

OCaml utop (part 31)

```
# let is_ocaml_source s =
    match String.rsplit2 s ~on:'.' with
    | Some (_,("ml"|"mli")) -> true
    | _ -> false
  ;;
val is_ocaml_source : string -> bool = <fun>
# let (ml_files,other_files) =
    List.partition_tf (Sys.ls_dir ".") ~f:is_ocaml_source;;
val ml_files : string list = ["example.mli"; "example.ml"]
val other_files : string list = ["main.topscript"; "lists_layout.ascii"]
```

Combining lists

Another very common operation on lists is concatenation. The list module actually comes with a few different ways of doing this. First, there's `List.append`, for concatenating a pair of lists:

OCaml utop (part 32)

```
# List.append [1;2;3] [4;5;6];;
- : int list = [1; 2; 3; 4; 5; 6]
```

There's also @, an operator equivalent of `List.append`:

OCaml utop (part 33)

```
# [1;2;3] @ [4;5;6];;
- : int list = [1; 2; 3; 4; 5; 6]
```

In addition, there is `List.concat`, for concatenating a list of lists:

OCaml utop (part 34)

```
# List.concat [[1;2];[3;4;5];[6];[]];;
- : int list = [1; 2; 3; 4; 5; 6]
```

Here's an example of using `List.concat` along with `List.map` to compute a recursive listing of a directory tree:

OCaml utop (part 35)

```
# let rec ls_rec s =
    if Sys.is_file_exn ~follow_symlinks:true s
    then [s]
    else
      Sys.ls_dir s
      |> List.map ~f:(fun sub -> ls_rec (s ^/ sub))
      |> List.concat
```

```
  ;;
val ls_rec : string -> string list = <fun>
```

Note that ^/ is an infix operator provided by Core for adding a new element to a string representing a file path. It is equivalent to Core's Filename.concat.

The preceding combination of List.map and List.concat is common enough that there is a function List.concat_map that combines these into one, more efficient operation:

OCaml utop (part 36)

```
# let rec ls_rec s =
    if Sys.is_file_exn ~follow_symlinks:true s
    then [s]
    else
      Sys.ls_dir s
      |> List.concat_map ~f:(fun sub -> ls_rec (s ^/ sub))
  ;;
val ls_rec : string -> string list = <fun>
```

Tail Recursion

The only way to compute the length of an OCaml list is to walk the list from beginning to end. As a result, computing the length of a list takes time linear in the size of the list. Here's a simple function for doing so:

OCaml utop (part 37)

```
# let rec length = function
    | [] -> 0
    | _ :: tl -> 1 + length tl
  ;;
val length : 'a list -> int = <fun>
# length [1;2;3];;
- : int = 3
```

This looks simple enough, but you'll discover that this implementation runs into problems on very large lists, as we'll show in the following code:

OCaml utop (part 38)

```
# let make_list n = List.init n ~f:(fun x -> x);;
val make_list : int -> int list = <fun>
# length (make_list 10);;
- : int = 10
# length (make_list 10_000_000);;
Stack overflow during evaluation (looping recursion?).
```

The preceding example creates lists using List.init, which takes an integer n and a function f and creates a list of length n, where the data for each element is created by calling f on the index of that element.

To understand where the error in the above example comes from, you need to learn a bit more about how function calls work. Typically, a function call needs some space to keep track of information associated with the call, such as the arguments passed to the function, or the location of the code that needs to start executing when the function call is complete. To allow for nested function calls, this information is typically organized in a stack, where a new *stack frame* is allocated for each nested function call, and then deallocated when the function call is complete.

And that's the problem with our call to length: it tried to allocate 10 million stack frames, which exhausted the available stack space. Happily, there's a way around this problem. Consider the following alternative implementation:

OCaml utop (part 39)

```
# let rec length_plus_n l n =
    match l with
    | [] -> n
    | _ :: tl -> length_plus_n tl (n + 1)
  ;;
val length_plus_n : 'a list -> int -> int = <fun>
# let length l = length_plus_n l 0 ;;
val length : 'a list -> int = <fun>
# length [1;2;3;4];;
- : int = 4
```

This implementation depends on a helper function, length_plus_n, that computes the length of a given list plus a given n. In practice, n acts as an accumulator in which the answer is built up, step by step. As a result, we can do the additions along the way rather than doing them as we unwind the nested sequence of function calls, as we did in our first implementation of length.

The advantage of this approach is that the recursive call in length_plus_n is a *tail call*. We'll explain more precisely what it means to be a tail call shortly, but the reason it's important is that tail calls don't require the allocation of a new stack frame, due to what is called the *tail-call optimization*. A recursive function is said to be *tail recursive* if all of its recursive calls are tail calls. length_plus_n is indeed tail recursive, and as a result, length can take a long list as input without blowing the stack:

OCaml utop (part 40)

```
# length (make_list 10_000_000);;
- : int = 10000000
```

So when is a call a tail call? Let's think about the situation where one function (the *caller*) invokes another (the *callee*). The invocation is considered a tail call when the caller doesn't do anything with the value returned by the callee except to return it. The tail-call optimization makes sense because, when a caller makes a tail call, the caller's stack frame need never be used again, and so you don't need to keep it around. Thus, instead of allocating a new stack frame for the callee, the compiler is free to reuse the caller's stack frame.

Tail recursion is important for more than just lists. Ordinary nontail recursive calls are reasonable when dealing with data structures like binary trees, where the depth of the tree is logarithmic in the size of your data. But when dealing with situations where the depth of the sequence of nested calls is on the order of the size of your data, tail recursion is usually the right approach.

Terser and Faster Patterns

Now that we know more about how lists and patterns work, let's consider how we can improve on an example from "Recursive list functions" on page 14: the function des tutter, which removes sequential duplicates from a list. Here's the implementation that was described earlier:

OCaml utop (part 41)

```
# let rec destutter list =
    match list with
    | [] -> []
    | [hd] -> [hd]
    | hd :: hd' :: tl ->
      if hd = hd' then destutter (hd' :: tl)
      else hd :: destutter (hd' :: tl)
  ;;
val destutter : 'a list -> 'a list = <fun>
```

We'll consider some ways of making this code more concise and more efficient.

First, let's consider efficiency. One problem with the destutter code above is that it in some cases re-creates on the righthand side of the arrow a value that already existed on the lefthand side. Thus, the pattern [hd] -> [hd] actually allocates a new list element, when really, it should be able to just return the list being matched. We can reduce allocation here by using an as pattern, which allows us to declare a name for the thing matched by a pattern or subpattern. While we're at it, we'll use the function keyword to eliminate the need for an explicit match:

OCaml utop (part 42)

```
# let rec destutter = function
    | [] as l -> l
    | [_] as l -> l
    | hd :: (hd' :: _ as tl) ->
      if hd = hd' then destutter tl
      else hd :: destutter tl
  ;;
val destutter : 'a list -> 'a list = <fun>
```

We can further collapse this by combining the first two cases into one, using an Or pattern:

OCaml utop (part 43)

```
# let rec destutter = function
    | [] | [_] as l -> l
```

```
    | hd :: (hd' :: _ as tl) ->
      if hd = hd' then destutter tl
      else hd :: destutter tl
  ;;
val destutter : 'a list -> 'a list = <fun>
```

We can make the code slightly terser now by using a when clause. A when clause allows us to add an extra precondition to a pattern in the form of an arbitrary OCaml expression. In this case, we can use it to include the check on whether the first two elements are equal:

OCaml utop (part 44)

```
# let rec destutter = function
  | [] | [_] as l -> l
  | hd :: (hd' :: _ as tl) when hd = hd' -> destutter tl
  | hd :: tl -> hd :: destutter tl
;;
val destutter : 'a list -> 'a list = <fun>
```

Polymorphic Compare

In the preceding destutter example, we made use of the fact that OCaml lets us test equality between values of any type, using the = operator. Thus, we can write:

OCaml utop (part 45)

```
# 3 = 4;;
- : bool = false
# [3;4;5] = [3;4;5];;
- : bool = true
# [Some 3; None] = [None; Some 3];;
- : bool = false
```

Indeed, if we look at the type of the equality operator, we'll see that it is polymorphic:

OCaml utop (part 46)

```
# (=);;
- : 'a -> 'a -> bool = <fun>
```

OCaml comes with a whole family of polymorphic comparison operators, including the standard infix comparators, <, >=, etc., as well as the function compare that returns -1, 0, or 1 to flag whether the first operand is smaller than, equal to, or greater than the second, respectively.

You might wonder how you could build functions like these yourself if OCaml didn't come with them built in. It turns out that you *can't* build these functions on your own. OCaml's polymorphic comparison functions are built into the runtime to a low level. These comparisons are polymorphic on the basis of ignoring almost everything about the types of the values that are being compared, paying attention only to the structure of the values as they're laid out in memory.

Polymorphic compare does have some limitations. For example, it will fail at runtime if it encounters a function value:

OCaml utop (part 47)

```
# (fun x -> x + 1) = (fun x -> x + 1);;
Exception: (Invalid_argument "equal: functional value").
```

Similarly, it will fail on values that come from outside the OCaml heap, like values from C bindings. But it will work in a reasonable way for other kinds of values.

For simple atomic types, polymorphic compare has the semantics you would expect: for floating-point numbers and integers, polymorphic compare corresponds to the expected numerical comparison functions. For strings, it's a lexicographic comparison.

Sometimes, however, the type-ignoring nature of polymorphic compare is a problem, particularly when you have your own notion of equality and ordering that you want to impose. We'll discuss this issue more, as well as some of the other downsides of polymorphic compare, in Chapter 13.

Note that when clauses have some downsides. As we noted earlier, the static checks associated with pattern matches rely on the fact that patterns are restricted in what they can express. Once we add the ability to add an arbitrary condition to a pattern, something will be lost. In particular, the ability of the compiler to determine if a match is exhaustive, or if some case is redundant, is compromised.

Consider the following function, which takes a list of optional values, and returns the number of those values that are Some. Because this implementation uses when clauses, the compiler can't tell that the code is exhaustive:

OCaml utop (part 48)

```
# let rec count_some list =
    match list with
    | [] -> 0
    | x :: tl when Option.is_none x -> count_some tl
    | x :: tl when Option.is_some x -> 1 + count_some tl
  ;;
Characters 30-169:
Warning 8: this pattern-matching is not exhaustive.
Here is an example of a value that is not matched:
_::_
(However, some guarded clause may match this value.)
val count_some : 'a option list -> int = <fun>
```

Despite the warning, the function does work fine:

OCaml utop (part 49)

```
# count_some [Some 3; None; Some 4];;
- : int = 2
```

If we add another redundant case without a when clause, the compiler will stop complaining about exhaustiveness and won't produce a warning about the redundancy.

OCaml utop (part 50)

```
# let rec count_some list =
    match list with
    | [] -> 0
    | x :: tl when Option.is_none x -> count_some tl
    | x :: tl when Option.is_some x -> 1 + count_some tl
    | x :: tl -> -1 (* unreachable *)
  ;;
val count_some : 'a option list -> int = <fun>
```

Probably a better approach is to simply drop the second when clause:

OCaml utop (part 51)

```
# let rec count_some list =
    match list with
    | [] -> 0
    | x :: tl when Option.is_none x -> count_some tl
    | _ :: tl -> 1 + count_some tl
  ;;
val count_some : 'a option list -> int = <fun>
```

This is a little less clear, however, than the direct pattern-matching solution, where the meaning of each pattern is clearer on its own:

OCaml utop (part 52)

```
# let rec count_some list =
    match list with
    | [] -> 0
    | None    :: tl -> count_some tl
    | Some _ :: tl -> 1 + count_some tl
  ;;
val count_some : 'a option list -> int = <fun>
```

The takeaway from all of this is although when clauses can be useful, we should prefer patterns wherever they are sufficient.

As a side note, the above implementation of count_some is longer than necessary; even worse, it is not tail recursive. In real life, you would probably just use the List.count function from Core:

OCaml utop (part 53)

```
# let count_some l = List.count ~f:Option.is_some l;;
val count_some : 'a option list -> int = <fun>
```

## CHAPTER 4

Files, Modules, and Programs

We've so far experienced OCaml largely through the toplevel. As you move from exercises to real-world programs, you'll need to leave the toplevel behind and start building programs from files. Files are more than just a convenient way to store and manage your code; in OCaml, they also correspond to modules, which act as boundaries that divide your program into conceptual units.

In this chapter, we'll show you how to build an OCaml program from a collection of files, as well as the basics of working with modules and module signatures.

Single-File Programs

We'll start with an example: a utility that reads lines from stdin and computes a frequency count of the lines. At the end, the 10 lines with the highest frequency counts are written out. We'll start with a simple implementation, which we'll save as the file *freq.ml*.

This implementation will use two functions from the List.Assoc module, which provides utility functions for interacting with association lists, i.e., lists of key/value pairs. In particular, we use the function List.Assoc.find, which looks up a key in an association list; and List.Assoc.add, which adds a new binding to an association list, as shown here:

OCaml utop

```
# let assoc = [("one", 1); ("two",2); ("three",3)] ;;
val assoc : (string * int) list = [("one", 1); ("two", 2); ("three", 3)]
# List.Assoc.find assoc "two" ;;
- : int option = Some 2
# List.Assoc.add assoc "four" 4 (* add a new key *) ;;
- : (string, int) List.Assoc.t =
[("four", 4); ("one", 1); ("two", 2); ("three", 3)]
# List.Assoc.add assoc "two"  4 (* overwrite an existing key *) ;;
- : (string, int) List.Assoc.t = [("two", 4); ("one", 1); ("three", 3)]
```

Note that List.Assoc.add doesn't modify the original list, but instead allocates a new list with the requisite key/value pair added.

Now we can write freq.ml:

OCaml

```
open Core.Std

let build_counts () =
  In_channel.fold_lines stdin ~init:[] ~f:(fun counts line ->
    let count =
      match List.Assoc.find counts line with
      | None -> 0
      | Some x -> x
    in
    List.Assoc.add counts line (count + 1)
  )

let () =
  build_counts ()
  |> List.sort ~cmp:(fun (_,x) (_,y) -> Int.descending x y)
  |> (fun l -> List.take l 10)
  |> List.iter ~f:(fun (line,count) -> printf "%3d: %s\n" count line)
```

The function build_counts reads in lines from stdin, constructing from those lines an association list with the frequencies of each line. It does this by invoking In_channel.fold_lines (similar to the function List.fold described in Chapter 3), which reads through the lines one by one, calling the provided fold function for each line to update the accumulator. That accumulator is initialized to the empty list.

With build_counts defined, we then call the function to build the association list, sort that list by frequency in descending order, grab the first 10 elements off the list, and then iterate over those 10 elements and print them to the screen. These operations are tied together using the |> operator described in Chapter 2.

Where Is the Main Function?

Unlike C, programs in OCaml do not have a unique main function. When an OCaml program is evaluated, all the statements in the implementation files are evaluated in the order in which they were linked together. These implementation files can contain arbitrary expressions, not just function definitions. In this example, the declaration starting with let () = plays the role of the main function, kicking off the processing. But really the entire file is evaluated at startup, and so in some sense the full codebase is one big main function.

The idiom of writing let () = may seem a bit odd, but it has a purpose. The let binding here is a pattern-match to a value of type unit, which is there to ensure that the expression on the righthand side returns unit, as is common for functions that operate primarily by side effect.

If we weren't using Core or any other external libraries, we could build the executable like this:

Terminal

```
$ ocamlc freq.ml -o freq.byte
File "freq.ml", line 1, characters 0-13:
Error: Unbound module Core
```

But as you can see, it fails because it can't find Core. We need a somewhat more complex invocation to get Core linked in:

Terminal

```
$ ocamlfind ocamlc -linkpkg -thread -package core freq.ml -o freq.byte
```

This uses *ocamlfind*, a tool which itself invokes other parts of the OCaml toolchain (in this case, *ocamlc*) with the appropriate flags to link in particular libraries and packages. Here, -package core is asking *ocamlfind* to link in the Core library; -linkpkg asks ocamlfind to link in the packages as is necessary for building an executable, while -thread turns on threading support (which is required for Core).

While this works well enough for a one-file project, more complicated projects require a tool to orchestrate the build. One good tool for this task is *ocamlbuild*, which is shipped with the OCaml compiler. We'll talk more about *ocamlbuild* in Chapter 22, but for now, we'll just use a simple wrapper around *ocamlbuild* called *corebuild* that sets build parameters appropriately for building against Core and its related libraries:

Terminal

```
$ corebuild freq.byte
```

If we'd invoked *corebuild* with a target of freq.native instead of freq.byte, we would have gotten native code instead.

We can run the resulting executable from the command line. The following line extracts strings from the *ocamlopt* binary, reporting the most frequently occurring ones. Note that the specific results will vary from platform to platform, since the binary itself will differ between platforms:

Terminal

```
$ strings `which ocamlopt` | ./freq.byte
  6: +pci_expr =
  6: -pci_params =
  6: .pci_virt = %a
  4: #lsr
  4: #lsl
  4: $lxor
  4: #lor
  4: $land
```

```
4: #mod
3: 6 .section .rdata,"dr"
```

Bytecode Versus Native Code

OCaml ships with two compilers: the *ocamlc* bytecode compiler and the *ocamlopt* native-code compiler. Programs compiled with *ocamlc* are interpreted by a virtual machine, while programs compiled with *ocamlopt* are compiled to native machine code to be run on a specific operating system and processor architecture. With *ocamlbuild*, targets ending with .byte are build as bytecode executables, and those ending with .native are built as native code.

Aside from performance, executables generated by the two compilers have nearly identical behavior. There are a few things to be aware of. First, the bytecode compiler can be used on more architectures, and has some tools that are not available for native code. For example, the OCaml debugger only works with bytecode (although *gdb*, the GNU Debugger, works with OCaml native-code applications). The bytecode compiler is also quicker than the native-code compiler. In addition, in order to run a bytecode executable, you typically need to have OCaml installed on the system in question. That's not strictly required, though, since you can build a bytecode executable with an embedded runtime, using the -custom compiler flag.

As a general matter, production executables should usually be built using the native-code compiler, but it sometimes makes sense to use bytecode for development builds. And, of course, bytecode makes sense when targeting a platform not supported by the native-code compiler. We'll cover both compilers in more detail in Chapter 23.

Multifile Programs and Modules

Source files in OCaml are tied into the module system, with each file compiling down into a module whose name is derived from the name of the file. We've encountered modules before, such as when we used functions like find and add from the List.Assoc module. At its simplest, you can think of a module as a collection of definitions that are stored within a namespace.

Let's consider how we can use modules to refactor the implementation of freq.ml. Remember that the variable counts contains an association list representing the counts of the lines seen so far. But updating an association list takes time linear in the length of the list, meaning that the time complexity of processing a file is quadratic in the number of distinct lines in the file.

We can fix this problem by replacing association lists with a more efficient data structure. To do that, we'll first factor out the key functionality into a separate module with an explicit interface. We can consider alternative (and more efficient) implementations once we have a clear interface to program against.

We'll start by creating a file, counter.ml, that contains the logic for maintaining the association list used to represent the frequency counts. The key function, called touch, bumps the frequency count of a given line by one:

OCaml

```
open Core.Std

let touch t s =
  let count =
    match List.Assoc.find t s with
    | None -> 0
    | Some x -> x
  in
  List.Assoc.add t s (count + 1)
```

The file *counter.ml* will be compiled into a module named Counter, where the name of the module is derived automatically from the filename. The module name is capitalized even if the file is not. Indeed, module names are always capitalized.

We can now rewrite freq.ml to use Counter. Note that the resulting code can still be built with *ocamlbuild*, which will discover dependencies and realize that counter.ml needs to be compiled:

OCaml

```
open Core.Std

let build_counts () =
  In_channel.fold_lines stdin ~init:[] ~f:Counter.touch

let () =
  build_counts ()
  |> List.sort ~cmp:(fun (_,x) (_,y) -> Int.descending x y)
  |> (fun l -> List.take l 10)
  |> List.iter ~f:(fun (line,count) -> printf "%3d: %s\n" count line)
```

Signatures and Abstract Types

While we've pushed some of the logic to the Counter module, the code in freq.ml can still depend on the details of the implementation of Counter. Indeed, if you look at the definition of build_counts, you'll see that it depends on the fact that the empty set of frequency counts is represented as an empty list. We'd like to prevent this kind of dependency, so we can change the implementation of Counter without needing to change client code like that in freq.ml.

The implementation details of a module can be hidden by attaching an *interface*. (Note that in the context of OCaml, the terms *interface*, *signature*, and *module type* are all used interchangeably.) A module defined by a file `filename.ml` can be constrained by a signature placed in a file called `filename.mli`.

For `counter.mli`, we'll start by writing down an interface that describes what's currently available in `counter.ml`, without hiding anything. `val` declarations are used to specify values in a signature. The syntax of a `val` declaration is as follows:

Syntax

```
val <identifier> : <type>
```

Using this syntax, we can write the signature of `counter.ml` as follows:

OCaml

```
open Core.Std

(** Bump the frequency count for the given string. *)
val touch : (string * int) list -> string -> (string * int) list
```

Note that *ocamlbuild* will detect the presence of the `mli` file automatically and include it in the build.

Autogenerating mli Files

If you don't want to construct an `mli` entirely by hand, you can ask OCaml to autogenerate one for you from the source, which you can then adjust to fit your needs. Here's how you can do that using *corebuild*:

Terminal

```
$ corebuild counter.inferred.mli
$ cat _build/counter.inferred.mli
val touch :
  ('a, int) Core.Std.List.Assoc.t -> 'a -> ('a, int) Core.Std.List.Assoc.t
```

The generated code is basically equivalent to the `mli` that we wrote by hand but is a bit uglier and more verbose and, of course, has no comments. In general, autogenerated `mli`s are only useful as a starting point. In OCaml, the `mli` is the key place where you present and document your interface, and there's no replacement for careful human editing and organization.

To hide the fact that frequency counts are represented as association lists, we'll need to make the type of frequency counts *abstract*. A type is abstract if its name is exposed in the interface, but its definition is not. Here's an abstract interface for `Counter`:

OCaml

```
open Core.Std

(** A collection of string frequency counts *)
type t

(** The empty set of frequency counts  *)
val empty : t
```

```
(** Bump the frequency count for the given string. *)
val touch : t -> string -> t

(** Converts the set of frequency counts to an association list.  A string shows
    up at most once, and the counts are >= 1. *)
val to_list : t -> (string * int) list
```

Note that we needed to add empty and to_list to Counter, since otherwise there would be no way to create a Counter.t or get data out of one.

We also used this opportunity to document the module. The mli file is the place where you specify your module's interface, and as such is a natural place to put documentation. We started our comments with a double asterisk to cause them to be picked up by the *ocamldoc* tool when generating API documentation. We'll discuss *ocamldoc* more in Chapter 22.

Here's a rewrite of counter.ml to match the new counter.mli:

OCaml

```
open Core.Std

type t = (string * int) list

let empty = []

let to_list x = x

let touch t s =
  let count =
    match List.Assoc.find t s with
    | None -> 0
    | Some x -> x
  in
  List.Assoc.add t s (count + 1)
```

If we now try to compile freq.ml, we'll get the following error:

Terminal

```
$ corebuild freq.byte
File "freq.ml", line 4, characters 42-55:
Error: This expression has type Counter.t -> string -> Counter.t
       but an expression was expected of type 'a list -> string -> 'a list
       Type Counter.t is not compatible with type 'a list
Command exited with code 2.
```

This is because freq.ml depends on the fact that frequency counts are represented as association lists, a fact that we've just hidden. We just need to fix build_counts to use Counter.empty instead of [] and Counter.to_list to get the association list out at the end for processing and printing. The resulting implementation is shown below:

```
open Core.Std

let build_counts () =
  In_channel.fold_lines stdin ~init:Counter.empty ~f:Counter.touch

let () =
  build_counts ()
  |> Counter.to_list
  |> List.sort ~cmp:(fun (_,x) (_,y) -> Int.descending x y)
  |> (fun counts -> List.take counts 10)
  |> List.iter ~f:(fun (line,count) -> printf "%3d: %s\n" count line)
```

Now we can turn to optimizing the implementation of `Counter`. Here's an alternate and far more efficient implementation, based on the `Map` data structure in Core:

```
open Core.Std

type t = int String.Map.t

let empty = String.Map.empty

let to_list t = Map.to_alist t

let touch t s =
  let count =
    match Map.find t s with
    | None -> 0
    | Some x -> x
  in
  Map.add t ~key:s ~data:(count + 1)
```

Note that in the preceding example we use `String.Map` in some places and simply `Map` in others. This has to do with the fact that for some operations, like creating a `Map.t`, you need access to type-specialized information, and for others, like looking something up in `Map.t`, you don't. This is covered in more detail in Chapter 13.

Concrete Types in Signatures

In our frequency-count example, the module `Counter` had an abstract type `Counter.t` for representing a collection of frequency counts. Sometimes, you'll want to make a type in your interface *concrete*, by including the type definition in the interface.

For example, imagine we wanted to add a function to `Counter` for returning the line with the median frequency count. If the number of lines is even, then there is no precise median, and the function would return the lines before and after the median instead. We'll use a custom type to represent the fact that there are two possible return values. Here's a possible implementation:

```
type median = | Median of string
              | Before_and_after of string * string

let median t =
  let sorted_strings = List.sort (Map.to_alist t)
                         ~cmp:(fun (_,x) (_,y) -> Int.descending x y)
  in
  let len = List.length sorted_strings in
  if len = 0 then failwith "median: empty frequency count";
  let nth n = fst (List.nth_exn sorted_strings n) in
  if len mod 2 = 1
  then Median (nth (len/2))
  else Before_and_after (nth (len/2 - 1), nth (len/2));;
```

In the preceding implementation, we use `failwith` to throw an exception for the case of the empty list. We'll discuss exceptions more in Chapter 7. Note also that the function `fst` simply returns the first element of any two-tuple.

Now, to expose this usefully in the interface, we need to expose both the function and the type `median` with its definition. Note that values (of which functions are an example) and types have distinct namespaces, so there's no name clash here. Adding the following two lines added to `counter.mli` does the trick:

```
(** Represents the median computed from a set of strings.  In the case where
    there is an even number of choices, the one before and after the median is
    returned.  *)
type median = | Median of string
              | Before_and_after of string * string

val median : t -> median
```

The decision of whether a given type should be abstract or concrete is an important one. Abstract types give you more control over how values are created and accessed, and make it easier to enforce invariants beyond what is enforced by the type itself; concrete types let you expose more detail and structure to client code in a lightweight way. The right choice depends very much on the context.

Nested Modules

Up until now, we've only considered modules that correspond to files, like `counter.ml`. But modules (and module signatures) can be nested inside other modules. As a simple example, consider a program that needs to deal with multiple identifiers like usernames and hostnames. If you just represent these as strings, then it becomes easy to confuse one with the other.

A better approach is to mint new abstract types for each identifier, where those types are under the covers just implemented as strings. That way, the type system will prevent you from confusing a username with a hostname, and if you do need to convert, you can do so using explicit conversions to and from the string type.

Here's how you might create such an abstract type, within a submodule:

OCaml

```
open Core.Std

module Username : sig
  type t
  val of_string : string -> t
  val to_string : t -> string
end = struct
  type t = string
  let of_string x = x
  let to_string x = x
end
```

Note that the `to_string` and `of_string` functions above are implemented simply as the identity function, which means they have no runtime effect. They are there purely as part of the discipline that they enforce on the code through the type system.

The basic structure of a module declaration like this is:

Syntax

```
module <name> : <signature> = <implementation>
```

We could have written this slightly differently, by giving the signature its own top-level `module type` declaration, making it possible to create multiple distinct types with the same underlying implementation in a lightweight way:

OCaml

```
open Core.Std

module type ID = sig
  type t
  val of_string : string -> t
  val to_string : t -> string
end

module String_id = struct
  type t = string
  let of_string x = x
  let to_string x = x
end

module Username : ID = String_id
module Hostname : ID = String_id

type session_info = { user: Username.t;
                      host: Hostname.t;
                      when_started: Time.t;
                    }
```

```
let sessions_have_same_user s1 s2 =
  s1.user = s2.host
```

The preceding code has a bug: it compares the username in one session to the host in the other session, when it should be comparing the usernames in both cases. Because of how we defined our types, however, the compiler will flag this bug for us:

```
$ corebuild session_info.native
File "session_info.ml", line 24, characters 12-19:
Error: This expression has type Hostname.t
       but an expression was expected of type Username.t
Command exited with code 2.
```

This is a trivial example, but confusing different kinds of identifiers is a very real source of bugs, and the approach of minting abstract types for different classes of identifiers is an effective way of avoiding such issues.

Opening Modules

Most of the time, you refer to values and types within a module by using the module name as an explicit qualifier. For example, you write List.map to refer to the map function in the List module. Sometimes, though, you want to be able to refer to the contents of a module without this explicit qualification. That's what the open statement is for.

We've encountered open already, specifically where we've written open Core.Std to get access to the standard definitions in the Core library. In general, opening a module adds the contents of that module to the environment that the compiler looks at to find the definition of various identifiers. Here's an example:

```
# module M = struct let foo = 3 end;;
module M : sig val foo : int end
# foo;;
Characters -1-3:
Error: Unbound value foo
# open M;;
# foo;;
- : int = 3
```

open is essential when you want to modify your environment for a standard library like Core, but it's generally good style to keep the opening of modules to a minimum. Opening a module is basically a trade-off between terseness and explicitness—the more modules you open, the fewer module qualifications you need, and the harder it is to look at an identifier and figure out where it comes from.

Here's some general advice on how to deal with opens:

- Opening modules at the toplevel of a module should be done quite sparingly, and generally only with modules that have been specifically designed to be opened, like `Core.Std` or `Option.Monad_infix`.

- If you do need to do an open, it's better to do a *local open*. There are two syntaxes for local opens. For example, you can write:

OCaml utop (part 1)

```
# let average x y =
    let open Int64 in
    x + y / of_int 2;;
val average : int64 -> int64 -> int64 = <fun>
```

Here, of_int and the infix operators are the ones from the `Int64` module.

There's another, even more lightweight syntax for local opens, which is particularly useful for small expressions:

OCaml utop (part 2)

```
# let average x y =
    Int64.(x + y / of_int 2);;
val average : int64 -> int64 -> int64 = <fun>
```

- An alternative to local opens that makes your code terser without giving up on explicitness is to locally rebind the name of a module. So, when using the `Counter.median` type, instead of writing:

OCaml (part 1)

```
let print_median m =
  match m with
  | Counter.Median string -> printf "True median:\n   %s\n" string
  | Counter.Before_and_after (before, after) ->
    printf "Before and after median:\n   %s\n   %s\n" before after
```

you could write:

OCaml (part 1)

```
let print_median m =
  let module C = Counter in
  match m with
  | C.Median string -> printf "True median:\n   %s\n" string
  | C.Before_and_after (before, after) ->
    printf "Before and after median:\n   %s\n   %s\n" before after
```

Because the module name C only exists for a short scope, it's easy to read and remember what C stands for. Rebinding modules to very short names at the top level of your module is usually a mistake.

Including Modules

While opening a module affects the environment used to search for identifiers, *including* a module is a way of actually adding new identifiers to a module proper. Consider the following simple module for representing a range of integer values:

OCaml utop (part 3)

```
# module Interval = struct
    type t = | Interval of int * int
             | Empty

    let create low high =
      if high < low then Empty else Interval (low,high)
  end;;
module Interval :
  sig type t = Interval of int * int | Empty val create : int -> int -> t end
```

We can use the `include` directive to create a new, extended version of the `Interval` module:

OCaml utop (part 4)

```
# module Extended_interval = struct
    include Interval

    let contains t x =
      match t with
      | Empty -> false
      | Interval (low,high) -> x >= low && x <= high
  end;;
module Extended_interval :
  sig
    type t = Interval.t = Interval of int * int | Empty
    val create : int -> int -> t
    val contains : t -> int -> bool
  end
# Extended_interval.contains (Extended_interval.create 3 10) 4;;
- : bool = true
```

The difference between `include` and `open` is that we've done more than change how identifiers are searched for: we've changed what's in the module. If we'd used `open`, we'd have gotten a quite different result:

OCaml utop (part 5)

```
# module Extended_interval = struct
    open Interval

    let contains t x =
      match t with
      | Empty -> false
      | Interval (low,high) -> x >= low && x <= high
  end;;
module Extended_interval :
```

```
  sig val contains : Extended_interval.t -> int -> bool end
# Extended_interval.contains (Extended_interval.create 3 10) 4;;
Characters 28-52:
Error: Unbound value Extended_interval.create
```

To consider a more realistic example, imagine you wanted to build an extended version of the List module, where you've added some functionality not present in the module as distributed in Core. include allows us to do just that:

OCaml

```
open Core.Std

(* The new function we're going to add *)
let rec intersperse list el =
  match list with
  | [] | [ _ ]   -> list
  | x :: y :: tl -> x :: el :: intersperse (y::tl) el

(* The remainder of the list module *)
include List
```

Now, how do we write an interface for this new module? It turns out that include works on signatures as well, so we can pull essentially the same trick to write our mli. The only issues is that we need to get our hands on the signature for the List module. This can be done using module type of, which computes a signature from a module:

OCaml

```
open Core.Std

(* Include the interface of the list module from Core *)
include (module type of List)

(* Signature of function we're adding *)
val intersperse : 'a list -> 'a -> 'a list
```

Note that the order of declarations in the mli does not need to match the order of declarations in the ml. The order of declarations in the ml mostly matters insofar as it affects which values are shadowed. If we wanted to replace a function in List with a new function of the same name, the declaration of that function in the ml would have to come after the include List declaration.

We can now use Ext_list as a replacement for List. If we want to use Ext_list in preference to List in our project, we can create a file of common definitions:

OCaml

```
module List = Ext_list
```

And if we then put open Common after open Core.Std at the top of each file in our project, then references to List will automatically go to Ext_list instead.

Common Errors with Modules

When OCaml compiles a program with an `ml` and an `mli`, it will complain if it detects a mismatch between the two. Here are some of the common errors you'll run into.

Type Mismatches

The simplest kind of error is where the type specified in the signature does not match the type in the implementation of the module. As an example, if we replace the `val` declaration in `counter.mli` by swapping the types of the first two arguments:

OCaml (part 1)

```
(** Bump the frequency count for the given string. *)
val touch : string -> t -> t
```

and we try to compile, we'll get the following error:

Terminal

```
$ corebuild freq.byte
File "freq.ml", line 4, characters 53-66:
Error: This expression has type string -> Counter.t -> Counter.t
       but an expression was expected of type
         Counter.t -> string -> Counter.t
       Type string is not compatible with type Counter.t
Command exited with code 2.
```

Missing Definitions

We might decide that we want a new function in `Counter` for pulling out the frequency count of a given string. We can update the `mli` by adding the following line:

OCaml (part 1)

```
val count : t -> string -> int
```

Now, if we try to compile without actually adding the implementation, we'll get this error:

Terminal

```
$ corebuild freq.byte
File "counter.ml", line 1:
Error: The implementation counter.ml
       does not match the interface counter.cmi:
       The field `count' is required but not provided
Command exited with code 2.
```

A missing type definition will lead to a similar error.

Type Definition Mismatches

Type definitions that show up in an `mli` need to match up with corresponding definitions in the `ml`. Consider again the example of the type `median`. The order of the declaration of variants matters to the OCaml compiler, so the definition of median in the implementation listing those options in a different order:

OCaml (part 1)

```
(** Represents the median computed from a set of strings.  In the case where
    there is an even number of choices, the one before and after the median is
    returned.  *)
type median = | Before_and_after of string * string
              | Median of string
```

will lead to a compilation error:

Terminal

```
$ corebuild freq.byte
File "counter.ml", line 1:
Error: The implementation counter.ml
       does not match the interface counter.cmi:
       Type declarations do not match:
         type median = Median of string | Before_and_after of string * string
       is not included in
         type median = Before_and_after of string * string | Median of string
       File "counter.ml", line 18, characters 5-84: Actual declaration
       Fields number 1 have different names, Median and Before_and_after.
Command exited with code 2.
```

Order is similarly important to other type declarations, including the order in which record fields are declared and the order of arguments (including labeled and optional arguments) to a function.

Cyclic Dependencies

In most cases, OCaml doesn't allow cyclic dependencies, i.e., a collection of definitions that all refer to one another. If you want to create such definitions, you typically have to mark them specially. For example, when defining a set of mutually recursive values (like the definition of is_even and is_odd in "Recursive Functions" on page 34), you need to define them using let rec rather than ordinary let.

The same is true at the module level. By default, cyclic dependencies between modules are not allowed, and cyclic dependencies among files are never allowed. Recursive modules are possible but are a rare case, and we won't discuss them further here.

The simplest example of a forbidden circular reference is a module referring to its own module name. So, if we tried to add a reference to Counter from within counter.ml:

OCaml (part 1)

```
let singleton l = Counter.touch Counter.empty
```

we'll see this error when we try to build:

Terminal

```
$ corebuild freq.byte
File "counter.ml", line 18, characters 18-31:
```

```
Error: Unbound module Counter
Command exited with code 2.
```

The problem manifests in a different way if we create cyclic references between files. We could create such a situation by adding a reference to `Freq` from `counter.ml`, e.g., by adding the following line:

OCaml (part 1)

```
let _build_counts = Freq.build_counts
```

In this case, *ocamlbuild* (which is invoked by the *corebuild* script) will notice the error and complain explicitly about the cycle:

Terminal

```
$ corebuild freq.byte
Circular dependencies: "freq.cmo" already seen in
  [ "counter.cmo"; "freq.cmo" ]
```

Designing with Modules

The module system is a key part of how an OCaml program is structured. As such, we'll close this chapter with some advice on how to think about designing that structure effectively.

Expose Concrete Types Rarely

When designing an `mli`, one choice that you need to make is whether to expose the concrete definition of your types or leave them abstract. Most of the time, abstraction is the right choice, for two reasons: it enhances the flexibility of your design, and it makes it possible to enforce invariants on the use of your module.

Abstraction enhances flexibility by restricting how users can interact with your types, thus reducing the ways in which users can depend on the details of your implementation. If you expose types explicitly, then users can depend on any and every detail of the types you choose. If they're abstract, then only the specific operations you want to expose are available. This means that you can freely change the implementation without affecting clients, as long as you preserve the semantics of those operations.

In a similar way, abstraction allows you to enforce invariants on your types. If your types are exposed, then users of the module can create new instances of that type (or if mutable, modify existing instances) in any way allowed by the underlying type. That may violate a desired invariant *i.e.*, a property about your type that is always supposed to be true. Abstract types allow you to protect invariants by making sure that you only expose functions that preserves your invariants.

Despite these benefits, there is a trade-off here. In particular, exposing types concretely makes it possible to use pattern-matching with those types, which as we saw in Chapter 3 is a powerful and important tool. You should generally only expose the concrete implementation of your types when there's significant value in the ability to pattern match, and when the invariants that you care about are already enforced by the data type itself.

Design for the Call Site

When writing an interface, you should think not just about how easy it is to understand the interface for someone who reads your carefully documented mli file, but more importantly, you want the call to be as obvious as possible for someone who is reading it at the call site.

The reason for this is that most of the time, people interacting with your API will be doing so by reading and modifying code that uses the API, not by reading the interface definition. By making your API as obvious as possible from that perspective, you simplify the lives of your users.

There are many ways of improving readability at the call site. One example is labeled arguments (discussed in "Labeled Arguments" on page 40), which act as documentation that is available at the call site.

You can also improve readability simply by choosing good names for your functions, variant tags and record fields. Good names aren't always long, to be clear. If you wanted to write an anonymous function for doubling a number: (fun x -> x * 2), a short variable name like x is best. A good rule of thumb is that names that have a small scope should be short, whereas names that have a large scope, like the name of a function in an a module interface, should be longer and more explicit.

There is of course a tradeoff here, in that making your APIs more explicit tends to make them more verbose as well. Another useful rule of thumb is that more rarely used names should be longer and more explicit, since the cost of concision and the benefit of explicitness become more important the more often a name is used.

Create Uniform Interfaces

Designing the interface of a module is a task that should not be thought of in isolation. The interfaces that appear in your codebase should play together harmoniously. Part of achieving that is standardizing aspects of those interfaces.

Core itself is a library that works hard to create uniform interfaces. Here are some of the guidelines that are used in Core.

- *A module for (almost) every type.* You should mint a module for almost every type in your program, and the primary type of a given module should be called t.
- *Put t first.* If you have a module M whose primary type is M.t, the functions in M that take a value of M.t should take it as their first argument.

- Functions that routinely throw an exception should end in _exn. Otherwise, errors should be signaled by returning an option or an Or_error.t (both of which are discussed in Chapter 7).

There are also standards in Core about what the type signature for specific functions should be. For example, the signature for map is always essentially the same, no matter what the underlying type it is applied to. This kind of function-by-function API uniformity is achieved through the use of *signature includes*, which allow for different modules to share components of their interface. This approach is described in "Using Multiple Interfaces" on page 185.

Core's standards may or may not fit your projects, but you can improve the usability of your codebase by finding some consistent set of standards to apply.

Interfaces before implementations

OCaml's concise and flexible type language enables a type-oriented approach to software design. Such an approach involves thinking through and writing out the types you're going to use before embarking on the implementation itself.

This is a good approach both when working in the core language, where you would write your type definitions before writing the logic of your computations, as well as at the module level, where you would write a first draft of your mli before working on the ml.

Of course, the design process goes in both directions. You'll often find yourself going back and modifying your types in response to things you learn by working on the implementation. But types and signatures provide a lightweight tool for constructing a skeleton of your design in a way that helps clarify your goals and intent, before you spend a lot of time and effort fleshing it out.

## CHAPTER 5

Records

One of OCaml's best features is its concise and expressive system for declaring new data types, and records are a key element of that system. We discussed records briefly in Chapter 1, but this chapter will go into more depth, covering the details of how records work, as well as advice on how to use them effectively in your software designs.

A record represents a collection of values stored together as one, where each component is identified by a different field name. The basic syntax for a record type declaration is as follows:

Syntax

```
type <record-name> =
    { <field> : <type> ;
    <field> : <type> ;
    ...
    }
```

Note that record field names must start with a lowercase letter.

Here's a simple example, a host_info record that summarizes information about a given computer:

OCaml utop

```
# type host_info =
    { hostname   : string;
      os_name    : string;
      cpu_arch   : string;
      timestamp  : Time.t;
    };;
type host_info = {
  hostname : string;
  os_name : string;
  cpu_arch : string;
  timestamp : Time.t;
}
```

We can construct a `host_info` just as easily. The following code uses the `Shell` module from `Core_extended` to dispatch commands to the shell to extract the information we need about the computer we're running on. It also uses the `Time.now` call from Core's `Time` module:

OCaml utop (part 1)

```
# #require "core_extended";;
# open Core_extended.Std;;
# let my_host =
    let sh = Shell.sh_one_exn in
    { hostname    = sh "hostname";
      os_name     = sh "uname -s";
      cpu_arch    = sh "uname -p";
      timestamp   = Time.now ();
    };;
val my_host : host_info =
  {hostname = "ocaml-www1"; os_name = "Linux"; cpu_arch = "unknown";
   timestamp = 2013-08-18 14:50:48.986085+01:00}
```

You might wonder how the compiler inferred that `my_host` is of type `host_info`. The hook that the compiler uses in this case to figure out the type is the record field name. Later in the chapter, we'll talk about what happens when there is more than one record type in scope with the same field name.

Once we have a record value in hand, we can extract elements from the record field using dot notation:

OCaml utop (part 2)

```
# my_host.cpu_arch;;
- : string = "unknown"
```

When declaring an OCaml type, you always have the option of parameterizing it by a polymorphic type. Records are no different in this regard. So, for example, here's a type one might use to timestamp arbitrary items:

OCaml utop (part 3)

```
# type 'a timestamped = { item: 'a; time: Time.t };;
type 'a timestamped = { item : 'a; time : Time.t; }
```

We can then write polymorphic functions that operate over this parameterized type:

OCaml utop (part 4)

```
# let first_timestamped list =
    List.reduce list ~f:(fun a b -> if a.time < b.time then a else b)
  ;;
val first_timestamped : 'a timestamped list -> 'a timestamped option = <fun>
```

Patterns and Exhaustiveness

Another way of getting information out of a record is by using a pattern match, as in the definition of `host_info_to_string`:

```
# let host_info_to_string { hostname = h; os_name = os;
                            cpu_arch = c; timestamp = ts;
                          } =
     sprintf "%s (%s / %s, on %s)" h os c (Time.to_sec_string ts);;
val host_info_to_string : host_info -> string = <fun>
# host_info_to_string my_host;;
- : string = "ocaml-www1 (Linux / unknown, on 2013-08-18 14:50:48)"
```

Note that the pattern we used had only a single case, rather than using several cases separated by |'s. We needed only one pattern because record patterns are *irrefutable*, meaning that a record pattern match will never fail at runtime. This makes sense, because the set of fields available in a record is always the same. In general, patterns for types with a fixed structure, like records and tuples, are irrefutable, unlike types with variable structures like lists and variants.

Another important characteristic of record patterns is that they don't need to be complete; a pattern can mention only a subset of the fields in the record. This can be convenient, but it can also be error prone. In particular, this means that when new fields are added to the record, code that should be updated to react to the presence of those new fields will not be flagged by the compiler.

As an example, imagine that we wanted to add a new field to our host_info record called os_release:

```
# type host_info =
    { hostname   : string;
      os_name    : string;
      cpu_arch   : string;
      os_release : string;
      timestamp  : Time.t;
    } ;;
type host_info = {
  hostname : string;
  os_name : string;
  cpu_arch : string;
  os_release : string;
  timestamp : Time.t;
}
```

The code for host_info_to_string would continue to compile without change. In this particular case, it's pretty clear that you might want to update host_info_to_string in order to include os_release, and it would be nice if the type system would give you a warning about the change.

Happily, OCaml does offer an optional warning for missing fields in a record pattern. With that warning turned on (which you can do in the toplevel by typing #warnings "+9"), the compiler will warn about the missing field:

```
# #warnings "+9";;
# let host_info_to_string { hostname = h; os_name = os;
                            cpu_arch = c; timestamp = ts;
                          } =
    sprintf "%s (%s / %s, on %s)" h os c (Time.to_sec_string ts);;
Characters 24-139:
Warning 9: the following labels are not bound in this record pattern:
os_release
Either bind these labels explicitly or add '; _' to the pattern.
val host_info_to_string : host_info -> string = <fun>
```

We can disable the warning for a given pattern by explicitly acknowledging that we are ignoring extra fields. This is done by adding an underscore to the pattern:

```
# let host_info_to_string { hostname = h; os_name = os;
                            cpu_arch = c; timestamp = ts; _
                          } =
    sprintf "%s (%s / %s, on %s)" h os c (Time.to_sec_string ts);;
val host_info_to_string : host_info -> string = <fun>
```

It's a good idea to enable the warning for incomplete record matches and to explicitly disable it with an _ where necessary.

Compiler Warnings

The OCaml compiler is packed full of useful warnings that can be enabled and disabled separately. These are documented in the compiler itself, so we could have found out about warning 9 as follows:

```
$ ocaml -warn-help | egrep '\b9\b'
  9 Missing fields in a record pattern.
  R Synonym for warning 9.
```

You should think of OCaml's warnings as a powerful set of optional static analysis tools, and you should eagerly enable them in your build environment. You don't typically enable all warnings, but the defaults that ship with the compiler are pretty good.

The warnings used for building the examples in this book are specified with the following flag: -w @A-4-33-41-42-43-34-44.

The syntax of this can be found by running ocaml -help, but this particular invocation turns on all warnings as errors, disabling only the numbers listed explicitly after the A.

Treating warnings as errors (i.e., making OCaml fail to compile any code that triggers a warning) is good practice, since without it, warnings are too often ignored during development. When preparing a package for distribution, however, this is a bad idea, since the list of warnings may grow from one release of the compiler to another, and so this may lead your package to fail to compile on newer compiler releases.

Field Punning

When the name of a variable coincides with the name of a record field, OCaml provides some handy syntactic shortcuts. For example, the pattern in the following function binds all of the fields in question to variables of the same name. This is called *field punning*:

OCaml utop (part 9)

```
# let host_info_to_string { hostname; os_name; cpu_arch; timestamp; _ } =
    sprintf "%s (%s / %s) <%s>" hostname os_name cpu_arch
      (Time.to_string timestamp);;
val host_info_to_string : host_info -> string = <fun>
```

Field punning can also be used to construct a record. Consider the following code for generating a host_info record:

OCaml utop (part 10)

```
# let my_host =
    let sh cmd = Shell.sh_one_exn cmd in
    let hostname   = sh "hostname" in
    let os_name    = sh "uname -s" in
    let cpu_arch   = sh "uname -p" in
    let os_release = sh "uname -r" in
    let timestamp  = Time.now () in
    { hostname; os_name; cpu_arch; os_release; timestamp };;
val my_host : host_info =
  {hostname = "ocaml-www1"; os_name = "Linux"; cpu_arch = "unknown";
   os_release = "3.2.0-1-amd64";
   timestamp = 2013-08-18 14:50:55.287342+01:00}
```

In the preceding code, we defined variables corresponding to the record fields first, and then the record declaration itself simply listed the fields that needed to be included.

You can take advantage of both field punning and label punning when writing a function for constructing a record from labeled arguments:

OCaml utop (part 11)

```
# let create_host_info ~hostname ~os_name ~cpu_arch ~os_release =
    { os_name; cpu_arch; os_release;
      hostname = String.lowercase hostname;
      timestamp = Time.now () };;
val create_host_info :
  hostname:string ->
  os_name:string -> cpu_arch:string -> os_release:string -> host_info = <fun>
```

This is considerably more concise than what you would get without punning:

OCaml utop (part 12)

```
# let create_host_info
    ~hostname:hostname ~os_name:os_name
```

```
                 ~cpu_arch:cpu_arch ~os_release:os_release =
               { os_name = os_name;
                 cpu_arch = cpu_arch;
                 os_release = os_release;
                 hostname = String.lowercase hostname;
                 timestamp = Time.now () };;
  val create_host_info :
    hostname:string ->
    os_name:string -> cpu_arch:string -> os_release:string -> host_info = <fun>
```

Together, labeled arguments, field names, and field and label punning encourage a style where you propagate the same names throughout your codebase. This is generally good practice, since it encourages consistent naming, which makes it easier to navigate the source.

Reusing Field Names

Defining records with the same field names can be problematic. Let's consider a simple example: building types to represent the protocol used for a logging server.

We'll describe three message types: log_entry, heartbeat, and logon. The log_en try message is used to deliver a log entry to the server; the logon message is sent to initiate a connection and includes the identity of the user connecting and credentials used for authentication; and the heartbeat message is periodically sent by the client to demonstrate to the server that the client is alive and connected. All of these messages include a session ID and the time the message was generated:

OCaml utop (part 13)

```
# type log_entry =
    { session_id: string;
      time: Time.t;
      important: bool;
      message: string;
    }
  type heartbeat =
    { session_id: string;
      time: Time.t;
      status_message: string;
    }
  type logon =
    { session_id: string;
      time: Time.t;
      user: string;
      credentials: string;
    }
;;
type log_entry = {
  session_id : string;
  time : Time.t;
  important : bool;
```

```
    message : string;
}
type heartbeat = {
  session_id : string;
  time : Time.t;
  status_message : string;
}
type logon = {
  session_id : string;
  time : Time.t;
  user : string;
  credentials : string;
}
```

Reusing field names can lead to some ambiguity. For example, if we want to write a function to grab the session_id from a record, what type will it have?

OCaml utop (part 14)

```
# let get_session_id t = t.session_id;;
val get_session_id : logon -> string = <fun>
```

In this case, OCaml just picks the most recent definition of that record field. We can force OCaml to assume we're dealing with a different type (say, a heartbeat) using a type annotation:

OCaml utop (part 15)

```
# let get_heartbeat_session_id (t:heartbeat) = t.session_id;;
val get_heartbeat_session_id : heartbeat -> string = <fun>
```

While it's possible to resolve ambiguous field names using type annotations, the ambiguity can be a bit confusing. Consider the following functions for grabbing the session ID and status from a heartbeat:

OCaml utop (part 16)

```
# let status_and_session t = (t.status_message, t.session_id);;
val status_and_session : heartbeat -> string * string = <fun>
# let session_and_status t = (t.session_id, t.status_message);;
Characters 44-58:
Error: The record type logon has no field status_message
# let session_and_status (t:heartbeat) = (t.session_id, t.status_message);;
val session_and_status : heartbeat -> string * string = <fun>
```

Why did the first definition succeed without a type annotation and the second one fail? The difference is that in the first case, the type-checker considered the status_message field first and thus concluded that the record was a heartbeat. When the order was switched, the session_id field was considered first, and so that drove the type to be considered to be a logon, at which point t.status_message no longer made sense.

We can avoid this ambiguity altogether, either by using nonoverlapping field names or, more generally, by minting a module for each type. Packing types into modules is a broadly useful idiom (and one used quite extensively by Core), providing for each type a namespace within which to put related values. When using this style, it is standard practice to name the type associated with the module t. Using this style we would write:

OCaml utop (part 17)

```
# module Log_entry = struct
    type t =
      { session_id: string;
        time: Time.t;
        important: bool;
        message: string;
      }
  end
  module Heartbeat = struct
    type t =
      { session_id: string;
        time: Time.t;
        status_message: string;
      }
  end
  module Logon = struct
    type t =
      { session_id: string;
        time: Time.t;
        user: string;
        credentials: string;
      }
  end;;
module Log_entry :
  sig
    type t = {
      session_id : string;
      time : Time.t;
      important : bool;
      message : string;
    }
  end
module Heartbeat :
  sig
    type t = { session_id : string; time : Time.t; status_message : string; }
  end
module Logon :
  sig
    type t = {
      session_id : string;
      time : Time.t;
      user : string;
      credentials : string;
    }
  end
```

Now, our log-entry-creation function can be rendered as follows:

```
# let create_log_entry ~session_id ~important message =
    { Log_entry.time = Time.now (); Log_entry.session_id;
      Log_entry.important; Log_entry.message }
  ;;
val create_log_entry :
  session_id:string -> important:bool -> string -> Log_entry.t = <fun>
```

The module name Log_entry is required to qualify the fields, because this function is outside of the Log_entry module where the record was defined. OCaml only requires the module qualification for one record field, however, so we can write this more concisely. Note that we are allowed to insert whitespace between the module path and the field name:

```
# let create_log_entry ~session_id ~important message =
    { Log_entry.
      time = Time.now (); session_id; important; message }
  ;;
val create_log_entry :
  session_id:string -> important:bool -> string -> Log_entry.t = <fun>
```

This is not restricted to constructing a record; we can use the same trick when pattern matching:

```
# let message_to_string { Log_entry.important; message; _ } =
    if important then String.uppercase message else message
  ;;
val message_to_string : Log_entry.t -> string = <fun>
```

When using dot notation for accessing record fields, we can qualify the field by the module directly:

```
# let is_important t = t.Log_entry.important;;
val is_important : Log_entry.t -> bool = <fun>
```

The syntax here is a little surprising when you first encounter it. The thing to keep in mind is that the dot is being used in two ways: the first dot is a record field access, with everything to the right of the dot being interpreted as a field name; the second dot is accessing the contents of a module, referring to the record field important from within the module Log_entry. The fact that Log_entry is capitalized and so can't be a field name is what disambiguates the two uses.

For functions defined within the module where a given record is defined, the module qualification goes away entirely.

Functional Updates

Fairly often, you will find yourself wanting to create a new record that differs from an existing record in only a subset of the fields. For example, imagine our logging server had a record type for representing the state of a given client, including when the last heartbeat was received from that client. The following defines a type for representing this information, as well as a function for updating the client information when a new heartbeat arrives:

OCaml utop (part 22)

```
# type client_info =
    { addr: Unix.Inet_addr.t;
      port: int;
      user: string;
      credentials: string;
      last_heartbeat_time: Time.t;
    };;
type client_info = {
  addr : UnixLabels.inet_addr;
  port : int;
  user : string;
  credentials : string;
  last_heartbeat_time : Time.t;
}
# let register_heartbeat t hb =
      { addr = t.addr;
        port = t.port;
        user = t.user;
        credentials = t.credentials;
        last_heartbeat_time = hb.Heartbeat.time;
      };;
val register_heartbeat : client_info -> Heartbeat.t -> client_info = <fun>
```

This is fairly verbose, given that there's only one field that we actually want to change, and all the others are just being copied over from t. We can use OCaml's *functional update* syntax to do this more tersely. The syntax of a functional update is as follows:

Syntax

```
{ <record> with <field> = <value>;
    <field> = <value>;
    ...
}
```

The purpose of the functional update is to create a new record based on an existing one, with a set of field changes layered on top.

Given this, we can rewrite register_heartbeat more concisely:

OCaml utop (part 23)

```
# let register_heartbeat t hb =
    { t with last_heartbeat_time = hb.Heartbeat.time };;
val register_heartbeat : client_info -> Heartbeat.t -> client_info = <fun>
```

Functional updates make your code independent of the identity of the fields in the record that are not changing. This is often what you want, but it has downsides as well. In particular, if you change the definition of your record to have more fields, the type system will not prompt you to reconsider whether your code needs to change to accommodate the new fields. Consider what happens if we decided to add a field for the status message received on the last heartbeat:

OCaml utop (part 24)

```
# type client_info =
   { addr: Unix.Inet_addr.t;
     port: int;
     user: string;
     credentials: string;
     last_heartbeat_time: Time.t;
     last_heartbeat_status: string;
   };;
type client_info = {
  addr : UnixLabels.inet_addr;
  port : int;
  user : string;
  credentials : string;
  last_heartbeat_time : Time.t;
  last_heartbeat_status : string;
}
```

The original implementation of `register_heartbeat` would now be invalid, and thus the compiler would effectively warn us to think about how to handle this new field. But the version using a functional update continues to compile as is, even though it incorrectly ignores the new field. The correct thing to do would be to update the code as follows:

OCaml utop (part 25)

```
# let register_heartbeat t hb =
   { t with last_heartbeat_time   = hb.Heartbeat.time;
            last_heartbeat_status = hb.Heartbeat.status_message;
   };;
val register_heartbeat : client_info -> Heartbeat.t -> client_info = <fun>
```

Mutable Fields

Like most OCaml values, records are immutable by default. You can, however, declare individual record fields as mutable. In the following code, we've made the last two fields of `client_info` mutable:

OCaml utop (part 26)

```
# type client_info =
   { addr: Unix.Inet_addr.t;
     port: int;
     user: string;
     credentials: string;
```

```
      mutable last_heartbeat_time: Time.t;
      mutable last_heartbeat_status: string;
    };;
  type client_info = {
    addr : UnixLabels.inet_addr;
    port : int;
    user : string;
    credentials : string;
    mutable last_heartbeat_time : Time.t;
    mutable last_heartbeat_status : string;
  }
```

The <- operator is used for setting a mutable field. The side-effecting version of regis
ter_heartbeat would be written as follows:

OCaml utop (part 27)

```
# let register_heartbeat t hb =
    t.last_heartbeat_time   <- hb.Heartbeat.time;
    t.last_heartbeat_status <- hb.Heartbeat.status_message
  ;;
val register_heartbeat : client_info -> Heartbeat.t -> unit = <fun>
```

Note that mutable assignment, and thus the <- operator, is not needed for initialization because all fields of a record, including mutable ones, are specified when the record is created.

OCaml's policy of immutable-by-default is a good one, but imperative programming is an important part of programming in OCaml. We go into more depth about how (and when) to use OCaml's imperative features in "Imperative Programming" on page 20.

First-Class Fields

Consider the following function for extracting the usernames from a list of Logon messages:

OCaml utop (part 28)

```
# let get_users logons =
    List.dedup (List.map logons ~f:(fun x -> x.Logon.user));;
val get_users : Logon.t list -> string list = <fun>
```

Here, we wrote a small function (fun x -> x.Logon.user) to access the user field. This kind of accessor function is a common enough pattern that it would be convenient to generate it automatically. The fieldslib syntax extension that ships with Core does just that.

The with fields annotation at the end of the declaration of a record type will cause the extension to be applied to a given type declaration. So, for example, we could have defined Logon as follows:

```
# module Logon = struct
    type t =
      { session_id: string;
        time: Time.t;
        user: string;
        credentials: string;
      }
    with fields
  end;;
module Logon :
  sig
    type t = {
      session_id : string;
      time : Time.t;
      user : string;
      credentials : string;
    }
    val credentials : t -> string
    val user : t -> string
    val time : t -> Time.t
    val session_id : t -> string
    module Fields :
      sig
        val names : string list
        val credentials :
          ([< `Read | `Set_and_create ], t, string) Field.t_with_perm
        val user :
          ([< `Read | `Set_and_create ], t, string) Field.t_with_perm
        val time :
          ([< `Read | `Set_and_create ], t, Time.t) Field.t_with_perm
        val session_id :
          ([< `Read | `Set_and_create ], t, string) Field.t_with_perm

        [ ... many definitions omitted ... ]

      end
  end
```

Note that this will generate *a lot* of output because fieldslib generates a large collection of helper functions for working with record fields. We'll only discuss a few of these; you can learn about the remainder from the documentation that comes with fieldslib.

One of the functions we obtain is Logon.user, which we can use to extract the user field from a logon message:

```
# let get_users logons = List.dedup (List.map logons ~f:Logon.user);;
val get_users : Logon.t list -> string list = <fun>
```

In addition to generating field accessor functions, `fieldslib` also creates a submodule called `Fields` that contains a first-class representative of each field, in the form of a value of type `Field.t`. The `Field` module provides the following functions:

`Field.name`
> Returns the name of a field

`Field.get`
> Returns the content of a field

`Field.fset`
> Does a functional update of a field

`Field.setter`
> Returns `None` if the field is not mutable or `Some f` if it is, where `f` is a function for mutating that field

A `Field.t` has two type parameters: the first for the type of the record, and the second for the type of the field in question. Thus, the type of `Logon.Fields.session_id` is `(Logon.t, string) Field.t`, whereas the type of `Logon.Fields.time` is `(Logon.t, Time.t) Field.t`. Thus, if you call `Field.get` on `Logon.Fields.user`, you'll get a function for extracting the user field from a `Logon.t`:

OCaml utop (part 31)

```
# Field.get Logon.Fields.user;;
- : Logon.t -> string = <fun>
```

Thus, the first parameter of the `Field.t` corresponds to the record you pass to `get`, and the second parameter corresponds to the value contained in the field, which is also the return type of `get`.

The type of `Field.get` is a little more complicated than you might naively expect from the preceding one:

OCaml utop (part 32)

```
# Field.get;;
- : ('b, 'r, 'a) Field.t_with_perm -> 'r -> 'a = <fun>
```

The type is `Field.t_with_perm` rather than `Field.t` because fields have a notion of access control that comes up in some special cases where we expose the ability to read a field from a record, but not the ability to create new records, and so we can't expose functional updates.

We can use first-class fields to do things like write a generic function for displaying a record field:

OCaml utop (part 33)

```
# let show_field field to_string record =
    let name = Field.name field in
    let field_string = to_string (Field.get field record) in
    name ^ ": " ^ field_string
```

```
;;
val show_field :
  ('a, 'b, 'c) Field.t_with_perm -> ('c -> string) -> 'b -> string = <fun>
```

This takes three arguments: the `Field.t`, a function for converting the contents of the field in question to a string, and a record from which the field can be grabbed.

Here's an example of `show_field` in action:

OCaml utop (part 34)

```
# let logon = { Logon.
                session_id = "26685";
                time = Time.now ();
                user = "yminsky";
                credentials = "Xy2d9W"; }
  ;;
val logon : Logon.t =
  {Logon.session_id = "26685"; time = 2013-08-18 14:51:00.509463+01:00;
   user = "yminsky"; credentials = "Xy2d9W"}
# show_field Logon.Fields.user Fn.id logon;;
- : string = "user: yminsky"
# show_field Logon.Fields.time Time.to_string logon;;
- : string = "time: 2013-08-18 14:51:00.509463+01:00"
```

As a side note, the preceding example is our first use of the `Fn` module (short for "function"), which provides a collection of useful primitives for dealing with functions. `Fn.id` is the identity function.

`fieldslib` also provides higher-level operators, like `Fields.fold` and `Fields.iter`, which let you walk over the fields of a record. So, for example, in the case of `Logon.t`, the field iterator has the following type:

OCaml utop (part 35)

```
# Logon.Fields.iter;;
- : session_id:((([< `Read | `Set_and_create ], Logon.t, string)
                 Field.t_with_perm -> 'a) ->
    time:((([< `Read | `Set_and_create ], Logon.t, Time.t) Field.t_with_perm ->
          'b) ->
    user:((([< `Read | `Set_and_create ], Logon.t, string) Field.t_with_perm ->
          'c) ->
    credentials:((([< `Read | `Set_and_create ], Logon.t, string)
                  Field.t_with_perm -> 'd) ->
    'd
= <fun>
```

This is a bit daunting to look at, largely because of the access control markers, but the structure is actually pretty simple. Each labeled argument is a function that takes a first-class field of the necessary type as an argument. Note that `iter` passes each of these callbacks the `Field.t`, not the contents of the specific record field. The contents of the field, though, can be looked up using the combination of the record and the `Field.t`.

Now, let's use `Logon.Fields.iter` and `show_field` to print out all the fields of a `Log on` record:

```
# let print_logon logon =
    let print to_string field =
      printf "%s\n" (show_field field to_string logon)
    in
    Logon.Fields.iter
      ~session_id:(print Fn.id)
      ~time:(print Time.to_string)
      ~user:(print Fn.id)
      ~credentials:(print Fn.id)
  ;;
val print_logon : Logon.t -> unit = <fun>
# print_logon logon;;
session_id: 26685
time: 2013-08-18 14:51:00.509463+01:00
user: yminsky
credentials: Xy2d9W
- : unit = ()
```

One nice side effect of this approach is that it helps you adapt your code when the fields of a record change. If you were to add a field to `Logon.t`, the type of `Log on.Fields.iter` would change along with it, acquiring a new argument. Any code using `Logon.Fields.iter` won't compile until it's fixed to take this new argument into account.

Field iterators are useful for a variety of record-related tasks, from building record-validation functions to scaffolding the definition of a web form from a record type. Such applications can benefit from the guarantee that all fields of the record type in question have been considered.

## CHAPTER 6

Variants

Variant types are one of the most useful features of OCaml and also one of the most unusual. They let you represent data that may take on multiple different forms, where each form is marked by an explicit tag. As we'll see, when combined with pattern matching, variants give you a powerful way of representing complex data and of organizing the case-analysis on that information.

The basic syntax of a variant type declaration is as follows:

Syntax

```
type <variant> =
  | <Tag> [ of <type> [* <type>]... ]
  | <Tag> [ of <type> [* <type>]... ]
  | ...
```

Each row essentially represents a case of the variant. Each case has an associated tag and may optionally have a sequence of fields, where each field has a specified type.

Let's consider a concrete example of how variants can be useful. Almost all terminals support a set of eight basic colors, and we can represent those colors using a variant. Each color is declared as a simple tag, with pipes used to separate the different cases. Note that variant tags must be capitalized:

OCaml utop

```
# type basic_color =
  | Black | Red | Green | Yellow | Blue | Magenta | Cyan | White ;;
type basic_color =
    Black
  | Red
  | Green
  | Yellow
  | Blue
  | Magenta
  | Cyan
  | White
```

```
# Cyan ;;
- : basic_color = Cyan
# [Blue; Magenta; Red] ;;
- : basic_color list = [Blue; Magenta; Red]
```

The following function uses pattern matching to convert a `basic_color` to a corre-sponding integer. The exhaustiveness checking on pattern matches means that the compiler will warn us if we miss a color:

OCaml utop (part 1)

```
# let basic_color_to_int = function
  | Black -> 0 | Red     -> 1 | Green -> 2 | Yellow -> 3
  | Blue  -> 4 | Magenta -> 5 | Cyan  -> 6 | White  -> 7 ;;
val basic_color_to_int : basic_color -> int = <fun>
# List.map ~f:basic_color_to_int [Blue;Red];;
- : int list = [4; 1]
```

Using the preceding function, we can generate escape codes to change the color of a given string displayed in a terminal:

OCaml utop

```
# let color_by_number number text =
    sprintf "\027[38;5;%dm%s\027[0m" number text;;
val color_by_number : int -> string -> string = <fun>
# let blue = color_by_number (basic_color_to_int Blue) "Blue";;
val blue : string = "\027[38;5;4mBlue\027[0m"
# printf "Hello %s World!\n" blue;;
Hello Blue World!
```

On most terminals, that word "Blue" will be rendered in blue.

In this example, the cases of the variant are simple tags with no associated data. This is substantively the same as the enumerations found in languages like C and Java. But as we'll see, variants can do considerably more than represent a simple enumeration. As it happens, an enumeration isn't enough to effectively describe the full set of colors that a modern terminal can display. Many terminals, including the venerable xterm, support 256 different colors, broken up into the following groups:

- The eight basic colors, in regular and bold versions
- A $6 \times 6 \times 6$ RGB color cube
- A 24-level grayscale ramp

We'll also represent this more complicated color space as a variant, but this time, the different tags will have arguments that describe the data available in each case. Note that variants can have multiple arguments, which are separated by *s:

OCaml utop (part 3)

```
# type weight = Regular | Bold
  type color =
  | Basic of basic_color * weight (* basic colors, regular and bold *)
```

```
  | RGB   of int * int * int      (* 6x6x6 color cube *)
  | Gray  of int                  (* 24 grayscale levels *)
;;
type weight = Regular | Bold
type color =
    Basic of basic_color * weight
  | RGB of int * int * int
  | Gray of int
# [RGB (250,70,70); Basic (Green, Regular)];;
- : color list = [RGB (250, 70, 70); Basic (Green, Regular)]
```

Once again, we'll use pattern matching to convert a color to a corresponding integer. But in this case, the pattern matching does more than separate out the different cases; it also allows us to extract the data associated with each tag:

OCaml utop (part 4)

```
# let color_to_int = function
    | Basic (basic_color,weight) ->
      let base = match weight with Bold -> 8 | Regular -> 0 in
      base + basic_color_to_int basic_color
    | RGB (r,g,b) -> 16 + b + g * 6 + r * 36
    | Gray i -> 232 + i ;;
val color_to_int : color -> int = <fun>
```

Now, we can print text using the full set of available colors:

OCaml utop

```
# let color_print color s =
    printf "%s\n" (color_by_number (color_to_int color) s);;
val color_print : color -> string -> unit = <fun>
# color_print (Basic (Red,Bold)) "A bold red!";;
A bold red!
# color_print (Gray 4) "A muted gray...";;
A muted gray...
```

Catch-All Cases and Refactoring

OCaml's type system can act as a refactoring tool, warning you of places where your code needs to be updated to match an interface change. This is particularly valuable in the context of variants.

Consider what would happen if we were to change the definition of color to the following:

OCaml utop (part 1)

```
# type color =
    | Basic of basic_color     (* basic colors *)
    | Bold  of basic_color     (* bold basic colors *)
    | RGB   of int * int * int (* 6x6x6 color cube *)
    | Gray  of int             (* 24 grayscale levels *)
;;
type color =
```

```
  Basic of basic_color
| Bold of basic_color
| RGB of int * int * int
| Gray of int
```

We've essentially broken out the Basic case into two cases, Basic and Bold, and Ba
sic has changed from having two arguments to one. color_to_int as we wrote it still
expects the old structure of the variant, and if we try to compile that same code again,
the compiler will notice the discrepancy:

OCaml utop (part 2)

```
# let color_to_int = function
    | Basic (basic_color,weight) ->
      let base = match weight with Bold -> 8 | Regular -> 0 in
      base + basic_color_to_int basic_color
    | RGB (r,g,b) -> 16 + b + g * 6 + r * 36
    | Gray i -> 232 + i ;;
Characters 34-60:
Error: This pattern matches values of type 'a * 'b
       but a pattern was expected which matches values of type basic_color
```

Here, the compiler is complaining that the Basic tag is used with the wrong number of
arguments. If we fix that, however, the compiler flag will flag a second problem, which
is that we haven't handled the new Bold tag:

OCaml utop (part 3)

```
# let color_to_int = function
    | Basic basic_color -> basic_color_to_int basic_color
    | RGB (r,g,b) -> 16 + b + g * 6 + r * 36
    | Gray i -> 232 + i ;;
Characters 19-154:
Warning 8: this pattern-matching is not exhaustive.
Here is an example of a value that is not matched:
Bold _
val color_to_int : color -> int = <fun>
```

Fixing this now leads us to the correct implementation:

OCaml utop (part 4)

```
# let color_to_int = function
    | Basic basic_color -> basic_color_to_int basic_color
    | Bold  basic_color -> 8 + basic_color_to_int basic_color
    | RGB (r,g,b) -> 16 + b + g * 6 + r * 36
    | Gray i -> 232 + i ;;
val color_to_int : color -> int = <fun>
```

As we've seen, the type errors identified the things that needed to be fixed to complete
the refactoring of the code. This is fantastically useful, but for it to work well and reliably,
you need to write your code in a way that maximizes the compiler's chances of helping
you find the bugs. To this end, a useful rule of thumb is to avoid catch-all cases in pattern
matches.

Here's an example that illustrates how catch-all cases interact with exhaustion checks. Imagine we wanted a version of color_to_int that works on older terminals by rendering the first 16 colors (the eight basic_colors in regular and bold) in the normal way, but renders everything else as white. We might have written the function as follows:

OCaml utop (part 5)

```
# let oldschool_color_to_int = function
  | Basic (basic_color,weight) ->
    let base = match weight with Bold -> 8 | Regular -> 0 in
    base + basic_color_to_int basic_color
  | _ -> basic_color_to_int White;;
Characters 44-70:
Error: This pattern matches values of type 'a * 'b
       but a pattern was expected which matches values of type basic_color
```

But because the catch-all case encompasses all possibilities, the type system will no longer warn us that we have missed the new Bold case when we change the type to include it. We can get this check back by avoiding the catch-all case, and instead being explicit about the tags that are ignored.

Combining Records and Variants

The term *algebraic data types* is often used to describe a collection of types that includes variants, records, and tuples. Algebraic data types act as a peculiarly useful and powerful language for describing data. At the heart of their utility is the fact that they combine two different kinds of types: *product types*, like tuples and records, which combine multiple different types together and are mathematically similar to Cartesian products; and *sum types*, like variants, which let you combine multiple different possibilities into one type, and are mathematically similar to disjoint unions.

Algebraic data types gain much of their power from the ability to construct layered combinations of sums and products. Let's see what we can achieve with this by revisiting the logging server types that were described in Chapter 5. We'll start by reminding ourselves of the definition of Log_entry.t:

OCaml utop (part 1)

```
# module Log_entry = struct
    type t =
      { session_id: string;
        time: Time.t;
        important: bool;
        message: string;
      }
  end
  ;;
module Log_entry :
  sig
    type t = {
      session_id : string;
```

```
      time : Time.t;
      important : bool;
      message : string;
    }
  end
```

This record type combines multiple pieces of data into one value. In particular, a single
Log_entry.t has a session_id *and* a time *and* an important flag *and* a message. More
generally, you can think of record types as conjunctions. Variants, on the other hand,
are disjunctions, letting you represent multiple possibilities, as in the following example:

OCaml utop (part 2)

```
# type client_message = | Logon of Logon.t
                        | Heartbeat of Heartbeat.t
                        | Log_entry of Log_entry.t
  ;;
type client_message =
    Logon of Logon.t
  | Heartbeat of Heartbeat.t
  | Log_entry of Log_entry.t
```

A client_message is a Logon *or* a Heartbeat *or* a Log_entry. If we want to write code
that processes messages generically, rather than code specialized to a fixed message type,
we need something like client_message to act as one overarching type for the different
possible messages. We can then match on the client_message to determine the type of
the particular message being dealt with.

You can increase the precision of your types by using variants to represent differences
between types, and records to represent shared structure. Consider the following function that takes a list of client_messages and returns all messages generated by a given
user. The code in question is implemented by folding over the list of messages, where
the accumulator is a pair of:

- The set of session identifiers for the user that have been seen thus far
- The set of messages so far that are associated with the user

Here's the concrete code:

OCaml utop (part 3)

```
# let messages_for_user user messages =
    let (user_messages,_) =
      List.fold messages ~init:([],String.Set.empty)
        ~f:(fun ((messages,user_sessions) as acc) message ->
          match message with
          | Logon m ->
            if m.Logon.user = user then
              (message::messages, Set.add user_sessions m.Logon.session_id)
            else acc
          | Heartbeat _ | Log_entry _ ->
            let session_id = match message with
```

108 | Chapter 6: Variants

```
                | Logon     m -> m.Logon.session_id
                | Heartbeat m -> m.Heartbeat.session_id
                | Log_entry m -> m.Log_entry.session_id
             in
             if Set.mem user_sessions session_id then
               (message::messages,user_sessions)
             else acc
          )
     in
     List.rev user_messages
   ;;
 val messages_for_user : string -> client_message list -> client_message list =
   <fun>
```

There's one awkward part of the preceding code, which is the logic that determines the session ID. The code is somewhat repetitive, contemplating each of the possible message types (including the Logon case, which isn't actually possible at that point in the code) and extracting the session ID in each case. This per-message-type handling seems unnecessary, since the session ID works the same way for all of the message types.

We can improve the code by refactoring our types to explicitly reflect the information that's shared between the different messages. The first step is to cut down the definitions of each per-message record to contain just the information unique to that record:

OCaml utop (part 4)

```
# module Log_entry = struct
    type t = { important: bool;
               message: string;
             }
  end
  module Heartbeat = struct
    type t = { status_message: string; }
  end
  module Logon = struct
    type t = { user: string;
               credentials: string;
             }
  end ;;
module Log_entry : sig type t = { important : bool; message : string; } end
module Heartbeat : sig type t = { status_message : string; } end
module Logon : sig type t = { user : string; credentials : string; } end
```

We can then define a variant type that combines these types:

OCaml utop (part 5)

```
# type details =
    | Logon of Logon.t
    | Heartbeat of Heartbeat.t
    | Log_entry of Log_entry.t
  ;;
type details =
    Logon of Logon.t
```

```
| Heartbeat of Heartbeat.t
| Log_entry of Log_entry.t
```

Separately, we need a record that contains the fields that are common across all messages:

OCaml utop (part 6)

```
# module Common = struct
    type t = { session_id: string;
               time: Time.t;
             }
  end ;;
module Common : sig type t = { session_id : string; time : Time.t; } end
```

A full message can then be represented as a pair of a `Common.t` and a `details`. Using this, we can rewrite our preceding example as follows:

OCaml utop (part 7)

```
# let messages_for_user user messages =
    let (user_messages,_) =
      List.fold messages ~init:([],String.Set.empty)
        ~f:(fun ((messages,user_sessions) as acc) ((common,details) as message) ->
          let session_id = common.Common.session_id in
          match details with
          | Logon m ->
            if m.Logon.user = user then
              (message::messages, Set.add user_sessions session_id)
            else acc
          | Heartbeat _ | Log_entry _ ->
            if Set.mem user_sessions session_id then
              (message::messages,user_sessions)
            else acc
        )
    in
    List.rev user_messages
  ;;
val messages_for_user :
  string -> (Common.t * details) list -> (Common.t * details) list = <fun>
```

As you can see, the code for extracting the session ID has been replaced with the simple expression `common.Common.session_id`.

In addition, this design allows us to essentially downcast to the specific message type once we know what it is and then dispatch code to handle just that message type. In particular, while we use the type `Common.t * details` to represent an arbitrary message, we can use `Common.t * Logon.t` to represent a logon message. Thus, if we had functions for handling individual message types, we could write a dispatch function as follows:

OCaml utop (part 8)

```
# let handle_message server_state (common,details) =
    match details with
    | Log_entry m -> handle_log_entry server_state (common,m)
    | Logon     m -> handle_logon     server_state (common,m)
```

```
  | Heartbeat m -> handle_heartbeat server_state (common,m)
;;
```

And it's explicit at the type level that `handle_log_entry` sees only `Log_entry` messages, `handle_logon` sees only `Logon` messages, etc.

Variants and Recursive Data Structures

Another common application of variants is to represent tree-like recursive data structures. We'll show how this can be done by walking through the design of a simple Boolean expression language. Such a language can be useful anywhere you need to specify filters, which are used in everything from packet analyzers to mail clients.

An expression in this language will be defined by the variant `expr`, with one tag for each kind of expression we want to support:

OCaml utop

```
# type 'a expr =
    | Base  of 'a
    | Const of bool
    | And   of 'a expr list
    | Or    of 'a expr list
    | Not   of 'a expr
  ;;
type 'a expr =
    Base of 'a
  | Const of bool
  | And of 'a expr list
  | Or of 'a expr list
  | Not of 'a expr
```

Note that the definition of the type `expr` is recursive, meaning that a `expr` may contain other `expr`s. Also, `expr` is parameterized by a polymorphic type `'a` which is used for specifying the type of the value that goes under the `Base` tag.

The purpose of each tag is pretty straightforward. `And`, `Or`, and `Not` are the basic operators for building up Boolean expressions, and `Const` lets you enter the constants `true` and `false`.

The `Base` tag is what allows you to tie the `expr` to your application, by letting you specify an element of some base predicate type, whose truth or falsehood is determined by your application. If you were writing a filter language for an email processor, your base predicates might specify the tests you would run against an email, as in the following example:

OCaml utop (part 1)

```
# type mail_field = To | From | CC | Date | Subject
  type mail_predicate = { field: mail_field;
                          contains: string }
  ;;
```

```
type mail_field = To | From | CC | Date | Subject
type mail_predicate = { field : mail_field; contains : string; }
```

Using the preceding code, we can construct a simple expression with `mail_predi cate` as its base predicate:

OCaml utop (part 2)

```
# let test field contains = Base { field; contains };;
val test : mail_field -> string -> mail_predicate expr = <fun>
# And [ Or [ test To "doligez"; test CC "doligez" ];
        test Subject "runtime";
      ]
  ;;
- : mail_predicate expr =
And
 [Or
   [Base {field = To; contains = "doligez"};
    Base {field = CC; contains = "doligez"}];
  Base {field = Subject; contains = "runtime"}]
```

Being able to construct such expressions isn't enough; we also need to be able to evaluate them. Here's a function for doing just that:

OCaml utop (part 3)

```
# let rec eval expr base_eval =
    (* a shortcut, so we don't need to repeatedly pass [base_eval]
       explicitly to [eval] *)
    let eval' expr = eval expr base_eval in
    match expr with
    | Base  base  -> base_eval base
    | Const bool  -> bool
    | And   exprs -> List.for_all exprs ~f:eval'
    | Or    exprs -> List.exists  exprs ~f:eval'
    | Not   expr  -> not (eval' expr)
  ;;
val eval : 'a expr -> ('a -> bool) -> bool = <fun>
```

The structure of the code is pretty straightforward—we're just pattern matching over the structure of the data, doing the appropriate calculation based on which tag we see. To use this evaluator on a concrete example, we just need to write the `base_eval` function, which is capable of evaluating a base predicate.

Another useful operation on expressions is simplification. The following is a set of simplifying construction functions that mirror the tags of an `expr`:

OCaml utop (part 4)

```
# let and_ l =
    if List.mem l (Const false) then Const false
    else
      match List.filter l ~f:((<>) (Const true)) with
      | [] -> Const true
      | [ x ] -> x
      | l -> And l
```

```
    let or_ l =
      if List.mem l (Const true) then Const true
      else
        match List.filter l ~f:((<>) (Const false)) with
        | [] -> Const false
        | [x] -> x
        | l -> Or l

    let not_ = function
      | Const b -> Const (not b)
      | e -> Not e
   ;;
val and_ : 'a expr list -> 'a expr = <fun>
val or_ : 'a expr list -> 'a expr = <fun>
val not_ : 'a expr -> 'a expr = <fun>
```

We can now write a simplification routine that is based on the preceding functions.

OCaml utop (part 5)

```
# let rec simplify = function
    | Base _ | Const _ as x -> x
    | And l -> and_ (List.map ~f:simplify l)
    | Or l  -> or_  (List.map ~f:simplify l)
    | Not e -> not_ (simplify e)
  ;;
val simplify : 'a expr -> 'a expr = <fun>
```

We can apply this to a Boolean expression and see how good a job it does at simplifying it:

OCaml utop (part 6)

```
# simplify (Not (And [ Or [Base "it's snowing"; Const true];
                       Base "it's raining"]));;
- : string expr = Not (Base "it's raining")
```

Here, it correctly converted the Or branch to Const true and then eliminated the And entirely, since the And then had only one nontrivial component.

There are some simplifications it misses, however. In particular, see what happens if we add a double negation in:

OCaml utop (part 7)

```
# simplify (Not (And [ Or [Base "it's snowing"; Const true];
                       Not (Not (Base "it's raining"))]));;
- : string expr = Not (Not (Not (Base "it's raining")))
```

It fails to remove the double negation, and it's easy to see why. The not_ function has a catch-all case, so it ignores everything but the one case it explicitly considers, that of the negation of a constant. Catch-all cases are generally a bad idea, and if we make the code more explicit, we see that the missing of the double negation is more obvious:

```
# let not_ = function
    | Const b -> Const (not b)
    | (Base _ | And _ | Or _ | Not _) as e -> Not e
  ;;
val not_ : 'a expr -> 'a expr = <fun>
```

We can of course fix this by simply adding an explicit case for double negation:

```
# let not_ = function
    | Const b -> Const (not b)
    | Not e -> e
    | (Base _ | And _ | Or _ ) as e -> Not e
  ;;
val not_ : 'a expr -> 'a expr = <fun>
```

The example of a Boolean expression language is more than a toy. There's a module very much in this spirit in Core called Blang (short for "Boolean language"), and it gets a lot of practical use in a variety of applications. The simplification algorithm in particular is useful when you want to use it to specialize the evaluation of expressions for which the evaluation of some of the base predicates is already known.

More generally, using variants to build recursive data structures is a common technique, and shows up everywhere from designing little languages to building complex data structures.

Polymorphic Variants

In addition to the ordinary variants we've seen so far, OCaml also supports so-called *polymorphic variants*. As we'll see, polymorphic variants are more flexible and syntactically more lightweight than ordinary variants, but that extra power comes at a cost.

Syntactically, polymorphic variants are distinguished from ordinary variants by the leading backtick. And unlike ordinary variants, polymorphic variants can be used without an explicit type declaration:

```
# let three = `Int 3;;
val three : [> `Int of int ] = `Int 3
# let four = `Float 4.;;
val four : [> `Float of float ] = `Float 4.
# let nan = `Not_a_number;;
val nan : [> `Not_a_number ] = `Not_a_number
# [three; four; nan];;
- : [> `Float of float | `Int of int | `Not_a_number ] list =
[`Int 3; `Float 4.; `Not_a_number]
```

As you can see, polymorphic variant types are inferred automatically, and when we combine variants with different tags, the compiler infers a new type that knows about all of those tags. Note that in the preceding example, the tag name (e.g., `Int) matches the type name (int). This is a common convention in OCaml.

The type system will complain if it sees incompatible uses of the same tag:

```
# let five = `Int "five";;
val five : [> `Int of string ] = `Int "five"
# [three; four; five];;
Characters 14-18:
Error: This expression has type [> `Int of string ]
       but an expression was expected of type
         [> `Float of float | `Int of int ]
       Types for tag `Int are incompatible
```

The > at the beginning of the variant types above is critical because it marks the types as being open to combination with other variant types. We can read the type [> `Int of string | `Float of float] as describing a variant whose tags include `Int of string and `Float of float, but may include more tags as well. In other words, you can roughly translate > to mean: "these tags or more."

OCaml will in some cases infer a variant type with <, to indicate "these tags or less," as in the following example:

```
# let is_positive = function
    | `Int   x -> x > 0
    | `Float x -> x > 0.
  ;;
val is_positive : [< `Float of float | `Int of int ] -> bool = <fun>
```

The < is there because is_positive has no way of dealing with values that have tags other than `Float of float or `Int of int.

We can think of these < and > markers as indications of upper and lower bounds on the tags involved. If the same set of tags are both an upper and a lower bound, we end up with an *exact* polymorphic variant type, which has neither marker. For example:

```
# let exact = List.filter ~f:is_positive [three;four];;
val exact : [ `Float of float | `Int of int ] list = [`Int 3; `Float 4.]
```

Perhaps surprisingly, we can also create polymorphic variant types that have different upper and lower bounds. Note that Ok and Error in the following example come from the Result.t type from Core:

```
# let is_positive = function
    | `Int   x -> Ok (x > 0)
    | `Float x -> Ok (x > 0.)
    | `Not_a_number -> Error "not a number";;
val is_positive :
```

```
    [< `Float of float | `Int of int | `Not_a_number ] ->
    (bool, string) Result.t = <fun>
# List.filter [three; four] ~f:(fun x ->
    match is_positive x with Error _ -> false | Ok b -> b);;
- : [< `Float of float | `Int of int | `Not_a_number > `Float `Int ] list =
[`Int 3; `Float 4.]
```

Here, the inferred type states that the tags can be no more than `Float, `Int, and
`Not_a_number, and must contain at least `Float and `Int. As you can already start to
see, polymorphic variants can lead to fairly complex inferred types.

Example: Terminal Colors Redux

To see how to use polymorphic variants in practice, we'll return to terminal colors.
Imagine that we have a new terminal type that adds yet more colors, say, by adding an
alpha channel so you can specify translucent colors. We could model this extended set
of colors as follows, using an ordinary variant:

OCaml utop (part 11)

```
# type extended_color =
    | Basic of basic_color * weight  (* basic colors, regular and bold *)
    | RGB   of int * int * int       (* 6x6x6 color space *)
    | Gray  of int                   (* 24 grayscale levels *)
    | RGBA  of int * int * int * int (* 6x6x6x6 color space *)
  ;;
type extended_color =
    Basic of basic_color * weight
  | RGB of int * int * int
  | Gray of int
  | RGBA of int * int * int * int
```

We want to write a function extended_color_to_int, that works like color_to_int
for all of the old kinds of colors, with new logic only for handling colors that include an
alpha channel. One might try to write such a function as follows.

OCaml utop (part 12)

```
# let extended_color_to_int = function
    | RGBA (r,g,b,a) -> 256 + a + b * 6 + g * 36 + r * 216
    | (Basic _ | RGB _ | Gray _) as color -> color_to_int color
  ;;
Characters 154-159:
Error: This expression has type extended_color
       but an expression was expected of type color
```

The code looks reasonable enough, but it leads to a type error because extended_col
or and color are in the compiler's view distinct and unrelated types. The compiler
doesn't, for example, recognize any equality between the Basic tag in the two types.

What we want to do is to share tags between two different variant types, and polymorphic variants let us do this in a natural way. First, let's rewrite basic_color_to_int and

color_to_int using polymorphic variants. The translation here is pretty straightforward:

OCaml utop (part 13)

```
# let basic_color_to_int = function
    | `Black -> 0 | `Red     -> 1 | `Green -> 2 | `Yellow -> 3
    | `Blue  -> 4 | `Magenta -> 5 | `Cyan  -> 6 | `White  -> 7

  let color_to_int = function
    | `Basic (basic_color,weight) ->
      let base = match weight with `Bold -> 8 | `Regular -> 0 in
      base + basic_color_to_int basic_color
    | `RGB (r,g,b) -> 16 + b + g * 6 + r * 36
    | `Gray i -> 232 + i
  ;;
val basic_color_to_int :
  [< `Black | `Blue | `Cyan | `Green | `Magenta | `Red | `White | `Yellow ] ->
  int = <fun>
val color_to_int :
  [< `Basic of
       [< `Black
        | `Blue
        | `Cyan
        | `Green
        | `Magenta
        | `Red
        | `White
        | `Yellow ] *
       [< `Bold | `Regular ]
   | `Gray of int
   | `RGB of int * int * int ] ->
  int = <fun>
```

Now we can try writing extended_color_to_int. The key issue with this code is that
extended_color_to_int needs to invoke color_to_int with a narrower type, i.e., one
that includes fewer tags. Written properly, this narrowing can be done via a pattern
match. In particular, in the following code, the type of the variable color includes only
the tags `Basic, `RGB, and `Gray, and not `RGBA:

OCaml utop (part 14)

```
# let extended_color_to_int = function
    | `RGBA (r,g,b,a) -> 256 + a + b * 6 + g * 36 + r * 216
    | (`Basic _ | `RGB _ | `Gray _) as color -> color_to_int color
  ;;
val extended_color_to_int :
  [< `Basic of
       [< `Black
        | `Blue
        | `Cyan
        | `Green
        | `Magenta
        | `Red
```

```
      |  `White
      |  `Yellow ] *
     [< `Bold | `Regular ]
  | `Gray of int
  | `RGB of int * int * int
  | `RGBA of int * int * int * int ] ->
 int = <fun>
```

The preceding code is more delicately balanced than one might imagine. In particular,
if we use a catch-all case instead of an explicit enumeration of the cases, the type is no
longer narrowed, and so compilation fails:

OCaml utop (part 15)

```
# let extended_color_to_int = function
   | `RGBA (r,g,b,a) -> 256 + a + b * 6 + g * 36 + r * 216
   | color -> color_to_int color
 ;;
Characters 125-130:
Error: This expression has type [> `RGBA of int * int * int * int ]
       but an expression was expected of type
         [< `Basic of
             [< `Black
              | `Blue
              | `Cyan
              | `Green
              | `Magenta
              | `Red
              | `White
              | `Yellow ] *
             [< `Bold | `Regular ]
          | `Gray of int
          | `RGB of int * int * int ]
       The second variant type does not allow tag(s) `RGBA
```

Polymorphic Variants and Catch-all Cases
As we saw with the definition of is_positive, a match statement can lead to
the inference of an upper bound on a variant type, limiting the possible tags
to those that can be handled by the match. If we add a catch-all case to our
match statement, we end up with a type with a lower bound:

OCaml utop (part 16)

```
# let is_positive_permissive = function
    | `Int   x -> Ok (x > 0)
    | `Float x -> Ok (x > 0.)
    | _ -> Error "Unknown number type"
  ;;
val is_positive_permissive :
  [> `Float of float | `Int of int ] -> (bool, string) Result.t = <fun>
# is_positive_permissive (`Int 0);;
- : (bool, string) Result.t = Ok false
# is_positive_permissive (`Ratio (3,4));;
- : (bool, string) Result.t = Error "Unknown number type"
```

Catch-all cases are error-prone even with ordinary variants, but they are especially so with polymorphic variants. That's because you have no way of bounding what tags your function might have to deal with. Such code is particularly vulnerable to typos. For instance, if code that uses is_posi tive_permissive passes in Float misspelled as Floot, the erroneous code will compile without complaint:

OCaml utop (part 17)

```
# is_positive_permissive (`Floot 3.5);;
- : (bool, string) Result.t = Error "Unknown number type"
```

With ordinary variants, such a typo would have been caught as an un-known tag. As a general matter, one should be wary about mixing catch-all cases and polymorphic variants.

Let's consider how we might turn our code into a proper library with an implementation in an ml file and an interface in a separate mli, as we saw in Chapter 4. Let's start with the mli:

OCaml: OCaml

```
open Core.Std

type basic_color =
  [ `Black   | `Blue | `Cyan  | `Green
  | `Magenta | `Red  | `White | `Yellow ]

type color =
  [ `Basic of basic_color * [ `Bold | `Regular ]
  | `Gray of int
  | `RGB  of int * int * int ]

type extended_color =
  [ color
  | `RGBA of int * int * int * int ]

val color_to_int          : color -> int
val extended_color_to_int : extended_color -> int
```

Here, extended_color is defined as an explicit extension of color. Also, notice that we defined all of these types as exact variants. We can implement this library as follows:

OCaml: OCaml

```
open Core.Std

type basic_color =
  [ `Black   | `Blue | `Cyan  | `Green
  | `Magenta | `Red  | `White | `Yellow ]

type color =
  [ `Basic of basic_color * [ `Bold | `Regular ]
  | `Gray of int
  | `RGB  of int * int * int ]
```

```
type extended_color =
  [ color
  | `RGBA of int * int * int * int ]

let basic_color_to_int = function
  | `Black -> 0 | `Red     -> 1 | `Green -> 2 | `Yellow -> 3
  | `Blue  -> 4 | `Magenta -> 5 | `Cyan  -> 6 | `White  -> 7

let color_to_int = function
  | `Basic (basic_color,weight) ->
    let base = match weight with `Bold -> 8 | `Regular -> 0 in
    base + basic_color_to_int basic_color
  | `RGB (r,g,b) -> 16 + b + g * 6 + r * 36
  | `Gray i -> 232 + i

let extended_color_to_int = function
  | `RGBA (r,g,b,a) -> 256 + a + b * 6 + g * 36 + r * 216
  | `Grey x -> 2000 + x
  | (`Basic _ | `RGB _ | `Gray _) as color -> color_to_int color
```

In the preceding code, we did something funny to the definition of `extended_col or_to_int` that underlines some of the downsides of polymorphic variants. In particular, we added some special-case handling for the color gray, rather than using `col or_to_int`. Unfortunately, we misspelled `Gray` as `Grey`. This is exactly the kind of error that the compiler would catch with ordinary variants, but with polymorphic variants, this compiles without issue. All that happened was that the compiler inferred a wider type for `extended_color_to_int`, which happens to be compatible with the narrower type that was listed in the `mli`.

If we add an explicit type annotation to the code itself (rather than just in the `mli`), then the compiler has enough information to warn us:

OCaml: OCaml (part 1)

```
let extended_color_to_int : extended_color -> int = function
  | `RGBA (r,g,b,a) -> 256 + a + b * 6 + g * 36 + r * 216
  | `Grey x -> 2000 + x
  | (`Basic _ | `RGB _ | `Gray _) as color -> color_to_int color
```

In particular, the compiler will complain that the `Grey` case is unused:

Terminal

```
$ corebuild terminal_color.native
File "terminal_color.ml", line 30, characters 4-11:
Error: This pattern matches values of type [? `Grey of 'a ]
       but a pattern was expected which matches values of type extended_color
       The second variant type does not allow tag(s) `Grey
Command exited with code 2.
```

Once we have type definitions at our disposal, we can revisit the question of how we write the pattern match that narrows the type. In particular, we can explicitly use the type name as part of the pattern match, by prefixing it with a #:

OCaml: OCaml (part 1)

```
let extended_color_to_int : extended_color -> int = function
  | `RGBA (r,g,b,a) -> 256 + a + b * 6 + g * 36 + r * 216
  | #color as color -> color_to_int color
```

This is useful when you want to narrow down to a type whose definition is long, and you don't want the verbosity of writing the tags down explicitly in the match.

When to Use Polymorphic Variants

At first glance, polymorphic variants look like a strict improvement over ordinary variants. You can do everything that ordinary variants can do, plus it's more flexible and more concise. What's not to like?

In reality, regular variants are the more pragmatic choice most of the time. That's because the flexibility of polymorphic variants comes at a price. Here are some of the downsides:

Complexity
> As we've seen, the typing rules for polymorphic variants are a lot more complicated than they are for regular variants. This means that heavy use of polymorphic variants can leave you scratching your head trying to figure out why a given piece of code did or didn't compile. It can also lead to absurdly long and hard to decode error messages. Indeed, concision at the value level is often balanced out by more verbosity at the type level.

Error-finding
> Polymorphic variants are type-safe, but the typing discipline that they impose is, by dint of its flexibility, less likely to catch bugs in your program.

Efficiency
> This isn't a huge effect, but polymorphic variants are somewhat heavier than regular variants, and OCaml can't generate code for matching on polymorphic variants that is quite as efficient as what it generated for regular variants.

All that said, polymorphic variants are still a useful and powerful feature, but it's worth understanding their limitations and how to use them sensibly and modestly.

Probably the safest and most common use case for polymorphic variants is where ordinary variants would be sufficient but are syntactically too heavyweight. For example, you often want to create a variant type for encoding the inputs or outputs to a function, where it's not worth declaring a separate type for it. Polymorphic variants are very useful here, and as long as there are type annotations that constrain these to have explicit, exact types, this tends to work well.

Variants are most problematic exactly where you take full advantage of their power; in particular, when you take advantage of the ability of polymorphic variant types to overlap in the tags they support. This ties into OCaml's support for subtyping. As we'll discuss further when we cover objects in Chapter 11, subtyping brings in a lot of complexity, and most of the time, that's complexity you want to avoid.

## CHAPTER 7

Error Handling

Nobody likes dealing with errors. It's tedious, it's easy to get wrong, and it's usually just not as fun as planning out how your program is going to succeed. But error handling is important, and however much you don't like thinking about it, having your software fail due to poor error handling is worse.

Thankfully, OCaml has powerful tools for handling errors reliably and with a minimum of pain. In this chapter we'll discuss some of the different approaches in OCaml to handling errors, and give some advice on how to design interfaces that make error handling easier.

We'll start by describing the two basic approaches for reporting errors in OCaml: error-aware return types and exceptions.

Error-Aware Return Types

The best way in OCaml to signal an error is to include that error in your return value. Consider the type of the find function in the List module:

OCaml utop

```
# List.find;;
- : 'a list -> f:('a -> bool) -> 'a option = <fun>
```

The option in the return type indicates that the function may not succeed in finding a suitable element:

OCaml utop (part 1)

```
# List.find [1;2;3] ~f:(fun x -> x >= 2) ;;
- : int option = Some 2
# List.find [1;2;3] ~f:(fun x -> x >= 10) ;;
- : int option = None
```

Including errors in the return values of your functions requires the caller to handle the error explicitly, allowing the caller to make the choice of whether to recover from the error or propagate it onward.

Consider the `compute_bounds` function. The function takes a list and a comparison function and returns upper and lower bounds for the list by finding the smallest and largest element on the list. `List.hd` and `List.last`, which return `None` when they encounter an empty list, are used to extract the largest and smallest element of the list:

OCaml utop (part 2)

```
# let compute_bounds ~cmp list =
    let sorted = List.sort ~cmp list in
    match List.hd sorted, List.last sorted with
    | None,_ | _, None -> None
    | Some x, Some y -> Some (x,y)
  ;;
val compute_bounds : cmp:('a -> 'a -> int) -> 'a list -> ('a * 'a) option =
  <fun>
```

The `match` statement is used to handle the error cases, propagating a `None` in hd or last into the return value of `compute_bounds`.

On the other hand, in the `find_mismatches` that follows, errors encountered during the computation do not propagate to the return value of the function. `find_mismatches` takes two hash tables as arguments and searches for keys that have different data in one table than in the other. As such, the failure to find a key in one table isn't a failure of any sort:

OCaml utop (part 3)

```
# let find_mismatches table1 table2 =
    Hashtbl.fold table1 ~init:[] ~f:(fun ~key ~data mismatches ->
      match Hashtbl.find table2 key with
      | Some data' when data' <> data -> key :: mismatches
      | _ -> mismatches
    )
  ;;
val find_mismatches : ('a, 'b) Hashtbl.t -> ('a, 'b) Hashtbl.t -> 'a list =
  <fun>
```

The use of options to encode errors underlines the fact that it's not clear whether a particular outcome, like not finding something on a list, is an error or is just another valid outcome. This depends on the larger context of your program, and thus is not something that a general-purpose library can know in advance. One of the advantages of error-aware return types is that they work well in both situations.

Encoding Errors with Result

Options aren't always a sufficiently expressive way to report errors. Specifically, when you encode an error as None, there's nowhere to say anything about the nature of the error.

Result.t is meant to address this deficiency. The type is defined as follows:

```
module Result : sig
  type ('a,'b) t = | Ok of 'a
                   | Error of 'b
end
```

A Result.t is essentially an option augmented with the ability to store other information in the error case. Like Some and None for options, the constructors Ok and Error are promoted to the toplevel by Core.Std. As such, we can write:

```
# [ Ok 3; Error "abject failure"; Ok 4 ];;
- : (int, string) Result.t list = [Ok 3; Error "abject failure"; Ok 4]
```

without first opening the Result module.

Error and Or_error

Result.t gives you complete freedom to choose the type of value you use to represent errors, but it's often useful to standardize on an error type. Among other things, this makes it easier to write utility functions to automate common error handling patterns.

But which type to choose? Is it better to represent errors as strings? Some more structured representation like XML? Or something else entirely?

Core's answer to this question is the Error.t type, which tries to forge a good compromise between efficiency, convenience, and control over the presentation of errors.

It might not be obvious at first why efficiency is an issue at all. But generating error messages is an expensive business. An ASCII representation of a value can be quite time-consuming to construct, particularly if it includes expensive-to-convert numerical data.

Error gets around this issue through laziness. In particular, an Error.t allows you to put off generation of the error string until and unless you need it, which means a lot of the time you never have to construct it at all. You can of course construct an error directly from a string:

```
# Error.of_string "something went wrong";;
- : Error.t = something went wrong
```

But you can also construct an Error.t from a *thunk*, i.e., a function that takes a single argument of type unit:

```
# Error.of_thunk (fun () ->
    sprintf "something went wrong: %f" 32.3343);;
- : Error.t = something went wrong: 32.334300
```

In this case, we can benefit from the laziness of Error, since the thunk won't be called unless the Error.t is converted to a string.

The most common way to create Error.ts is using *s-expressions*. An s-expression is a balanced parenthetical expression where the leaves of the expressions are strings. Here's a simple example:

```
(This (is an) (s expression))
```

S-expressions are supported by the Sexplib package that is distributed with Core and is the most common serialization format used in Core. Indeed, most types in Core come with built-in s-expression converters. Here's an example of creating an error using the sexp converter for times, Time.sexp_of_t:

```
# Error.create "Something failed a long time ago" Time.epoch Time.sexp_of_t;;
- : Error.t =
Something failed a long time ago: (1970-01-01 01:00:00.000000+01:00)
```

Note that the time isn't actually serialized into an s-expression until the error is printed out.

We're not restricted to doing this kind of error reporting with built-in types. This will be discussed in more detail in Chapter 17, but Sexplib comes with a language extension that can autogenerate sexp converters for newly generated types:

```
# let custom_to_sexp = <:sexp_of<float * string list * int>>;;
val custom_to_sexp : float * string list * int -> Sexp.t = <fun>
# custom_to_sexp (3.5, ["a";"b";"c"], 6034);;
- : Sexp.t = (3.5 (a b c) 6034)
```

We can use this same idiom for generating an error:

```
# Error.create "Something went terribly wrong"
    (3.5, ["a";"b";"c"], 6034)
    <:sexp_of<float * string list * int>> ;;
- : Error.t = Something went terribly wrong: (3.5(a b c)6034)
```

Error also supports operations for transforming errors. For example, it's often useful to augment an error with information about the context of the error or to combine multiple errors together. Error.tag and Error.of_list fulfill these roles:

```
# Error.tag
    (Error.of_list [ Error.of_string "Your tires were slashed";
```

```
                Error.of_string "Your windshield was smashed" ])
    "over the weekend"
  ;;
- : Error.t =
over the weekend: Your tires were slashed; Your windshield was smashed
```

The type `'a Or_error.t` is just a shorthand for `('a,Error.t) Result.t`, and it is, after `option`, the most common way of returning errors in Core.

bind and Other Error Handling Idioms

As you write more error handling code in OCaml, you'll discover that certain patterns start to emerge. A number of these common patterns have been codified by functions in modules like `Option` and `Result`. One particularly useful pattern is built around the function `bind`, which is both an ordinary function and an infix operator `>>=`. Here's the definition of `bind` for options:

OCaml utop (part 11)

```
# let bind option f =
    match option with
    | None -> None
    | Some x -> f x
  ;;
val bind : 'a option -> ('a -> 'b option) -> 'b option = <fun>
```

As you can see, `bind None f` returns `None` without calling `f`, and `bind (Some x) f` returns `f x`. `bind` can be used as a way of sequencing together error-producing functions so that the first one to produce an error terminates the computation. Here's a rewrite of `compute_bounds` to use a nested series of `bind`s:

OCaml utop (part 12)

```
# let compute_bounds ~cmp list =
    let sorted = List.sort ~cmp list in
    Option.bind (List.hd sorted) (fun first ->
      Option.bind (List.last sorted) (fun last ->
        Some (first,last)))
  ;;
val compute_bounds : cmp:('a -> 'a -> int) -> 'a list -> ('a * 'a) option =
  <fun>
```

The preceding code is a little bit hard to swallow, however, on a syntactic level. We can make it easier to read and drop some of the parentheses, by using the infix operator form of `bind`, which we get access to by locally opening `Option.Monad_infix`. The module is called `Monad_infix` because the `bind` operator is part of a subinterface called `Monad`, which we'll see again in Chapter 18:

OCaml utop (part 13)

```
# let compute_bounds ~cmp list =
    let open Option.Monad_infix in
    let sorted = List.sort ~cmp list in
    List.hd sorted   >>= fun first ->
```

```
    List.last sorted >>= fun last  ->
    Some (first,last)
  ;;
val compute_bounds : cmp:('a -> 'a -> int) -> 'a list -> ('a * 'a) option =
  <fun>
```

This use of bind isn't really materially better than the one we started with, and indeed, for small examples like this, direct matching of options is generally better than using bind. But for large, complex examples with many stages of error handling, the bind idiom becomes clearer and easier to manage.

There are other useful idioms encoded in the functions in Option. One example is Option.both, which takes two optional values and produces a new optional pair that is None if either of its arguments are None. Using Option.both, we can make com pute_bounds even shorter:

OCaml utop (part 14)

```
# let compute_bounds ~cmp list =
    let sorted = List.sort ~cmp list in
    Option.both (List.hd sorted) (List.last sorted)
  ;;
val compute_bounds : cmp:('a -> 'a -> int) -> 'a list -> ('a * 'a) option =
  <fun>
```

These error-handling functions are valuable because they let you express your error handling both explicitly and concisely. We've only discussed these functions in the context of the Option module, but more functionality of this kind can be found in the Result and Or_error modules.

Exceptions

Exceptions in OCaml are not that different from exceptions in many other languages, like Java, C#, and Python. Exceptions are a way to terminate a computation and report an error, while providing a mechanism to catch and handle (and possibly recover from) exceptions that are triggered by subcomputations.

You can trigger an exception by, for example, dividing an integer by zero:

OCaml utop (part 15)

```
# 3 / 0;;
Exception: Division_by_zero.
```

And an exception can terminate a computation even if it happens nested somewhere deep within it:

OCaml utop (part 16)

```
# List.map ~f:(fun x -> 100 / x) [1;3;0;4];;
Exception: Division_by_zero.
```

If we put a `printf` in the middle of the computation, we can see that `List.map` is interrupted partway through its execution, never getting to the end of the list:

OCaml utop (part 17)

```
# List.map ~f:(fun x -> printf "%d\n%!" x; 100 / x) [1;3;0;4];;
1
3
0
Exception: Division_by_zero.
```

In addition to built-in exceptions like `Divide_by_zero`, OCaml lets you define your own:

OCaml utop (part 18)

```
# exception Key_not_found of string;;
exception Key_not_found of string
# raise (Key_not_found "a");;
Exception: Key_not_found("a").
```

Exceptions are ordinary values and can be manipulated just like other OCaml values:

OCaml utop (part 19)

```
# let exceptions = [ Not_found; Division_by_zero; Key_not_found "b" ];;
val exceptions : exn list = [Not_found; Division_by_zero; Key_not_found("b")]
# List.filter exceptions  ~f:(function
    | Key_not_found _ | Not_found -> true
    | _ -> false);;
- : exn list = [Not_found; Key_not_found("b")]
```

Exceptions are all of the same type, exn. The exn type is something of a special case in the OCaml type system. It is similar to the variant types we encountered in Chapter 6, except that it is *open*, meaning that it's not fully defined in any one place. In particular, new tags (specifically, new exceptions) can be added to it by different parts of the program. This is in contrast to ordinary variants, which are defined with a closed universe of available tags. One result of this is that you can never have an exhaustive match on an exn, since the full set of possible exceptions is not known.

The following function uses the Key_not_found exception we defined above to signal an error:

OCaml utop (part 20)

```
# let rec find_exn alist key = match alist with
    | [] -> raise (Key_not_found key)
    | (key',data) :: tl -> if key = key' then data else find_exn tl key
  ;;
val find_exn : (string * 'a) list -> string -> 'a = <fun>
# let alist = [("a",1); ("b",2)];;
val alist : (string * int) list = [("a", 1); ("b", 2)]
# find_exn alist "a";;
- : int = 1
# find_exn alist "c";;
Exception: Key_not_found("c").
```

Note that we named the function `find_exn` to warn the user that the function routinely throws exceptions, a convention that is used heavily in Core.

In the preceding example, `raise` throws the exception, thus terminating the computation. The type of raise is a bit surprising when you first see it:

OCaml utop (part 21)

```
# raise;;
- : exn -> 'a = <fun>
```

The return type of `'a` makes it look like `raise` manufactures a value to return that is completely unconstrained in its type. That seems impossible, and it is. Really, `raise` has a return type of `'a` because it never returns at all. This behavior isn't restricted to functions like `raise` that terminate by throwing exceptions. Here's another example of a function that doesn't return a value:

OCaml utop (part 22)

```
# let rec forever () = forever ();;
val forever : unit -> 'a = <fun>
```

`forever` doesn't return a value for a different reason: it's an infinite loop.

This all matters because it means that the return type of `raise` can be whatever it needs to be to fit into the context it is called in. Thus, the type system will let us throw an exception anywhere in a program.

Declaring Exceptions Using with sexp

OCaml can't always generate a useful textual representation of an exception. For example:

OCaml utop (part 23)

```
# exception Wrong_date of Date.t;;
exception Wrong_date of Date.t
# Wrong_date (Date.of_string "2011-02-23");;
- : exn = Wrong_date(_)
```

But if we declare the exception using `with sexp` (and the constituent types have sexp converters), we'll get something with more information:

OCaml utop (part 24)

```
# exception Wrong_date of Date.t with sexp;;
exception Wrong_date of Date.t
# Wrong_date (Date.of_string "2011-02-23");;
- : exn = (//toplevel//.Wrong_date 2011-02-23)
```

The period in front of `Wrong_date` is there because the representation generated by `with sexp` includes the full module path of the module where the exception in question is defined. In this case, the string `//toplevel//` is used to indicate that this was declared at the toplevel, rather than in a module.

This is all part of the support for s-expressions provided by the Sex-plib library and syntax extension, which is described in more detail in Chapter 17.

Helper Functions for Throwing Exceptions

OCaml and Core provide a number of helper functions to simplify the task of throwing exceptions. The simplest one is `failwith`, which could be defined as follows:

OCaml utop (part 25)

```
# let failwith msg = raise (Failure msg);;
val failwith : string -> 'a = <fun>
```

There are several other useful functions for raising exceptions, which can be found in the API documentation for the Common and Exn modules in Core.

Another important way of throwing an exception is the `assert` directive. `assert` is used for situations where a violation of the condition in question indicates a bug. Consider the following piece of code for zipping together two lists:

OCaml utop (part 26)

```
# let merge_lists xs ys ~f =
    if List.length xs <> List.length ys then None
    else
      let rec loop xs ys =
        match xs,ys with
        | [],[] -> []
        | x::xs, y::ys -> f x y :: loop xs ys
        | _ -> assert false
      in
      Some (loop xs ys)
  ;;
val merge_lists : 'a list -> 'b list -> f:('a -> 'b -> 'c) -> 'c list option =
  <fun>
# merge_lists [1;2;3] [-1;1;2] ~f:(+);;
- : int list option = Some [0; 3; 5]
# merge_lists [1;2;3] [-1;1] ~f:(+);;
- : int list option = None
```

Here we use `assert false`, which means that the `assert` is guaranteed to trigger. In general, one can put an arbitrary condition in the assertion.

In this case, the `assert` can never be triggered because we have a check that makes sure that the lists are of the same length before we call `loop`. If we change the code so that we drop this test, then we can trigger the `assert`:

OCaml utop (part 27)

```
# let merge_lists xs ys ~f =
    let rec loop xs ys =
      match xs,ys with
      | [],[] -> []
```

```
      | x::xs, y::ys -> f x y :: loop xs ys
      | _ -> assert false
    in
    loop xs ys
  ;;
val merge_lists : 'a list -> 'b list -> f:('a -> 'b -> 'c) -> 'c list = <fun>
# merge_lists [1;2;3] [-1] ~f:(+);;
Exception: (Assert_failure //toplevel// 5 13).
```

This shows what's special about `assert`: it captures the line number and character offset of the source location from which the assertion was made.

Exception Handlers

So far, we've only seen exceptions fully terminate the execution of a computation. But often, we want a program to be able to respond to and recover from an exception. This is achieved through the use of *exception handlers*.

In OCaml, an exception handler is declared using a `try/with` statement. Here's the basic syntax.

Syntax

```
try <expr> with
| <pat1> -> <expr1>
| <pat2> -> <expr2>
...
```

A `try/with` clause first evaluates its body, *expr*. If no exception is thrown, then the result of evaluating the body is what the entire `try/with` clause evaluates to.

But if the evaluation of the body throws an exception, then the exception will be fed to the pattern-match statements following the `with`. If the exception matches a pattern, then we consider the exception caught, and the `try/with` clause evaluates to the expression on the righthand side of the matching pattern.

Otherwise, the original exception continues up the stack of function calls, to be handled by the next outer exception handler. If the exception is never caught, it terminates the program.

Cleaning Up in the Presence of Exceptions

One headache with exceptions is that they can terminate your execution at unexpected places, leaving your program in an awkward state. Consider the following function for loading a file full of reminders, formatted as s-expressions:

OCaml utop (part 28)

```
# let reminders_of_sexp =
    <:of_sexp<(Time.t * string) list>>
  ;;
val reminders_of_sexp : Sexp.t -> (Time.t * string) list = <fun>
```

```
# let load_reminders filename =
    let inc = In_channel.create filename in
    let reminders = reminders_of_sexp (Sexp.input_sexp inc) in
    In_channel.close inc;
    reminders
  ;;
val load_reminders : string -> (Time.t * string) list = <fun>
```

The problem with this code is that the function that loads the s-expression and parses it into a list of Time.t/string pairs might throw an exception if the file in question is malformed. Unfortunately, that means that the In_channel.t that was opened will never be closed, leading to a file-descriptor leak.

We can fix this using Core's protect function, which takes two arguments: a thunk f, which is the main body of the computation to be run; and a thunk finally, which is to be called when f exits, whether it exits normally or with an exception. This is similar to the try/finally construct available in many programming languages, but it is implemented in a library, rather than being a built-in primitive. Here's how it could be used to fix load_reminders:

OCaml utop (part 29)

```
# let load_reminders filename =
    let inc = In_channel.create filename in
    protect ~f:(fun () -> reminders_of_sexp (Sexp.input_sexp inc))
      ~finally:(fun () -> In_channel.close inc)
  ;;
val load_reminders : string -> (Time.t * string) list = <fun>
```

This is a common enough problem that In_channel has a function called with_file that automates this pattern:

OCaml utop (part 30)

```
# let reminders_of_sexp filename =
    In_channel.with_file filename ~f:(fun inc ->
      reminders_of_sexp (Sexp.input_sexp inc))
  ;;
val reminders_of_sexp : string -> (Time.t * string) list = <fun>
```

In_channel.with_file is built on top of protect so that it can clean up after itself in the presence of exceptions.

Catching Specific Exceptions

OCaml's exception-handling system allows you to tune your error-recovery logic to the particular error that was thrown. For example, List.find_exn throws Not_found when the element in question can't be found. Let's look at an example of how you could take advantage of this. In particular, consider the following function:

OCaml utop (part 31)

```
# let lookup_weight ~compute_weight alist key =
    try
```

```
    let data = List.Assoc.find_exn alist key in
    compute_weight data
  with
    Not_found -> 0. ;;
val lookup_weight :
  compute_weight:('a -> float) -> ('b, 'a) List.Assoc.t -> 'b -> float =
  <fun>
```

As you can see from the type, `lookup_weight` takes an association list, a key for looking up a corresponding value in that list, and a function for computing a floating-point weight from the looked-up value. If no value is found, then a weight of `0.` should be returned.

The use of exceptions in this code, however, presents some problems. In particular, what happens if `compute_weight` throws an exception? Ideally, `lookup_weight` should propagate that exception on, but if the exception happens to be `Not_found`, then that's not what will happen:

OCaml utop (part 32)

```
# lookup_weight ~compute_weight:(fun _ -> raise Not_found)
    ["a",3; "b",4] "a" ;;
- : float = 0.
```

This kind of problem is hard to detect in advance because the type system doesn't tell you what exceptions a given function might throw. For this reason, it's generally better to avoid relying on the identity of the exception to determine the nature of a failure. A better approach is to narrow the scope of the exception handler, so that when it fires it's very clear what part of the code failed:

OCaml utop (part 33)

```
# let lookup_weight ~compute_weight alist key =
    match
      try Some (List.Assoc.find_exn alist key)
      with _ -> None
    with
    | None -> 0.
    | Some data -> compute_weight data ;;
val lookup_weight :
  compute_weight:('a -> float) -> ('b, 'a) List.Assoc.t -> 'b -> float =
  <fun>
```

At this point, it makes sense to simply use the nonexception-throwing function, `List.Assoc.find`, instead:

OCaml utop (part 34)

```
# let lookup_weight ~compute_weight alist key =
    match List.Assoc.find alist key with
    | None -> 0.
    | Some data -> compute_weight data ;;
val lookup_weight :
  compute_weight:('a -> float) -> ('b, 'a) List.Assoc.t -> 'b -> float =
  <fun>
```

Backtraces

A big part of the value of exceptions is that they provide useful debugging information in the form of a stack backtrace. Consider the following simple program:

OCaml

```
open Core.Std
exception Empty_list

let list_max = function
  | [] -> raise Empty_list
  | hd :: tl -> List.fold tl ~init:hd ~f:(Int.max)

let () =
  printf "%d\n" (list_max [1;2;3]);
  printf "%d\n" (list_max [])
```

If we build and run this program, we'll get a stack backtrace that will provide some information about where the error occurred and the stack of function calls that were in place at the time of the error:

Terminal

```
$ corebuild blow_up.byte
$ ./blow_up.byte
3
Fatal error: exception Blow_up.Empty_list
Raised at file "blow_up.ml", line 5, characters 16-26
Called from file "blow_up.ml", line 10, characters 17-28
```

You can also capture a backtrace within your program by calling Exn.backtrace, which returns the backtrace of the most recently thrown exception. This is useful for reporting detailed information on errors that did not cause your program to fail.

This works well if you have backtraces enabled, but that isn't always the case. In fact, by default, OCaml has backtraces turned off, and even if you have them turned on at runtime, you can't get backtraces unless you have compiled with debugging symbols. Core reverses the default, so if you're linking in Core, you will have backtraces enabled by default.

Even using Core and compiling with debugging symbols, you can turn backtraces off by setting the OCAMLRUNPARAM environment variable to be empty:

Terminal

```
$ corebuild blow_up.byte
$ OCAMLRUNPARAM= ./blow_up.byte
3
Fatal error: exception Blow_up.Empty_list
```

The resulting error message is considerably less informative. You can also turn backtraces off in your code by calling Backtrace.Exn.set_recording false.

There is a legitimate reasons to run without backtraces: speed. OCaml's exceptions are fairly fast, but they're even faster still if you disable backtraces. Here's a simple benchmark that shows the effect, using the core_bench package:

OCaml

```ocaml
open Core.Std
open Core_bench.Std

let simple_computation () =
  List.range 0 10
  |> List.fold ~init:0 ~f:(fun sum x -> sum + x * x)
  |> ignore

let simple_with_handler () =
  try simple_computation () with Exit -> ()

let end_with_exn () =
  try
    simple_computation ();
    raise Exit
  with Exit -> ()

let () =
  [ Bench.Test.create ~name:"simple computation"
      (fun () -> simple_computation ());
    Bench.Test.create ~name:"simple computation w/handler"
      (fun () -> simple_with_handler ());
    Bench.Test.create ~name:"end with exn"
      (fun () -> end_with_exn ());
  ]
  |> Bench.make_command
  |> Command.run
```

We're testing three cases here: a simple computation with no exceptions; the same computation with an exception handler but no thrown exceptions; and finally the same computation where we use the exception to do the control flow back to the caller.

If we run this with stacktraces on, the benchmark results look like this:

Terminal

```
$ corebuild -pkg core_bench exn_cost.native
$ ./exn_cost.native -ascii cycles
Estimated testing time 30s (change using -quota SECS).

  Name                              Cycles   Time (ns)   % of max
  ----------------------------      -------  ----------  ----------
  simple computation                  279         117      76.40
  simple computation w/handler        308         129      84.36
  end with exn                        366         153     100.00
```

Here, we see that we lose something like 30 cycles to adding an exception handler, and 60 more to actually throwing and catching an exception. If we turn backtraces off, then the results look like this:

```
$ OCAMLRUNPARAM= ./exn_cost.native -ascii cycles
Estimated testing time 30s (change using -quota SECS).

  Name                         Cycles   Time (ns)   % of max
  ---------------------------- -------- ----------- ----------
  simple computation              279         116      83.50
  simple computation w/handler    308         128      92.09
  end with exn                    334         140     100.00
```

Here, the handler costs about the same, but the exception itself costs only 25, as opposed to 60 additional cycles. All told, this should only matter if you're using exceptions routinely as part of your flow control, which is in most cases a stylistic mistake anyway.

From Exceptions to Error-Aware Types and Back Again

Both exceptions and error-aware types are necessary parts of programming in OCaml. As such, you often need to move between these two worlds. Happily, Core comes with some useful helper functions to help you do just that. For example, given a piece of code that can throw an exception, you can capture that exception into an option as follows:

OCaml utop (part 35)

```
# let find alist key =
    Option.try_with (fun () -> find_exn alist key) ;;
val find : (string * 'a) list -> string -> 'a option = <fun>
# find ["a",1; "b",2] "c";;
- : int option = None
# find ["a",1; "b",2] "b";;
- : int option = Some 2
```

And Result and Or_error have similar try_with functions. So, we could write:

OCaml utop (part 36)

```
# let find alist key =
    Or_error.try_with (fun () -> find_exn alist key) ;;
val find : (string * 'a) list -> string -> 'a Or_error.t = <fun>
# find ["a",1; "b",2] "c";;
- : int Or_error.t = Core_kernel.Result.Error ("Key_not_found(\"c\")")
```

And then we can reraise that exception:

OCaml utop (part 37)

```
# Or_error.ok_exn (find ["a",1; "b",2] "b");;
- : int = 2
# Or_error.ok_exn (find ["a",1; "b",2] "c");;
Exception: ("Key_not_found(\"c\")").
```

Choosing an Error-Handling Strategy

Given that OCaml supports both exceptions and error-aware return types, how do you choose between them? The key is to think about the trade-off between concision and explicitness.

Exceptions are more concise because they allow you to defer the job of error handling to some larger scope, and because they don't clutter up your types. But this concision comes at a cost: exceptions are all too easy to ignore. Error-aware return types, on the other hand, are fully manifest in your type definitions, making the errors that your code might generate explicit and impossible to ignore.

The right trade-off depends on your application. If you're writing a rough-and-ready program where getting it done quickly is key and failure is not that expensive, then using exceptions extensively may be the way to go. If, on the other hand, you're writing production software whose failure is costly, then you should probably lean in the direction of using error-aware return types.

To be clear, it doesn't make sense to avoid exceptions entirely. The maxim of "use exceptions for exceptional conditions" applies. If an error occurs sufficiently rarely, then throwing an exception is often the right behavior.

Also, for errors that are omnipresent, error-aware return types may be overkill. A good example is out-of-memory errors, which can occur anywhere, and so you'd need to use error-aware return types everywhere to capture those. Having every operation marked as one that might fail is no more explicit than having none of them marked.

In short, for errors that are a foreseeable and ordinary part of the execution of your production code and that are not omnipresent, error-aware return types are typically the right solution.

## CHAPTER 8

Imperative Programming

Most of the code shown so far in this book, and indeed, most OCaml code in general, is *pure*. Pure code works without mutating the program's internal state, performing I/O, reading the clock, or in any other way interacting with changeable parts of the world. Thus, a pure function behaves like a mathematical function, always returning the same results when given the same inputs, and never affecting the world except insofar as it returns the value of its computation. *Imperative* code, on the other hand, operates by side effects that modify a program's internal state or interact with the outside world. An imperative function has a new effect, and potentially returns different results, every time it's called.

Pure code is the default in OCaml, and for good reason—it's generally easier to reason about, less error prone and more composable. But imperative code is of fundamental importance to any practical programming language, because real-world tasks require that you interact with the outside world, which is by its nature imperative. Imperative programming can also be important for performance. While pure code is quite efficient in OCaml, there are many algorithms that can only be implemented efficiently using imperative techniques.

OCaml offers a happy compromise here, making it easy and natural to program in a pure style, but also providing great support for imperative programming. This chapter will walk you through OCaml's imperative features, and help you use them to their fullest.

Example: Imperative Dictionaries

We'll start with the implementation of a simple imperative dictionary, i.e., a mutable mapping from keys to values. This is really for illustration purposes; both Core and the standard library provide imperative dictionaries, and for most real-world tasks, you should use one of those implementations. There's more advice on using Core's implementation in particular in Chapter 13.

The dictionary we'll describe now, like those in Core and the standard library, will be implemented as a hash table. In particular, we'll use an *open hashing* scheme, where the hash table will be an array of buckets, each bucket containing a list of key/value pairs that have been hashed into that bucket.

Here's the interface we'll match, provided as an `mli`. The type `('a, 'b) t` represents a dictionary with keys of type `'a` and data of type `'b`:

OCaml (part 1)

```
(* file: dictionary.mli *)
open Core.Std

type ('a, 'b) t

val create : unit -> ('a, 'b) t
val length : ('a, 'b) t -> int
val add    : ('a, 'b) t -> key:'a -> data:'b -> unit
val find   : ('a, 'b) t -> 'a -> 'b option
val iter   : ('a, 'b) t -> f:(key:'a -> data:'b -> unit) -> unit
val remove : ('a, 'b) t -> 'a -> unit
```

The `mli` also includes a collection of helper functions whose purpose and behavior should be largely inferrable from their names and type signatures. Notice that a number of the functions, in particular, ones like `add` that modify the dictionary, return `unit`. This is typical of functions that act by side effect.

We'll now walk through the implementation (contained in the corresponding `ml` file) piece by piece, explaining different imperative constructs as they come up.

Our first step is to define the type of a dictionary as a record with two fields:

OCaml (part 1)

```
(* file: dictionary.ml *)
open Core.Std

type ('a, 'b) t = { mutable length: int;
                    buckets: ('a * 'b) list array;
                  }
```

The first field, `length`, is declared as mutable. In OCaml, records are immutable by default, but individual fields are mutable when marked as such. The second field, buckets, is immutable but contains an array, which is itself a mutable data structure.

Now we'll start putting together the basic functions for manipulating a dictionary:

OCaml (part 2)

```
let num_buckets = 17

let hash_bucket key = (Hashtbl.hash key) mod num_buckets
```

```
let create () =
  { length = 0;
    buckets = Array.create ~len:num_buckets [];
  }

let length t = t.length

let find t key =
  List.find_map t.buckets.(hash_bucket key)
    ~f:(fun (key',data) -> if key' = key then Some data else None)
```

Note that num_buckets is a constant, which means our bucket array is of fixed length. A practical implementation would need to be able to grow the array as the number of elements in the dictionary increases, but we'll omit this to simplify the presentation.

The function hash_bucket is used throughout the rest of the module to choose the position in the array that a given key should be stored at. It is implemented on top of Hashtbl.hash, which is a hash function provided by the OCaml runtime that can be applied to values of any type. Thus, its own type is polymorphic: 'a -> int.

The other functions defined above are fairly straightforward:

create
> Creates an empty dictionary.

length
> Grabs the length from the corresponding record field, thus returning the number of entries stored in the dictionary.

find
> Looks for a matching key in the table and returns the corresponding value if found as an option.

Another important piece of imperative syntax shows up in find: we write array.(index) to grab a value from an array. find also uses List.find_map, which you can see the type of by typing it into the toplevel:

OCaml utop (part 1)

```
# List.find_map;;
- : 'a list -> f:('a -> 'b option) -> 'b option = <fun>
```

List.find_map iterates over the elements of the list, calling f on each one until a Some is returned by f, at which point that value is returned. If f returns None on all values, then None is returned.

Now let's look at the implementation of iter:

OCaml (part 3)

```
let iter t ~f =
  for i = 0 to Array.length t.buckets - 1 do
```

```
    List.iter t.buckets.(i) ~f:(fun (key, data) -> f ~key ~data)
  done
```

iter is designed to walk over all the entries in the dictionary. In particular, iter t ~f
will call f for each key/value pair in dictionary t. Note that f must return unit, since it
is expected to work by side effect rather than by returning a value, and the overall iter
function returns unit as well.

The code for iter uses two forms of iteration: a for loop to walk over the array of
buckets; and within that loop a call to List.iter to walk over the values in a given
bucket. We could have done the outer loop with a recursive function instead of a for
loop, but for loops are syntactically convenient, and are more familiar and idiomatic
in imperative contexts.

The following code is for adding and removing mappings from the dictionary:

OCaml (part 4)

```
let bucket_has_key t i key =
  List.exists t.buckets.(i) ~f:(fun (key',_) -> key' = key)

let add t ~key ~data =
  let i = hash_bucket key in
  let replace = bucket_has_key t i key in
  let filtered_bucket =
    if replace then
      List.filter t.buckets.(i) ~f:(fun (key',_) -> key' <> key)
    else
      t.buckets.(i)
  in
  t.buckets.(i) <- (key, data) :: filtered_bucket;
  if not replace then t.length <- t.length + 1

let remove t key =
  let i = hash_bucket key in
  if bucket_has_key t i key then (
    let filtered_bucket =
      List.filter t.buckets.(i) ~f:(fun (key',_) -> key' <> key)
    in
    t.buckets.(i) <- filtered_bucket;
    t.length <- t.length - 1
  )
```

This preceding code is made more complicated by the fact that we need to detect whether
we are overwriting or removing an existing binding, so we can decide whether t.length
needs to be changed. The helper function bucket_has_key is used for this purpose.

Another piece of syntax shows up in both add and remove: the use of the <- operator to
update elements of an array (array.(i) <- expr) and for updating a record field
(record.field <- expression).

We also use ;, the sequencing operator, to express a sequence of imperative actions. We could have done the same using `let` bindings:

OCaml (part 1)

```
let () = t.buckets.(i) <- (key, data) :: filtered_bucket in
  if not replace then t.length <- t.length + 1
```

but ; is more concise and idiomatic. More generally,

Syntax

```
<expr1>;
<expr2>;
...
<exprN>
```

is equivalent to

Syntax

```
let () = <expr1> in
let () = <expr2> in
...
<exprN>
```

When a sequence expression `expr1; expr2` is evaluated, `expr1` is evaluated first, and then `expr2`. The expression `expr1` should have type `unit` (though this is a warning rather than a hard restriction. The `-strict-sequence` compiler flag makes this a hard restriction, which is generally a good idea), and the value of `expr2` is returned as the value of the entire sequence. For example, the sequence `print_string "hello world"; 1 + 2` first prints the string `"hello world"`, then returns the integer 3.

Note also that we do all of the side-effecting operations at the very end of each function. This is good practice because it minimizes the chance that such operations will be interrupted with an exception, leaving the data structure in an inconsistent state.

Primitive Mutable Data

Now that we've looked at a complete example, let's take a more systematic look at imperative programming in OCaml. We encountered two different forms of mutable data above: records with mutable fields and arrays. We'll now discuss these in more detail, along with the other primitive forms of mutable data that are available in OCaml.

Array-Like Data

OCaml supports a number of array-like data structures; i.e., mutable integer-indexed containers that provide constant-time access to their elements. We'll discuss several of them in this section.

Ordinary arrays

The `array` type is used for general-purpose polymorphic arrays. The `Array` module has a variety of utility functions for interacting with arrays, including a number of mutating operations. These include `Array.set`, for setting an individual element, and `Array.blit`, for efficiently copying values from one range of indices to another.

Arrays also come with special syntax for retrieving an element from an array:

Syntax

```
<array_expr>.(<index_expr>)
```

and for setting an element in an array:

Syntax

```
<array_expr>.(<index_expr>) <- <value_expr>
```

Out-of-bounds accesses for arrays (and indeed for all the array-like data structures) will lead to an exception being thrown.

Array literals are written using [| and |] as delimiters. Thus, [| 1; 2; 3 |] is a literal integer array.

Strings

Strings are essentially byte arrays which are often used for textual data. The main advantage of using a `string` in place of a `Char.t array` (a `Char.t` is an 8-bit character) is that the former is considerably more space-efficient; an array uses one word—8 bytes on a 64-bit machine—to store a single entry, whereas strings use 1 byte per character.

Strings also come with their own syntax for getting and setting values:

Syntax

```
<string_expr>.[<index_expr>]
        <string_expr>.[<index_expr>] <- <char_expr>
```

And string literals are bounded by quotes. There's also a module `String` where you'll find useful functions for working with strings.

Bigarrays

A `Bigarray.t` is a handle to a block of memory stored outside of the OCaml heap. These are mostly useful for interacting with C or Fortran libraries, and are discussed in Chapter 20. Bigarrays too have their own getting and setting syntax:

Syntax

```
<bigarray_expr>.{<index_expr>}
        <bigarray_expr>.{<index_expr>} <- <value_expr>
```

Mutable Record and Object Fields and Ref Cells

As we've seen, records are immutable by default, but individual record fields can be declared as mutable. These mutable fields can be set using the <- operator, i.e., re cord.field <- expr.

As we'll see in Chapter 11, fields of an object can similarly be declared as mutable, and can then be modified in much the same way as record fields.

Ref cells

Variables in OCaml are never mutable—they can refer to mutable data, but what the variable points to can't be changed. Sometimes, though, you want to do exactly what you would do with a mutable variable in another language: define a single, mutable value. In OCaml this is typically achieved using a ref, which is essentially a container with a single mutable polymorphic field.

The definition for the ref type is as follows:

OCaml utop (part 1)

```
# type 'a ref = { mutable contents : 'a };;
type 'a ref = { mutable contents : 'a; }
```

The standard library defines the following operators for working with refs.

ref expr
    Constructs a reference cell containing the value defined by the expression expr.

!refcell
    Returns the contents of the reference cell.

refcell := expr
    Replaces the contents of the reference cell.

You can see these in action:

OCaml utop (part 3)

```
# let x = ref 1;;
val x : int ref = {contents = 1}
#   !x;;
- : int = 1
#   x := !x + 1;;
- : unit = ()
#   !x;;
- : int = 2
```

The preceding are just ordinary OCaml functions, which could be defined as follows:

OCaml utop (part 2)

```
# let ref x = { contents = x };;
val ref : 'a -> 'a ref = <fun>
#   let (!) r = r.contents;;
val ( ! ) : 'a ref -> 'a = <fun>
```

```
#   let (:=) r x = r.contents <- x;;
val ( := ) : 'a ref -> 'a -> unit = <fun>
```

Foreign Functions

Another source of imperative operations in OCaml is resources that come from interfacing with external libraries through OCaml's foreign function interface (FFI). The FFI
opens OCaml up to imperative constructs that are exported by system calls or other
external libraries. Many of these come built in, like access to the write system call or to
the clock, while others come from user libraries, like LAPACK bindings. OCaml's FFI
is discussed in more detail in Chapter 19.

for and while Loops

OCaml provides support for traditional imperative looping constructs, in particular,
for and while loops. Neither of these constructs is strictly necessary, since they can be
simulated with recursive functions. Nonetheless, explicit for and while loops are both
more concise and more idiomatic when programming imperatively.

The for loop is the simpler of the two. Indeed, we've already seen the for loop in action
—the iter function in Dictionary is built using it. Here's a simple example of for:

OCaml utop (part 1)

```
# for i = 0 to 3 do printf "i = %d\n" i done;;
i = 0
i = 1
i = 2
i = 3
- : unit = ()
```

As you can see, the upper and lower bounds are inclusive. We can also use downto to
iterate in the other direction:

OCaml utop (part 2)

```
# for i = 3 downto 0 do printf "i = %d\n" i done;;
i = 3
i = 2
i = 1
i = 0
- : unit = ()
```

Note that the loop variable of a for loop, i in this case, is immutable in the scope of the
loop and is also local to the loop, i.e., it can't be referenced outside of the loop.

OCaml also supports while loops, which include a condition and a body. The loop first
evaluates the condition, and then, if it evaluates to true, evaluates the body and starts
the loop again. Here's a simple example of a function for reversing an array in place:

```
# let rev_inplace ar =
    let i = ref 0 in
    let j = ref (Array.length ar - 1) in
    (* terminate when the upper and lower indices meet *)
    while !i < !j do
      (* swap the two elements *)
      let tmp = ar.(!i) in
      ar.(!i) <- ar.(!j);
      ar.(!j) <- tmp;
      (* bump the indices *)
      incr i;
      decr j
    done
  ;;
val rev_inplace : 'a array -> unit = <fun>
# let nums = [|1;2;3;4;5|];;
val nums : int array = [|1; 2; 3; 4; 5|]
# rev_inplace nums;;
- : unit = ()
# nums;;
- : int array = [|5; 4; 3; 2; 1|]
```

In the preceding example, we used incr and decr, which are built-in functions for incrementing and decrementing an int ref by one, respectively.

Example: Doubly Linked Lists

Another common imperative data structure is the doubly linked list. Doubly linked lists can be traversed in both directions, and elements can be added and removed from the list in constant time. Core defines a doubly linked list (the module is called Dou bly_linked), but we'll define our own linked list library as an illustration.

Here's the mli of the module we'll build:

```
(* file: dlist.mli *)
open Core.Std

type 'a t
type 'a element

(** Basic list operations  *)
val create   : unit -> 'a t
val is_empty : 'a t -> bool

(** Navigation using [element]s *)
val first : 'a t -> 'a element option
val next  : 'a element -> 'a element option
val prev  : 'a element -> 'a element option
val value : 'a element -> 'a
```

```
(** Whole-data-structure iteration *)
val iter   : 'a t -> f:('a -> unit) -> unit
val find_el : 'a t -> f:('a -> bool) -> 'a element option

(** Mutation *)
val insert_first : 'a t -> 'a -> 'a element
val insert_after : 'a element -> 'a -> 'a element
val remove : 'a t -> 'a element -> unit
```

Note that there are two types defined here: `'a t`, the type of a list; and `'a element`, the type of an element. Elements act as pointers to the interior of a list and allow us to navigate the list and give us a point at which to apply mutating operations.

Now let's look at the implementation. We'll start by defining `'a element` and `'a t`:

OCaml (part 1)

```
(* file: dlist.ml *)
open Core.Std

type 'a element =
  { value : 'a;
    mutable next : 'a element option;
    mutable prev : 'a element option
  }

type 'a t = 'a element option ref
```

An `'a element` is a record containing the value to be stored in that node as well as optional (and mutable) fields pointing to the previous and next elements. At the beginning of the list, the `prev` field is None, and at the end of the list, the `next` field is None.

The type of the list itself, `'a t`, is a mutable reference to an optional `element`. This reference is None if the list is empty, and Some otherwise.

Now we can define a few basic functions that operate on lists and elements:

OCaml (part 2)

```
let create () = ref None
let is_empty t = !t = None

let value elt = elt.value

let first t = !t
let next elt = elt.next
let prev elt = elt.prev
```

These all follow relatively straightforwardly from our type definitions.

Cyclic Data Structures

Doubly linked lists are a cyclic data structure, meaning that it is possible to follow a nontrivial sequence of pointers that closes in on itself. In general, building cyclic data structures requires the use of side effects. This is done by constructing the data elements first, and then adding cycles using assignment afterward.

There is an exception to this, though: you can construct fixed-size cyclic data structures using `let rec`:

OCaml utop (part 2)

```
# let rec endless_loop = 1 :: 2 :: 3 :: endless_loop;;
val endless_loop : int list =
  [1; 2; 3; 1; 2; 3; 1; 2; 3;
   1; 2; 3; 1; 2; 3; 1; 2; 3;
   1; 2; 3; 1; 2; 3; 1; 2; 3;
   ...]
```

This approach is quite limited, however. General-purpose cyclic data structures require mutation.

Modifying the List

Now, we'll start considering operations that mutate the list, starting with `insert_first`, which inserts an element at the front of the list:

OCaml (part 3)

```
let insert_first t value =
  let new_elt = { prev = None; next = !t; value } in
  begin match !t with
  | Some old_first -> old_first.prev <- Some new_elt
  | None -> ()
  end;
  t := Some new_elt;
  new_elt
```

`insert_first` first defines a new element `new_elt`, and then links it into the list, finally setting the list itself to point to `new_elt`. Note that the precedence of a `match` expression is very low, so to separate it from the following assignment (`t := Some new_elt`), we surround the match with `begin ... end`. We could have used parentheses for the same purpose. Without some kind of bracketing, the final assignment would incorrectly become part of the `None` case.

We can use `insert_after` to insert elements later in the list. `insert_after` takes as arguments both an `element` after which to insert the new node and a value to insert:

OCaml (part 4)

```
let insert_after elt value =
  let new_elt = { value; prev = Some elt; next = elt.next } in
  begin match elt.next with
  | Some old_next -> old_next.prev <- Some new_elt
```

```
  | None -> ()
  end;
  elt.next <- Some new_elt;
  new_elt
```

Finally, we need a `remove` function:

OCaml (part 5)

```
let remove t elt =
  let { prev; next; _ } = elt in
  begin match prev with
  | Some prev -> prev.next <- next
  | None -> t := next
  end;
  begin match next with
  | Some next -> next.prev <- prev;
  | None -> ()
  end;
  elt.prev <- None;
  elt.next <- None
```

Note that the preceding code is careful to change the `prev` pointer of the following element and the `next` pointer of the previous element, if they exist. If there's no previous element, then the list pointer itself is updated. In any case, the next and previous pointers of the element itself are set to `None`.

These functions are more fragile than they may seem. In particular, misuse of the interface may lead to corrupted data. For example, double-removing an element will cause the main list reference to be set to `None`, thus emptying the list. Similar problems arise from removing an element from a list it doesn't belong to.

This shouldn't be a big surprise. Complex imperative data structures can be quite tricky, considerably trickier than their pure equivalents. The issues described previously can be dealt with by more careful error detection, and such error correction is taken care of in modules like Core's `Doubly_linked`. You should use imperative data structures from a well-designed library when you can. And when you can't, you should make sure to put great care into your error handling.

Iteration Functions

When defining containers like lists, dictionaries, and trees, you'll typically want to define a set of iteration functions like `iter`, `map`, and `fold`, which let you concisely express common iteration patterns.

`Dlist` has two such iterators: `iter`, the goal of which is to call a `unit`-producing function on every element of the list, in order; and `find_el`, which runs a provided test function on each values stored in the list, returning the first `element` that passes the test. Both `iter` and `find_el` are implemented using simple recursive loops that use `next` to walk from element to element and `value` to extract the element from a given node:

```
let iter t ~f =
  let rec loop = function
    | None -> ()
    | Some el -> f (value el); loop (next el)
  in
  loop !t

let find_el t ~f =
  let rec loop = function
    | None -> None
    | Some elt ->
      if f (value elt) then Some elt
      else loop (next elt)
  in
  loop !t
```

This completes our implementation, but there's still considerably more work to be done to make a really usable doubly linked list. As mentioned earlier, you're probably better off using something like Core's `Doubly_linked` module that has a more complete interface and has more of the tricky corner cases worked out. Nonetheless, this example should serve to demonstrate some of the techniques you can use to build nontrivial imperative data structure in OCaml, as well as some of the pitfalls.

Laziness and Other Benign Effects

There are many instances where you basically want to program in a pure style, but you want to make limited use of side effects to improve the performance of your code. Such side effects are sometimes called *benign effects*, and they are a useful way of leveraging OCaml's imperative features while still maintaining most of the benefits of pure programming.

One of the simplest benign effects is *laziness*. A lazy value is one that is not computed until it is actually needed. In OCaml, lazy values are created using the `lazy` keyword, which can be used to convert any expression of type s into a lazy value of type s `Lazy.t`. The evaluation of that expression is delayed until forced with `Lazy.force`:

```
# let v = lazy (print_string "performing lazy computation\n"; sqrt 16.);;
val v : float lazy_t = <lazy>
# Lazy.force v;;
performing lazy computation
- : float = 4.
# Lazy.force v;;
- : float = 4.
```

You can see from the `print` statement that the actual computation was performed only once, and only after `force` had been called.

To better understand how laziness works, let's walk through the implementation of our own lazy type. We'll start by declaring types to represent a lazy value:

OCaml utop (part 2)

```
# type 'a lazy_state =
    | Delayed of (unit -> 'a)
    | Value of 'a
    | Exn of exn
  ;;
type 'a lazy_state = Delayed of (unit -> 'a) | Value of 'a | Exn of exn
```

A `lazy_state` represents the possible states of a lazy value. A lazy value is `Delayed` before it has been run, where `Delayed` holds a function for computing the value in question. A lazy value is in the `Value` state when it has been forced and the computation ended normally. The `Exn` case is for when the lazy value has been forced, but the computation ended with an exception. A lazy value is simply a `ref` containing a `lazy_state`, where the `ref` makes it possible to change from being in the `Delayed` state to being in the `Value` or `Exn` states.

We can create a lazy value from a thunk, i.e., a function that takes a unit argument. Wrapping an expression in a thunk is another way to suspend the computation of an expression:

OCaml utop (part 3)

```
# let create_lazy f = ref (Delayed f);;
val create_lazy : (unit -> 'a) -> 'a lazy_state ref = <fun>
# let v = create_lazy
    (fun () -> print_string "performing lazy computation\n"; sqrt 16.);;
val v : float lazy_state ref = {contents = Delayed <fun>}
```

Now we just need a way to force a lazy value. The following function does just that:

OCaml utop (part 4)

```
# let force v =
    match !v with
    | Value x -> x
    | Exn e -> raise e
    | Delayed f ->
      try
        let x = f () in
        v := Value x;
        x
      with exn ->
        v := Exn exn;
        raise exn
    ;;
val force : 'a lazy_state ref -> 'a = <fun>
```

Which we can use in the same way we used `Lazy.force`:

```
# force v;;
performing lazy computation
- : float = 4.
# force v;;
- : float = 4.
```

The main user-visible difference between our implementation of laziness and the built-in version is syntax. Rather than writing `create_lazy (fun () -> sqrt 16.)`, we can (with the built-in `lazy`) just write `lazy (sqrt 16.)`.

Memoization and Dynamic Programming

Another benign effect is *memoization*. A memoized function remembers the result of previous invocations of the function so that they can be returned without further computation when the same arguments are presented again.

Here's a function that takes as an argument an arbitrary single-argument function and returns a memoized version of that function. Here we'll use Core's `Hashtbl` module, rather than our toy `Dictionary`:

```
# let memoize f =
    let table = Hashtbl.Poly.create () in
    (fun x ->
      match Hashtbl.find table x with
      | Some y -> y
      | None ->
        let y = f x in
        Hashtbl.add_exn table ~key:x ~data:y;
        y
    );;
val memoize : ('a -> 'b) -> 'a -> 'b = <fun>
```

The preceding code is a bit tricky. `memoize` takes as its argument a function `f` and then allocates a hash table (called `table`) and returns a new function as the memoized version of `f`. When called, this new function looks in `table` first, and if it fails to find a value, calls `f` and stashes the result in `table`. Note that `table` doesn't go out of scope as long as the function returned by `memoize` is in scope.

Memoization can be useful whenever you have a function that is expensive to recompute and you don't mind caching old values indefinitely. One important caution: a memoized function by its nature leaks memory. As long as you hold on to the memoized function, you're holding every result it has returned thus far.

Memoization is also useful for efficiently implementing some recursive algorithms. One good example is the algorithm for computing the *edit distance* (also called the Levenshtein distance) between two strings. The edit distance is the number of single-character changes (including letter switches, insertions, and deletions) required to convert one string to the other. This kind of distance metric can be useful for a variety of approximate string-matching problems, like spellcheckers.

Consider the following code for computing the edit distance. Understanding the algorithm isn't important here, but you should pay attention to the structure of the recursive calls:

OCaml utop (part 2)

```ocaml
# let rec edit_distance s t =
    match String.length s, String.length t with
    | (0,x) | (x,0) -> x
    | (len_s,len_t) ->
      let s' = String.drop_suffix s 1 in
      let t' = String.drop_suffix t 1 in
      let cost_to_drop_both =
        if s.[len_s - 1] = t.[len_t - 1] then 0 else 1
      in
      List.reduce_exn ~f:Int.min
        [ edit_distance s' t  + 1
        ; edit_distance s  t' + 1
        ; edit_distance s' t' + cost_to_drop_both
        ]
  ;;
val edit_distance : string -> string -> int = <fun>
# edit_distance "OCaml" "ocaml";;
- : int = 2
```

The thing to note is that if you call `edit_distance "OCaml" "ocaml"`, then that will in turn dispatch the following calls:

Diagram

```
edit_distance "OCam" "ocaml"
edit_distance "OCaml" "ocam"
edit_distance "OCam" "ocam"
```

And these calls will in turn dispatch other calls:

Diagram

```
edit_distance "OCam" "ocaml"
  edit_distance "OCa" "ocaml"
  edit_distance "OCam" "ocam"
  edit_distance "OCa" "ocam"
edit_distance "OCaml" "ocam"
  edit_distance "OCam" "ocam"
  edit_distance "OCaml" "oca"
  edit_distance "OCam" "oca"
edit_distance "OCam" "ocam"
  edit_distance "OCa" "ocam"
  edit_distance "OCam" "oca"
  edit_distance "OCa" "oca"
```

As you can see, some of these calls are repeats. For example, there are two different calls to `edit_distance "OCam" "oca"`. The number of redundant calls grows exponentially with the size of the strings, meaning that our implementation of `edit_distance` is brutally slow for large strings. We can see this by writing a small timing function:

OCaml utop (part 3)

```
# let time f =
    let start = Time.now () in
    let x = f () in
    let stop = Time.now () in
    printf "Time: %s\n" (Time.Span.to_string (Time.diff stop start));
    x ;;
val time : (unit -> 'a) -> 'a = <fun>
```

And now we can use this to try out some examples:

OCaml utop (part 4)

```
# time (fun () -> edit_distance "OCaml" "ocaml");;
Time: 1.40405ms
- : int = 2
# time (fun () -> edit_distance "OCaml 4.01" "ocaml 4.01");;
Time: 6.79065s
- : int = 2
```

Just those few extra characters made it thousands of times slower!

Memoization would be a huge help here, but to fix the problem, we need to memoize the calls that `edit_distance` makes to itself. This technique is sometimes referred to as *dynamic programming*. To see how to do this, let's step away from `edit_distance` and instead consider a much simpler example: computing the *n*th element of the Fibonacci sequence. The Fibonacci sequence by definition starts out with two 1s, with every subsequent element being the sum of the previous two. The classic recursive definition of Fibonacci is as follows:

OCaml utop (part 1)

```
# let rec fib i =
    if i <= 1 then 1 else fib (i - 1) + fib (i - 2);;
val fib : int -> int = <fun>
```

This is, however, exponentially slow, for the same reason that `edit_distance` was slow: we end up making many redundant calls to `fib`. It shows up quite dramatically in the performance:

OCaml utop (part 2)

```
# time (fun () -> fib 20);;
Time: 0.844955ms
- : int = 10946
# time (fun () -> fib 40);;
Time: 12.7751s
- : int = 165580141
```

As you can see, `fib 40` takes thousands of times longer to compute than `fib 20`.

So, how can we use memoization to make this faster? The tricky bit is that we need to insert the memoization before the recursive calls within `fib`. We can't just define `fib` in the ordinary way and memoize it after the fact and expect the first call to `fib` to be improved:

OCaml utop (part 3)

```
# let fib = memoize fib;;
val fib : int -> int = <fun>
# time (fun () -> fib 40);;
Time: 12.774s
- : int = 165580141
# time (fun () -> fib 40);;
Time: 0.00309944ms
- : int = 165580141
```

In order to make `fib` fast, our first step will be to rewrite `fib` in a way that unwinds the recursion. The following version expects as its first argument a function (called `fib`) that will be called in lieu of the usual recursive call:

OCaml utop (part 4)

```
# let fib_norec fib i =
    if i <= 1 then i
    else fib (i - 1) + fib (i - 2) ;;
val fib_norec : (int -> int) -> int -> int = <fun>
```

We can now turn this back into an ordinary Fibonacci function by tying the recursive knot:

OCaml utop (part 5)

```
# let rec fib i = fib_norec fib i;;
val fib : int -> int = <fun>
# fib 20;;
- : int = 6765
```

We can even write a polymorphic function that we'll call `make_rec` that can tie the recursive knot for any function of this form:

OCaml utop (part 6)

```
# let make_rec f_norec =
    let rec f x = f_norec f x in
    f
  ;;
val make_rec : (('a -> 'b) -> 'a -> 'b) -> 'a -> 'b = <fun>
# let fib = make_rec fib_norec;;
val fib : int -> int = <fun>
# fib 20;;
- : int = 6765
```

This is a pretty strange piece of code, and it may take a few moments of thought to figure out what's going on. Like `fib_norec`, the function `f_norec` passed into `make_rec` is a function that isn't recursive but takes as an argument a function that it will call. What `make_rec` does is to essentially feed `f_norec` to itself, thus making it a true recursive function.

This is clever enough, but all we've really done is find a new way to implement the same old slow Fibonacci function. To make it faster, we need a variant of `make_rec` that inserts memoization when it ties the recursive knot. We'll call that function `memo_rec`:

OCaml utop (part 7)

```
# let memo_rec f_norec x =
    let fref = ref (fun _ -> assert false) in
    let f = memoize (fun x -> f_norec !fref x) in
    fref := f;
    f x
  ;;
val memo_rec : (('a -> 'b) -> 'a -> 'b) -> 'a -> 'b = <fun>
```

Note that `memo_rec` has the same signature as `make_rec`.

We're using the reference here as a way of tying the recursive knot without using a `let rec`, which for reasons we'll describe later wouldn't work here.

Using `memo_rec`, we can now build an efficient version of `fib`:

OCaml utop (part 8)

```
# let fib = memo_rec fib_norec;;
val fib : int -> int = <fun>
# time (fun () -> fib 40);;
Time: 0.0591278ms
- : int = 102334155
```

And as you can see, the exponential time complexity is now gone.

The memory behavior here is important. If you look back at the definition of `memo_rec`, you'll see that the call `memo_rec fib_norec` does not trigger a call to `memoize`. Only when `fib` is called and thereby the final argument to `memo_rec` is presented does `memoize` get called. The result of that call falls out of scope when the `fib` call returns, and so calling `memo_rec` on a function does not create a memory leak—the memoization table is collected after the computation completes.

We can use `memo_rec` as part of a single declaration that makes this look like it's little more than a special form of `let rec`:

OCaml utop (part 9)

```
# let fib = memo_rec (fun fib i ->
    if i <= 1 then 1 else fib (i - 1) + fib (i - 2));;
val fib : int -> int = <fun>
```

Memoization is overkill for implementing Fibonacci, and indeed, the `fib` defined above is not especially efficient, allocating space linear in the number passed in to `fib`. It's easy enough to write a Fibonacci function that takes a constant amount of space.

But memoization is a good approach for optimizing `edit_distance`, and we can apply the same approach we used on `fib` here. We will need to change `edit_distance` to take a pair of strings as a single argument, since `memo_rec` only works on single-argument functions. (We can always recover the original interface with a wrapper function.) With just that change and the addition of the `memo_rec` call, we can get a memoized version of `edit_distance`:

OCaml utop (part 6)

```
# let edit_distance = memo_rec (fun edit_distance (s,t) ->
    match String.length s, String.length t with
    | (0,x) | (x,0) -> x
    | (len_s,len_t) ->
      let s' = String.drop_suffix s 1 in
      let t' = String.drop_suffix t 1 in
      let cost_to_drop_both =
        if s.[len_s - 1] = t.[len_t - 1] then 0 else 1
      in
      List.reduce_exn ~f:Int.min
        [ edit_distance (s',t ) + 1
        ; edit_distance (s ,t') + 1
        ; edit_distance (s',t') + cost_to_drop_both
        ]) ;;
val edit_distance : string * string -> int = <fun>
```

This new version of `edit_distance` is much more efficient than the one we started with; the following call is many thousands of times faster than it was without memoization:

OCaml utop (part 7)

```
# time (fun () -> edit_distance ("OCaml 4.01","ocaml 4.01"));;
Time: 0.500917ms
- : int = 2
```

Limitations of let rec

You might wonder why we didn't tie the recursive knot in `memo_rec` using `let rec`, as we did for `make_rec` earlier. Here's code that tries to do just that:

OCaml utop (part 1)

```
# let memo_rec f_norec =
    let rec f = memoize (fun x -> f_norec f x) in
    f
  ;;
Characters 39-69:
Error: This kind of expression is not allowed as right-hand side of `let rec'
```

OCaml rejects the definition because OCaml, as a strict language, has limits on what it can put on the righthand side of a `let rec`. In particular, imagine how the following code snippet would be compiled:

OCaml

```
let rec x = x + 1
```

Note that x is an ordinary value, not a function. As such, it's not clear how this definition should be handled by the compiler. You could imagine it compiling down to an infinite loop, but x is of type int, and there's no int that corresponds to an infinite loop. As such, this construct is effectively impossible to compile.

To avoid such impossible cases, the compiler only allows three possible constructs to show up on the righthand side of a let rec: a function definition, a constructor, or the lazy keyword. This excludes some reasonable things, like our definition of memo_rec, but it also blocks things that don't make sense, like our definition of x.

It's worth noting that these restrictions don't show up in a lazy language like Haskell. Indeed, we can make something like our definition of x work if we use OCaml's laziness:

OCaml utop (part 2)

```
# let rec x = lazy (Lazy.force x + 1);;
val x : int lazy_t = <lazy>
```

Of course, actually trying to compute this will fail. OCaml's lazy throws an exception when a lazy value tries to force itself as part of its own evaluation.

OCaml utop (part 3)

```
# Lazy.force x;;
Exception: Lazy.Undefined.
```

But we can also create useful recursive definitions with lazy. In particular, we can use laziness to make our definition of memo_rec work without explicit mutation:

OCaml utop (part 5)

```
# let lazy_memo_rec f_norec x =
    let rec f = lazy (memoize (fun x -> f_norec (Lazy.force f) x)) in
    (Lazy.force f) x
  ;;
val lazy_memo_rec : (('a -> 'b) -> 'a -> 'b) -> 'a -> 'b = <fun>
# time (fun () -> lazy_memo_rec fib_norec 40);;
Time: 0.0650883ms
- : int = 102334155
```

Laziness is more constrained than explicit mutation, and so in some cases can lead to code whose behavior is easier to think about.

Input and Output

Imperative programming is about more than modifying in-memory data structures. Any function that doesn't boil down to a deterministic transformation from its arguments to its return value is imperative in nature. That includes not only things that mutate your program's data, but also operations that interact with the world outside of your program. An important example of this kind of interaction is I/O, i.e., operations for reading or writing data to things like files, terminal input and output, and network sockets.

There are multiple I/O libraries in OCaml. In this section we'll discuss OCaml's buffered I/O library that can be used through the `In_channel` and `Out_channel` modules in Core. Other I/O primitives are also available through the `Unix` module in Core as well as `Async`, the asynchronous I/O library that is covered in Chapter 18. Most of the functionality in Core's `In_channel` and `Out_channel` (and in Core's `Unix` module) derives from the standard library, but we'll use Core's interfaces here.

Terminal I/O

OCaml's buffered I/O library is organized around two types: `in_channel`, for channels you read from, and `out_channel`, for channels you write to. The `In_channel` and `Out_channel` modules only have direct support for channels corresponding to files and terminals; other kinds of channels can be created through the `Unix` module.

We'll start our discussion of I/O by focusing on the terminal. Following the UNIX model, communication with the terminal is organized around three channels, which correspond to the three standard file descriptors in Unix:

`In_channel.stdin`
> The "standard input" channel. By default, input comes from the terminal, which handles keyboard input.

`Out_channel.stdout`
> The "standard output" channel. By default, output written to `stdout` appears on the user terminal.

`Out_channel.stderr`
> The "standard error" channel. This is similar to `stdout` but is intended for error messages.

The values `stdin`, `stdout`, and `stderr` are useful enough that they are also available in the global namespace directly, without having to go through the `In_channel` and `Out_channel` modules.

Let's see this in action in a simple interactive application. The following program, `time_converter`, prompts the user for a time zone, and then prints out the current time in that time zone. Here, we use Core's `Zone` module for looking up a time zone, and the `Time` module for computing the current time and printing it out in the time zone in question:

OCaml

```
open Core.Std

let () =
  Out_channel.output_string stdout "Pick a timezone: ";
  Out_channel.flush stdout;
  match In_channel.input_line stdin with
  | None -> failwith "No timezone provided"
```

```
| Some zone_string ->
  let zone = Zone.find_exn zone_string in
  let time_string = Time.to_string_abs (Time.now ()) ~zone in
  Out_channel.output_string stdout
    (String.concat
       ["The time in ";Zone.to_string zone;" is ";time_string;".\n"]);
  Out_channel.flush stdout
```

We can build this program using *corebuild* and run it. You'll see that it prompts you for input, as follows:

Terminal

```
$ corebuild time_converter.byte
$ ./time_converter.byte
Pick a timezone:
```

You can then type in the name of a time zone and hit Return, and it will print out the current time in the time zone in question:

Terminal

```
Pick a timezone: Europe/London
The time in Europe/London is 2013-08-15 00:03:10.666220+01:00.
```

We called Out_channel.flush on stdout because out_channels are buffered, which is to say that OCaml doesn't immediately do a write every time you call output_string. Instead, writes are buffered until either enough has been written to trigger the flushing of the buffers, or until a flush is explicitly requested. This greatly increases the efficiency of the writing process by reducing the number of system calls.

Note that In_channel.input_line returns a string option, with None indicating that the input stream has ended (i.e., an end-of-file condition). Out_channel.out put_string is used to print the final output, and Out_channel.flush is called to flush that output to the screen. The final flush is not technically required, since the program ends after that instruction, at which point all remaining output will be flushed anyway, but the explicit flush is nonetheless good practice.

Formatted Output with printf

Generating output with functions like Out_channel.output_string is simple and easy to understand, but can be a bit verbose. OCaml also supports formatted output using the printf function, which is modeled after printf in the C standard library. printf takes a *format string* that describes what to print and how to format it, as well as arguments to be printed, as determined by the formatting directives embedded in the format string. So, for example, we can write:

OCaml utop (part 1)

```
# printf "%i is an integer, %F is a float, \"%s\" is a string\n"
    3 4.5 "five";;
3 is an integer, 4.5 is a float, "five" is a string
- : unit = ()
```

Unlike C's printf, the printf in OCaml is type-safe. In particular, if we provide an argument whose type doesn't match what's presented in the format string, we'll get a type error:

```
# printf "An integer: %i\n" 4.5;;
Characters 26-29:
Error: This expression has type float but an expression was expected of type
       int
```

Understanding Format Strings

The format strings used by printf turn out to be quite different from ordinary strings. This difference ties to the fact that OCaml format strings, unlike their equivalent in C, are type-safe. In particular, the compiler checks that the types referred to by the format string match the types of the rest of the arguments passed to printf.

To check this, OCaml needs to analyze the contents of the format string at compile time, which means the format string needs to be available as a string literal at compile time. Indeed, if you try to pass an ordinary string to printf, the compiler will complain:

OCaml utop (part 3)

```
# let fmt = "%i is an integer, %F is a float, \"%s\" is a string\n";;
val fmt : string = "%i is an integer, %F is a float, \"%s\" is a string\n"
# printf fmt 3 4.5 "five";;
Characters 9-12:
Error: This expression has type string but an expression was expected of type
         ('a -> 'b -> 'c -> 'd, out_channel, unit) format =
           ('a -> 'b -> 'c -> 'd, out_channel, unit, unit, unit, unit)
           format6
```

If OCaml infers that a given string literal is a format string, then it parses it at compile time as such, choosing its type in accordance with the formatting directives it finds. Thus, if we add a type annotation indicating that the string we're defining is actually a format string, it will be interpreted as such:

OCaml utop (part 4)

```
# let fmt : ('a, 'b, 'c) format =
    "%i is an integer, %F is a float, \"%s\" is a string\n";;
val fmt : (int -> float -> string -> 'c, 'b, 'c) format = <abstr>
```

And accordingly, we can pass it to printf:

OCaml utop (part 5)

```
# printf fmt 3 4.5 "five";;
3 is an integer, 4.5 is a float, "five" is a string - : unit = ()
```

> If this looks different from everything else you've seen so far, that's because it is. This is really a special case in the type system. Most of the time, you don't need to worry about this special handling of format strings—you can just use `printf` and not worry about the details. But it's useful to keep the broad outlines of the story in the back of your head.

Now let's see how we can rewrite our time conversion program to be a little more concise using `printf`:

OCaml

```
open Core.Std

let () =
  printf "Pick a timezone: %!";
  match In_channel.input_line stdin with
  | None -> failwith "No timezone provided"
  | Some zone_string ->
    let zone = Zone.find_exn zone_string in
    let time_string = Time.to_string_abs (Time.now ()) ~zone in
    printf "The time in %s is %s.\n%!" (Zone.to_string zone) time_string
```

In the preceding example, we've used only two formatting directives: `%s`, for including a string, and `%!` which causes `printf` to flush the channel.

`printf`'s formatting directives offer a significant amount of control, allowing you to specify things like:

- Alignment and padding
- Escaping rules for strings
- Whether numbers should be formatted in decimal, hex, or binary
- Precision of float conversions

There are also `printf`-style functions that target outputs other than `stdout`, including:

- `eprintf`, which prints to `stderr`
- `fprintf`, which prints to an arbitrary `out_channel`
- `sprintf`, which returns a formatted string

All of this, and a good deal more, is described in the API documentation for the `Printf` module in the OCaml Manual.

File I/O

Another common use of `in_channels` and `out_channels` is for working with files. Here are a couple of functions—one that creates a file full of numbers, and the other that reads in such a file and returns the sum of those numbers:

```
# let create_number_file filename numbers =
    let outc = Out_channel.create filename in
    List.iter numbers ~f:(fun x -> fprintf outc "%d\n" x);
    Out_channel.close outc
  ;;
val create_number_file : string -> int list -> unit = <fun>
# let sum_file filename =
    let file = In_channel.create filename in
    let numbers = List.map ~f:Int.of_string (In_channel.input_lines file) in
    let sum = List.fold ~init:0 ~f:(+) numbers in
    In_channel.close file;
    sum
  ;;
val sum_file : string -> int = <fun>
# create_number_file "numbers.txt" [1;2;3;4;5];;
- : unit = ()
# sum_file "numbers.txt";;
- : int = 15
```

For both of these functions, we followed the same basic sequence: we first create the channel, then use the channel, and finally close the channel. The closing of the channel is important, since without it, we won't release resources associated with the file back to the operating system.

One problem with the preceding code is that if it throws an exception in the middle of its work, it won't actually close the file. If we try to read a file that doesn't actually contain numbers, we'll see such an error:

```
# sum_file "/etc/hosts";;
Exception: (Failure "Int.of_string: \"127.0.0.1    localhost\"").
```

And if we do this over and over in a loop, we'll eventually run out of file descriptors:

```
# for i = 1 to 10000 do try ignore (sum_file "/etc/hosts") with _ -> () done;;
- : unit = ()
# sum_file "numbers.txt";;
Exception: (Sys_error "numbers.txt: Too many open files").
```

And now, you'll need to restart your toplevel if you want to open any more files!

To avoid this, we need to make sure that our code cleans up after itself. We can do this using the protect function described in Chapter 7, as follows:

```
# let sum_file filename =
    let file = In_channel.create filename in
    protect ~f:(fun () ->
        let numbers = List.map ~f:Int.of_string (In_channel.input_lines file) in
        List.fold ~init:0 ~f:(+) numbers)
      ~finally:(fun () -> In_channel.close file)
```

```
  ;;
val sum_file : string -> int = <fun>
```

And now, the file descriptor leak is gone:

```
# for i = 1 to 10000 do try ignore (sum_file "/etc/hosts") with _ -> () done;;
- : unit = ()
# sum_file "numbers.txt";;
- : int = 15
```

This is really an example of a more general issue with imperative programming. When programming imperatively, you need to be quite careful to make sure that exceptions don't leave you in an awkward state.

In_channel has functions that automate the handling of some of these details. For example, In_channel.with_file takes a filename and a function for processing data from an in_channel and takes care of the bookkeeping associated with opening and closing the file. We can rewrite sum_file using this function, as shown here:

```
# let sum_file filename =
    In_channel.with_file filename ~f:(fun file ->
      let numbers = List.map ~f:Int.of_string (In_channel.input_lines file) in
      List.fold ~init:0 ~f:(+) numbers)
  ;;
val sum_file : string -> int = <fun>
```

Another misfeature of our implementation of sum_file is that we read the entire file into memory before processing it. For a large file, it's more efficient to process a line at a time. You can use the In_channel.fold_lines function to do just that:

```
# let sum_file filename =
    In_channel.with_file filename ~f:(fun file ->
      In_channel.fold_lines file ~init:0 ~f:(fun sum line ->
        sum + Int.of_string line))
  ;;
val sum_file : string -> int = <fun>
```

This is just a taste of the functionality of In_channel and Out_channel. To get a fuller understanding, you should review the API documentation for those modules.

Order of Evaluation

The order in which expressions are evaluated is an important part of the definition of a programming language, and it is particularly important when programming imperatively. Most programming languages you're likely to have encountered are *strict*, and OCaml is, too. In a strict language, when you bind an identifier to the result of some expression, the expression is evaluated before the variable is bound. Similarly, if you call a function on a set of arguments, those arguments are evaluated before they are passed to the function.

Consider the following simple example. Here, we have a collection of angles, and we want to determine if any of them have a negative sin. The following snippet of code would answer that question:

OCaml utop (part 1)

```
# let x = sin 120. in
  let y = sin 75.  in
  let z = sin 128. in
  List.exists ~f:(fun x -> x < 0.) [x;y;z]
  ;;
- : bool = true
```

In some sense, we don't really need to compute the sin 128. because sin 75. is negative, so we could know the answer before even computing sin 128..

It doesn't have to be this way. Using the lazy keyword, we can write the original computation so that sin 128. won't ever be computed:

OCaml utop (part 2)

```
# let x = lazy (sin 120.) in
  let y = lazy (sin 75.) in
  let z = lazy (sin 128.) in
  List.exists ~f:(fun x -> Lazy.force x < 0.) [x;y;z]
  ;;
- : bool = true
```

We can confirm that fact by a few well-placed printfs:

OCaml utop (part 3)

```
# let x = lazy (printf "1\n"; sin 120.) in
  let y = lazy (printf "2\n"; sin 75.)  in
  let z = lazy (printf "3\n"; sin 128.) in
  List.exists ~f:(fun x -> Lazy.force x < 0.) [x;y;z]
  ;;
1
2
- : bool = true
```

OCaml is strict by default for a good reason: lazy evaluation and imperative programming generally don't mix well because laziness makes it harder to reason about when a given side effect is going to occur. Understanding the order of side effects is essential to reasoning about the behavior of an imperative program.

In a strict language, we know that expressions that are bound by a sequence of let bindings will be evaluated in the order that they're defined. But what about the evaluation order within a single expression? Officially, the answer is that evaluation order within an expression is undefined. In practice, OCaml has only one compiler, and that behavior is a kind of de facto standard. Unfortunately, the evaluation order in this case is often the opposite of what one might expect.

Consider the following example:

OCaml utop (part 4)

```
# List.exists ~f:(fun x -> x < 0.)
  [ (printf "1\n"; sin 120.);
    (printf "2\n"; sin 75.);
    (printf "3\n"; sin 128.); ]
  ;;
3
2
1
- : bool = true
```

Here, you can see that the subexpression that came last was actually evaluated first! This is generally the case for many different kinds of expressions. If you want to make sure of the evaluation order of different subexpressions, you should express them as a series of let bindings.

Side Effects and Weak Polymorphism

Consider the following simple, imperative function:

OCaml utop (part 1)

```
# let remember =
    let cache = ref None in
    (fun x ->
      match !cache with
      | Some y -> y
      | None -> cache := Some x; x)
  ;;
val remember : '_a -> '_a = <fun>
```

remember simply caches the first value that's passed to it, returning that value on every call. That's because cache is created and initialized once and is shared across invocations of remember.

remember is not a terribly useful function, but it raises an interesting question: what is its type?

On its first call, remember returns the same value it's passed, which means its input type and return type should match. Accordingly, remember should have type t -> t for some type t. There's nothing about remember that ties the choice of t to any particular type, so you might expect OCaml to generalize, replacing t with a polymorphic type variable. It's this kind of generalization that gives us polymorphic types in the first place. The identity function, as an example, gets a polymorphic type in this way:

```
# let identity x = x;;
val identity : 'a -> 'a = <fun>
# identity 3;;
- : int = 3
# identity "five";;
- : string = "five"
```

As you can see, the polymorphic type of identity lets it operate on values with different types.

This is not what happens with remember, though. As you can see from the above examples, the type that OCaml infers for remember looks almost, but not quite, like the type of the identity function. Here it is again:

```
val remember : '_a -> '_a = <fun>
```

The underscore in the type variable '_a tells us that the variable is only *weakly polymorphic*, which is to say that it can be used with any *single* type. That makes sense because, unlike identity, remember always returns the value it was passed on its first invocation, which means its return value must always have the same type.

OCaml will convert a weakly polymorphic variable to a concrete type as soon as it gets a clue as to what concrete type it is to be used as:

```
# let remember_three () = remember 3;;
val remember_three : unit -> int = <fun>
# remember;;
- : int -> int = <fun>
# remember "avocado";;
Characters 9-18:
Error: This expression has type string but an expression was expected of type
          int
```

Note that the type of remember was settled by the definition of remember_three, even though remember_three was never called!

The Value Restriction

So, when does the compiler infer weakly polymorphic types? As we've seen, we need weakly polymorphic types when a value of unknown type is stored in a persistent mutable cell. Because the type system isn't precise enough to determine all cases where this might happen, OCaml uses a rough rule to flag cases that don't introduce any persistent mutable cells, and to only infer polymorphic types in those cases. This rule is called *the value restriction*.

The core of the value restriction is the observation that some kinds of expressions, which we'll refer to as *simple values*, by their nature can't introduce persistent mutable cells, including:

- Constants (i.e., things like integer and floating-point literals)
- Constructors that only contain other simple values
- Function declarations, i.e., expressions that begin with `fun` or `function`, or the equivalent let binding, `let f x = ...`
- let bindings of the form `let var = expr1 in expr2`, where both *expr1* and *expr2* are simple values

Thus, the following expression is a simple value, and as a result, the types of values contained within it are allowed to be polymorphic:

OCaml utop (part 1)

```
# (fun x -> [x;x]);;
- : 'a -> 'a list = <fun>
```

But, if we write down an expression that isn't a simple value by the preceding definition, we'll get different results. For example, consider what happens if we try to memoize the function defined previously.

OCaml utop (part 2)

```
# memoize (fun x -> [x;x]);;
- : '_a -> '_a list = <fun>
```

The memoized version of the function does in fact need to be restricted to a single type because it uses mutable state behind the scenes to cache values returned by previous invocations of the function. But OCaml would make the same determination even if the function in question did no such thing. Consider this example:

OCaml utop (part 3)

```
# identity (fun x -> [x;x]);;
- : '_a -> '_a list = <fun>
```

It would be safe to infer a fully polymorphic variable here, but because OCaml's type system doesn't distinguish between pure and impure functions, it can't separate those two cases.

The value restriction doesn't require that there is no mutable state, only that there is no *persistent* mutable state that could share values between uses of the same function. Thus, a function that produces a fresh reference every time it's called can have a fully polymorphic type:

OCaml utop (part 4)

```
# let f () = ref None;;
val f : unit -> 'a option ref = <fun>
```

But a function that has a mutable cache that persists across calls, like `memoize`, can only be weakly polymorphic.

Partial Application and the Value Restriction

Most of the time, when the value restriction kicks in, it's for a good reason, i.e., it's because the value in question can actually only safely be used with a single type. But sometimes, the value restriction kicks in when you don't want it. The most common such case is partially applied functions. A partially applied function, like any function application, is not a simple value, and as such, functions created by partial application are sometimes less general than you might expect.

Consider the `List.init` function, which is used for creating lists where each element is created by calling a function on the index of that element:

OCaml utop (part 5)

```
# List.init;;
- : int -> f:(int -> 'a) -> 'a list = <fun>
# List.init 10 ~f:Int.to_string;;
- : string list = ["0"; "1"; "2"; "3"; "4"; "5"; "6"; "7"; "8"; "9"]
```

Imagine we wanted to create a specialized version of `List.init` that always created lists of length 10. We could do that using partial application, as follows:

OCaml utop (part 6)

```
# let list_init_10 = List.init 10;;
val list_init_10 : f:(int -> '_a) -> '_a list = <fun>
```

As you can see, we now infer a weakly polymorphic type for the resulting function. That's because there's nothing that guarantees that `List.init` isn't creating a persistent `ref` somewhere inside of it that would be shared across multiple calls to `list_init_10`. We can eliminate this possibility, and at the same time get the compiler to infer a polymorphic type, by avoiding partial application:

OCaml utop (part 7)

```
# let list_init_10 ~f = List.init 10 ~f;;
val list_init_10 : f:(int -> 'a) -> 'a list = <fun>
```

This transformation is referred to as *eta expansion* and is often useful to resolve problems that arise from the value restriction.

Relaxing the Value Restriction

OCaml is actually a little better at inferring polymorphic types than was suggested previously. The value restriction as we described it is basically a syntactic check: you can do a few operations that count as simple values, and anything that's a simple value can be generalized.

But OCaml actually has a relaxed version of the value restriction that can make use of type information to allow polymorphic types for things that are not simple values.

For example, we saw that a function application, even a simple application of the identity function, is not a simple value and thus can turn a polymorphic value into a weakly polymorphic one:

OCaml utop (part 8)

```
# identity (fun x -> [x;x]);;
- : '_a -> '_a list = <fun>
```

But that's not always the case. When the type of the returned value is immutable, then OCaml can typically infer a fully polymorphic type:

OCaml utop (part 9)

```
# identity [];;
- : 'a list = []
```

On the other hand, if the returned type is potentially mutable, then the result will be weakly polymorphic:

OCaml utop (part 10)

```
# [||];;
- : 'a array = [||]
# identity [||];;
- : '_a array = [||]
```

A more important example of this comes up when defining abstract data types. Consider the following simple data structure for an immutable list type that supports constant-time concatenation:

OCaml utop (part 11)

```
# module Concat_list : sig
    type 'a t
    val empty : 'a t
    val singleton : 'a -> 'a t
    val concat  : 'a t -> 'a t -> 'a t  (* constant time *)
    val to_list : 'a t -> 'a list       (* linear time   *)
  end = struct

    type 'a t = Empty | Singleton of 'a | Concat of 'a t * 'a t

    let empty = Empty
    let singleton x = Singleton x
    let concat x y = Concat (x,y)

    let rec to_list_with_tail t tail =
      match t with
      | Empty -> tail
      | Singleton x -> x :: tail
      | Concat (x,y) -> to_list_with_tail x (to_list_with_tail y tail)

    let to_list t =
```

```
        to_list_with_tail t []

  end;;
module Concat_list :
  sig
    type 'a t
    val empty : 'a t
    val singleton : 'a -> 'a t
    val concat : 'a t -> 'a t -> 'a t
    val to_list : 'a t -> 'a list
  end
```

The details of the implementation don't matter so much, but it's important to note that a `Concat_list.t` is unquestionably an immutable value. However, when it comes to the value restriction, OCaml treats it as if it were mutable:

OCaml utop (part 12)

```
# Concat_list.empty;;
- : 'a Concat_list.t = <abstr>
# identity Concat_list.empty;;
- : '_a Concat_list.t = <abstr>
```

The issue here is that the signature, by virtue of being abstract, has obscured the fact that `Concat_list.t` is in fact an immutable data type. We can resolve this in one of two ways: either by making the type concrete (i.e., exposing the implementation in the mli), which is often not desirable; or by marking the type variable in question as *covariant*. We'll learn more about covariance and contravariance in Chapter 11, but for now, you can think of it as an annotation that can be put in the interface of a pure data structure.

In particular, if we replace `type 'a t` in the interface with `type +'a t`, that will make it explicit in the interface that the data structure doesn't contain any persistent references to values of type `'a`, at which point, OCaml can infer polymorphic types for expressions of this type that are not simple values:

OCaml utop

```
# module Concat_list : sig
    type +'a t
    val empty : 'a t
    val singleton : 'a -> 'a t
    val concat  : 'a t -> 'a t -> 'a t  (* constant time *)
    val to_list : 'a t -> 'a list       (* linear time   *)
  end = struct

    type 'a t = Empty | Singleton of 'a | Concat of 'a t * 'a t

    ...

  end;;
module Concat_list :
  sig
```

```
    type '+a t
    val empty : 'a t
    val singleton : 'a -> 'a t
    val concat : 'a t -> 'a t -> 'a t
    val to_list : 'a t -> 'a list
end
```

Now, we can apply the identity function to `Concat_list.empty` without without losing any polymorphism:

OCaml utop (part 14)

```
# identity Concat_list.empty;;
- : 'a Concat_list.t = <abstr>
```

Summary

This chapter has covered quite a lot of ground, including:

- Discussing the building blocks of mutable data structures as well as the basic imperative constructs like `for` loops, `while` loops, and the sequencing operator `;`
- Walking through the implementation of a couple of classic imperative data structures
- Discussing so-called benign effects like memoization and laziness
- Covering OCaml's API for blocking I/O
- Discussing how language-level issues like order of evaluation and weak polymorphism interact with OCaml's imperative features

The scope and sophistication of the material here is an indication of the importance of OCaml's imperative features. The fact that OCaml defaults to immutability shouldn't obscure the fact that imperative programming is a fundamental part of building any serious application, and that if you want to be an effective OCaml programmer, you need to understand OCaml's approach to imperative programming.

## CHAPTER 9

Functors

Up until now, we've seen OCaml's modules play an important but limited role. In particular, we've seen them as a mechanism for organizing code into units with specified interfaces. But OCaml's module system can do much more than that, serving as a powerful tool for building generic code and structuring large-scale systems. Much of that power comes from functors.

Functors are, roughly speaking, functions from modules to modules, and they can be used to solve a variety of code-structuring problems, including:

Dependency injection

    Makes the implementations of some components of a system swappable. This is particularly useful when you want to mock up parts of your system for testing and simulation purposes.

Autoextension of modules

    Functors give you a way of extending existing modules with new functionality in a standardized way. For example, you might want to add a slew of comparison operators derived from a base comparison function. To do this by hand would require a lot of repetitive code for each type, but functors let you write this logic just once and apply it to many different types.

Instantiating modules with state

    Modules can contain mutable states, and that means that you'll occasionally want to have multiple instantiations of a particular module, each with its own separate and independent mutable state. Functors let you automate the construction of such modules.

These are really just some of the uses that you can put functors to. We'll make no attempt to provide examples of all of the uses of functors here. Instead, this chapter will try to provide examples that illuminate the language features and design patterns that you need to master in order to use functors effectively.

A Trivial Example

Let's create a functor that takes a module containing a single integer variable x and returns a new module with x incremented by one. This is intended to serve as a way to walk through the basic mechanics of functors, even though it's not something you'd want to do in practice.

First, let's define a signature for a module that contains a single value of type int:

OCaml utop

```
# module type X_int = sig val x : int end;;
module type X_int = sig val x : int end
```

Now we can define our functor. We'll use X_int both to constrain the argument to the functor and to constrain the module returned by the functor:

OCaml utop (part 1)

```
# module Increment (M : X_int) : X_int = struct
    let x = M.x + 1
  end;;
module Increment : functor (M : X_int) -> X_int
```

One thing that immediately jumps out is that functors are more syntactically heavy-weight than ordinary functions. For one thing, functors require explicit (module) type annotations, which ordinary functions do not. Technically, only the type on the input is mandatory, although in practice, you should usually constrain the module returned by the functor, just as you should use an mli, even though it's not mandatory.

The following shows what happens when we omit the module type for the output of the functor:

OCaml utop (part 2)

```
# module Increment (M : X_int) = struct
    let x = M.x + 1
  end;;
module Increment : functor (M : X_int) -> sig val x : int end
```

We can see that the inferred module type of the output is now written out explicitly, rather than being a reference to the named signature X_int.

We can use Increment to define new modules:

OCaml utop (part 3)

```
# module Three = struct let x = 3 end;;
module Three : sig val x : int end
# module Four = Increment(Three);;
module Four : sig val x : int end
# Four.x - Three.x;;
- : int = 1
```

In this case, we applied Increment to a module whose signature is exactly equal to X_int. But we can apply Increment to any module that *satisfies* the interface X_int, in the same way that the contents of an `ml` file must satisfy the `mli`. That means that the module type can omit some information available in the module, either by dropping fields or by leaving some fields abstract. Here's an example:

OCaml utop (part 4)

```
# module Three_and_more = struct
    let x = 3
    let y = "three"
  end;;
module Three_and_more : sig val x : int val y : string end
# module Four = Increment(Three_and_more);;
module Four : sig val x : int end
```

The rules for determining whether a module matches a given signature are similar in spirit to the rules in an object-oriented language that determine whether an object satisfies a given interface. As in an object-oriented context, the extra information that doesn't match the signature you're looking for (in this case, the variable y) is simply ignored.

A Bigger Example: Computing with Intervals

Let's consider a more realistic example of how to use functors: a library for computing with intervals. Intervals are a common computational object, and they come up in different contexts and for different types. You might need to work with intervals of floating-point values or strings or times, and in each of these cases, you want similar operations: testing for emptiness, checking for containment, intersecting intervals, and so on.

Let's see how to use functors to build a generic interval library that can be used with any type that supports a total ordering on the underlying set over which you want to build intervals.

First we'll define a module type that captures the information we'll need about the endpoints of the intervals. This interface, which we'll call Comparable, contains just two things: a comparison function and the type of the values to be compared:

OCaml utop (part 5)

```
# module type Comparable = sig
    type t
    val compare : t -> t -> int
  end ;;
module type Comparable = sig type t val compare : t -> t -> int end
```

The comparison function follows the standard OCaml idiom for such functions, returning 0 if the two elements are equal, a positive number if the first element is larger than the second, and a negative number if the first element is smaller than the second. Thus, we could rewrite the standard comparison functions on top of compare.

```
compare x y < 0      (* x < y *)
compare x y = 0      (* x = y *)
compare x y > 0      (* x > y *)
```

(This idiom is a bit of a historical error. It would be better if compare returned a variant with three cases for less than, greater than, and equal. But it's a well-established idiom at this point, and unlikely to change.)

The functor for creating the interval module follows. We represent an interval with a variant type, which is either Empty or Interval (x,y), where x and y are the bounds of the interval. In addition to the type, the body of the functor contains implementations of a number of useful primitives for interacting with intervals:

OCaml utop (part 6)

```
# module Make_interval(Endpoint : Comparable) = struct

    type t = | Interval of Endpoint.t * Endpoint.t
             | Empty

    (** [create low high] creates a new interval from [low] to
        [high].  If [low > high], then the interval is empty *)
    let create low high =
      if Endpoint.compare low high > 0 then Empty
      else Interval (low,high)

    (** Returns true iff the interval is empty *)
    let is_empty = function
      | Empty -> true
      | Interval _ -> false

    (** [contains t x] returns true iff [x] is contained in the
        interval [t] *)
    let contains t x =
      match t with
      | Empty -> false
      | Interval (l,h) ->
        Endpoint.compare x l >= 0 && Endpoint.compare x h <= 0

    (** [intersect t1 t2] returns the intersection of the two input
        intervals *)
    let intersect t1 t2 =
      let min x y = if Endpoint.compare x y <= 0 then x else y in
      let max x y = if Endpoint.compare x y >= 0 then x else y in
      match t1,t2 with
      | Empty, _ | _, Empty -> Empty
      | Interval (l1,h1), Interval (l2,h2) ->
        create (max l1 l2) (min h1 h2)

  end ;;
module Make_interval :
  functor (Endpoint : Comparable) ->
```

```
sig
  type t = Interval of Endpoint.t * Endpoint.t | Empty
  val create : Endpoint.t -> Endpoint.t -> t
  val is_empty : t -> bool
  val contains : t -> Endpoint.t -> bool
  val intersect : t -> t -> t
end
```

We can instantiate the functor by applying it to a module with the right signature. In the following code, rather than name the module first and then call the functor, we provide the functor input as an anonymous module:

OCaml utop (part 7)

```
# module Int_interval =
    Make_interval(struct
      type t = int
      let compare = Int.compare
    end);;
module Int_interval :
  sig
    type t = Interval of int * int | Empty
    val create : int -> int -> t
    val is_empty : t -> bool
    val contains : t -> int -> bool
    val intersect : t -> t -> t
  end
```

If the input interface for your functor is aligned with the standards of the libraries you use, then you don't need to construct a custom module to feed to the functor. In this case, we can directly use the Int or String modules provided by Core:

OCaml utop (part 8)

```
# module Int_interval = Make_interval(Int) ;;
module Int_interval :
  sig
    type t = Make_interval(Core.Std.Int).t = Interval of int * int | Empty
    val create : int -> int -> t
    val is_empty : t -> bool
    val contains : t -> int -> bool
    val intersect : t -> t -> t
  end
# module String_interval = Make_interval(String) ;;
module String_interval :
  sig
    type t =
      Make_interval(Core.Std.String).t =
        Interval of string * string
      | Empty
    val create : string -> string -> t
    val is_empty : t -> bool
    val contains : t -> string -> bool
    val intersect : t -> t -> t
  end
```

This works because many modules in Core, including `Int` and `String`, satisfy an extended version of the `Comparable` signature described previously. Such standardized signatures are good practice, both because they make functors easier to use, and because they encourage standardization that makes your codebase easier to navigate.

We can use the newly defined `Int_interval` module like any ordinary module:

OCaml utop (part 9)

```
# let i1 = Int_interval.create 3 8;;
val i1 : Int_interval.t = Int_interval.Interval (3, 8)
# let i2 = Int_interval.create 4 10;;
val i2 : Int_interval.t = Int_interval.Interval (4, 10)
# Int_interval.intersect i1 i2;;
- : Int_interval.t = Int_interval.Interval (4, 8)
```

This design gives us the freedom to use any comparison function we want for comparing the endpoints. We could, for example, create a type of integer interval with the order of the comparison reversed, as follows:

OCaml utop (part 10)

```
# module Rev_int_interval =
    Make_interval(struct
      type t = int
      let compare x y = Int.compare y x
    end);;
module Rev_int_interval :
  sig
    type t = Interval of int * int | Empty
    val create : int -> int -> t
    val is_empty : t -> bool
    val contains : t -> int -> bool
    val intersect : t -> t -> t
  end
```

The behavior of `Rev_int_interval` is of course different from `Int_interval`:

OCaml utop (part 11)

```
# let interval = Int_interval.create 4 3;;
val interval : Int_interval.t = Int_interval.Empty
# let rev_interval = Rev_int_interval.create 4 3;;
val rev_interval : Rev_int_interval.t = Rev_int_interval.Interval (4, 3)
```

Importantly, `Rev_int_interval.t` is a different type than `Int_interval.t`, even though its physical representation is the same. Indeed, the type system will prevent us from confusing them.

OCaml utop (part 12)

```
# Int_interval.contains rev_interval 3;;
Characters 22-34:
Error: This expression has type Rev_int_interval.t
       but an expression was expected of type Int_interval.t
```

This is important, because confusing the two kinds of intervals would be a semantic error, and it's an easy one to make. The ability of functors to mint new types is a useful trick that comes up a lot.

Making the Functor Abstract

There's a problem with `Make_interval`. The code we wrote depends on the invariant that the upper bound of an interval is greater than its lower bound, but that invariant can be violated. The invariant is enforced by the `create` function, but because `Interval.t` is not abstract, we can bypass the `create` function:

OCaml utop (part 13)

```
# Int_interval.is_empty (* going through create *)
    (Int_interval.create 4 3) ;;
- : bool = true
# Int_interval.is_empty (* bypassing create *)
    (Int_interval.Interval (4,3)) ;;
- : bool = false
```

To make `Int_interval.t` abstract, we need to restrict the output of `Make_interval` with an interface. Here's an explicit interface that we can use for that purpose:

OCaml utop (part 14)

```
# module type Interval_intf = sig
    type t
    type endpoint
    val create : endpoint -> endpoint -> t
    val is_empty : t -> bool
    val contains : t -> endpoint -> bool
    val intersect : t -> t -> t
  end;;
module type Interval_intf =
  sig
    type t
    type endpoint
    val create : endpoint -> endpoint -> t
    val is_empty : t -> bool
    val contains : t -> endpoint -> bool
    val intersect : t -> t -> t
  end
```

This interface includes the type `endpoint` to give us a way of referring to the endpoint type. Given this interface, we can redo our definition of `Make_interval`. Notice that we added the type `endpoint` to the implementation of the module to match `Interval_intf`:

OCaml utop

```
# module Make_interval(Endpoint : Comparable) : Interval_intf = struct
    type endpoint = Endpoint.t
    type t = | Interval of Endpoint.t * Endpoint.t
             | Empty
```

```
    ...
  end ;;
module Make_interval : functor (Endpoint : Comparable) -> Interval_intf
```

Sharing Constraints

The resulting module is abstract, but it's unfortunately too abstract. In particular, we haven't exposed the type endpoint, which means that we can't even construct an interval anymore:

OCaml utop (part 16)

```
# module Int_interval = Make_interval(Int);;
module Int_interval :
  sig
    type t = Make_interval(Core.Std.Int).t
    type endpoint = Make_interval(Core.Std.Int).endpoint
    val create : endpoint -> endpoint -> t
    val is_empty : t -> bool
    val contains : t -> endpoint -> bool
    val intersect : t -> t -> t
  end
# Int_interval.create 3 4;;
Characters 20-21:
Error: This expression has type int but an expression was expected of type
        Int_interval.endpoint
```

To fix this, we need to expose the fact that endpoint is equal to Int.t (or more generally, Endpoint.t, where Endpoint is the argument to the functor). One way of doing this is through a *sharing constraint*, which allows you to tell the compiler to expose the fact that a given type is equal to some other type. The syntax for a simple sharing constraint is as follows:

Syntax

```
<Module_type> with type <type> = <type'>
```

The result of this expression is a new signature that's been modified so that it exposes the fact that *type* defined inside of the module type is equal to *type'* whose definition is outside of it. One can also apply multiple sharing constraints to the same signature:

Syntax

```
<Module_type> with type <type1> = <type1'> and <type2> = <type2'>
```

We can use a sharing constraint to create a specialized version of Interval_intf for integer intervals:

OCaml utop (part 17)

```
# module type Int_interval_intf =
    Interval_intf with type endpoint = int;;
module type Int_interval_intf =
  sig
    type t
```

```
    type endpoint = int
    val create : endpoint -> endpoint -> t
    val is_empty : t -> bool
    val contains : t -> endpoint -> bool
    val intersect : t -> t -> t
  end
```

We can also use sharing constraints in the context of a functor. The most common use case is where you want to expose that some of the types of the module being generated by the functor are related to the types in the module fed to the functor.

In this case, we'd like to expose an equality between the type endpoint in the new module and the type Endpoint.t, from the module Endpoint that is the functor argument. We can do this as follows:

OCaml utop

```
# module Make_interval(Endpoint : Comparable)
    : (Interval_intf with type endpoint = Endpoint.t)
  = struct

    type endpoint = Endpoint.t
    type t = | Interval of Endpoint.t * Endpoint.t
             | Empty

    ...

  end ;;
module Make_interval :
  functor (Endpoint : Comparable) ->
    sig
      type t
      type endpoint = Endpoint.t
      val create : endpoint -> endpoint -> t
      val is_empty : t -> bool
      val contains : t -> endpoint -> bool
      val intersect : t -> t -> t
    end
```

So now, the interface is as it was, except that endpoint is known to be equal to End point.t. As a result of that type equality, we can again do things that require that endpoint be exposed, like constructing intervals:

OCaml utop (part 19)

```
# module Int_interval = Make_interval(Int);;
module Int_interval :
  sig
    type t = Make_interval(Core.Std.Int).t
    type endpoint = int
    val create : endpoint -> endpoint -> t
    val is_empty : t -> bool
    val contains : t -> endpoint -> bool
    val intersect : t -> t -> t
```

```
  end
# let i = Int_interval.create 3 4;;
val i : Int_interval.t = <abstr>
# Int_interval.contains i 5;;
- : bool = false
```

Destructive Substitution

Sharing constraints basically do the job, but they have some downsides. In particular,
we've now been stuck with the useless type declaration of endpoint that clutters up both
the interface and the implementation. A better solution would be to modify the Inter
val_intf signature by replacing endpoint with Endpoint.t everywhere it shows up,
and deleting the definition of endpoint from the signature. We can do just this using
what's called *destructive substitution*. Here's the basic syntax:

Syntax

```
<Module_type> with type <type> := <type'>
```

The following shows how we could use this with Make_interval:

OCaml utop (part 20)

```
# module type Int_interval_intf =
    Interval_intf with type endpoint := int;;
module type Int_interval_intf =
  sig
    type t
    val create : int -> int -> t
    val is_empty : t -> bool
    val contains : t -> int -> bool
    val intersect : t -> t -> t
  end
```

There's now no endpoint type: all of its occurrences of have been replaced by int. As
with sharing constraints, we can also use this in the context of a functor:

OCaml utop

```
# module Make_interval(Endpoint : Comparable)
    : Interval_intf with type endpoint := Endpoint.t =
  struct

    type t = | Interval of Endpoint.t * Endpoint.t
             | Empty

    ...

  end ;;
module Make_interval :
  functor (Endpoint : Comparable) ->
  sig
    type t
    val create : Endpoint.t -> Endpoint.t -> t
    val is_empty : t -> bool
```

```
      val contains : t -> Endpoint.t -> bool
      val intersect : t -> t -> t
    end
```

The interface is precisely what we want: the type t is abstract, and the type of the endpoint is exposed; so we can create values of type Int_interval.t using the creation function, but not directly using the constructors and thereby violating the invariants of the module:

OCaml utop (part 22)

```
# module Int_interval = Make_interval(Int);;
module Int_interval :
  sig
    type t = Make_interval(Core.Std.Int).t
    val create : int -> int -> t
    val is_empty : t -> bool
    val contains : t -> int -> bool
    val intersect : t -> t -> t
  end
# Int_interval.is_empty
    (Int_interval.create 3 4);;
- : bool = false
# Int_interval.is_empty
    (Int_interval.Interval (4,3));;
Characters 40-48:
Error: Unbound constructor Int_interval.Interval
```

In addition, the endpoint type is gone from the interface, meaning we no longer need to define the endpoint type alias in the body of the module.

It's worth noting that the name is somewhat misleading, in that there's nothing destructive about destructive substitution; it's really just a way of creating a new signature by transforming an existing one.

Using Multiple Interfaces

Another feature that we might want for our interval module is the ability to *serialize*, i.e., to be able to read and write intervals as a stream of bytes. In this case, we'll do this by converting to and from s-expressions, which were mentioned already in Chapter 7. To recall, an s-expression is essentially a parenthesized expression whose atoms are strings, and it is a serialization format that is used commonly in Core. Here's an example:

OCaml utop (part 23)

```
# Sexp.of_string "(This is (an s-expression))";;
- : Sexp.t = (This is (an s-expression))
```

Core comes with a syntax extension called Sexplib which can autogenerate s-expression conversion functions from a type declaration. Attaching with sexp to a type definition signals to the extension to generate the converters. Thus, we can write:

```
# type some_type = int * string list with sexp;;
type some_type = int * string list
val some_type_of_sexp : Sexp.t -> int * string list = <fun>
val sexp_of_some_type : int * string list -> Sexp.t = <fun>
# sexp_of_some_type (33, ["one"; "two"]);;
- : Sexp.t = (33 (one two))
# Sexp.of_string "(44 (five six))" |> some_type_of_sexp;;
- : int * string list = (44, ["five"; "six"])
```

We'll discuss s-expressions and Sexplib in more detail in Chapter 17, but for now, let's see what happens if we attach the `with sexp` declaration to the definition of `t` within the functor:

```
# module Make_interval(Endpoint : Comparable)
    : (Interval_intf with type endpoint := Endpoint.t) = struct

    type t = | Interval of Endpoint.t * Endpoint.t
             | Empty
    with sexp

    ...

  end ;;
Characters 136-146:
  Error: Unbound value Endpoint.t_of_sexp
```

The problem is that `with sexp` adds code for defining the s-expression converters, and that code assumes that `Endpoint` has the appropriate sexp-conversion functions for `Endpoint.t`. But all we know about `Endpoint` is that it satisfies the `Comparable` interface, which doesn't say anything about s-expressions.

Happily, Core comes with a built-in interface for just this purpose called `Sexpable`, which is defined as follows:

```
module type Sexpable = sig
  type t
  val sexp_of_t : t -> Sexp.t
  val t_of_sexp : Sexp.t -> t
end
```

We can modify `Make_interval` to use the `Sexpable` interface, for both its input and its output. First, let's create an extended version of the `Interval_intf` interface that includes the functions from the `Sexpable` interface. We can do this using destructive substitution on the `Sexpable` interface, to avoid having multiple distinct type `t`'s clashing with each other:

```
# module type Interval_intf_with_sexp = sig
    include Interval_intf
```

```
    include Sexpable with type t := t
  end;;
module type Interval_intf_with_sexp =
  sig
    type t
    type endpoint
    val create : endpoint -> endpoint -> t
    val is_empty : t -> bool
    val contains : t -> endpoint -> bool
    val intersect : t -> t -> t
    val t_of_sexp : Sexp.t -> t
    val sexp_of_t : t -> Sexp.t
  end
```

Equivalently, we can define a type t within our new module, and apply destructive substitutions to all of the included interfaces, Interval_intf included, as shown in the following example. This is somewhat cleaner when combining multiple interfaces, since it correctly reflects that all of the signatures are being handled equivalently:

OCaml utop (part 27)

```
# module type Interval_intf_with_sexp = sig
    type t
    include Interval_intf with type t := t
    include Sexpable      with type t := t
  end;;
module type Interval_intf_with_sexp =
  sig
    type t
    type endpoint
    val create : endpoint -> endpoint -> t
    val is_empty : t -> bool
    val contains : t -> endpoint -> bool
    val intersect : t -> t -> t
    val t_of_sexp : Sexp.t -> t
    val sexp_of_t : t -> Sexp.t
  end
```

Now we can write the functor itself. We have been careful to override the sexp converter here to ensure that the data structure's invariants are still maintained when reading in from an s-expression:

OCaml utop (part 28)

```
# module Make_interval(Endpoint : sig
                          type t
                          include Comparable with type t := t
                          include Sexpable   with type t := t
                        end)
    : (Interval_intf_with_sexp with type endpoint := Endpoint.t)
  = struct

    type t = | Interval of Endpoint.t * Endpoint.t
             | Empty
```

A Bigger Example: Computing with Intervals | 187

```
    with sexp

    (** [create low high] creates a new interval from [low] to
        [high].  If [low > high], then the interval is empty *)
    let create low high =
      if Endpoint.compare low high > 0 then Empty
      else Interval (low,high)

    (* put a wrapper around the autogenerated [t_of_sexp] to enforce
       the invariants of the data structure *)
    let t_of_sexp sexp =
      match t_of_sexp sexp with
      | Empty -> Empty
      | Interval (x,y) -> create x y

    (** Returns true iff the interval is empty *)
    let is_empty = function
      | Empty -> true
      | Interval _ -> false

    (** [contains t x] returns true iff [x] is contained in the
        interval [t] *)
    let contains t x =
      match t with
      | Empty -> false
      | Interval (l,h) ->
        Endpoint.compare x l >= 0 && Endpoint.compare x h <= 0

    (** [intersect t1 t2] returns the intersection of the two input
        intervals *)
    let intersect t1 t2 =
      let min x y = if Endpoint.compare x y <= 0 then x else y in
      let max x y = if Endpoint.compare x y >= 0 then x else y in
      match t1,t2 with
      | Empty, _ | _, Empty -> Empty
      | Interval (l1,h1), Interval (l2,h2) ->
        create (max l1 l2) (min h1 h2)
  end;;
module Make_interval :
  functor
    (Endpoint : sig
                  type t
                  val compare : t -> t -> int
                  val t_of_sexp : Sexp.t -> t
                  val sexp_of_t : t -> Sexp.t
                end) ->
    sig
      type t
      val create : Endpoint.t -> Endpoint.t -> t
      val is_empty : t -> bool
      val contains : t -> Endpoint.t -> bool
      val intersect : t -> t -> t
```

```
      val t_of_sexp : Sexp.t -> t
      val sexp_of_t : t -> Sexp.t
    end
```

And now, we can use that sexp converter in the ordinary way:

OCaml utop (part 29)

```
# module Int_interval = Make_interval(Int) ;;
module Int_interval :
  sig
    type t = Make_interval(Core.Std.Int).t
    val create : int -> int -> t
    val is_empty : t -> bool
    val contains : t -> int -> bool
    val intersect : t -> t -> t
    val t_of_sexp : Sexp.t -> t
    val sexp_of_t : t -> Sexp.t
  end
# Int_interval.sexp_of_t (Int_interval.create 3 4);;
- : Sexp.t = (Interval 3 4)
# Int_interval.sexp_of_t (Int_interval.create 4 3);;
- : Sexp.t = Empty
```

Extending Modules

Another common use of functors is to generate type-specific functionality for a given module in a standardized way. Let's see how this works in the context of a functional queue, which is just a functional version of a FIFO (first-in, first-out) queue. Being functional, operations on the queue return new queues, rather than modifying the queues that were passed in.

Here's a reasonable mli for such a module:

OCaml

```
type 'a t

val empty : 'a t

(** [enqueue q el] adds [el] to the back of [q] *)
val enqueue : 'a t -> 'a -> 'a t

(** [dequeue q] returns None if the [q] is empty, otherwise returns
    the first element of the queue and the remainder of the queue *)
val dequeue : 'a t -> ('a * 'a t) option

(** Folds over the queue, from front to back *)
val fold : 'a t -> init:'acc -> f:('acc -> 'a -> 'acc) -> 'acc
```

The preceding Fqueue.fold function requires some explanation. It follows the same pattern as the List.fold function we described in "Using the List Module Effectively" on page 55. Essentially, Fqueue.fold q ~init ~f walks over the elements of q from front to back, starting with an accumulator of `init` and using `f` to update the accumulator value as it walks over the queue, returning the final value of the accumulator at the end of the computation. `fold` is a quite powerful operation, as we'll see.

We'll implement `Fqueue` the well known trick of maintaining an input and an output list so that one can efficiently enqueue on the input list and efficiently dequeue from the output list. If you attempt to dequeue when the output list is empty, the input list is reversed and becomes the new output list. Here's the implementation:

OCaml

```
open Core.Std

type 'a t = 'a list * 'a list

let empty = ([],[])

let enqueue (in_list, out_list) x =
  (x :: in_list,out_list)

let dequeue (in_list, out_list) =
  match out_list with
  | hd :: tl -> Some (hd, (in_list, tl))
  | [] ->
    match List.rev in_list with
    | [] -> None
    | hd :: tl -> Some (hd, ([], tl))

let fold (in_list, out_list) ~init ~f =
  let after_out = List.fold ~init ~f out_list in
  List.fold_right ~init:after_out ~f:(fun x acc -> f acc x) in_list
```

One problem with `Fqueue` is that the interface is quite skeletal. There are lots of useful helper functions that one might want that aren't there. The `List` module, by way of contrast, has functions like `List.iter`, which runs a function on each element; and `List.for_all`, which returns true if and only if the given predicate evaluates to `true` on every element of the list. Such helper functions come up for pretty much every container type, and implementing them over and over is a dull and repetitive affair.

As it happens, many of these helper functions can be derived mechanically from the `fold` function we already implemented. Rather than write all of these helper functions by hand for every new container type, we can instead use a functor to add this functionality to any container that has a `fold` function.

We'll create a new module, `Foldable`, that automates the process of adding helper functions to a `fold`-supporting container. As you can see, `Foldable` contains a module signature `S` which defines the signature that is required to support folding; and a functor `Extend` that allows one to extend any module that matches `Foldable.S`:

```ocaml
open Core.Std

module type S = sig
  type 'a t
  val fold : 'a t -> init:'acc -> f:('acc -> 'a -> 'acc) -> 'acc
end

module type Extension = sig
  type 'a t
  val iter    : 'a t -> f:('a -> unit) -> unit
  val length  : 'a t -> int
  val count   : 'a t -> f:('a -> bool) -> int
  val for_all : 'a t -> f:('a -> bool) -> bool
  val exists  : 'a t -> f:('a -> bool) -> bool
end

(* For extending a Foldable module *)
module Extend(Arg : S)
  : (Extension with type 'a t := 'a Arg.t) =
struct
  open Arg

  let iter t ~f =
    fold t ~init:() ~f:(fun () a -> f a)

  let length t =
    fold t ~init:0  ~f:(fun acc _ -> acc + 1)

  let count t ~f =
    fold t ~init:0  ~f:(fun count x -> count + if f x then 1 else 0)

  exception Short_circuit

  let for_all c ~f =
    try iter c ~f:(fun x -> if not (f x) then raise Short_circuit); true
    with Short_circuit -> false

  let exists c ~f =
    try iter c ~f:(fun x -> if f x then raise Short_circuit); false
    with Short_circuit -> true
end
```

Now we can apply this to Fqueue. We can create an interface for an extended version of Fqueue as follows:

```ocaml
type 'a t
include (module type of Fqueue) with type 'a t := 'a t
include Foldable.Extension with type 'a t := 'a t
```

In order to apply the functor, we'll put the definition of Fqueue in a submodule called T, and then call Foldable.Extend on T:

```
include Fqueue
include Foldable.Extend(Fqueue)
```

Core comes with a number of functors for extending modules that follow this same basic pattern, including:

Container.Make

> Very similar to Foldable.Extend.

Comparable.Make

> Adds support for functionality that depends on the presence of a comparison function, including support for containers like maps and sets.

Hashable.Make

> Adds support for hashing-based data structures including hash tables, hash sets, and hash heaps.

Monad.Make

> For so-called monadic libraries, like those discussed in Chapters 7 and 18. Here, the functor is used to provide a collection of standard helper functions based on the bind and return operators.

These functors come in handy when you want to add the same kind of functionality that is commonly available in Core to your own types.

We've really only covered some of the possible uses of functors. Functors are really a quite powerful tool for modularizing your code. The cost is that functors are syntactically heavyweight compared to the rest of the language, and that there are some tricky issues you need to understand to use them effectively, with sharing constraints and destructive substitution being high on that list.

All of this means that for small and simple programs, heavy use of functors is probably a mistake. But as your programs get more complicated and you need more effective modular architectures, functors become a highly valuable tool.

## CHAPTER 10

First-Class Modules

You can think of OCaml as being broken up into two parts: a core language that is concerned with values and types, and a module language that is concerned with modules and module signatures. These sublanguages are stratified, in that modules can contain types and values, but ordinary values can't contain modules or module types. That means you can't do things like define a variable whose value is a module, or a function that takes a module as an argument.

OCaml provides a way around this stratification in the form of *first-class modules*. First-class modules are ordinary values that can be created from and converted back to regular modules.

First-class modules are a sophisticated technique, and you'll need to get comfortable with some advanced aspects of the language to use them effectively. But it's worth learning, because letting modules into the core language is quite powerful, increasing the range of what you can express and making it easier to build flexible and modular systems.

Working with First-Class Modules

We'll start out by covering the basic mechanics of first-class modules by working through some toy examples. We'll get to more realistic examples in the next section.

In that light, consider the following signature of a module with a single integer variable:

OCaml utop

```
# module type X_int = sig val x : int end;;
module type X_int = sig val x : int end
```

We can also create a module that matches this signature:

```
# module Three : X_int = struct let x = 3 end;;
module Three : X_int
# Three.x;;
- : int = 3
```

A first-class module is created by packaging up a module with a signature that it satisfies. This is done using the module keyword, using the following syntax:

```
(module <Module> : <Module_type>)
```

So, we can convert Three into a first-class module as follows:

```
# let three = (module Three : X_int);;
val three : (module X_int) = <module>
```

The module type doesn't need to be part of the construction of a first-class module if it can be inferred. Thus, we can write:

```
# module Four = struct let x = 4 end;;
module Four : sig val x : int end
# let numbers = [ three; (module Four) ];;
val numbers : (module X_int) list = [<module>; <module>]
```

We can also create a first-class module from an anonymous module:

```
# let numbers = [three; (module struct let x = 4 end)];;
val numbers : (module X_int) list = [<module>; <module>]
```

In order to access the contents of a first-class module, you need to unpack it into an ordinary module. This can be done using the val keyword, using this syntax:

```
(val <first_class_module> : <Module_type>)
```

And here's an example:

```
# module New_three = (val three : X_int) ;;
module New_three : X_int
# New_three.x;;
- : int = 3
```

Equality of First-Class Module Types

The type of the first-class module, e.g., (module X_int), is based on the fully qualified name of the signature that was used to construct it. A first-class module based on a signature with a different name, even if it is substantively the same signature, will result in a distinct type:

OCaml utop (part 6)

```
# module type Y_int = X_int;;
module type Y_int = X_int
# let five = (module struct let x = 5 end : Y_int);;
val five : (module Y_int) = <module>
# [three; five];;
Characters 8-12:
Error: This expression has type (module Y_int)
       but an expression was expected of type (module X_int)
```

Even though their types as first-class modules are distinct, the underlying module types are compatible (indeed, identical), so we can unify the types by unpacking and repacking the module:

OCaml utop (part 7)

```
# [three; (module (val five))];;
- : (module X_int) list = [<module>; <module>]
```

The way in which type equality for first-class modules is determined can be confusing. One common and problematic case is that of creating an alias of a module type defined elsewhere. This is often done to improve readability and can happen both through an explicit declaration of a module type or implicitly through an include declaration. In both cases, this has the unintended side effect of making first-class modules built off the alias incompatible with those built off the original module type. To deal with this, we should be disciplined in how we refer to signatures when constructing first-class modules.

We can also write ordinary functions which consume and create first-class modules. The following shows the definition of two functions: to_int, which converts a (module X_int) into an int; and plus, which returns the sum of two (module X_int):

OCaml utop (part 8)

```
# let to_int m =
    let module M = (val m : X_int) in
    M.x
  ;;
val to_int : (module X_int) -> int = <fun>
# let plus m1 m2 =
    (module struct
       let x = to_int m1 + to_int m2
     end : X_int)
```

```
  ;;
val plus : (module X_int) -> (module X_int) -> (module X_int) = <fun>
```

With these functions in hand, we can now work with values of type (module X_int) in a more natural style, taking advantage of the concision and simplicity of the core language:

OCaml utop (part 9)

```
# let six = plus three three;;
val six : (module X_int) = <module>
# to_int (List.fold ~init:six ~f:plus [three;three]);;
- : int = 12
```

There are some useful syntactic shortcuts when dealing with first-class modules. One notable one is that you can do the conversion to an ordinary module within a pattern match. Thus, we can rewrite the to_int function as follows:

OCaml utop (part 10)

```
# let to_int (module M : X_int) = M.x ;;
val to_int : (module X_int) -> int = <fun>
```

First-class modules can contain types and functions in addition to simple values like int. Here's an interface that contains a type and a corresponding bump operation that takes a value of the type and produces a new one:

OCaml utop (part 11)

```
# module type Bumpable = sig
    type t
    val bump : t -> t
  end;;
module type Bumpable = sig type t val bump : t -> t end
```

We can create multiple instances of this module with different underlying types:

OCaml utop (part 12)

```
# module Int_bumper = struct
    type t = int
    let bump n = n + 1
  end;;
module Int_bumper : sig type t = int val bump : t -> t end
# module Float_bumper = struct
    type t = float
    let bump n = n +. 1.
  end;;
module Float_bumper : sig type t = float val bump : t -> t end
```

And we can convert these to first-class modules:

OCaml utop (part 13)

```
# let int_bumper = (module Int_bumper : Bumpable);;
val int_bumper : (module Bumpable) = <module>
```

But you can't do much with int_bumper, since int_bumper is fully abstract, so that we can no longer recover the fact that the type in question is int.

```
# let (module Bumpable) = int_bumper in Bumpable.bump 3;;
Characters 52-53:
Error: This expression has type int but an expression was expected of type
       Bumpable.t
```

To make `int_bumper` usable, we need to expose the type, which we can do as follows:

```
# let int_bumper = (module Int_bumper : Bumpable with type t = int);;
val int_bumper : (module Bumpable with type t = int) = <module>
# let float_bumper = (module Float_bumper : Bumpable with type t = float);;
val float_bumper : (module Bumpable with type t = float) = <module>
```

The sharing constraints we've added above make the resulting first-class modules polymorphic in the type t. As a result, we can now use these values on values of the matching type:

```
# let (module Bumpable) = int_bumper in Bumpable.bump 3;;
- : int = 4
# let (module Bumpable) = float_bumper in Bumpable.bump 3.5;;
- : float = 4.5
```

We can also write functions that use such first-class modules polymorphically. The following function takes two arguments: a `Bumpable` module and a list of elements of the same type as the type t of the module:

```
# let bump_list
      (type a)
      (module B : Bumpable with type t = a)
      (l: a list)
    =
    List.map ~f:B.bump l
  ;;
val bump_list : (module Bumpable with type t = 'a) -> 'a list -> 'a list =
  <fun>
```

Here, we used a feature of OCaml that hasn't come up before: a *locally abstract type*. For any function, you can declare a pseudoparameter of the form (type a) for any type name a which introduces a fresh type. This type acts like an abstract type within the context of the function. In the example above, the locally abstract type was used as part of a sharing constraint that ties the type B.t with the type of the elements of the list passed in.

The resulting function is polymorphic in both the type of the list element and the type `Bumpable.t`. We can see this function in action:

```
# bump_list int_bumper [1;2;3];;
- : int list = [2; 3; 4]
```

```
# bump_list float_bumper [1.5;2.5;3.5];;
- : float list = [2.5; 3.5; 4.5]
```

Polymorphic first-class modules are important because they allow you to connect the types associated with a first-class module to the types of other values you're working with.

More on Locally Abstract Types

One of the key properties of locally abstract types is that they're dealt with as abstract types in the function they're defined within, but are polymorphic from the outside. Consider the following example:

OCaml utop (part 19)

```
# let wrap_in_list (type a) (x:a) = [x];;
val wrap_in_list : 'a -> 'a list = <fun>
```

This compiles successfully because the type a is used in a way that is compatible with it being abstract, but the type of the function that is inferred is polymorphic.

If, on the other hand, we try to use the type a as equivalent to some concrete type, say, int, then the compiler will complain:

OCaml utop (part 20)

```
# let double_int (type a) (x:a) = x + x;;
Characters 38-39:
Error: This expression has type a but an expression was expected of type int
```

One common use of locally abstract types is to create a new type that can be used in constructing a module. Here's an example of doing this to create a new first-class module:

OCaml utop (part 21)

```
# module type Comparable = sig
    type t
    val compare : t -> t -> int
  end ;;
module type Comparable = sig type t val compare : t -> t -> int end
# let create_comparable (type a) compare =
    (module struct
      type t = a
      let compare = compare
    end : Comparable with type t = a)
  ;;
val create_comparable :
  ('a -> 'a -> int) -> (module Comparable with type t = 'a) = <fun>
# create_comparable Int.compare;;
- : (module Comparable with type t = int) = <module>
# create_comparable Float.compare;;
- : (module Comparable with type t = float) = <module>
```

Here, what we effectively do is capture a polymorphic type and export it as a concrete type within a module.

This technique is useful beyond first-class modules. For example, we can use the same approach to construct a local module to be fed to a functor.

Example: A Query-Handling Framework

Now let's look at first-class modules in the context of a more complete and realistic example. In particular, consider the following signature for a module that implements a system for responding to user-generated queries.

OCaml utop

```
# module type Query_handler = sig

    (** Configuration for a query handler.  Note that this can be
        converted to and from an s-expression *)
    type config with sexp

    (** The name of the query-handling service *)
    val name : string

    (** The state of the query handler *)
    type t

    (** Creates a new query handler from a config *)
    val create : config -> t

    (** Evaluate a given query, where both input and output are
        s-expressions *)
    val eval : t -> Sexp.t -> Sexp.t Or_error.t
  end;;
module type Query_handler =
  sig
    type config
    val name : string
    type t
    val create : config -> t
    val eval : t -> Sexp.t -> Sexp.t Or_error.t
    val config_of_sexp : Sexp.t -> config
    val sexp_of_config : config -> Sexp.t
  end
```

Here, we used s-expressions as the format for queries and responses, as well as the configuration for the query handler. S-expressions are a simple, flexible, and human-readable serialization format commonly used in Core. For now, it's enough to think of them as balanced parenthetical expressions whose atomic values are strings, e.g., (this (is an) (s expression)).

In addition, we use the Sexplib syntax extension which extends OCaml by adding the with sexp declaration. When attached to a type in a signature, with sexp adds declarations of s-expression converters, for example:

OCaml utop (part 1)

```
# module type M = sig type t with sexp end;;
module type M =
  sig type t val t_of_sexp : Sexp.t -> t val sexp_of_t : t -> Sexp.t end
```

In a module, with sexp adds the implementation of those functions. Thus, we can write:

OCaml utop (part 2)

```
# type u = { a: int; b: float } with sexp;;
type u = { a : int; b : float; }
val u_of_sexp : Sexp.t -> u = <fun>
val sexp_of_u : u -> Sexp.t = <fun>
# sexp_of_u {a=3;b=7.};;
- : Sexp.t = ((a 3) (b 7))
# u_of_sexp (Sexp.of_string "((a 43) (b 3.4))");;
- : u = {a = 43; b = 3.4}
```

This is all described in more detail in Chapter 17.

Implementing a Query Handler

Let's look at some examples of query handlers that satisfy the Query_handler interface. The first example is a handler that produces unique integer IDs. It works by keeping an internal counter which it bumps every time it produces a new value. The input to the query in this case is just the trivial s-expression (), otherwise known as Sexp.unit:

OCaml utop (part 3)

```
# module Unique = struct
    type config = int with sexp
    type t = { mutable next_id: int }

    let name = "unique"
    let create start_at = { next_id = start_at }

    let eval t sexp =
      match Or_error.try_with (fun () -> unit_of_sexp sexp) with
      | Error _ as err -> err
      | Ok () ->
        let response = Ok (Int.sexp_of_t t.next_id) in
        t.next_id <- t.next_id + 1;
        response
  end;;
module Unique :
  sig
    type config = int
    val config_of_sexp : Sexp.t -> config
    val sexp_of_config : config -> Sexp.t
    type t = { mutable next_id : config; }
    val name : string
    val create : config -> t
    val eval : t -> Sexp.t -> (Sexp.t, Error.t) Result.t
  end
```

We can use this module to create an instance of the Unique query handler and interact with it directly:

```
# let unique = Unique.create 0;;
val unique : Unique.t = {Unique.next_id = 0}
# Unique.eval unique Sexp.unit;;
- : (Sexp.t, Error.t) Result.t = Ok 0
# Unique.eval unique Sexp.unit;;
- : (Sexp.t, Error.t) Result.t = Ok 1
```

Here's another example: a query handler that does directory listings. Here, the config is the default directory that relative paths are interpreted within:

```
# module List_dir = struct
    type config = string with sexp
    type t = { cwd: string }

    (** [is_abs p] Returns true if [p] is an absolute path  *)
    let is_abs p =
      String.length p > 0 && p.[0] = '/'

    let name = "ls"
    let create cwd = { cwd }

    let eval t sexp =
      match Or_error.try_with (fun () -> string_of_sexp sexp) with
      | Error _ as err -> err
      | Ok dir ->
        let dir =
          if is_abs dir then dir
          else Filename.concat t.cwd dir
        in
        Ok (Array.sexp_of_t String.sexp_of_t (Sys.readdir dir))
  end;;
module List_dir :
  sig
    type config = string
    val config_of_sexp : Sexp.t -> config
    val sexp_of_config : config -> Sexp.t
    type t = { cwd : config; }
    val is_abs : config -> bool
    val name : config
    val create : config -> t
    val eval : t -> Sexp.t -> (Sexp.t, Error.t) Result.t
  end
```

Again, we can create an instance of this query handler and interact with it directly:

```
# let list_dir = List_dir.create "/var";;
val list_dir : List_dir.t = {List_dir.cwd = "/var"}
# List_dir.eval list_dir (sexp_of_string ".");;
- : (Sexp.t, Error.t) Result.t =
Ok (lib mail cache www spool run log lock opt local backups tmp)
```

```
# List_dir.eval list_dir (sexp_of_string "yp");;
Exception: (Sys_error "/var/yp: No such file or directory").
```

Dispatching to Multiple Query Handlers

Now, what if we want to dispatch queries to any of an arbitrary collection of handlers?
Ideally, we'd just like to pass in the handlers as a simple data structure like a list. This is
awkward to do with modules and functors alone, but it's quite natural with first-class
modules. The first thing we'll need to do is create a signature that combines a Query_han
dler module with an instantiated query handler:

OCaml utop (part 7)

```
# module type Query_handler_instance = sig
    module Query_handler : Query_handler
    val this : Query_handler.t
  end;;
module type Query_handler_instance =
  sig module Query_handler : Query_handler val this : Query_handler.t end
```

With this signature, we can create a first-class module that encompasses both an instance
of the query and the matching operations for working with that query.

We can create an instance as follows:

OCaml utop (part 8)

```
# let unique_instance =
    (module struct
       module Query_handler = Unique
       let this = Unique.create 0
     end : Query_handler_instance);;
val unique_instance : (module Query_handler_instance) = <module>
```

Constructing instances in this way is a little verbose, but we can write a function that
eliminates most of this boilerplate. Note that we are again making use of a locally abstract
type:

OCaml utop (part 9)

```
# let build_instance
      (type a)
      (module Q : Query_handler with type config = a)
      config
  =
  (module struct
     module Query_handler = Q
     let this = Q.create config
   end : Query_handler_instance)
  ;;
val build_instance :
  (module Query_handler with type config = 'a) ->
  'a -> (module Query_handler_instance) = <fun>
```

Using build_instance, constructing a new instance becomes a one-liner:

```
# let unique_instance = build_instance (module Unique) 0;;
val unique_instance : (module Query_handler_instance) = <module>
# let list_dir_instance = build_instance (module List_dir)  "/var";;
val list_dir_instance : (module Query_handler_instance) = <module>
```

We can now write code that lets you dispatch queries to one of a list of query handler instances. We assume that the shape of the query is as follows:

```
(query-name query)
```

where *query-name* is the name used to determine which query handler to dispatch the query to, and *query* is the body of the query.

The first thing we'll need is a function that takes a list of query handler instances and constructs a dispatch table from it:

```
# let build_dispatch_table handlers =
    let table = String.Table.create () in
    List.iter handlers
      ~f:(fun ((module I : Query_handler_instance) as instance) ->
        Hashtbl.replace table ~key:I.Query_handler.name ~data:instance);
    table
  ;;
val build_dispatch_table :
  (module Query_handler_instance) list ->
  (module Query_handler_instance) String.Table.t = <fun>
```

Now, we need a function that dispatches to a handler using a dispatch table:

```
# let dispatch dispatch_table name_and_query =
    match name_and_query with
    | Sexp.List [Sexp.Atom name; query] ->
      begin match Hashtbl.find dispatch_table name with
      | None ->
        Or_error.error "Could not find matching handler"
          name String.sexp_of_t
      | Some (module I : Query_handler_instance) ->
        I.Query_handler.eval I.this query
      end
    | _ ->
      Or_error.error_string "malformed query"
  ;;
val dispatch :
  (string, (module Query_handler_instance)) Hashtbl.t ->
  Sexp.t -> Sexp.t Or_error.t = <fun>
```

This function interacts with an instance by unpacking it into a module I and then using the query handler instance (I.this) in concert with the associated module (I.Query_handler).

The bundling together of the module and the value is in many ways reminiscent of object-oriented languages. One key difference, is that first-class modules allow you to package up more than just functions or methods. As we've seen, you can also include types and even modules. We've only used it in a small way here, but this extra power allows you to build more sophisticated components that involve multiple interdependent types and values.

Now let's turn this into a complete, running example by adding a command-line interface:

OCaml utop (part 13)

```
# let rec cli dispatch_table =
    printf ">>> %!";
    let result =
      match In_channel.input_line stdin with
      | None -> `Stop
      | Some line ->
        match Or_error.try_with (fun () -> Sexp.of_string line) with
        | Error e -> `Continue (Error.to_string_hum e)
        | Ok (Sexp.Atom "quit") -> `Stop
        | Ok query ->
          begin match dispatch dispatch_table query with
          | Error e -> `Continue (Error.to_string_hum e)
          | Ok s    -> `Continue (Sexp.to_string_hum s)
          end;
    in
    match result with
    | `Stop -> ()
    | `Continue msg ->
      printf "%s\n%!" msg;
      cli dispatch_table
  ;;
val cli : (string, (module Query_handler_instance)) Hashtbl.t -> unit = <fun>
```

We can most effectively run this command-line interface from a standalone program, which we can do by putting the above code in a file along with following command to launch the interface:

OCaml (part 1)

```
let () =
  cli (build_dispatch_table [unique_instance; list_dir_instance])
```

Here's an example of a session with this program:

OCaml utop

```
$ ./query_handler.byte
>>> (unique ())
0
>>> (unique ())
1
>>> (ls .)
(agentx at audit backups db empty folders jabberd lib log mail msgs named
```

```
    netboot pgsql_socket_alt root rpc run rwho spool tmp vm yp)
>>> (ls vm)
(sleepimage swapfile0 swapfile1 swapfile2 swapfile3 swapfile4 swapfile5
  swapfile6)
```

Loading and Unloading Query Handlers

One of the advantages of first-class modules is that they afford a great deal of dynamism
and flexibility. For example, it's a fairly simple matter to change our design to allow
query handlers to be loaded and unloaded at runtime.

We'll do this by creating a query handler whose job is to control the set of active query
handlers. The module in question will be called Loader, and its configuration is a list
of known Query_handler modules. Here are the basic types:

OCaml (part 1)

```
module Loader = struct
  type config = (module Query_handler) list sexp_opaque
  with sexp

  type t = { known  : (module Query_handler)          String.Table.t
           ; active : (module Query_handler_instance) String.Table.t
           }

  let name = "loader"
```

Note that a Loader.t has two tables: one containing the known query handler modules,
and one containing the active query handler instances. The Loader.t will be responsible
for creating new instances and adding them to the table, as well as for removing instances, all in response to user queries.

Next, we'll need a function for creating a Loader.t. This function requires the list of
known query handler modules. Note that the table of active modules starts out as empty:

OCaml (part 2)

```
  let create known_list =
    let active = String.Table.create () in
    let known  = String.Table.create () in
    List.iter known_list
      ~f:(fun ((module Q : Query_handler) as q) ->
        Hashtbl.replace known ~key:Q.name ~data:q);
    { known; active }
```

Now we'll start writing out the functions for manipulating the table of active query
handlers. We'll start with the function for loading an instance. Note that it takes as an
argument both the name of the query handler and the configuration for instantiating
that handler in the form of an s-expression. These are used for creating a first-class
module of type (module Query_handler_instance), which is then added to the active
table:

```
let load t handler_name config =
    if Hashtbl.mem t.active handler_name then
      Or_error.error "Can't re-register an active handler"
        handler_name String.sexp_of_t
    else
      match Hashtbl.find t.known handler_name with
      | None ->
        Or_error.error "Unknown handler" handler_name String.sexp_of_t
      | Some (module Q : Query_handler) ->
        let instance =
          (module struct
             module Query_handler = Q
             let this = Q.create (Q.config_of_sexp config)
           end : Query_handler_instance)
        in
        Hashtbl.replace t.active ~key:handler_name ~data:instance;
        Ok Sexp.unit
```

Since the load function will refuse to load an already active handler, we also need the ability to unload a handler. Note that the handler explicitly refuses to unload itself:

```
let unload t handler_name =
    if not (Hashtbl.mem t.active handler_name) then
      Or_error.error "Handler not active" handler_name String.sexp_of_t
    else if handler_name = name then
      Or_error.error_string "It's unwise to unload yourself"
    else (
      Hashtbl.remove t.active handler_name;
      Ok Sexp.unit
    )
```

Finally, we need to implement the eval function, which will determine the query interface presented to the user. We'll do this by creating a variant type, and using the s-expression converter generated for that type to parse the query from the user:

```
type request =
    | Load of string * Sexp.t
    | Unload of string
    | Known_services
    | Active_services
  with sexp
```

The eval function itself is fairly straightforward, dispatching to the appropriate functions to respond to each type of query. Note that we write <:sexp_of<string list>> to autogenerate a function for converting a list of strings to an s-expression, as described in Chapter 17.

This function ends the definition of the Loader module:

```
let eval t sexp =
    match Or_error.try_with (fun () -> request_of_sexp sexp) with
    | Error _ as err -> err
    | Ok resp ->
      match resp with
      | Load (name,config) -> load    t name config
      | Unload name         -> unload t name
      | Known_services ->
        Ok (<:sexp_of<string list>> (Hashtbl.keys t.known))
      | Active_services ->
        Ok (<:sexp_of<string list>> (Hashtbl.keys t.active))
end
```

Finally, we can put this all together with the command-line interface. We first create an instance of the loader query handler and then add that instance to the loader's active table. We can then just launch the command-line interface, passing it the active table:

```
let () =
  let loader = Loader.create [(module Unique); (module List_dir)] in
  let loader_instance =
    (module struct
       module Query_handler = Loader
       let this = loader
     end : Query_handler_instance)
  in
  Hashtbl.replace loader.Loader.active
    ~key:Loader.name ~data:loader_instance;
  cli loader.Loader.active
```

Now build this into a command-line interface to experiment with it:

```
$ corebuild query_handler_loader.byte
```

The resulting command-line interface behaves much as you'd expect, starting out with no query handlers available but giving you the ability to load and unload them. Here's an example of it in action. As you can see, we start out with loader itself as the only active handler:

```
$ ./query_handler_loader.byte
>>> (loader known_services)
(ls unique)
>>> (loader active_services)
(loader)
```

Any attempt to use an inactive query handler will fail:

```
>>> (ls .)
Could not find matching handler: ls
```

But, we can load the `ls` handler with a config of our choice, at which point it will be available for use. And once we unload it, it will be unavailable yet again and could be reloaded with a different config:

Terminal

```
>>> (loader (load ls /var))
()
>>> (ls /var)
(agentx at audit backups db empty folders jabberd lib log mail msgs named
 netboot pgsql_socket_alt root rpc run rwho spool tmp vm yp)
>>> (loader (unload ls))
()
>>> (ls /var)
Could not find matching handler: ls
```

Notably, the loader can't be loaded (since it's not on the list of known handlers) and can't be unloaded either:

Terminal

```
>>> (loader (unload loader))
It's unwise to unload yourself
```

Although we won't describe the details here, we can push this dynamism yet further using OCaml's dynamic linking facilities, which allow you to compile and link in new code to a running program. This can be automated using libraries like `ocaml_plugin`, which can be installed via OPAM, and which automates much of the workflow around setting up dynamic linking.

Living Without First-Class Modules

It's worth noting that most designs that can be done with first-class modules can be simulated without them, with some level of awkwardness. For example, we could rewrite our query handler example without first-class modules using the following types:

OCaml utop (part 14)

```
# type query_handler_instance = { name : string
                                ; eval : Sexp.t -> Sexp.t Or_error.t
                                }
  type query_handler = Sexp.t -> query_handler_instance
  ;;
type query_handler_instance = {
  name : string;
  eval : Sexp.t -> Sexp.t Or_error.t;
}
type query_handler = Sexp.t -> query_handler_instance
```

The idea here is that we hide the true types of the objects in question behind the functions stored in the closure. Thus, we could put the `Unique` query handler into this framework as follows:

```
# let unique_handler config_sexp =
    let config = Unique.config_of_sexp config_sexp in
    let unique = Unique.create config in
    { name = Unique.name
    ; eval = (fun config -> Unique.eval unique config)
    }
  ;;
val unique_handler : Sexp.t -> query_handler_instance = <fun>
```

For an example on this scale, the preceding approach is completely reasonable, and first-class modules are not really necessary. But the more functionality you need to hide away behind a set of closures, and the more complicated the relationships between the different types in question, the more awkward this approach becomes, and the better it is to use first-class modules.

CHAPTER 11

Objects

We've already seen several tools that OCaml provides for organizing programs, particularly modules. In addition, OCaml also supports object-oriented programming. There are objects, classes, and their associated types. In this chapter, we'll introduce you to OCaml objects and subtyping. In the next chapter, Chapter 12, we'll introduce you to classes and inheritance.

What Is Object-Oriented Programming?

Object-oriented programming (often shorted to OOP) is a programming style that encapsulates computation and data within logical *objects*. Each object contains some data stored in *fields* and has *method* functions that can be invoked against the data within the object (also called "sending a message" to the object). The code definition behind an object is called a *class*, and objects are constructed from a class definition by calling a constructor with the data that the object will use to build itself.

There are five fundamental properties that differentiate OOP from other styles:

Abstraction
> The details of the implementation are hidden in the object, and the external interface is just the set of publicly accessible methods.

Dynamic lookup
> When a message is sent to an object, the method to be executed is determined by the implementation of the object, not by some static property of the program. In other words, different objects may react to the same message in different ways.

Subtyping
> If an object a has all the functionality of an object b, then we may use a in any context where b is expected.

Inheritance

> The definition of one kind of object can be reused to produce a new kind of object. This new definition can override some behavior, but also share code with its parent.

Open recursion

> An object's methods can invoke another method in the same object using a special variable (often called self or this). When objects are created from classes, these calls use dynamic lookup, allowing a method defined in one class to invoke methods defined in another class that inherits from the first.

Almost every notable modern programming language has been influenced by OOP, and you'll have run across these terms if you've ever used C++, Java, C#, Ruby, Python, or JavaScript.

OCaml Objects

If you already know about object-oriented programming in a language like Java or C++, the OCaml object system may come as a surprise. Foremost is the complete separation of objects and their types from the class system. In a language like Java, a class name is also used as the type of objects created by instantiating it, and the relationships between these object types correspond to inheritance. For example, if we implement a class Deque in Java by inheriting from a class Stack, we would be allowed to pass a deque anywhere a stack is expected.

OCaml is entirely different. Classes are used to construct objects and support inheritance, but classes are not types. Instead, objects have *object types*, and if you want to use objects, you aren't required to use classes at all. Here's an example of a simple object:

OCaml utop (part 1)

```
# let s = object
    val mutable v = [0; 2]

    method pop =
      match v with
      | hd :: tl ->
        v <- tl;
        Some hd
      | [] -> None

    method push hd =
      v <- hd :: v
  end ;;
val s : < pop : int option; push : int -> unit > = <obj>
```

The object has an integer list value v, a method pop that returns the head of v, and a method push that adds an integer to the head of v.

The object type is enclosed in angle brackets < ... >, containing just the types of the methods. Fields, like v, are not part of the public interface of an object. All interaction with an object is through its methods. The syntax for a method invocation uses the # character:

OCaml utop (part 2)

```
# s#pop ;;
- : int option = Some 0
# s#push 4 ;;
- : unit = ()
# s#pop ;;
- : int option = Some 4
```

Note that unlike functions, methods can have zero parameters, since the method call is routed to a concrete object instance. That's why the pop method doesn't have a unit argument, as the equivalent functional version would.

Objects can also be constructed by functions. If we want to specify the initial value of the object, we can define a function that takes the value and returns an object:

OCaml utop (part 3)

```
# let stack init = object
    val mutable v = init

    method pop =
      match v with
      | hd :: tl ->
        v <- tl;
        Some hd
      | [] -> None

    method push hd =
      v <- hd :: v
  end ;;
val stack : 'a list -> < pop : 'a option; push : 'a -> unit > = <fun>
# let s = stack [3; 2; 1] ;;
val s : < pop : int option; push : int -> unit > = <obj>
# s#pop ;;
- : int option = Some 3
```

Note that the types of the function stack and the returned object now use the polymorphic type 'a. When stack is invoked on a concrete value [3; 2; 1], we get the same object type as before, with type int for the values on the stack.

Object Polymorphism

Like polymorphic variants, methods can be used without an explicit type declaration:

OCaml utop (part 1)

```
# let area sq = sq#width * sq#width ;;
val area : < width : int; .. > -> int = <fun>
```

```
# let minimize sq : unit = sq#resize 1 ;;
val minimize : < resize : int -> unit; .. > -> unit = <fun>
# let limit sq =
    if (area sq) > 100 then minimize sq ;;
val limit : < resize : int -> unit; width : int; .. > -> unit = <fun>
```

As you can see, object types are inferred automatically from the methods that are invoked on them.

The type system will complain if it sees incompatible uses of the same method:

OCaml utop (part 2)

```
# let toggle sq b : unit =
    if b then sq#resize `Fullscreen
    else minimize sq ;;
Characters 80-82:
Error: This expression has type < resize : [> `Fullscreen ] -> unit; .. >
       but an expression was expected of type < resize : int -> unit; .. >
       Types for method resize are incompatible
```

The .. in the inferred object types are ellipses, standing for other unspecified methods that the object may have. The type < width : float; .. > specifies an object that must have at least a width method, and possibly some others as well. Such object types are said to be *open*.

We can manually *close* an object type using a type annotation:

OCaml utop (part 3)

```
# let area_closed (sq: < width : int >) = sq#width * sq#width ;;
val area_closed : < width : int > -> int = <fun>
# let sq = object
    method width = 30
    method name = "sq"
  end ;;
val sq : < name : string; width : int > = <obj>
# area_closed sq ;;
Characters 12-14:
Error: This expression has type < name : string; width : int >
       but an expression was expected of type < width : int >
       The second object type has no method name
```

Elisions Are Polymorphic

The .. in an open object type is an elision, standing for "possibly more methods." It may not be apparent from the syntax, but an elided object type is actually polymorphic. For example, if we try to write a type definition, we get an "unbound type variable" error:

OCaml utop (part 4)

```
# type square = < width : int; ..> ;;
Characters 5-32:
Error: A type variable is unbound in this type declaration.
In type < width : int; .. > as 'a the variable 'a is unbound
```

This is because .. is really a special kind of type variable called a *row variable*.

This kind of typing scheme using row variables is called *row polymorphism*. Row polymorphism is also used in polymorphic variant types, and there is a close relationship between objects and polymorphic variants: objects are to records what polymorphic variants are to ordinary variants.

An object of type < pop : int option; .. > can be any object with a method pop : int option; it doesn't matter how it is implemented. When the method #pop is invoked, the actual method that is run is determined by the object:

OCaml utop (part 4)

```
# let print_pop st = Option.iter ~f:(printf "Popped: %d\n") st#pop ;;
val print_pop : < pop : int option; .. > -> unit = <fun>
# print_pop (stack [5;4;3;2;1]) ;;
Popped: 5
- : unit = ()
# let t = object
    method pop = Some (Float.to_int (Time.to_float (Time.now ())))
  end ;;
val t : < pop : int option > = <obj>
# print_pop t ;;
Popped: 1376833904
- : unit = ()
```

Immutable Objects

Many people consider object-oriented programming to be intrinsically imperative, where an object is like a state machine. Sending a message to an object causes it to change state, possibly sending messages to other objects.

Indeed, in many programs this makes sense, but it is by no means required. Let's define a function that creates immutable stack objects:

```
# let imm_stack init = object
  val v = init

  method pop =
    match v with
    | hd :: tl -> Some (hd, {< v = tl >})
    | [] -> None

  method push hd =
    {< v = hd :: v >}
  end ;;
val imm_stack :
  'a list -> (< pop : ('a * 'b) option; push : 'a -> 'b > as 'b) = <fun>
```

The key parts of this implementation are in the pop and push methods. The expression {< ... >} produces a copy of the current object, with the same type, and the specified fields updated. In other words, the push hd method produces a copy of the object, with v replaced by hd :: v. The original object is not modified:

```
# let s = imm_stack [3; 2; 1] ;;
val s : < pop : (int * 'a) option; push : int -> 'a > as 'a = <obj>
# let t = s#push 4 ;;
val t : < pop : (int * 'a) option; push : int -> 'a > as 'a = <obj>
# s#pop ;;
- : (int * (< pop : 'a; push : int -> 'b > as 'b)) option as 'a =
Some (3, <obj>)
# t#pop ;;
- : (int * (< pop : 'a; push : int -> 'b > as 'b)) option as 'a =
Some (4, <obj>)
```

There are some restrictions on the use of the expression {< ... >}. It can be used only within a method body, and only the values of fields may be updated. Method implementations are fixed at the time the object is created; they cannot be changed dynamically.

When to Use Objects

You might wonder when to use objects in OCaml, which has a multitude of alternative mechanisms to express the similar concepts. First-class modules are more expressive (a module can include types, while classes and objects cannot). Modules, functors, and data types also offer a wide range of ways to express program structure. In fact, many seasoned OCaml programmers rarely use classes and objects, if at all.

Objects have some advantages over records: they don't require type definitions, and their support for row polymorphism makes them more flexible. However, the heavy syntax and additional runtime cost means that objects are rarely used in place of records.

The real benefits of objects come from the class system. Classes support inheritance and open recursion. Open recursion allows interdependent parts of an object to be defined separately. This works because calls between the methods of an object are determined when the object is instantiated, a form of *late* binding. This makes it possible (and necessary) for one method to refer to other methods in the object without knowing statically how they will be implemented.

In contrast, modules use early binding. If you want to parameterize your module code so that some part of it can be implemented later, you would write a function or functor. This is more explicit, but often more verbose than overriding a method in a class.

In general, a rule of thumb is: use classes and objects in situations where open recursion is a big win. Two good examples are Xavier Leroy's Cryptokit (*http://gallium.inria.fr/~xleroy/software.html#cryptokit*), which provides a variety of cryptographic primitives that can be combined in building-block style; and the Camlimages (*http://cristal.inria.fr/camlimages/*) library, which manipulates various graphical file formats. Camlimages also provides a module-based version of the same library, letting you choose between functional and object-oriented styles depending on your problem domain.

We'll introduce you to classes, and examples using open recursion, in Chapter 12.

Subtyping

Subtyping is a central concept in object-oriented programming. It governs when an object with one type *A* can be used in an expression that expects an object of another type *B*. When this is true, we say that *A* is a *subtype* of *B*. More concretely, subtyping restricts when the coercion operator e :> t can be applied. This coercion works only if the type of e is a subtype of t.

Width Subtyping

To explore this, let's define some simple object types for geometric shapes. The generic type shape has a method to compute the area, and square and circle are specific kinds of shapes:

OCaml (part 1)

```
type shape = < area : float >

type square = < area : float; width : int >

let square w = object
  method area = Float.of_int (w * w)
  method width = w
end

type circle = < area : float; radius : int >
```

```
let circle r = object
  method area = 3.14 *. (Float.of_int r) ** 2.0
  method radius = r
end
```

A square has a method area just like a shape, and an additional method width. Still, we expect a square to be a shape, and it is. The coercion :> must be explicit:

OCaml utop (part 1)

```
# let shape w : shape = square w ;;
Characters 22-30:
Error: This expression has type < area : float; width : int >
       but an expression was expected of type shape
       The second object type has no method width
# let shape w : shape = (square w :> shape) ;;
val shape : int -> shape = <fun>
```

This form of object subtyping is called *width* subtyping. Width subtyping means that an object type *A* is a subtype of *B*, if *A* has all of the methods of *B*, and possibly more. A square is a subtype of shape because it implements all of the methods of shape (the area method).

Depth Subtyping

We can also use *depth* subtyping with objects. Depth subtyping allows us coerce an object if its individual methods could safely be coerced. So an object type < m: t1 > is a subtype of < m: t2 > if t1 is a subtype of t2.

For example, we can create two objects with a shape method:

OCaml utop (part 2)

```
# let coin = object
    method shape = circle 5
    method color = "silver"
  end ;;
val coin : < color : string; shape : < area : float; radius : int > > = <obj>
# let map = object
    method shape = square 10
  end ;;
val map : < shape : < area : float; width : int > > = <obj>
```

Both these objects have a shape method whose type is a subtype of the shape type, so they can both be coerced into the object type < shape : shape >:

OCaml utop (part 3)

```
# type item = < shape : shape > ;;
type item = < shape : shape >
# let items = [ (coin :> item) ; (map :> item) ] ;;
val items : item list = [<obj>; <obj>]
```

Polymorphic Variant Subtyping

Subtyping can also be used to coerce a polymorphic variant into a larger polymorphic variant type. A polymorphic variant type *A* is a subtype of *B*, if the tags of *A* are a subset of the tags of *B*:

OCaml utop (part 4)

```
# type num = [ `Int of int | `Float of float ] ;;
type num = [ `Float of float | `Int of int ]
# type const = [ num | `String of string ] ;;
type const = [ `Float of float | `Int of int | `String of string ]
# let n : num = `Int 3 ;;
val n : num = `Int 3
# let c : const = (n :> const) ;;
val c : const = `Int 3
```

Variance

What about types built from object types? If a square is a shape, we expect a square
list to be a shape list. OCaml does indeed allow such coercions:

OCaml utop (part 5)

```
# let squares: square list = [ square 10; square 20 ] ;;
val squares : square list = [<obj>; <obj>]
# let shapes: shape list = (squares :> shape list) ;;
val shapes : shape list = [<obj>; <obj>]
```

Note that this relies on lists being immutable. It would not be safe to treat a square
array as a shape array because it would allow you to store nonsquare shapes into what
should be an array of squares. OCaml recognizes this and does not allow the coercion:

OCaml utop (part 6)

```
# let square_array: square array = [| square 10; square 20 |] ;;
val square_array : square array = [|<obj>; <obj>|]
# let shape_array: shape array = (square_array :> shape array) ;;
Characters 31-60:
Error: Type square array is not a subtype of shape array
       Type square = < area : float, width : int >
       is not compatible with type shape = < area : float >
       The second object type has no method width
```

We say that 'a list is *covariant* (in 'a), while 'a array is *invariant*.

Subtyping function types requires a third class of variance. A function with type square
-> string cannot be used with type shape -> string because it expects its argument
to be a square and would not know what to do with a circle. However, a function with
type shape -> string *can* safely be used with type square -> string:

OCaml utop (part 7)

```
# let shape_to_string: shape -> string =
    fun s -> sprintf "Shape(%F)" s#area ;;
val shape_to_string : shape -> string = <fun>
# let square_to_string: square -> string =
```

```
    (shape_to_string :> square -> string) ;;
val square_to_string : square -> string = <fun>
```

We say that `'a -> string` is *contravariant* in `'a`. In general, function types are contravariant in their arguments and covariant in their results.

Variance Annotations

OCaml works out the variance of a type using that type's definition:

OCaml utop (part 8)

```
# module Either = struct
    type ('a, 'b) t =
      | Left of 'a
      | Right of 'b
    let left x = Left x
    let right x = Right x
  end ;;
module Either :
  sig
    type ('a, 'b) t = Left of 'a | Right of 'b
    val left : 'a -> ('a, 'b) t
    val right : 'a -> ('b, 'a) t
  end
# (Either.left (square 40) :> (shape, shape) Either.t) ;;
- : (shape, shape) Either.t = Either.Left <obj>
```

However, if the definition is hidden by a signature, then OCaml is forced to assume that the type is invariant:

OCaml utop (part 9)

```
# module AbstractEither : sig
    type ('a, 'b) t
    val left: 'a -> ('a, 'b) t
    val right: 'b -> ('a, 'b) t
  end = Either ;;
module AbstractEither :
  sig
    type ('a, 'b) t
    val left : 'a -> ('a, 'b) t
    val right : 'b -> ('a, 'b) t
  end
# (AbstractEither.left (square 40) :> (shape, shape) AbstractEither.t) ;;
Characters 1-32:
Error: This expression cannot be coerced to type
         (shape, shape) AbstractEither.t;
       it has type (< area : float; width : int >, 'a) AbstractEither.t
       but is here used with type (shape, shape) AbstractEither.t
       Type < area : float; width : int > is not compatible with type
         shape = < area : float >
       The second object type has no method width
```

We can fix this by adding *variance annotations* to the type's parameters in the signature:
+ for covariance or - for contravariance:

```
# module VarEither : sig
    type (+'a, +'b) t
    val left: 'a -> ('a, 'b) t
    val right: 'b -> ('a, 'b) t
  end = Either ;;
module VarEither :
  sig
    type (+'a, +'b) t
    val left : 'a -> ('a, 'b) t
    val right : 'b -> ('a, 'b) t
  end
# (VarEither.left (square 40) :> (shape, shape) VarEither.t) ;;
- : (shape, shape) VarEither.t = <abstr>
```

For a more concrete example of variance, let's create some stacks containing shapes by
applying our stack function to some squares and some circles:

OCaml (part 2)

```
type 'a stack = < pop: 'a option; push: 'a -> unit >

let square_stack: square stack = stack [square 30; square 10]

let circle_stack: circle stack = stack [circle 20; circle 40]
```

If we wanted to write a function that took a list of such stacks and found the total area
of their shapes, we might try:

OCaml utop (part 11)

```
# let total_area (shape_stacks: shape stack list) =
    let stack_area acc st =
      let rec loop acc =
        match st#pop with
        | Some s -> loop (acc +. s#area)
        | None -> acc
      in
      loop acc
    in
      List.fold ~init:0.0 ~f:stack_area shape_stacks ;;
val total_area : shape stack list -> float = <fun>
```

However, when we try to apply this function to our objects, we get an error:

OCaml utop (part 12)

```
# total_area [(square_stack :> shape stack); (circle_stack :> shape stack)] ;;
Characters 12-41:
Error: Type square stack = < pop : square option; push : square -> unit >
       is not a subtype of
         shape stack = < pop : shape option; push : shape -> unit >
```

```
        Type shape = < area : float > is not a subtype of
           square = < area : float; width : int >
```

As you can see, `square stack` and `circle stack` are not subtypes of `shape stack`. The problem is with the push method. For `shape stack`, the push method takes an arbitrary shape. So if we could coerce a `square stack` to a `shape stack`, then it would be possible to push an arbitrary shape onto `square stack`, which would be an error.

Another way of looking at this is that `< push: 'a -> unit; .. >` is contravariant in `'a`, so `< push: square -> unit; pop: square option >` cannot be a subtype of `< push: shape -> unit; pop: shape option >`.

Still, the `total_area` function should be fine, in principle. It doesn't call push, so it isn't making that error. To make it work, we need to use a more precise type that indicates we are not going to be using the `set` method. We define a type `readonly_stack` and confirm that we can coerce the list of `stacks` to it:

OCaml utop (part 13)

```
# type 'a readonly_stack = < pop : 'a option > ;;
type 'a readonly_stack = < pop : 'a option >
# let total_area (shape_stacks: shape readonly_stack list) =
    let stack_area acc st =
      let rec loop acc =
        match st#pop with
        | Some s -> loop (acc +. s#area)
        | None -> acc
      in
        loop acc
    in
      List.fold ~init:0.0 ~f:stack_area shape_stacks ;;
val total_area : shape readonly_stack list -> float = <fun>
# total_area [(square_stack :> shape readonly_stack); (circle_stack :>
    shape readonly_stack)] ;;
- : float = 7280.
```

Aspects of this section may seem fairly complicated, but it should be pointed out that this typing *works*, and in the end, the type annotations are fairly minor. In most typed object-oriented languages, these coercions would simply not be possible. For example, in C++, a STL type `list<T>` is invariant in `T`, so it is simply not possible to use `list<square>` where `list<shape>` is expected (at least safely). The situation is similar in Java, although Java has an escape hatch that allows the program to fall back to dynamic typing. The situation in OCaml is much better: it works, it is statically checked, and the annotations are pretty simple.

Narrowing

Narrowing, also called *down casting*, is the ability to coerce an object to one of its subtypes. For example, if we have a list of shapes `shape list`, we might know (for some reason) what the actual type of each shape is. Perhaps we know that all objects in the list have type `square`. In this case, *narrowing* would allow the recasting of the object from type `shape` to type `square`. Many languages support narrowing through dynamic type checking. For example, in Java, a coercion `(Square)` x is allowed if the value x has type `Square` or one of its subtypes; otherwise the coercion throws an exception.

Narrowing is *not permitted* in OCaml. Period.

Why? There are two reasonable explanations, one based on a design principle, and another technical (the technical reason is simple: it is hard to implement).

The design argument is this: narrowing violates abstraction. In fact, with a structural typing system like in OCaml, narrowing would essentially provide the ability to enumerate the methods in an object. To check whether an object `obj` has some method `foo : int`, one would attempt a coercion `(obj :> < foo : int >)`.

More pragmatically, narrowing leads to poor object-oriented style. Consider the following Java code, which returns the name of a shape object:

Java: objects/Shape.java

```Java
String GetShapeName(Shape s) {
  if (s instanceof Square) {
    return "Square";
  } else if (s instanceof Circle) {
    return "Circle";
  } else {
    return "Other";
  }
}
```

Most programmers would consider this code to be "wrong." Instead of performing a case analysis on the type of object, it would be better to define a method to return the name of the shape. Instead of calling `GetShapeName(s)`, we should call `s.Name()` instead.

However, the situation is not always so obvious. The following code checks whether an array of shapes looks like a "barbell," composed of two `Circle` objects separated by a `Line`, where the circles have the same radius:

Java

```Java
boolean IsBarbell(Shape[] s) {
  return s.length == 3 && (s[0] instanceof Circle) &&
    (s[1] instanceof Line) && (s[2] instanceof Circle) &&
      ((Circle) s[0]).radius() == ((Circle) s[2]).radius();
}
```

In this case, it is much less clear how to augment the `Shape` class to support this kind of pattern analysis. It is also not obvious that object-oriented programming is well-suited for this situation. Pattern matching seems like a better fit:

```
let is_barbell = function
| [Circle r1; Line _; Circle r2] when r1 = r2 -> true
| _ -> false
```

Regardless, there is a solution if you find yourself in this situation, which is to augment the classes with variants. You can define a method `variant` that injects the actual object into a variant type:

```
type shape = < variant : repr; area : float>
and circle = < variant : repr; area : float; radius : int >
and line = < variant : repr; area : float; length : int >
and repr =
  | Circle of circle
  | Line of line;;

let is_barbell = function
| [s1; s2; s3] ->
    (match s1#variant, s2#variant, s3#variant with
     | Circle c1, Line _, Circle c2 when c1#radius = c2#radius -> true
     | _ -> false)
| _ -> false;;
```

This pattern works, but it has drawbacks. In particular, the recursive type definition should make it clear that this pattern is essentially equivalent to using variants, and that objects do not provide much value here.

Subtyping Versus Row Polymorphism

There is considerable overlap between subtyping and row polymorphism. Both mechanisms allow you to write functions that can be applied to objects of different types. In these cases, row polymorphism is usually preferred over subtyping because it does not require explicit coercions, and it preserves more type information, allowing functions like the following:

```
# let remove_large l =
    List.filter ~f:(fun s -> s#area <= 100.) l ;;
val remove_large : (< area : float; .. > as 'a) list -> 'a list = <fun>
```

The return type of this function is built from the open object type of its argument, preserving any additional methods that it may have:

```
# let squares : < area : float; width : int > list =
    [square 5; square 15; square 10] ;;
val squares : < area : float; width : int > list = [<obj>; <obj>; <obj>]
# remove_large squares ;;
- : < area : float; width : int > list = [<obj>; <obj>]
```

Writing a similar function with a closed type and applying it using subtyping does not preserve the methods of the argument: the returned object is only known to have an area method:

OCaml utop (part 3)

```
# let remove_large (l: < area : float > list) =
    List.filter ~f:(fun s -> s#area <= 100.) l ;;
val remove_large : < area : float > list -> < area : float > list = <fun>
# remove_large (squares :> < area : float > list ) ;;
- : < area : float > list = [<obj>; <obj>]
```

However, there are some situations where we cannot use row polymorphism. In particular, row polymorphism cannot be used to place different types of object in the same container. For example, lists of heterogeneous elements cannot be created using row polymorphism:

OCaml utop (part 4)

```
# let hlist: < area: float; ..> list = [square 10; circle 30] ;;
Characters 49-58:
Error: This expression has type < area : float; radius : int >
       but an expression was expected of type < area : float; width : int >
       The second object type has no method radius
```

Similarly, we cannot use row polymorphism to store different types of object in the same reference:

OCaml utop (part 5)

```
# let shape_ref: < area: float; ..> ref = ref (square 40) ;;
val shape_ref : < area : float; width : int > ref = {contents = <obj>}
# shape_ref := circle 20 ;;
Characters 13-22:
Error: This expression has type < area : float; radius : int >
       but an expression was expected of type < area : float; width : int >
       The second object type has no method radius
```

In both these cases we must use subtyping:

OCaml utop (part 6)

```
# let hlist: shape list = [(square 10 :> shape); (circle 30 :> shape)] ;;
val hlist : shape list = [<obj>; <obj>]
# let shape_ref: shape ref = ref (square 40 :> shape) ;;
val shape_ref : shape ref = {contents = <obj>}
# shape_ref := (circle 20 :> shape) ;;
- : unit = ()
```

Production Note

This chapter contains significant contributions from Leo White.

## CHAPTER 12

Classes

Programming with objects directly is great for encapsulation, but one of the main goals of object-oriented programming is code reuse through inheritance. For inheritance, we need to introduce *classes*. In object-oriented programming, a class is a "recipe" for creating objects. The recipe can be changed by adding new methods and fields, or it can be changed by modifying existing methods.

OCaml Classes

In OCaml, class definitions must be defined as toplevel statements in a module. The syntax for a class definition uses the keyword `class`:

OCaml utop

```
# class istack = object
    val mutable v = [0; 2]

    method pop =
      match v with
      | hd :: tl ->
          v <- tl;
          Some hd
      | [] -> None

    method push hd =
      v <- hd :: v
  end ;;
class istack :
  object
    val mutable v : int list
    method pop : int option
    method push : int -> unit
  end
```

The class istack : object ... end result shows that we have created a class istack with *class type* object ... end. Like module types, class types are completely separate from regular OCaml types (e.g., int, string, and list) and, in particular, should not be confused with object types (e.g., < get : int; .. >). The class type describes the class itself rather than the objects that the class creates. This particular class type specifies that the istack class defines a mutable field v, a method pop that returns an int option, and a method push with type int -> unit.

To produce an object, classes are instantiated with the keyword new:

OCaml utop (part 1)

```
# let s = new istack ;;
val s : istack = <obj>
# s#pop ;;
- : int option = Some 0
# s#push 5 ;;
- : unit = ()
# s#pop ;;
- : int option = Some 5
```

You may have noticed that the object s has been given the type istack. But wait, we've stressed *classes are not types*, so what's up with that? In fact, what we've said is entirely true: classes and class names *are not* types. However, for convenience, the definition of the class istack also defines an object type istack with the same methods as the class. This type definition is equivalent to:

OCaml utop (part 2)

```
# type istack = < pop: int option; push: int -> unit > ;;
type istack = < pop : int option; push : int -> unit >
```

Note that this type represents any object with these methods: objects created using the istack class will have this type, but objects with this type may not have been created by the istack class.

Class Parameters and Polymorphism

A class definition serves as the *constructor* for the class. In general, a class definition may have parameters that must be provided as arguments when the object is created with new.

Let's implement a variant of the istack class that can hold any values, not just integers. When defining the class, the type parameters are placed in square brackets before the class name in the class definition. We also add a parameter init for the initial contents of the stack:

OCaml utop

```
# class ['a] stack init = object
    val mutable v : 'a list = init
```

```
    method pop =
      match v with
      | hd :: tl ->
        v <- tl;
        Some hd
      | [] -> None

    method push hd =
      v <- hd :: v
  end ;;
class ['a] stack :
  'a list ->
  object
    val mutable v : 'a list
    method pop : 'a option
    method push : 'a -> unit
  end
```

Note that the type parameter ['a] in the definition uses square brackets, but for other uses of the type they are omitted (or replaced with parentheses if there is more than one type parameter).

The type annotation on the declaration of v is used to constrain type inference. If we omit this annotation, the type inferred for the class will be "too polymorphic": init could have some type 'b list:

OCaml utop (part 1)

```
# class ['a] stack init = object
    val mutable v = init

    method pop =
      match v with
      | hd :: tl ->
        v <- tl;
        Some hd
      | [] -> None

    method push hd =
      v <- hd :: v
  end ;;
Characters 6-16:
Error: Some type variables are unbound in this type:
        class ['a] stack :
          'b list ->
          object
            val mutable v : 'b list
            method pop : 'b option
            method push : 'b -> unit
          end
        The method pop has type 'b option where 'b is unbound
```

In general, we need to provide enough constraints so that the compiler will infer the correct type. We can add type constraints to the parameters, to the fields, and to the methods. It is a matter of preference how many constraints to add. You can add type constraints in all three places, but the extra text may not help clarity. A convenient middle ground is to annotate the fields and/or class parameters, and add constraints to methods only if necessary.

Object Types as Interfaces

We may wish to traverse the elements on our stack. One common style for doing this in object-oriented languages is to define a class for an `iterator` object. An iterator provides a generic mechanism to inspect and traverse the elements of a collection.

There are two common styles for defining abstract interfaces like this. In Java, an iterator would normally be specified with an interface, which specifies a set of method types:

Java

```
// Java-style iterator, specified as an interface.
interface <T> iterator {
  T Get();
  boolean HasValue();
  void Next();
};
```

In languages without interfaces, like C++, the specification would normally use *abstract* classes to specify the methods without implementing them (C++ uses the "= 0" definition to mean "not implemented"):

C

```
// Abstract class definition in C++.
template<typename T>
class Iterator {
 public:
  virtual ~Iterator() {}
  virtual T get() const = 0;
  virtual bool has_value() const = 0;
  virtual void next() = 0;
};
```

OCaml supports both styles. In fact, OCaml is more flexible than these approaches because an object type can be implemented by any object with the appropriate methods; it does not have to be specified by the object's class *a priori*. We'll leave abstract classes for later. Let's demonstrate the technique using object types.

First, we'll define an object type `iterator` that specifies the methods in an iterator:

OCaml utop

```
# type 'a iterator = < get : 'a; has_value : bool; next : unit > ;;
type 'a iterator = < get : 'a; has_value : bool; next : unit >
```

Next, we'll define an actual iterator for lists. We can use this to iterate over the contents of our stack:

OCaml utop (part 1)

```
# class ['a] list_iterator init = object
    val mutable current : 'a list = init

    method has_value = current <> []

    method get =
      match current with
      | hd :: tl -> hd
      | [] -> raise (Invalid_argument "no value")

    method next =
      match current with
      | hd :: tl -> current <- tl
      | [] -> raise (Invalid_argument "no value")
  end ;;
class ['a] list_iterator :
  'a list ->
  object
    val mutable current : 'a list
    method get : 'a
    method has_value : bool
    method next : unit
  end
```

Finally, we add a method iterator to the stack class to produce an iterator. To do so, we construct a list_iterator that refers to the current contents of the stack:

OCaml utop (part 2)

```
# class ['a] stack init = object
    val mutable v : 'a list = init

    method pop =
      match v with
      | hd :: tl ->
        v <- tl;
        Some hd
      | [] -> None

    method push hd =
      v <- hd :: v

    method iterator : 'a iterator =
      new list_iterator v
  end ;;
class ['a] stack :
  'a list ->
  object
    val mutable v : 'a list
    method iterator : 'a iterator
```

```
      method pop : 'a option
      method push : 'a -> unit
    end
```

Now we can build a new stack, push some values to it, and iterate over them:

OCaml utop (part 3)

```
# let s = new stack [] ;;
val s : '_a stack = <obj>
# s#push 5 ;;
- : unit = ()
# s#push 4 ;;
- : unit = ()
# let it = s#iterator ;;
val it : int iterator = <obj>
# it#get ;;
- : int = 4
# it#next ;;
- : unit = ()
# it#get ;;
- : int = 5
# it#next ;;
- : unit = ()
# it#has_value ;;
- : bool = false
```

Functional Iterators

In practice, most OCaml programmers avoid iterator objects in favor of functional-style techniques. For example, the alternative stack class that follows takes a function f and applies it to each of the elements on the stack:

OCaml utop (part 4)

```
# class ['a] stack init = object
    val mutable v : 'a list = init

    method pop =
      match v with
      | hd :: tl ->
        v <- tl;
        Some hd
      | [] -> None

    method push hd =
      v <- hd :: v

    method iter f =
      List.iter ~f v
  end ;;
class ['a] stack :
  'a list ->
  object
```

```
    val mutable v : 'a list
    method iter : ('a -> unit) -> unit
    method pop : 'a option
    method push : 'a -> unit
  end
```

What about functional operations like map and fold? In general, these methods take a
function that produces a value of some other type than the elements of the set.

For example, a fold method for our ['a] stack class should have type ('b -> 'a ->
'b) -> 'b -> 'b, where the 'b is polymorphic. To express a polymorphic method type
like this, we must use a type quantifier, as shown in the following example:

OCaml utop (part 5)

```
# class ['a] stack init = object
    val mutable v : 'a list = init

    method pop =
      match v with
      | hd :: tl ->
        v <- tl;
        Some hd
      | [] -> None

    method push hd =
      v <- hd :: v

    method fold : 'b. ('b -> 'a -> 'b) -> 'b -> 'b =
      (fun f init -> List.fold ~f ~init v)
  end ;;
class ['a] stack :
  'a list ->
  object
    val mutable v : 'a list
    method fold : ('b -> 'a -> 'b) -> 'b -> 'b
    method pop : 'a option
    method push : 'a -> unit
  end
```

The type quantifier 'b. can be read as "for all 'b." Type quantifiers can only be used
directly after the method name, which means that method parameters must be expressed
using a fun or function expression.

Inheritance

Inheritance uses an existing class to define a new one. For example, the following class
definition inherits from our stack class for strings and adds a new method print that
prints all the strings on the stack:

```
# class sstack init = object
    inherit [string] stack init

    method print =
        List.iter ~f:print_string v
  end ;;
class sstack :
  string list ->
  object
    val mutable v : string list
    method pop : string option
    method print : unit
    method push : string -> unit
  end
```

A class can override methods from classes it inherits. For example, this class creates
stacks of integers that double the integers before they are pushed onto the stack:

```
# class double_stack init = object
    inherit [int] stack init as super

    method push hd =
        super#push (hd * 2)
  end ;;
class double_stack :
  int list ->
  object
    val mutable v : int list
    method pop : int option
    method push : int -> unit
  end
```

The preceding as super statement creates a special object called super which can be
used to call superclass methods. Note that super is not a real object and can only be
used to call methods.

Class Types

To allow code in a different file or module to inherit from a class, we must expose it and
give it a class type. What is the class type?

As an example, let's wrap up our stack class in an explicit module (we'll use explicit
modules for illustration, but the process is similar when we want to define a .mli file).
In keeping with the usual style for modules, we define a type 'a t to represent the type
of our stacks:

```
module Stack = struct
  class ['a] stack init = object
```

```
      ...
   end

   type 'a t = 'a stack

   let make init = new stack init
end
```

We have multiple choices in defining the module type, depending on how much of the implementation we want to expose. At one extreme, a maximally abstract signature would completely hide the class definitions:

OCaml (part 1)

```
module AbstractStack : sig
   type 'a t = < pop: 'a option; push: 'a -> unit >

   val make : unit -> 'a t
end = Stack
```

The abstract signature is simple because we ignore the classes. But what if we want to include them in the signature so that other modules can inherit from the class definitions? For this, we need to specify types for the classes, called *class types*.

Class types do not appear in mainstream object-oriented programming languages, so you may not be familiar with them, but the concept is pretty simple. A class type specifies the type of each of the visible parts of the class, including both fields and methods. Just as with module types, you don't have to give a type for everything; anything you omit will be hidden:

OCaml (part 2)

```
module VisibleStack : sig

   type 'a t = < pop: 'a option; push: 'a -> unit >

   class ['a] stack : object
     val mutable v : 'a list
     method pop : 'a option
     method push : 'a -> unit
   end

   val make : unit -> 'a t
end = Stack
```

In this signature, we've chosen to make everything visible. The class type for stack specifies the types of the field v, as well as the types of each of the methods.

Open Recursion

Open recursion allows an object's methods to invoke other methods on the same object. These calls are looked up dynamically, allowing a method in one class to call a method from another class, if both classes are inherited by the same object. This allows mutually recursive parts of an object to be defined separately.

This ability to define mutually recursive methods from separate components is a key feature of classes: achieving similar functionality with data types or modules is much more cumbersome and verbose.

For example, consider writing recursive functions over a simple document format. This format is represented as a tree with three different types of node:

OCaml

```
type doc =
  | Heading of string
  | Paragraph of text_item list
  | Definition of string list_item list

and text_item =
  | Raw of string
  | Bold of text_item list
  | Enumerate of int list_item list
  | Quote of doc

and 'a list_item =
  { tag: 'a;
    text: text_item list }
```

It is quite easy to write a function that operates by recursively traversing this data. However, what if you need to write many similar recursive functions? How can you factor out the common parts of these functions to avoid repetitive boilerplate?

The simplest way is to use classes and open recursion. For example, the following class defines objects that fold over the document data:

OCaml (part 1)

```
open Core.Std

class ['a] folder = object(self)
  method doc acc = function
  | Heading _ -> acc
  | Paragraph text -> List.fold ~f:self#text_item ~init:acc text
  | Definition list -> List.fold ~f:self#list_item ~init:acc list

  method list_item: 'b. 'a -> 'b list_item -> 'a =
    fun acc {tag; text} ->
      List.fold ~f:self#text_item ~init:acc text

  method text_item acc = function
  | Raw _ -> acc
  | Bold text -> List.fold ~f:self#text_item ~init:acc text
  | Enumerate list -> List.fold ~f:self#list_item ~init:acc list
  | Quote doc -> self#doc acc doc
  end
```

The `object (self)` syntax binds `self` to the current object, allowing the `doc`, `list_item`, and `text_item` methods to call each other.

By inheriting from this class, we can create functions that fold over the document data. For example, the `count_doc` function counts the number of bold tags in the document that are not within a list:

OCaml (part 2)

```
class counter = object
  inherit [int] folder as super

  method list_item acc li = acc

  method text_item acc ti =
    let acc = super#text_item acc ti in
    match ti with
    | Bold _ -> acc + 1
    | _ -> acc
end

let count_doc = (new counter)#doc
```

Note how the `super` special object is used in `text_item` to call the `[int] folder` class's `text_item` method to fold over the children of the `text_item` node.

Private Methods

Methods can be declared *private*, which means that they may be called by subclasses, but they are not visible otherwise (similar to a *protected* method in C++).

For example, we may want to include methods in our `folder` class for handling each of the different cases in `doc` and `text_item`. However, we may not want to force subclasses of `folder` to expose these methods, as they probably shouldn't be called directly:

OCaml (part 3)

```
class ['a] folder2 = object(self)
  method doc acc = function
  | Heading str -> self#heading acc str
  | Paragraph text -> self#paragraph acc text
  | Definition list -> self#definition acc list

  method list_item: 'b. 'a -> 'b list_item -> 'a =
    fun acc {tag; text} ->
      List.fold ~f:self#text_item ~init:acc text

  method text_item acc = function
  | Raw str -> self#raw acc str
  | Bold text -> self#bold acc text
  | Enumerate list -> self#enumerate acc list
  | Quote doc -> self#quote acc doc
```

```
    method private heading acc str = acc
    method private paragraph acc text =
      List.fold ~f:self#text_item ~init:acc text
    method private definition acc list =
      List.fold ~f:self#list_item ~init:acc list

    method private raw acc str = acc
    method private bold acc text =
      List.fold ~f:self#text_item ~init:acc text
    method private enumerate acc list =
      List.fold ~f:self#list_item ~init:acc list
    method private quote acc doc = self#doc acc doc
  end

let f :
  < doc : int -> doc -> int;
    list_item : 'a . int -> 'a list_item -> int;
    text_item : int -> text_item -> int >  = new folder2
```

The final statement that builds the value f shows how the instantiation of a folder2 object has a type that hides the private methods.

To be precise, the private methods are part of the class type, but not part of the object type. This means, for example, that the object f has no method bold. However, the private methods are available to subclasses: we can use them to simplify our counter class:

OCaml (part 4)

```
class counter_with_private_method = object
  inherit [int] folder2 as super

  method list_item acc li = acc

  method private bold acc txt =
    let acc = super#bold acc txt in
    acc + 1
end
```

The key property of private methods is that they are visible to subclasses, but not anywhere else. If you want the stronger guarantee that a method is *really* private, not even accessible in subclasses, you can use an explicit class type that omits the method. In the following code, the private methods are explicitly omitted from the class type of counter_with_sig and can't be invoked in subclasses of counter_with_sig:

OCaml (part 5)

```
class counter_with_sig : object
  method doc : int -> doc -> int
  method list_item : int -> 'b list_item -> int
  method text_item : int -> text_item -> int
end = object
  inherit [int] folder2 as super
```

```
    method list_item acc li = acc

    method private bold acc txt =
      let acc = super#bold acc txt in
      acc + 1
  end
```

Binary Methods

A *binary method* is a method that takes an object of self type. One common example
is defining a method for equality:

OCaml utop

```
# class square w = object(self : 'self)
    method width = w
    method area = Float.of_int (self#width * self#width)
    method equals (other : 'self) = other#width = self#width
  end ;;
class square :
  int ->
  object ('a)
    method area : float
    method equals : 'a -> bool
    method width : int
  end
# class circle r = object(self : 'self)
    method radius = r
    method area = 3.14 *. (Float.of_int self#radius) ** 2.0
    method equals (other : 'self) = other#radius = self#radius
  end ;;
class circle :
  int ->
  object ('a)
    method area : float
    method equals : 'a -> bool
    method radius : int
  end
```

Note how we can use the type annotation (self: 'self) to obtain the type of the
current object.

We can now test different object instances for equality by using the equals binary
method:

OCaml utop (part 1)

```
# (new square 5)#equals (new square 5) ;;
- : bool = true
# (new circle 10)#equals (new circle 7) ;;
- : bool = false
```

This works, but there is a problem lurking here. The method `equals` takes an object of the exact type `square` or `circle`. Because of this, we can't define a common base class `shape` that also includes an equality method:

OCaml utop (part 2)

```
# type shape = < equals : shape -> bool; area : float > ;;
type shape = < area : float; equals : shape -> bool >
# (new square 5 :> shape) ;;
Characters -1-23:
Error: Type square = < area : float; equals : square -> bool; width : int >
       is not a subtype of shape = < area : float; equals : shape -> bool >
       Type shape = < area : float; equals : shape -> bool >
       is not a subtype of
         square = < area : float; equals : square -> bool; width : int >
```

The problem is that a `square` expects to be compared with a `square`, not an arbitrary `shape`; likewise for `circle`. This problem is fundamental. Many languages solve it either with narrowing (with dynamic type checking), or by method overloading. Since OCaml has neither of these, what can we do?

Since the problematic method is equality, one proposal we could consider is to just drop it from the base type `shape` and use polymorphic equality instead. However, the built-in polymorphic equality has very poor behavior when applied to objects:

OCaml utop (part 3)

```
# (object method area = 5 end) = (object method area = 5 end) ;;
- : bool = false
```

The problem here is that two objects are considered equal by the built-in polymorphic equality if and only if they are physically equal. There are other reasons not to use the built-in polymorphic equality, but these false negatives are a showstopper.

If we want to define equality for shapes in general, the remaining solution is to use the same approach as we described for narrowing. That is, introduce a *representation* type implemented using variants, and implement the comparison based on the representation type:

OCaml utop (part 4)

```
# type shape_repr =
  | Square of int
  | Circle of int ;;
type shape_repr = Square of int | Circle of int
# type shape =
  < repr : shape_repr; equals : shape -> bool; area : float > ;;
type shape = < area : float; equals : shape -> bool; repr : shape_repr >
# class square w = object(self)
    method width = w
    method area = Float.of_int (self#width * self#width)
    method repr = Square self#width
    method equals (other : shape) = other#repr = self#repr
  end ;;
```

```
class square :
  int ->
  object
    method area : float
    method equals : shape -> bool
    method repr : shape_repr
    method width : int
  end
```

The binary method `equals` is now implemented in terms of the concrete type `shape_repr`. When using this pattern, you will not be able to hide the `repr` method, but you can hide the type definition using the module system:

OCaml

```
module Shapes : sig
  type shape_repr
  type shape =
    < repr : shape_repr; equals : shape -> bool; area: float >

  class square : int ->
    object
      method width : int
      method area : float
      method repr : shape_repr
      method equals : shape -> bool
    end
end = struct
  type shape_repr =
  | Square of int
  | Circle of int
  ...
end
```

Note that this solution prevents us from adding new kinds of shapes without adding new constructors to the `shape_repr` type, which is quite restrictive. The objects created by these classes are also in one-to-one correspondence with members of the representation type, making the objects seem somewhat redundant.

However, equality is quite an extreme instance of a binary method: it needs access to all the information of the other object. Many other binary methods need only partial information about the object. For instance, a method that compares shapes by their sizes:

OCaml

```
class square w = object(self)
  method width = w
  method area = Float.of_int (self#width * self#width)
  method larger other = self#area > other#area
end
```

In this case, there is no one-to-one correspondence between the objects and their sizes, and we can still easily define new kinds of shape.

Virtual Classes and Methods

A *virtual* class is a class where some methods or fields are declared but not implemented. This should not be confused with the word `virtual` as it is used in C++. A `virtual` method in C++ uses dynamic dispatch, while regular, nonvirtual methods are statically dispatched. In OCaml, *all* methods use dynamic dispatch, but the keyword `virtual` means that the method or field is not implemented. A class containing virtual methods must also be flagged `virtual` and cannot be directly instantiated (i.e., no object of this class can be created).

To explore this, let's extend our shapes examples to simple, interactive graphics. We will use the Async concurrency library and the Async_graphics (*http://github.com/lpw25/async_graphics/*) library, which provides an asynchronous interface to OCaml's built-in Graphics library. Concurrent programming with Async will be explored later in Chapter 18; for now you can safely ignore the details. You just need to run `opam install async_graphics` to get the library installed on your system.

We will give each shape a `draw` method that describes how to draw the shape on the `Async_graphics` display:

OCaml

```
open Core.Std
open Async.Std
open Async_graphics

type drawable = < draw: unit >
```

Create Some Simple Shapes

Now let's add classes for making squares and circles. We include an `on_click` method for adding event handlers to the shapes:

OCaml (part 1)

```
class square w x y = object(self)
  val mutable x: int = x
  method x = x

  val mutable y: int = y
  method y = y

  val mutable width = w
  method width = width

  method draw = fill_rect x y width width

  method private contains x' y' =
    x <= x' && x' <= x + width &&
      y <= y' && y' <= y + width
```

```
    method on_click ?start ?stop f =
      on_click ?start ?stop
        (fun ev ->
           if self#contains ev.mouse_x ev.mouse_y then
             f ev.mouse_x ev.mouse_y)
  end
```

The `square` class is pretty straightforward, and the `circle` class below also looks very similar:

OCaml (part 2)

```
class circle r x y = object(self)
  val mutable x: int = x
  method x = x

  val mutable y: int = y
  method y = y

  val mutable radius = r
  method radius = radius

  method draw = fill_circle x y radius

  method private contains x' y' =
    let dx = abs (x' - x) in
    let dy = abs (y' - y) in
    let dist = sqrt (Float.of_int ((dx * dx) + (dy * dy))) in
      dist <= (Float.of_int radius)

  method on_click ?start ?stop f =
    on_click ?start ?stop
      (fun ev ->
         if self#contains ev.mouse_x ev.mouse_y then
           f ev.mouse_x ev.mouse_y)
  end
```

These classes have a lot in common, and it would be useful to factor out this common functionality into a superclass. We can easily move the definitions of x and y into a superclass, but what about `on_click`? Its definition depends on `contains`, which has a different definition in each class. The solution is to create a *virtual* class. This class will declare a `contains` method but leave its definition to the subclasses.

Here is the more succinct definition, starting with a virtual `shape` class that implements `on_click` and `on_mousedown`:

OCaml (part 1)

```
class virtual shape x y = object(self)
  method virtual private contains: int -> int -> bool

  val mutable x: int = x
  method x = x
```

```
    val mutable y: int = y
    method y = y

    method on_click ?start ?stop f =
      on_click ?start ?stop
        (fun ev ->
          if self#contains ev.mouse_x ev.mouse_y then
            f ev.mouse_x ev.mouse_y)

    method on_mousedown ?start ?stop f =
      on_mousedown ?start ?stop
        (fun ev ->
          if self#contains ev.mouse_x ev.mouse_y then
            f ev.mouse_x ev.mouse_y)
  end
```

Now we can define square and circle by inheriting from shape:

OCaml (part 2)

```
class square w x y = object
  inherit shape x y

  val mutable width = w
  method width = width

  method draw = fill_rect x y width width

  method private contains x' y' =
    x <= x' && x' <= x + width &&
    y <= y' && y' <= y + width
end

class circle r x y = object
  inherit shape x y

  val mutable radius = r
  method radius = radius

  method draw = fill_circle x y radius

  method private contains x' y' =
    let dx = abs (x' - x) in
    let dy = abs (y' - y) in
    let dist = sqrt (Float.of_int ((dx * dx) + (dy * dy))) in
    dist <= (Float.of_int radius)
end
```

One way to view a virtual class is that it is like a functor, where the "inputs" are the declared—but not defined—virtual methods and fields. The functor application is implemented through inheritance, when virtual methods are given concrete implementations.

Initializers

You can execute expressions during the instantiation of a class by placing them before the object expression or in the initial value of a field:

OCaml utop

```
# class obj x =
    let () = printf "Creating obj %d\n" x in
    object
      val field = printf "Initializing field\n"; x
    end ;;
class obj : int -> object val field : int end
# let o = new obj 3 ;;
Creating obj 3
Initializing field
val o : obj = <obj>
```

However, these expressions are executed before the object has been created and cannot refer to the methods of the object. If you need to use an object's methods during instantiation, you can use an initializer. An initializer is an expression that will be executed during instantiation but after the object has been created.

For example, suppose we wanted to extend our previous shapes module with a grow ing_circle class for circles that expand when clicked. We could inherit from circle and used the inherited on_click to add a handler for click events:

OCaml (part 3)

```
class growing_circle r x y = object(self)
  inherit circle r x y

  initializer
    self#on_click (fun _x _y -> radius <- radius * 2)
end
```

Multiple Inheritance

When a class inherits from more than one superclass, it is using *multiple inheritance*. Multiple inheritance extends the variety of ways that classes can be combined, and it can be quite useful, particularly with virtual classes. However, it can be tricky to use, particularly when the inheritance hierarchy is a graph rather than a tree, so it should be used with care.

How Names Are Resolved

The main trickiness of multiple inheritance is due to naming—what happens when a method or field with some name is defined in more than one class?

If there is one thing to remember about inheritance in OCaml, it is this: inheritance is like textual inclusion. If there is more than one definition for a name, the last definition wins.

For example, consider this class, which inherits from `square` and defines a new `draw` method that uses `draw_rect` instead of `fill_rect` to draw the square:

OCaml (part 1)

```
class square_outline w x y = object
  inherit square w x y
  method draw = draw_rect x y width width
end
```

Since the `inherit` declaration comes before the method definition, the new `draw` method overrides the old one, and the square is drawn using `draw_rect`. But, what if we had defined `square_outline` as follows?

OCaml (part 1)

```
class square_outline w x y = object
  method draw = draw_rect x y w w
  inherit square w x y
end
```

Here the `inherit` declaration comes after the method definition, so the `draw` method from `square` will override the other definition, and the square will be drawn using `fill_rect`.

To reiterate, to understand what inheritance means, replace each `inherit` directive with its definition, and take the last definition of each method or field. Note that the methods and fields added by an inheritance are those listed in its class type, so private methods that are hidden by the type will not be included.

Mixins

When should you use multiple inheritance? If you ask multiple people, you're likely to get multiple (perhaps heated) answers. Some will argue that multiple inheritance is overly complicated; others will argue that inheritance is problematic in general, and one should use object composition instead. But regardless of who you talk to, you will rarely hear that multiple inheritance is great and that you should use it widely.

In any case, if you're programming with objects, there's one general pattern for multiple inheritance that is both useful and reasonably simple: the *mixin* pattern. Generically, a *mixin* is just a virtual class that implements a feature based on another one. If you have a class that implements methods A, and you have a mixin M that provides methods B from A, then you can inherit from M—"mixing" it in—to get features B.

That's too abstract, so let's give some examples based on our interactive shapes. We may wish to allow a shape to be dragged by the mouse. We can define this functionality for any object that has mutable x and y fields and an on_mousedown method for adding event handlers:

OCaml (part 4)

```
class virtual draggable = object(self)
  method virtual on_mousedown:
    ?start:unit Deferred.t ->
    ?stop:unit Deferred.t ->
    (int -> int -> unit) -> unit
  val virtual mutable x: int
  val virtual mutable y: int

  val mutable dragging = false
  method dragging = dragging

  initializer
    self#on_mousedown
      (fun mouse_x mouse_y ->
        let offset_x = x - mouse_x in
        let offset_y = y - mouse_y in
        let mouse_up = Ivar.create () in
        let stop = Ivar.read mouse_up in
        dragging <- true;
        on_mouseup ~stop
          (fun _ ->
            Ivar.fill mouse_up ();
            dragging <- false);
        on_mousemove ~stop
          (fun ev ->
            x <- ev.mouse_x + offset_x;
            y <- ev.mouse_y + offset_y))
end
```

This allows us to create draggable shapes using multiple inheritance:

OCaml (part 5)

```
class small_square = object
  inherit square 20 40 40
  inherit draggable
end
```

We can also use mixins to create animated shapes. Each animated shape has a list of update functions to be called during animation. We create an animated mixin to provide this update list and ensure that the functions in it are called regular intervals when the shape is animated:

OCaml (part 6)

```
class virtual animated span = object(self)
  method virtual on_click:
    ?start:unit Deferred.t ->
    ?stop:unit Deferred.t ->
    (int -> int -> unit) -> unit
  val mutable updates: (int -> unit) list = []
```

```
      val mutable step = 0
      val mutable running = false

      method running = running

      method animate =
        step <- 0;
        running <- true;
        let stop =
          Clock.after span
          >>| fun () -> running <- false
        in
        Clock.every ~stop (Time.Span.of_sec (1.0 /. 24.0))
          (fun () ->
            step <- step + 1;
            List.iter ~f:(fun f -> f step) updates
          )

      initializer
        self#on_click (fun _x _y -> if not self#running then self#animate)
    end
```

We use initializers to add functions to this update list. For example, this class will produce circles that move to the right for a second when clicked:

OCaml (part 7)

```
class my_circle = object
  inherit circle 20 50 50
  inherit animated Time.Span.second
  initializer updates <- [fun _ -> x <- x + 5]
end
```

These initializers can also be added using mixins:

OCaml (part 8)

```
class virtual linear x' y' = object
  val virtual mutable updates: (int -> unit) list
  val virtual mutable x: int
  val virtual mutable y: int

  initializer
    let update _ =
      x <- x + x';
      y <- y + y'
    in
    updates <- update :: updates
end

let pi = (atan 1.0) *. 4.0

class virtual harmonic offset x' y' = object
  val virtual mutable updates: (int -> unit) list
  val virtual mutable x: int
```

```
    val virtual mutable y: int

    initializer
      let update step =
        let m = sin (offset +. ((Float.of_int step) *. (pi /. 64.))) in
        let x' = Float.to_int (m *. Float.of_int x') in
        let y' = Float.to_int (m *. Float.of_int y') in
        x <- x + x';
        y <- y + y'
      in
      updates <- update :: updates
end
```

Since the linear and harmonic mixins are only used for their side effects, they can be inherited multiple times within the same object to produce a variety of different animations:

OCaml (part 9)

```
class my_square x y = object
  inherit square 40 x y
  inherit draggable
  inherit animated (Time.Span.of_int_sec 5)
  inherit linear 5 0
  inherit harmonic 0.0 7 ~-10
end

let my_circle = object
  inherit circle 30 250 250
  inherit animated (Time.Span.minute)
  inherit harmonic 0.0 10 0
  inherit harmonic (pi /. 2.0) 0 10
end
```

Displaying the Animated Shapes

We finish our shapes module by creating a main function to draw some shapes on the graphical display and running that function using the Async scheduler:

OCaml (part 10)

```
let main () =
  let shapes = [
    (my_circle :> drawable);
    (new my_square 50 350 :> drawable);
    (new my_square 50 200 :> drawable);
    (new growing_circle 20 70 70 :> drawable);
  ] in
  let repaint () =
    clear_graph ();
    List.iter ~f:(fun s -> s#draw) shapes;
    synchronize ()
  in
    open_graph "";
```

```
        auto_synchronize false;
        Clock.every (Time.Span.of_sec (1.0 /. 24.0)) repaint

    let () = never_returns (Scheduler.go_main ~main ())
```

Our main function creates a list of shapes to be displayed and defines a repaint function that actually draws them on the display. We then open a graphical display and ask Async to run repaint at regular intervals.

Finally, build the binary by linking against the async_graphics package, which will pull in all the other dependencies:

Terminal

```
    $ corebuild -pkg async_graphics shapes.native
```

When you run the binary, a new graphical window should appear (on Mac OS X, you will need to install the X11 package first, which you will be prompted for). Try clicking on the various widgets, and gasp in awe at the sophisticated animations that unfold as a result.

The graphics library described here is the one built into OCaml and is more useful as a learning tool than anything else. There are several third-party libraries that provide more sophisticated bindings to various graphics subsystems:

Lablgtk (http://lablgtk.forge.ocamlcore.org)
    A strongly typed interface to the GTK widget library.

LablGL (https://forge.ocamlcore.org/projects/lablgl/)
    An interface between OCaml and OpenGL, a widely supported standard for 3D rendering.

js_of_ocaml (http://ocsigen.org/js_of_ocaml/api/Js)
    Compiles OCaml code to JavaScript and has bindings to WebGL. This is the emerging standard for 3D rendering in web browsers.

Tools and Techniques

Part II builds on the basics by demonstrating more advanced tools and techniques that are useful for building real world programs. Here you'll learn about useful libraries for building practical applications, as well as design patterns that help combine different features of the language to good effect.

This part begins by introducing two of the most common datastructures used in OCaml: maps and hashtables. We then change gears and explain how to build expressive command-line interfaces, which is a good example of a sophisticated use of the type system to create a user friendly library.

Some of the examples in this part use the JSON interchange format, and so we first show how to use third-party tools to parse and generate JSON, as well as how to build a parser from scratch. Another interchange format used throughout OCaml are s-expressions, and this chapter shows how to turn any OCaml value into an s-expression by using the powerful camlp4 syntax preprocessor.

We close with a tour of the Async communications library, which lets you build scalable, high-performance networked applications in OCaml. By the end of the chapter, you will be able to run web queries against the DuckDuckGo engine by using Async, JSON and a HTTP library all written in OCaml.

## CHAPTER 13

Maps and Hash Tables

Lots of programming problems require dealing with data organized as key/value pairs. Maybe the simplest way of representing such data in OCaml is an *association list*, which is simply a list of pairs of keys and values. For example, you could represent a mapping between the 10 digits and their English names as follows:

OCaml utop (part 1)

```
# let digit_alist =
    [ 0, "zero"; 1, "one"; 2, "two"  ; 3, "three"; 4, "four"
    ; 5, "five"; 6, "six"; 7, "seven"; 8, "eight"; 9, "nine" ]
  ;;
val digit_alist : (int * string) list =
  [(0, "zero"); (1, "one"); (2, "two"); (3, "three"); (4, "four");
   (5, "five"); (6, "six"); (7, "seven"); (8, "eight"); (9, "nine")]
```

We can use functions from the List.Assoc module to manipulate this data:

OCaml utop (part 2)

```
# List.Assoc.find digit_alist 6;;
- : string option = Some "six"
# List.Assoc.find digit_alist 22;;
- : string option = None
# List.Assoc.add digit_alist 0 "zilch";;
- : (int, string) List.Assoc.t =
[(0, "zilch"); (1, "one"); (2, "two"); (3, "three"); (4, "four");
 (5, "five"); (6, "six"); (7, "seven"); (8, "eight"); (9, "nine")]
```

Association lists are simple and easy to use, but their performance is not ideal, since almost every nontrivial operation on an association list requires a linear-time scan of the list.

In this chapter, we'll talk about two more efficient alternatives to association lists: *maps* and *hash tables*. A map is an immutable tree-based data structure where most operations take time logarithmic in the size of the map, whereas a hash table is a mutable data structure where most operations have constant time complexity. We'll describe both of these data structures in detail and provide some advice as to how to choose between them.

Maps

Let's consider an example of how one might use a map in practice. In Chapter 4, we showed a module `Counter` for keeping frequency counts on a set of strings. Here's the interface:

OCaml

```
open Core.Std

(** A collection of string frequency counts *)
type t

(** The empty set of frequency counts  *)
val empty : t

(** Bump the frequency count for the given string. *)
val touch : t -> string -> t

(* Converts the set of frequency counts to an association list.  Every string
   in the list will show up at most once, and the integers will be at least
   1. *)
val to_list : t -> (string * int) list
```

The intended behavior here is straightforward. `Counter.empty` represents an empty collection of frequency counts; `touch` increments the frequency count of the specified string by 1; and `to_list` returns the list of nonzero frequencies.

Here's the implementation:

OCaml

```
open Core.Std

type t = int String.Map.t

let empty = String.Map.empty

let to_list t = Map.to_alist t

let touch t s =
  let count =
    match Map.find t s with
    | None -> 0
    | Some x -> x
  in
  Map.add t ~key:s ~data:(count + 1)
```

Note that in some places the preceding code refers to `String.Map.t`, and in others `Map.t`. This has to do with the fact that maps are implemented as ordered binary trees, and as such, need a way of comparing keys.

To deal with this, a map, once created, stores the necessary comparison function within the data structure. Thus, operations like `Map.find` or `Map.add` that access the contents of a map or create a new map from an existing one, do so by using the comparison function embedded within the map.

But in order to get a map in the first place, you need to get your hands on the comparison function somehow. For this reason, modules like `String` contain a `Map` submodule that has values like `String.Map.empty` and `String.Map.of_alist` that are specialized to strings, and thus have access to a string comparison function. Such a `Map` submodule is included in every module that satisfies the `Comparable.S` interface from Core.

Creating Maps with Comparators

The specialized `Map` submodule is convenient, but it's not the only way of creating a `Map.t`. The information required to compare values of a given type is wrapped up in a value called a *comparator* that can be used to create maps using the `Map` module directly:

OCaml utop (part 3)

```
# let digit_map = Map.of_alist_exn digit_alist
                       ~comparator:Int.comparator;;
val digit_map : (int, string, Int.comparator) Map.t = <abstr>
# Map.find digit_map 3;;
- : string option = Some "three"
```

The preceding code uses `Map.of_alist_exn`, which creates a map from an association list, throwing an exception if there are duplicate keys in the list.

The comparator is only required for operations that create maps from scratch. Operations that update an existing map simply inherit the comparator of the map they start with:

OCaml utop (part 4)

```
# let zilch_map = Map.add digit_map ~key:0 ~data:"zilch";;
val zilch_map : (int, string, Int.comparator) Map.t = <abstr>
```

The type `Map.t` has three type parameters: one for the key, one for the value, and one to identify the comparator. Indeed, the type `'a Int.Map.t` is just a type alias for `(int,'a,Int.comparator) Map.t`.

Including the comparator in the type is important because operations that work on multiple maps at the same time often require that the maps share their comparison function. Consider, for example, `Map.symmetric_diff`, which computes a summary of the differences between two maps:

```
# let left = String.Map.of_alist_exn ["foo",1; "bar",3; "snoo",0]
  let right = String.Map.of_alist_exn ["foo",0; "snoo",0]
  let diff = Map.symmetric_diff ~data_equal:Int.equal left right
  ;;
val left : int String.Map.t = <abstr>
val right : int String.Map.t = <abstr>
val diff :
  (string * [ `Left of int | `Right of int | `Unequal of int * int ]) list =
  [("foo", `Unequal (1, 0)); ("bar", `Left 3)]
```

The type of `Map.symmetric_diff`, which follows, requires that the two maps it compares have the same comparator type. Each comparator has a fresh abstract type, so the type of a comparator identifies the comparator uniquely:

```
# Map.symmetric_diff;;
- : ('k, 'v, 'cmp) Map.t ->
    ('k, 'v, 'cmp) Map.t ->
    data_equal:('v -> 'v -> bool) ->
    ('k * [ `Left of 'v | `Right of 'v | `Unequal of 'v * 'v ]) list
= <fun>
```

This constraint is important because the algorithm that `Map.symmetric_diff` uses depends for its correctness on the fact that both maps have the same comparator.

We can create a new comparator using the `Comparator.Make` functor, which takes as its input a module containing the type of the object to be compared, sexp converter functions, and a comparison function. The sexp converters are included in the comparator to make it possible for users of the comparator to generate better error messages. Here's an example:

```
# module Reverse = Comparator.Make(struct
    type t = string
    let sexp_of_t = String.sexp_of_t
    let t_of_sexp = String.t_of_sexp
    let compare x y = String.compare y x
  end);;
module Reverse :
  sig
    type t = string
    val compare : t -> t -> int
    val t_of_sexp : Sexp.t -> t
    val sexp_of_t : t -> Sexp.t
    type comparator
    val comparator : (t, comparator) Comparator.t_
  end
```

As you can see in the following code, both `Reverse.comparator` and `String.compara
tor` can be used to create maps with a key type of `string`:

```
# let alist = ["foo", 0; "snoo", 3];;
val alist : (string * int) list = [("foo", 0); ("snoo", 3)]
# let ord_map = Map.of_alist_exn ~comparator:String.comparator alist;;
val ord_map : (string, int, String.comparator) Map.t = <abstr>
# let rev_map = Map.of_alist_exn ~comparator:Reverse.comparator alist;;
val rev_map : (string, int, Reverse.comparator) Map.t = <abstr>
```

Map.min_elt returns the key and value for the smallest key in the map, which lets us
see that these two maps do indeed use different comparison functions:

```
# Map.min_elt ord_map;;
- : (string * int) option = Some ("foo", 0)
# Map.min_elt rev_map;;
- : (string * int) option = Some ("snoo", 3)
```

Accordingly, if we try to use Map.symmetric_diff on these two maps, we'll get a
compile-time error:

```
# Map.symmetric_diff ord_map rev_map;;
Characters 27-34:
Error: This expression has type (string, int, Reverse.comparator) Map.t
       but an expression was expected of type
         (string, int, String.comparator) Map.t
       Type Reverse.comparator is not compatible with type String.comparator
```

Trees

As we've discussed, maps carry within them the comparator that they were created with.
Sometimes, often for space efficiency reasons, you want a version of the map data
structure that doesn't include the comparator. You can get such a representation with
Map.to_tree, which returns just the tree underlying the map, without the comparator:

```
# let ord_tree = Map.to_tree ord_map;;
val ord_tree : (string, int, String.comparator) Map.Tree.t = <abstr>
```

Even though a Map.Tree.t doesn't physically include a comparator, it does include the
comparator in its type. This is what is known as a *phantom type*, because it reflects
something about the logic of the value in question, even though it doesn't correspond
to any values directly represented in the underlying physical structure of the value.

Since the comparator isn't included in the tree, we need to provide the comparator
explicitly when we, say, search for a key, as shown below:

```
# Map.Tree.find ~comparator:String.comparator ord_tree "snoo";;
- : int option = Some 3
```

The algorithm of `Map.Tree.find` depends on the fact that it's using the same comparator when looking up a value as you were when you stored it. That's the invariant that the phantom type is there to enforce. As you can see in the following example, using the wrong comparator will lead to a type error:

OCaml utop (part 13)

```
# Map.Tree.find ~comparator:Reverse.comparator ord_tree "snoo";;
Characters 45-53:
Error: This expression has type (string, int, String.comparator) Map.Tree.t
       but an expression was expected of type
         (string, int, Reverse.comparator) Map.Tree.t
       Type String.comparator is not compatible with type Reverse.comparator
```

The Polymorphic Comparator

We don't need to generate specialized comparators for every type we want to build a map on. We can instead use a comparator based on OCaml's built-in polymorphic comparison function, which was discussed in Chapter 3. This comparator is found in the `Comparator.Poly` module, allowing us to write:

OCaml utop (part 14)

```
# Map.of_alist_exn ~comparator:Comparator.Poly.comparator digit_alist;;
- : (int, string, Comparator.Poly.comparator) Map.t = <abstr>
```

Or, equivalently:

OCaml utop (part 15)

```
# Map.Poly.of_alist_exn digit_alist;;
- : (int, string) Map.Poly.t = <abstr>
```

Note that maps based on the polymorphic comparator are not equivalent to those based on the type-specific comparators from the point of view of the type system. Thus, the compiler rejects the following:

OCaml utop (part 16)

```
# Map.symmetric_diff (Map.Poly.singleton 3 "three")
                     (Int.Map.singleton  3 "four" ) ;;
Characters 72-99:
Error: This expression has type
         string Int.Map.t = (int, string, Int.comparator) Map.t
       but an expression was expected of type
         (int, string, Comparator.Poly.comparator) Map.t
       Type Int.comparator is not compatible with type
         Comparator.Poly.comparator
```

This is rejected for good reason: there's no guarantee that the comparator associated with a given type will order things in the same way that polymorphic compare does.

The Perils of Polymorphic Compare

Polymorphic compare is highly convenient, but it has serious downsides as well and should be used with care. In particular, polymorphic compare has a fixed algorithm for comparing values of any type, and that algorithm can sometimes yield surprising results.

To understand what's wrong with polymorphic compare, you need to understand a bit about how it works. Polymorphic compare is *structural*, in that it operates directly on the runtime representation of OCaml values, walking the structure of the values in question without regard for their type.

This is convenient because it provides a comparison function that works for most OCaml values and largely behaves as you would expect. For example, on ints and floats, it acts as you would expect a numeric comparison function to act. For simple containers like strings and lists and arrays, it operates as a lexicographic comparison. And except for functions and values from outside of the OCaml heap, it works on almost every OCaml type.

But sometimes, a structural comparison is not what you want. Sets are a great example of this. Consider the following two sets:

OCaml utop (part 18)

```
# let (s1,s2) = (Int.Set.of_list [1;2],
                 Int.Set.of_list [2;1]);;
val s1 : Int.Set.t = <abstr>
val s2 : Int.Set.t = <abstr>
```

Logically, these two sets should be equal, and that's the result that you get if you call Set.equal on them:

OCaml utop (part 19)

```
# Set.equal s1 s2;;
- : bool = true
```

But because the elements were added in different orders, the layout of the trees underlying the sets will be different. As such, a structural comparison function will conclude that they're different.

Let's see what happens if we use polymorphic compare to test for equality by way of the = operator. Comparing the maps directly will fail at runtime because the comparators stored within the sets contain function values:

OCaml utop (part 20)

```
# s1 = s2;;
Exception: (Invalid_argument "equal: functional value").
```

We can, however, use the function `Set.to_tree` to expose the underlying tree without the attached comparator:

```
# Set.to_tree s1 = Set.to_tree s2;;
- : bool = false
```

This can cause real and quite subtle bugs. If, for example, you use a map whose keys contain sets, then the map built with the polymorphic comparator will behave incorrectly, separating out keys that should be aggregated together. Even worse, it will work sometimes and fail others; since if the sets are built in a consistent order, then they will work as expected, but once the order changes, the behavior will change.

Sets

Sometimes, instead of keeping track of a set of key/value pairs, you just want a data type for keeping track of a set of keys. You could build this on top of a map by representing a set of values by a map whose data type is `unit`. But a more idiomatic (and efficient) solution is to use Core's set type, which is similar in design and spirit to the map type, while having an API better tuned to working with sets and a lower memory footprint. Here's a simple example:

```
# let dedup ~comparator l =
    List.fold l ~init:(Set.empty ~comparator) ~f:Set.add
    |> Set.to_list
  ;;
val dedup :
  comparator:('a, 'b) Core_kernel.Comparator.t_ -> 'a list -> 'a list = <fun>
# dedup ~comparator:Int.comparator [8;3;2;3;7;8;10];;
- : int list = [2; 3; 7; 8; 10]
```

In addition to the operators you would expect to have for maps, sets support the traditional set operations, including union, intersection, and set difference. And, as with maps, we can create sets based on type-specific comparators or on the polymorphic comparator.

Satisfying the Comparable.S Interface

Core's `Comparable.S` interface includes a lot of useful functionality, including support for working with maps and sets. In particular, `Comparable.S` requires the presence of the Map and Set submodules, as well as a comparator.

`Comparable.S` is satisfied by most of the types in Core, but the question arises of how to satisfy the comparable interface for a new type that you design. Certainly implementing all of the required functionality from scratch would be an absurd amount of work.

The module `Comparable` contains a number of functors to help you automate this task. The simplest one of these is `Comparable.Make`, which takes as an input any module that satisfies the following interface:

OCaml

```ocaml
module type Comparable = sig
  type t
  val sexp_of_t : t -> Sexp.t
  val t_of_sexp : Sexp.t -> t
  val compare : t -> t -> int
end
```

In other words, it expects a type with a comparison function, as well as functions for converting to and from *s-expressions*. S-expressions are a serialization format used commonly in Core and are required here to enable better error messages. We'll discuss s-expressions more in Chapter 17, but in the meantime, we'll use the `with sexp` declaration that comes from the Sexplib syntax extension. This declaration kicks off the automatic generation of s-expression conversion functions for the marked type.

The following example shows how this all fits together, following the same basic pattern for using functors described in "Extending Modules" on page 189:

OCaml utop

```ocaml
# module Foo_and_bar : sig
    type t = { foo: Int.Set.t; bar: string }
    include Comparable.S with type t := t
  end = struct
    module T = struct
      type t = { foo: Int.Set.t; bar: string } with sexp
      let compare t1 t2 =
        let c = Int.Set.compare t1.foo t2.foo in
        if c <> 0 then c else String.compare t1.bar t2.bar
    end
    include T
    include Comparable.Make(T)
  end;;
module Foo_and_bar :
sig
  type t = { foo : Int.Set.t; bar : string; }
  val ( >= ) : t -> t -> bool
  val ( <= ) : t -> t -> bool
  val ( = ) : t -> t -> bool

  ...

end
```

We don't include the full response from the toplevel because it is quite lengthy, but `Foo_and_bar` does satisfy `Comparable.S`.

In the preceding code we wrote the comparison function by hand, but this isn't strictly necessary. Core ships with a syntax extension called comparelib, which will create a comparison function from a type definition. Using it, we can rewrite the previous example as follows:

OCaml utop

```
# module Foo_and_bar : sig
    type t = { foo: Int.Set.t; bar: string }
    include Comparable.S with type t := t
  end = struct
    module T = struct
      type t = { foo: Int.Set.t; bar: string } with sexp, compare
    end
    include T
    include Comparable.Make(T)
  end;;
module Foo_and_bar :
sig
  type t = { foo : Int.Set.t; bar : string; }
  val ( >= ) : t -> t -> bool
  val ( <= ) : t -> t -> bool
  val ( = ) : t -> t -> bool

  ...

end
```

The comparison function created by comparelib for a given type will call out to the comparison functions for its component types. As a result, the foo field will be compared using Int.Set.compare. This is different, and saner than the structural comparison done by polymorphic compare.

If you want your comparison function to behave in a specific way, you should still write your own comparison function by hand; but if all you want is a total order suitable for creating maps and sets with, then comparelib is a good way to go.

You can also satisfy the Comparable.S interface using polymorphic compare:

OCaml utop

```
# module Foo_and_bar : sig
    type t = { foo: int; bar: string }
    include Comparable.S with type t := t
  end = struct
    module T = struct
      type t = { foo: int; bar: string } with sexp
    end
    include T
    include Comparable.Poly(T)
  end;;
module Foo_and_bar :
sig
  type t = { foo : int; bar : string; }
```

```
val ( >= ) : t -> t -> bool
val ( <= ) : t -> t -> bool
val ( = ) : t -> t -> bool

...

end
```

That said, for reasons we discussed earlier, polymorphic compare should be used sparingly.

=, ==, and phys_equal

If you come from a C/C++ background, you'll probably reflexively use == to test two values for equality. In OCaml, the == operator tests for *physical* equality, while the = operator tests for *structural* equality.

The physical equality test will match if two data structures have precisely the same pointer in memory. Two data structures that have identical contents but are constructed separately will not match using ==.

The = structural equality operator recursively inspects each field in the two values and tests them individually for equality. Crucially, if your data structure is cyclical (that is, a value recursively points back to another field within the same structure), the = operator will never terminate, and your program will hang! You therefore must use the physical equality operator or write a custom comparison function when comparing cyclic values.

It's quite easy to mix up the use of = and ==, so Core disables the == operator and provides the more explicit phys_equal function instead. You'll see a type error if you use == anywhere in code that opens Core.Std:

OCaml utop

```
# open Core.Std ;;
# 1 == 2 ;;
Characters -1-1:
Error: This expression has type int but an expression was expected of type
        [ `Consider_using_phys_equal ]
# phys_equal 1 2 ;;
- : bool = false
```

If you feel like hanging your OCaml interpreter, you can verify what happens with recursive values and structural equality for yourself:

OCaml utop

```
# type t1 = { foo1:int; bar1:t2 } and t2 = { foo2:int; bar2:t1 } ;;
type t1 = { foo1 : int; bar1 : t2; }
and t2 = { foo2 : int; bar2 : t1; }
# let rec v1 = { foo1=1; bar1=v2 } and v2 = { foo2=2; bar2=v1 } ;;
<lots of text>
# v1 == v1;;
- : bool = true
```

```
# phys_equal v1 v1;;
- : bool = true
# v1 = v1 ;;
<press ^Z and kill the process now>
```

Hash Tables

Hash tables are the imperative cousin of maps. We walked over a basic hash table implementation in Chapter 8, so in this section we'll mostly discuss the pragmatics of Core's Hashtbl module. We'll cover this material more briefly than we did with maps because many of the concepts are shared.

Hash tables differ from maps in a few key ways. First, hash tables are mutable, meaning that adding a key/value pair to a hash table modifies the table, rather than creating a new table with the binding added. Second, hash tables generally have better time-complexity than maps, providing constant-time lookup and modifications, as opposed to logarithmic for maps. And finally, just as maps depend on having a comparison function for creating the ordered binary tree that underlies a map, hash tables depend on having a *hash function*, i.e., a function for converting a key to an integer.

Time Complexity of Hash Tables

The statement that hash tables provide constant-time access hides some complexities. First of all, any hash table implementation, OCaml's included, needs to resize the table when it gets too full. A resize requires allocating a new backing array for the hash table and copying over all entries, and so it is quite an expensive operation. That means adding a new element to the table is only *amortized* constant, which is to say, it's constant on average over a long sequence of operations, but some of the individual operations can be quite expensive.

Another hidden cost of hash tables has to do with the hash function you use. If you end up with a pathologically bad hash function that hashes all of your data to the same number, then all of your insertions will hash to the same underlying bucket, meaning you no longer get constant-time access at all. Core's hash table implementation uses binary trees for the hash-buckets, so this case only leads to logarithmic time, rather than linear for a traditional hash table.

The logarithmic behavior of Core's hash tables in the presence of hash collisions also helps protect against some denial-of-service attacks. One well-known type of attack is to send queries to a service with carefully chosen keys to cause many collisions. This, in combination with the linear behavior of most hashtables, can cause the service to become unresponsive due to high CPU load. Core's hash tables would be much less susceptible to such an attack because the amount of degradation would be far less.

When creating a hash table, we need to provide a value of type *hashable*, which includes among other things the function for hashing the key type. This is analogous to the comparator used for creating maps:

OCaml utop (part 25)

```
# let table = Hashtbl.create ~hashable:String.hashable ();;
val table : (string, '_a) Hashtbl.t = <abstr>
# Hashtbl.replace table ~key:"three" ~data:3;;
- : unit = ()
# Hashtbl.find table "three";;
- : int option = Some 3
```

The `hashable` value is included as part of the `Hashable.S` interface, which is satisfied by most types in Core. The `Hashable.S` interface also includes a `Table` submodule which provides more convenient creation functions:

OCaml utop (part 26)

```
# let table = String.Table.create ();;
val table : '_a String.Table.t = <abstr>
```

There is also a polymorphic `hashable` value, corresponding to the polymorphic hash function provided by the OCaml runtime, for cases where you don't have a hash function for your specific type:

OCaml utop (part 27)

```
# let table = Hashtbl.create ~hashable:Hashtbl.Poly.hashable ();;
val table : ('_a, '_b) Hashtbl.t = <abstr>
```

Or, equivalently:

OCaml utop (part 28)

```
# let table = Hashtbl.Poly.create ();;
val table : ('_a, '_b) Hashtbl.t = <abstr>
```

Note that, unlike the comparators used with maps and sets, hashables don't show up in the type of a `Hashtbl.t`. That's because hash tables don't have operations that operate on multiple hash tables that depend on those tables having the same hash function, in the way that `Map.symmetric_diff` and `Set.union` depend on their arguments using the same comparison function.

Collisions with the Polymorphic Hash Function

OCaml's polymorphic hash function works by walking over the data structure it's given using a breadth-first traversal that is bounded in the number of nodes it's willing to traverse. By default, that bound is set at 10 "meaningful" nodes.

The bound on the traversal means that the hash function may ignore part of the data structure, and this can lead to pathological cases where every value you store has the same hash value. We'll demonstrate this below, using the function List.range to allocate lists of integers of different length:

OCaml utop (part 29)

```
# Caml.Hashtbl.hash (List.range 0 9);;
- : int = 209331808
# Caml.Hashtbl.hash (List.range 0 10);;
- : int = 182325193
# Caml.Hashtbl.hash (List.range 0 11);;
- : int = 182325193
# Caml.Hashtbl.hash (List.range 0 100);;
- : int = 182325193
```

As you can see, the hash function stops after the first 10 elements. The same can happen with any large data structure, including records and arrays. When building hash functions over large custom data structures, it is generally a good idea to write one's own hash function.

Satisfying the Hashable.S Interface

Most types in Core satisfy the Hashable.S interface, but as with the Comparable.S interface, the question remains of how one should satisfy this interface when writing a new module. Again, the answer is to use a functor to build the necessary functionality; in this case, Hashable.Make. Note that we use OCaml's lxor operator for doing the "logical" (i.e., bitwise) exclusive Or of the hashes from the component values:

OCaml utop

```
# module Foo_and_bar : sig
    type t = { foo: int; bar: string }
    include Hashable.S with type t := t
  end = struct
    module T = struct
      type t = { foo: int; bar: string } with sexp, compare
      let hash t =
        (Int.hash t.foo) lxor (String.hash t.bar)
    end
    include T
    include Hashable.Make(T)
  end;;
module Foo_and_bar :
sig
  type t = { foo : int; bar : string; }
```

```
module Hashable : sig type t = t end
val hash : t -> int
val compare : t -> t -> int
val hashable : t Pooled_hashtbl.Hashable.t

...

end
```

Note that in order to satisfy hashable, one also needs to provide a comparison function. That's because Core's hash tables use an ordered binary tree data structure for the hash-buckets, so that performance of the table degrades gracefully in the case of pathologically bad choice of hash function.

There is currently no analogue of comparelib for autogeneration of hash functions, so you do need to either write the hash function by hand, or use the built-in polymorphic hash function, Hashtbl.hash.

Choosing Between Maps and Hash Tables

Maps and hash tables overlap enough in functionality that it's not always clear when to choose one or the other. Maps, by virtue of being immutable, are generally the default choice in OCaml. OCaml also has good support for imperative programming, though, and when programming in an imperative idiom, hash tables are often the more natural choice.

Programming idioms aside, there are significant performance differences between maps and hash tables. For code that is dominated by updates and lookups, hash tables are a clear performance win, and the win is clearer the larger the amount of data.

The best way of answering a performance question is by running a benchmark, so let's do just that. The following benchmark uses the core_bench library, and it compares maps and hash tables under a very simple workload. Here, we're keeping track of a set of 1,000 different integer keys and cycling over the keys and updating the values they contain. Note that we use the Map.change and Hashtbl.change functions to update the respective data structures:

OCaml

```
open Core.Std
open Core_bench.Std

let map_iter ~num_keys ~iterations =
  let rec loop i map =
    if i <= 0 then ()
    else loop (i - 1)
           (Map.change map (i mod num_keys) (fun current ->
               Some (1 + Option.value ~default:0 current)))
  in
  loop iterations Int.Map.empty
```

```
let table_iter ~num_keys ~iterations =
  let table = Int.Table.create ~size:num_keys () in
  let rec loop i =
    if i <= 0 then ()
    else (
      Hashtbl.change table (i mod num_keys) (fun current ->
        Some (1 + Option.value ~default:0 current));
      loop (i - 1)
    )
  in
  loop iterations

let tests ~num_keys ~iterations =
  let test name f = Bench.Test.create f ~name in
  [ test "map"   (fun () -> map_iter   ~num_keys ~iterations)
  ; test "table" (fun () -> table_iter ~num_keys ~iterations)
  ]

let () =
  tests ~num_keys:1000 ~iterations:100_000
  |> Bench.make_command
  |> Command.run
```

The results show the hash table version to be around four times faster than the map version:

Terminal

```
$ corebuild -pkg core_bench map_vs_hash.native
$ ./map_vs_hash.native -ascii -clear-columns name time speedup
Estimated testing time 20s (change using -quota SECS).

  Name     Time (ns)   Speedup
 -------  -----------  ---------
  map      31_698_313    1.00
  table     7_202_631    4.40
```

We can make the speedup smaller or larger depending on the details of the test; for example, it will vary with the number of distinct keys. But overall, for code that is heavy on sequences of querying and updating a set of key/value pairs, hash tables will significantly outperform maps.

Hash tables are not always the faster choice, though. In particular, maps are often more performant in situations where you need to keep multiple related versions of the data structure in memory at once. That's because maps are immutable, and so operations like Map.add that modify a map do so by creating a new map, leaving the original undisturbed. Moreover, the new and old maps share most of their physical structure, so multiple versions can be kept around efficiently.

Here's a benchmark that demonstrates this. In it, we create a list of maps (or hash tables) that are built up by iteratively applying small updates, keeping these copies around. In the map case, this is done by using `Map.change` to update the map. In the hash table implementation, the updates are done using `Hashtbl.change`, but we also need to call `Hashtbl.copy` to take snapshots of the table:

OCaml

```ocaml
open Core.Std
open Core_bench.Std

let create_maps ~num_keys ~iterations =
  let rec loop i map =
    if i <= 0 then []
    else
      let new_map =
        Map.change map (i mod num_keys) (fun current ->
          Some (1 + Option.value ~default:0 current))
      in
      new_map :: loop (i - 1) new_map
  in
  loop iterations Int.Map.empty

let create_tables ~num_keys ~iterations =
  let table = Int.Table.create ~size:num_keys () in
  let rec loop i =
    if i <= 0 then []
    else (
      Hashtbl.change table (i mod num_keys) (fun current ->
        Some (1 + Option.value ~default:0 current));
      let new_table = Hashtbl.copy table in
      new_table :: loop (i - 1)
    )
  in
  loop iterations

let tests ~num_keys ~iterations =
  let test name f = Bench.Test.create f ~name in
  [ test "map"   (fun () -> ignore (create_maps   ~num_keys ~iterations))
  ; test "table" (fun () -> ignore (create_tables ~num_keys ~iterations))
  ]

let () =
  tests ~num_keys:50 ~iterations:1000
  |> Bench.make_command
  |> Command.run
```

Unsurprisingly, maps perform far better than hash tables on this benchmark, in this case by more than a factor of 10:

Terminal

```
$ corebuild -pkg core_bench map_vs_hash2.native
$ ./map_vs_hash2.native -ascii -clear-columns name time speedup
```

```
Estimated testing time 20s (change using -quota SECS).

  Name    Time (ns)   Speedup
  -------  -----------  ---------
  map        218_581     12.03
  table    2_628_423      1.00
```

These numbers can be made more extreme by increasing the size of the tables or the length of the list.

As you can see, the relative performance of trees and maps depends a great deal on the details of how they're used, and so whether to choose one data structure or the other will depend on the details of the application.

## CHAPTER 14

Command-Line Parsing

Many of the OCaml programs that you'll write will end up as binaries that need to be run from a command prompt. Any nontrivial command line should support a collection of basic features:

- Parsing of command-line arguments
- Generation of error messages in response to incorrect inputs
- Help for all the available options
- Interactive autocompletion

It's tedious and error-prone to code all of this manually for every program you write. Core provides the Command library, which simplifies all of this by letting you declare all your command-line options in one place and by deriving all of the above functionality from these declarations.

Command is simple to use for simple applications but also scales well as your needs grow more complex. In particular, Command provides a sophisticated subcommand mode that groups related commands together as the complexity of your user interface grows. You may already be familiar with this command-line style from the Git or Mercurial version control systems.

In this chapter, we'll:

- Learn how to use Command to construct basic and grouped command-line interfaces
- We will build simple equivalents to the cryptographic md5 and shasum utilities
- Demonstrate how *functional combinators* can be used to declare complex command-line interfaces in a type-safe and elegant way

Basic Command-Line Parsing

Let's start by working through a clone of the *md5sum* command that is present on most Linux installations (the equivalent command on Mac OS X is simply md5). The following function defined below reads in the contents of a file, applies the MD5 one-way cryptographic hash function to the data, and outputs an ASCII hex representation of the result:

OCaml

```
open Core.Std

let do_hash file =
  In_channel.with_file file ~f:(fun ic ->
    let open Cryptokit in
    hash_channel (Hash.md5 ()) ic
    |> transform_string (Hexa.encode ())
    |> print_endline
  )
```

The do_hash function accepts a filename parameter and prints the human-readable MD5 string to the console standard output. The first step toward turning this function into a command-line program is to declare all the possible command-line arguments in a *specification*. Command.Spec defines combinators that can be chained together to define optional flags and positional arguments, what types they should map to, and whether to take special actions (such as pausing for interactive input) if certain inputs are encountered.

Anonymous Arguments

Let's build the specification for a single argument that is passed directly on the command line. This is known as an *anonymous* argument:

OCaml (part 1)

```
let spec =
  let open Command.Spec in
  empty
  +> anon ("filename" %: string)
```

The Command.Spec module defines the tools you'll need to build up a command-line specification. We start with the empty value and add parameters to that using the +> combinator. (Both of these values come from Command.Spec.)

In this case, we defined a single anonymous argument called filename, which takes a value of type string. Anonymous parameters are created using the %: operator, which binds a textual name (used in the help text to identify the parameter) to an OCaml conversion function that parses the command-line string fragments into a higher-level OCaml data type. In the preceding example, this is just Command.Spec.string, but we'll see more complex conversion options later in the chapter.

Defining Basic Commands

Once we've defined a specification, we need to put it to work on real input. The simplest way is to directly create a command-line interface via the `Command.basic` module:

OCaml (part 2)

```
let command =
  Command.basic
    ~summary:"Generate an MD5 hash of the input data"
    ~readme:(fun () -> "More detailed information")
    spec
    (fun filename () -> do_hash filename)
```

`Command.basic` defines a complete command-line interface that takes the following extra arguments, in addition to the ones defined in the specification:

summary

A required one-line description to go at the top of the command help screen.

readme

For longer help text when the command is called with `-help`. The `readme` argument is a function that is only evaluated when the help text is actually needed.

The specification and the callback function follow as nonlabeled arguments.

The callback function is where all the work happens after the command-line parsing is complete. This function is applied with the arguments containing the parsed command-line values, and it takes over as the main thread of the application. The callback's arguments are passed in the same order as they were bound in the specification (using the `+>` operator).

The Extra unit Argument to Callbacks

The preceding callback needs an extra `unit` argument after `file name`. This is to ensure that specifications can work even when they are empty (i.e. the `Command.Spec.empty` value).

Every OCaml function needs at least one argument, so the final `unit` guarantees that it will not be evaluated immediately as a value if there are no other arguments.

Running Basic Commands

Once we've defined the basic command, running it is just one function call away:

OCaml (part 3)

```
let () =
  Command.run ~version:"1.0" ~build_info:"RWO" command
```

`Command.run` takes a couple of optional arguments that are useful to identify which version of the binary you are running in production. You'll need to install Cryptokit via `opam install cryptokit` before building this example. Once that's completed, run the following to compile the binary:

Terminal

```
$ corebuild -pkg cryptokit basic_md5.native
```

You can now query the version information for the binary you just compiled:

Terminal

```
$ ./basic_md5.native -version
1.0
$ ./basic_md5.native -build-info
RWO
```

The versions that you see in the output were defined via the optional arguments to `Command.run`. You can leave these blank in your own programs or get your build system to generate them directly from your version control system (e.g., by running `hg id` to generate a build revision number, in the case of Mercurial):

Terminal

```
$ ./basic_md5.native
Generate an MD5 hash of the input data

  basic_md5.native FILENAME

More detailed information

=== flags ===

  [-build-info]  print info about this build and exit
  [-version]     print the version of this build and exit
  [-help]        print this help text and exit
                 (alias: -?)

missing anonymous argument: FILENAME
```

When we invoke this binary without any arguments, it helpfully displays all of the command-line options available, along with a message to the standard error that informs you that a required argument `filename` is missing.

If you do supply the `filename` argument, then `do_hash` is called with the argument and the MD5 output is displayed to the standard output:

Terminal

```
$ ./basic_md5.native ./basic_md5.native
b5ee7de449a2e0c6c01d4f2d898926de
```

And that's all it took to build our little MD5 utility! Here's a complete version of the example we just walked through, made slightly more succinct by removing intermediate variables:

```
open Core.Std

let do_hash file () =
  In_channel.with_file file ~f:(fun ic ->
    let open Cryptokit in
    hash_channel (Hash.md5 ()) ic
    |> transform_string (Hexa.encode ())
    |> print_endline
  )

let command =
  Command.basic
    ~summary:"Generate an MD5 hash of the input data"
    ~readme:(fun () -> "More detailed information")
    Command.Spec.(empty +> anon ("filename" %: string))
    do_hash

let () =
  Command.run ~version:"1.0" ~build_info:"RWO" command
```

Now that we have the basics in place, the rest of the chapter will examine some of the more advanced features of Command.

Argument Types

You aren't just limited to parsing command lines as strings, of course. Command.Spec defines several other conversion functions (shown in Table 14-1) that validate and parse input into various types.

Table 14-1. Conversion functions defined by Command.spec

Argument type	OCaml type	Example
string	string	foo
int	int	123
float	float	123.01
bool	bool	true
date	Date.t	2013-12-25
time_span	Span.t	5s
file	string	/etc/passwd

We can tighten up the specification of the command to file to reflect that the argument must be a valid filename, and not just any string:

```
let command =
  Command.basic
    ~summary:"Generate an MD5 hash of the input data"
```

```
    ~readme:(fun () -> "More detailed information")
    Command.Spec.(empty +> anon ("filename" %: file))
    do_hash

let () =
  Command.run ~version:"1.0" ~build_info:"RWO" command
```

Running this with a nonexistent filename will now output an error if the file doesn't exist. As a bonus, it also enables interactive command-line completion to work on the filename argument (explained later in the chapter):

Terminal

```
$ ./basic_md5_as_filename.native nonexistent
Uncaught exception:

  (Sys_error "nonexistent: No such file or directory")

Raised by primitive operation at file "pervasives.ml", line 292, characters 20-46
Called from file "lib/in_channel.ml", line 19, characters 46-65
Called from file "lib/exn.ml", line 87, characters 6-10
```

Defining Custom Argument Types

We can also define our own argument types if the predefined ones aren't sufficient. For instance, let's make a `regular_file` argument type that ensures that the input file isn't a character device or some other odd UNIX file type that can't be fully read:

OCaml

```
open Core.Std

let do_hash file () =
  In_channel.with_file file ~f:(fun ic ->
    let open Cryptokit in
    hash_channel (Hash.md5 ()) ic
    |> transform_string (Hexa.encode ())
    |> print_endline
  )

let regular_file =
  Command.Spec.Arg_type.create
    (fun filename ->
      match Sys.is_file filename with
      | `Yes -> filename
      | `No | `Unknown ->
        eprintf "'%s' is not a regular file.\n%!" filename;
        exit 1
    )

let command =
  Command.basic
    ~summary:"Generate an MD5 hash of the input data"
    ~readme:(fun () -> "More detailed information")
```

```
Command.Spec.(empty +> anon ("filename" %: regular_file))
do_hash

let () =
  Command.run ~version:"1.0" ~build_info:"RWO" command
```

The `regular_file` function transforms a `filename` string parameter into the same string but first checks that the file exists and is a regular file type. When you build and run this code, you will see the new error messages if you try to open a special device such as /dev/null:

Terminal

```
$ ./basic_md5_with_custom_arg.native /etc/passwd
8cfb68a5622dd12932df658a54698aad
$ ./basic_md5_with_custom_arg.native /dev/null
'/dev/null' is not a regular file.
```

Optional and Default Arguments

A more realistic MD5 binary could also read from the standard input if a `filename` isn't specified:

OCaml (part 1)

```
let command =
  Command.basic
    ~summary:"Generate an MD5 hash of the input data"
    ~readme:(fun () -> "More detailed information")
    Command.Spec.(empty +> anon (maybe ("filename" %: string)))
    do_hash

let () =
  Command.run ~version:"1.0" ~build_info:"RWO" command
```

This just wraps the `filename` argument declaration in the `maybe` function to mark it as an optional argument. However, building this results in a compile-time error:

Terminal

```
$ corebuild -pkg cryptokit basic_md5_with_optional_file_broken.native
File "basic_md5_with_optional_file_broken.ml", line 18, characters 4-11:
Error: This expression has type string -> unit -> unit
       but an expression was expected of type string option -> unit -> unit
       Type string is not compatible with type string option
Command exited with code 2.
```

This is because changing the argument type has also changed the type of the callback function. It now wants a `string option` instead of a `string`, since the value has become optional. We can adapt our example to use the new information and read from standard input if no file is specified:

OCaml

```
open Core.Std
```

```
let get_inchan = function
  | None | Some "-" ->
    In_channel.stdin
  | Some filename ->
    In_channel.create ~binary:true filename

let do_hash filename () =
  let open Cryptokit in
  get_inchan filename
  |> hash_channel (Hash.md5 ())
  |> transform_string (Hexa.encode ())
  |> print_endline

let command =
  Command.basic
    ~summary:"Generate an MD5 hash of the input data"
    ~readme:(fun () -> "More detailed information")
    Command.Spec.(empty +> anon (maybe ("filename" %: file)))
    do_hash

let () =
  Command.run ~version:"1.0" ~build_info:"RWO" command
```

The `filename` parameter to do_hash is now a `string option` type. This is resolved into an input channel via `get_inchan` to determine whether to open the standard input or a file, and then the rest of the command is similar to our previous examples.

Another possible way to handle this would be to supply a dash as the default filename if one isn't specified. The `maybe_with_default` function can do just this, with the benefit of not having to change the callback parameter type (which may be a problem in more complex applications).

The following example behaves exactly the same as the previous example, but replaces `maybe` with `maybe_with_default`:

OCaml

```
open Core.Std

let get_inchan = function
  | "-"      -> In_channel.stdin
  | filename -> In_channel.create ~binary:true filename

let do_hash filename () =
  let open Cryptokit in
  get_inchan filename
  |> hash_channel (Hash.md5 ())
  |> transform_string (Hexa.encode ())
  |> print_endline

let command =
  Command.basic
    ~summary:"Generate an MD5 hash of the input data"
```

```
~readme:(fun () -> "More detailed information")
Command.Spec.(
  empty
  +> anon (maybe_with_default "-" ("filename" %: file))
)
do_hash

let () =
  Command.run ~version:"1.0" ~build_info:"RWO" command
```

Building and running both against a system file confirms that they have the same behavior:

Terminal

```
$ cat /etc/passwd | ./basic_md5_with_optional_file.native
8cfb68a5622dd12932df658a54698aad
$ cat /etc/passwd | ./basic_md5_with_default_file.native
8cfb68a5622dd12932df658a54698aad
```

Sequences of Arguments

One last transformation that's useful is to obtain lists of anonymous arguments rather than a single one. As an example, let's modify our MD5 code to take a collection of files to process on the command line:

OCaml

```
open Core.Std

let do_hash filename ic =
  let open Cryptokit in
  hash_channel (Hash.md5 ()) ic
  |> transform_string (Hexa.encode ())
  |> fun md5 -> printf "MD5 (%s) = %s\n" filename md5

let command =
  Command.basic
    ~summary:"Generate an MD5 hash of the input data"
    ~readme:(fun () -> "More detailed information")
    Command.Spec.(empty +> anon (sequence ("filename" %: file)))
    (fun files () ->
      match files with
      | [] -> do_hash "-" In_channel.stdin
      | _ ->
        List.iter files ~f:(fun file ->
          In_channel.with_file ~f:(do_hash file) file
        )
    )

let () =
  Command.run ~version:"1.0" ~build_info:"RWO" command
```

The callback function is a little more complex now, to handle the extra options. The files are now a `string list`, and an empty list reverts to using standard input, just as our previous `maybe` and `maybe_with_default` examples did. If the list of files isn't empty, then it opens up each file and runs them through do_hash sequentially.

Adding Labeled Flags to the Command Line

You aren't just limited to anonymous arguments on the command line. A *flag* is a named field that can be followed by an optional argument. These flags can appear in any order on the command line, or multiple times, depending on how they're declared in the specification.

Let's add two arguments to our md5 command that mimics the Mac OS X version. A -s flag specifies the string to be hashed directly on the command line and -t runs a self-test. The complete example follows:

OCaml

```
open Core.Std
open Cryptokit

let checksum_from_string buf =
  hash_string (Hash.md5 ()) buf
  |> transform_string (Hexa.encode ())
  |> print_endline

let checksum_from_file filename =
  let ic = match filename with
    | "-" -> In_channel.stdin
    | _   -> In_channel.create ~binary:true filename
  in
  hash_channel (Hash.md5 ()) ic
  |> transform_string (Hexa.encode ())
  |> print_endline

let command =
  Command.basic
    ~summary:"Generate an MD5 hash of the input data"
    Command.Spec.(
      empty
      +> flag "-s" (optional string) ~doc:"string Checksum the given string"
      +> flag "-t" no_arg ~doc:" run a built-in time trial"
      +> anon (maybe_with_default "-" ("filename" %: file))
    )
    (fun use_string trial filename () ->
      match trial with
      | true -> printf "Running time trial\n"
      | false -> begin
          match use_string with
          | Some buf -> checksum_from_string buf
          | None -> checksum_from_file filename
```

```
        end
    )

let () = Command.run command
```

The specification now uses the flag function to define the two new labeled, command-line arguments. The doc string is formatted so that the first word is the short name that appears in the usage text, with the remainder being the full help text. Notice that the -t flag has no argument, and so we prepend its doc text with a blank space. The help text for the preceding code looks like this:

Terminal

```
$ ./basic_md5_with_flags.native -help
Generate an MD5 hash of the input data

  basic_md5_with_flags.native [FILENAME]

=== flags ===

  [-s string]     Checksum the given string
  [-t]            run a built-in time trial
  [-build-info]   print info about this build and exit
  [-version]      print the version of this build and exit
  [-help]         print this help text and exit
                  (alias: -?)

$ ./basic_md5_with_flags.native -s "ocaml rocks"
5a118fe92ac3b6c7854c595ecf6419cb
```

The -s flag in our specification requires a string argument and isn't optional. The Command parser outputs an error message if the flag isn't supplied, as with the anonymous arguments in earlier examples. Table 14-2 contains a list of some of the functions that you can wrap flags in to control how they are parsed.

Table 14-2. Flag functions

Flag function	OCaml type
required *arg*	*arg* and error if not present
optional *arg*	*arg* option
optional_with_default *val arg*	*arg* with default *val* if not present
listed *arg*	*arg* list, flag may appear multiple times
no_arg	bool that is true if flag is present

The flags affect the type of the callback function in exactly the same way as anonymous arguments do. This lets you change the specification and ensure that all the callback functions are updated appropriately, without runtime errors.

Grouping Subcommands Together

You can get pretty far by using flags and anonymous arguments to assemble complex, command-line interfaces. After a while, though, too many options can make the program very confusing for newcomers to your application. One way to solve this is by grouping common operations together and adding some hierarchy to the command-line interface.

You'll have run across this style already when using the OPAM package manager (or, in the non-OCaml world, the Git or Mercurial commands). OPAM exposes commands in this form:

Terminal

```
$ opam config env
$ opam remote list -k git
$ opam install --help
$ opam install cryptokit --verbose
```

The `config`, `remote`, and `install` keywords form a logical grouping of commands that factor out a set of flags and arguments. This lets you prevent flags that are specific to a particular subcommand from leaking into the general configuration space.

This usually only becomes a concern when your application organically grows features. Luckily, it's simple to extend your application to do this in Command: just swap the `Command.basic` for `Command.group`, which takes an association list of specifications and handles the subcommand parsing and help output for you:

OCaml utop

```
# Command.basic ;;
- : summary:string ->
    ?readme:(unit -> string) ->
    ('main, unit -> unit) Command.Spec.t -> 'main -> Command.t
= <fun>
# Command.group ;;
- : summary:string ->
    ?readme:(unit -> string) -> (string * Command.t) list -> Command.t
= <fun>
```

The `group` signature accepts a list of basic `Command.t` values and their corresponding names. When executed, it looks for the appropriate subcommand from the name list, and dispatches it to the right command handler.

Let's build the outline of a calendar tool that does a few operations over dates from the command line. We first need to define a command that adds days to an input date and prints the resulting date:

OCaml

```
open Core.Std

let add =
```

```
Command.basic
  ~summary:"Add [days] to the [base] date and print day"
  Command.Spec.(
    empty
    +> anon ("base" %: date)
    +> anon ("days" %: int)
  )
  (fun base span () ->
    Date.add_days base span
    |> Date.to_string
    |> print_endline
  )

let () = Command.run add
```

Everything in this command should be familiar to you by now. Once you've tested it and made sure it works, we can define another new command that takes the difference of two dates. However, instead of creating a new binary, we group both operations as subcommands using Command.group:

OCaml

```
open Core.Std

let add =
  Command.basic ~summary:"Add [days] to the [base] date"
    Command.Spec.(
      empty
      +> anon ("base" %: date)
      +> anon ("days" %: int)
    )
    (fun base span () ->
      Date.add_days base span
      |> Date.to_string
      |> print_endline
    )

let diff =
  Command.basic ~summary:"Show days between [date1] and [date2]"
    Command.Spec.(
      empty
      +> anon ("date1" %: date)
      +> anon ("date2" %: date)
    )
    (fun date1 date2 () ->
      Date.diff date1 date2
      |> printf "%d days\n"
    )

let command =
  Command.group ~summary:"Manipulate dates"
    [ "add", add; "diff", diff ]
```

```
    let () = Command.run command
```

And that's all you really need to add subcommand support! Let's build the example first in the usual way and inspect the help output, which now reflects the subcommands we just added.

Terminal

```
$ corebuild cal_add_sub_days.native
$ ./cal_add_sub_days.native -help
Manipulate dates

  cal_add_sub_days.native SUBCOMMAND

=== subcommands ===

  add      Add [days] to the [base] date
  diff     Show days between [date1] and [date2]
  version  print version information
  help     explain a given subcommand (perhaps recursively)
```

We can invoke the two commands we just defined to verify that they work and see the date parsing in action:

Terminal

```
$ ./cal_add_sub_days.native add 2012-12-25 40
2013-02-03
$ ./cal_add_sub_days.native diff 2012-12-25 2012-11-01
54 days
```

Advanced Control over Parsing

The functions for generating a specification may seem like magic. In particular, even if you know how to use them, it's not entirely clear how they work, and in particular, why the types work out the way they do.

Understanding the details of how these specifications fit together becomes more useful as your command-line interfaces get more complex. In particular, you may want to factor out common functionality between specifications or interrupt the parsing to perform special processing, such as requesting an interactive passphrase from the user before proceeding. All of this is helped by a deeper understanding of the Command library.

In the following sections we'll explain the logic behind the combinators we've already described and show you some new combinators that let you use Command even more effectively.

The Types Behind Command.Spec

The Command module's safety relies on the specification's output values precisely matching the callback function which invokes the main program. In order to prevent any such mismatches, Command uses some interesting type machinery to guarantee they remain in sync. You don't have to understand this section to use the more advanced combinators, but it'll help you debug type errors as you use Command more.

The Command.Spec.t type looks deceptively simple: ('a, 'b) t. You can think of ('a, 'b) t here as a function of type 'a -> 'b, but embellished with information about:

- How to parse the command line
- What the command does and how to call it
- How to autocomplete a partial command line

The type of a specification transforms a 'a to a 'b value. For instance, a value of Spec.t might have type (arg1 -> ... -> argN -> 'r, 'r) Spec.t.

Such a value transforms a main function of type arg1 -> ... -> argN -> 'r by supplying all the argument values, leaving a main function that returns a value of type 'r. Let's look at some examples of specs, and their types:

OCaml utop

```
# Command.Spec.empty ;;
- : ('m, 'm) Command.Spec.t = <abstr>
# Command.Spec.(empty +> anon ("foo" %: int)) ;;
- : (int -> '_a, '_a) Command.Spec.t = <abstr>
```

The empty specification is simple, as it doesn't add any parameters to the callback type. The second example adds an int anonymous parameter that is reflected in the inferred type. One forms a command by combining a spec of type ('main, unit) Spec.t with a function of type 'main. The combinators we've shown so far incrementally build the type of 'main according to the command-line parameters it expects, so the resulting type of 'main is something like arg1 -> ... -> argN -> unit.

The type of Command.basic should make more sense now:

OCaml utop

```
# Command.basic ;;
- : summary:string ->
    ?readme:(unit -> string) ->
    ('main, unit -> unit) Command.Spec.t -> 'main -> Command.t
= <fun>
```

The parameters to Spec.t are important here. They show that the callback function for a spec should consume identical arguments to the supplied main function, except for an additional unit argument. This final unit is there to make sure the callback is evaluated as a function, since if zero command-line arguments are specified (i.e.,

`Spec.empty`), the callback would otherwise have no arguments and be evaluated immediately. That's why you have to supply an additional `()` to the callback function in all the previous examples.

Composing Specification Fragments Together

If you want to factor out common command-line operations, the `++` operator will append two specifications together. Let's add some dummy verbosity and debug flags to our calendar application to illustrate this.

OCaml

```
open Core.Std

let add ~common =
  Command.basic ~summary:"Add [days] to the [base] date"
    Command.Spec.(
      empty
      +> anon ("base" %: date)
      +> anon ("days" %: int)
      ++ common
    )
    (fun base span debug verbose () ->
       Date.add_days base span
       |> Date.to_string
       |> print_endline
    )

let diff ~common =
  Command.basic ~summary:"Show days between [date2] and [date1]"
    Command.Spec.(
      empty
      +> anon ("date1" %: date)
      +> anon ("date2" %: date)
      ++ common
    )
    (fun date1 date2 debug verbose () ->
       Date.diff date1 date2
       |> printf "%d days\n"
    )
```

The definitions of the specifications are very similar to the earlier example, except that they append a `common` parameter after each specification. We can supply these flags when defining the groups.

OCaml (part 1)

```
let () =
  let common =
    Command.Spec.(
      empty
      +> flag "-d" (optional_with_default false bool) ~doc:" Debug mode"
      +> flag "-v" (optional_with_default false bool) ~doc:" Verbose output"
```

```
    )
  in
  List.map ~f:(fun (name, cmd) -> (name, cmd ~common))
    [ "add", add; "diff", diff ]
  |> Command.group ~summary:"Manipulate dates"
  |> Command.run
```

Both of these flags will now be applied and passed to all the callback functions. This makes code refactoring a breeze by using the compiler to spot places where you use commands. Just add a parameter to the common definition, run the compiler, and fix type errors until everything works again.

For example, if we remove the `verbose` flag and recompile, we'll get this impressively long type error:

```
$ corebuild cal_append_broken.native
File "cal_append_broken.ml", line 38, characters 45-52:
Error: This expression has type
         (bool -> unit -> unit -> unit, unit -> unit -> unit) Command.Spec.t
       but an expression was expected of type
         (bool -> unit -> unit -> unit, unit -> unit) Command.Spec.t
       Type unit -> unit is not compatible with type unit
Command exited with code 2.
```

While this does look scary, the key line to scan is the last one, where it's telling you that you have supplied too many arguments in the callback function (`unit -> unit` versus `unit`). If you started with a working program and made this single change, you typically don't even need to read the type error, as the filename and location information is sufficient to make the obvious fix.

Prompting for Interactive Input

The `step` combinator lets you control the normal course of parsing by supplying a function that maps callback arguments to a new set of values. For instance, let's revisit our first calendar application that added a number of days onto a supplied base date:

```
open Core.Std

let add =
  Command.basic
    ~summary:"Add [days] to the [base] date and print day"
    Command.Spec.(
      empty
      +> anon ("base" %: date)
      +> anon ("days" %: int)
    )
    (fun base span () ->
       Date.add_days base span
       |> Date.to_string
```

```
      |> print_endline
    )

let () = Command.run add
```

This program requires you to specify both the **base** date and the number of **days** to add onto it. If **days** isn't supplied on the command line, an error is output. Now let's modify it to interactively prompt for a number of days if only the **base** date is supplied:

OCaml

```
open Core.Std

let add_days base span () =
  Date.add_days base span
  |> Date.to_string
  |> print_endline

let add =
  Command.basic
    ~summary:"Add [days] to the [base] date and print day"
    Command.Spec.(
      step
        (fun m base days ->
           match days with
           | Some days ->
             m base days
           | None ->
             print_endline "enter days: ";
             read_int ()
             |> m base
        )
      +> anon ("base" %: date)
      +> anon (maybe ("days" %: int))
    )
    add_days

let () = Command.run add
```

The **days** anonymous argument is now an optional integer in the spec, and we want to transform it into a nonoptional value before calling our **add_days** callback. The **step** combinator lets us perform this transformation by applying its supplied callback function first. In the example, the callback first checks if **days** is defined. If it's undefined, then it interactively reads an integer from the standard input.

The first **m** argument to the **step** callback is the next callback function in the chain. The transformation is completed by calling **m base days** to continue processing with the new values we've just calculated. The **days** value that is passed onto the next callback now has a nonoptional **int** type:

Terminal

```
$ ocamlbuild -use-ocamlfind -tag thread -pkg core cal_add_interactive.native
$ ./cal_add_interactive.native 2013-12-01
```

```
enter days:
35
2014-01-05
```

The transformation means that the add_days callback can just keep its original definition of Date.t -> int -> unit. The step function transformed the int option
argument from the parsing into an int suitable for add_days. This transformation is
explicitly represented in the type of the step return value:

OCaml utop

```
# open Command.Spec ;;
# step (fun m (base:Date.t) days ->
  match days with
  | Some days -> m base days
  | None ->
    print_endline "enter days: ";
    m base (read_int ())) ;;
- : (Date.t -> int -> '_a, Date.t -> int option -> '_a) t = <abstr>
```

The first half of the Spec.t shows that the callback type is Date.t -> int, whereas the
resulting value expected from the next specification in the chain is a Date.t -> int
option.

Adding Labeled Arguments to Callbacks

The step chaining lets you control the types of your callbacks very easily. This can help
you match existing interfaces or make things more explicit by adding labeled arguments:

OCaml

```
open Core.Std

let add_days ~base_date ~num_days () =
  Date.add_days base_date num_days
  |> Date.to_string
  |> print_endline

let add =
  Command.basic
    ~summary:"Add [days] to the [base] date and print day"
    Command.Spec.(
      step (fun m base days -> m ~base_date:base ~num_days:days)
      +> anon ("base" %: date)
      +> anon ("days" %: int)
    )
    add_days

let () = Command.run add
```

This cal_add_labels example goes back to our noninteractive calendar addition program, but the add_days main function now expects labeled arguments. The step

function in the specification simply converts the default `base` and `days` arguments into a labeled function.

Labeled arguments are more verbose but can also help prevent errors with command-line arguments with similar types but different names and purposes. It's good form to use labels when you have a lot of otherwise anonymous `int` and `string` arguments.

Command-Line Autocompletion with bash

Modern UNIX shells usually have a tab-completion feature to interactively help you figure out how to build a command line. These work by pressing the Tab key in the middle of typing a command, and seeing the options that pop up. You've probably used this most often to find the files in the current directory, but it can actually be extended for other parts of the command, too.

The precise mechanism for autocompletion varies depending on what shell you are using, but we'll assume you are using the most common one: *bash*. This is the default interactive shell on most Linux distributions and Mac OS X, but you may need to switch to it on *BSD or Windows (when using Cygwin). The rest of this section assumes that you're using *bash*.

Bash autocompletion isn't always installed by default, so check your OS package manager to see if you have it available.

Operating system	Package manager	Package
Debian Linux	apt	bash-completion
Mac OS X	Homebrew	bash-completion
FreeBSD	Ports system	*/usr/ports/shells/bash-completion*

Once *bash* completion is installed and configured, check that it works by typing the `ssh` command and pressing the Tab key. This should show you the list of known hosts from your *~/.ssh/known_hosts* file. If it lists some hosts that you've recently connected to, you can continue on. If it lists the files in your current directory instead, then check your OS documentation to configure completion correctly.

One last bit of information you'll need to find is the location of the *bash_completion.d* directory. This is where all the shell fragments that contain the completion logic are held. On Linux, this is often in */etc/bash_completion.d*, and in Homebrew on Mac OS X, it would be */usr/local/etc/bash_completion.d* by default.

Generating Completion Fragments from Command

The Command library has a declarative description of all the possible valid options, and it can use this information to generate a shell script that provides completion support

for that command. To generate the fragment, just run the command with the COM
MAND_OUTPUT_INSTALLATION_BASH environment variable set to any value.

For example, let's try it on our MD5 example from earlier, assuming that the binary is
called *basic_md5_with_flags* in the current directory:

```
$ env COMMAND_OUTPUT_INSTALLATION_BASH=1 ./basic_md5_with_flags.native
function _jsautocom_23343 {
  export COMP_CWORD
  COMP_WORDS[0]=./basic_md5_with_flags.native
  COMPREPLY=($("${COMP_WORDS[@]}"))
}
complete -F _jsautocom_23343 ./basic_md5_with_flags.native
```

Recall that we used the Arg_type.file to specify the argument type. This also supplies
the completion logic so that you can just press Tab to complete files in your current
directory.

Installing the Completion Fragment

You don't need to worry about what the preceding output script actually does (unless
you have an unhealthy fascination with shell scripting internals, that is). Instead, redirect
the output to a file in your current directory and source it into your current shell:

```
$ env COMMAND_OUTPUT_INSTALLATION_BASH=1 ./cal_add_sub_days.native > cal.cmd
$ . cal.cmd
$ ./cal_add_sub_days.native <tab>
add      diff      help      version
```

Command completion support works for flags and grouped commands and is very
useful when building larger command-line interfaces. Don't forget to install the shell
fragment into your global *bash_completion.d* directory if you want it to be loaded in all
of your login shells.

Installing a Generic Completion Handler

Sadly, *bash* doesn't support installing a generic handler for all
Command-based applications. This means you have to install the
completion script for every application, but you should be able to
automate this in the build and packaging system for your application.

It will help to check out how other applications install tab-
completion scripts and follow their lead, as the details are very OS-
specific.

Alternative Command-Line Parsers

This rounds up our tour of the Command library. This isn't the only way to parse command-line arguments of course; there are several alternatives available on OPAM. Three of the most prominent ones follow:

The Arg *module*
> The Arg module is from the OCaml standard library, which is used by the compiler itself to handle its command-line interface. Command is generally more featureful than Arg (mainly via support for subcommands, the step combinator to transform inputs, and help generation), but there's absolutely nothing wrong with using Arg either.
>
> You can use the Command.Spec.flags_of_args_exn function to convert Arg specifications into ones compatible with Command. This is quite often used to help port older non-Core code into the Core standard library world.

ocaml-getopt (https://forge.ocamlcore.org/projects/ocaml-getopt/)
> ocaml-getopt provides the general command-line syntax of GNU getopt and getopt_long. The GNU conventions are widely used in the open source world, and this library lets your OCaml programs obey the same rules.

Cmdliner (http://erratique.ch/software/cmdliner)
> Cmdliner is a mix between the Command and Getopt libraries. It allows for the declarative definition of command-line interfaces but exposes a more getopt-like interface. It also automates the generation of UNIX man pages as part of the specification. Cmdliner is the parser used by OPAM to manage its command line.

CHAPTER 15

Handling JSON Data

Data serialization, i.e., converting data to and from a sequence of bytes that's suitable for writing to disk or sending across the network, is an important and common programming task. You often have to match someone else's data format (such as XML), sometimes you need a highly efficient format, and other times you want something that is easy for humans to edit. To this end, OCaml libraries provide several techniques for data serialization depending on what your problem is.

We'll start by using the popular and simple JSON data format and then look at other serialization formats later in the book. This chapter introduces you to a couple of new techniques that glue together the basic ideas from Part I of the book by using:

- *Polymorphic variants* to write more extensible libraries and protocols (but still retain the ability to extend them if needed)

- *Functional combinators* to compose common operations over data structures in a type-safe way

- External tools to generate boilerplate OCaml modules and signatures from external specification files

JSON Basics

JSON is a lightweight data-interchange format often used in web services and browsers. It's described in RFC4627 (*http://www.ietf.org/rfc/rfc4627.txt*) and is easier to parse and generate than alternatives such as XML. You'll run into JSON very often when working with modern web APIs, so we'll cover several different ways to manipulate it in this chapter.

JSON consists of two basic structures: an unordered collection of key/value pairs, and an ordered list of values. Values can be strings, Booleans, floats, integers, or null. Let's see what a JSON record for an example book description looks like:

JSON

```
{
  "title": "Real World OCaml",
  "tags" : [ "functional programming", "ocaml", "algorithms" ],
  "pages": 450,
  "authors": [
    { "name": "Jason Hickey", "affiliation": "Google" },
    { "name": "Anil Madhavapeddy", "affiliation": "Cambridge"},
    { "name": "Yaron Minsky", "affiliation": "Jane Street"}
  ],
  "is_online": true
}
```

The outermost JSON value is usually a record (delimited by the curly braces) and contains an unordered set of key/value pairs. The keys must be strings, but values can be any JSON type. In the preceding example, `tags` is a string list, while the `authors` field contains a list of records. Unlike OCaml lists, JSON lists can contain multiple different JSON types within a single list.

This free-form nature of JSON types is both a blessing and a curse. It's very easy to generate JSON values, but code that parses them also has to handle subtle variations in how the values are represented. For example, what if the preceding `pages` value is actually represented as a string value of "450" instead of an integer?

Our first task is to parse the JSON into a more structured OCaml type so that we can use static typing more effectively. When manipulating JSON in Python or Ruby, you might write unit tests to check that you have handled unusual inputs. The OCaml model prefers compile-time static checking as well as unit tests. For example, using pattern matching can warn you if you've not checked that a value can be `Null` as well as contain an actual value.

 Installing the Yojson Library

There are several JSON libraries available for OCaml. For this chapter, we've picked the OCaml (*http://mjambon.com/yojson.html*) library by Martin Jambon. It's easiest to install via OPAM by running `opam install yojson`. See this Real World OCaml page (*http://realworldocaml.org/install*) for installation instructions if you haven't already got OPAM. Once installed, you can open it in the *utop* toplevel by:

OCaml utop

```
# #require "yojson" ;;
# open Yojson ;;
```

Parsing JSON with Yojson

The JSON specification has very few data types, and the `Yojson.Basic.json` type that follows is sufficient to express any valid JSON structure:

OCaml

```
type json = [
  | `Assoc of (string * json) list
  | `Bool of bool
  | `Float of float
  | `Int of int
  | `List of json list
  | `Null
  | `String of string
]
```

Some interesting properties should leap out at you after reading this definition:

- The `json` type is *recursive*, which is to say that some of the tags refer back to the overall `json` type. In particular, `Assoc` and `List` types can contain references to further JSON values of different types. This is unlike the OCaml lists, whose contents must be of a uniform type.

- The definition specifically includes a `Null` variant for empty fields. OCaml doesn't allow null values by default, so this must be encoded explicitly.

- The type definition uses polymorphic variants and not normal variants. This will become significant later, when we extend it with custom extensions to the JSON format.

Let's parse the earlier JSON example into this type now. The first stop is the `Yojson.Ba sic` documentation, where we find these helpful functions:

OCaml (part 1)

```
val from_string : ?buf:Bi_outbuf.t -> ?fname:string -> ?lnum:int ->
  string -> json
(* Read a JSON value from a string.
   [buf]   : use this buffer at will during parsing instead of
             creating a new one.
   [fname] : data file name to be used in error messages. It does not
             have to be a real file.
   [lnum]  : number of the first line of input. Default is 1. *)

val from_file : ?buf:Bi_outbuf.t -> ?fname:string -> ?lnum:int ->
  string -> json
(* Read a JSON value from a file. See [from_string] for the meaning of the optional
   arguments. *)

val from_channel : ?buf:Bi_outbuf.t -> ?fname:string -> ?lnum:int ->
  in_channel -> json
```

```
(** Read a JSON value from a channel.
    See [from_string] for the meaning of the optional arguments. *)
```

When first reading these interfaces, you can generally ignore the optional arguments (which have the question marks in the type signature), since they should have sensible defaults. In the preceding signature, the optional arguments offer finer control over the memory buffer allocation and error messages from parsing incorrect JSON.

The type signature for these functions with the optional elements removed makes their purpose much clearer. The three ways of parsing JSON are either directly from a string, from a file on a filesystem, or via a buffered input channel:

OCaml

```
val from_string  : string      -> json
val from_file    : string      -> json
val from_channel : in_channel  -> json
```

The next example shows both the `string` and `file` functions in action, assuming the JSON record is stored in a file called *book.json*:

OCaml

```
open Core.Std

let () =
  (* Read JSON file into an OCaml string *)
  let buf = In_channel.read_all "book.json" in
  (* Use the string JSON constructor *)
  let json1 = Yojson.Basic.from_string buf in
  (* Use the file JSON constructor *)
  let json2 = Yojson.Basic.from_file "book.json" in
  (* Test that the two values are the same *)
  print_endline (if json1 = json2 then "OK" else "FAIL")
```

You can build this by running *corebuild*:

Terminal

```
$ corebuild -pkg yojson read_json.native
$ ./read_json.native
OK
```

The `from_file` function accepts an input filename and takes care of opening and closing it for you. It's far more common to use `from_string` to construct JSON values though, since these strings come in via a network connection (we'll see more of this in Chapter 18) or a database. Finally, the example checks that the two input mechanisms actually resulted in the same OCaml data structure.

Selecting Values from JSON Structures

Now that we've figured out how to parse the example JSON into an OCaml value, let's manipulate it from OCaml code and extract specific fields:

```
open Core.Std

let () =
  (* Read the JSON file *)
  let json = Yojson.Basic.from_file "book.json" in

  (* Locally open the JSON manipulation functions *)
  let open Yojson.Basic.Util in
  let title = json |> member "title" |> to_string in
  let tags = json |> member "tags" |> to_list |> filter_string in
  let pages = json |> member "pages" |> to_int in
  let is_online = json |> member "is_online" |> to_bool_option in
  let is_translated = json |> member "is_translated" |> to_bool_option in
  let authors = json |> member "authors" |> to_list in
  let names = List.map authors ~f:(fun json -> member "name" json |> to_string) in

  (* Print the results of the parsing *)
  printf "Title: %s (%d)\n" title pages;
  printf "Authors: %s\n" (String.concat ~sep:", " names);
  printf "Tags: %s\n" (String.concat ~sep:", " tags);
  let string_of_bool_option =
    function
    | None -> "<unknown>"
    | Some true -> "yes"
    | Some false -> "no" in
  printf "Online: %s\n" (string_of_bool_option is_online);
  printf "Translated: %s\n" (string_of_bool_option is_translated)
```

Now build and run this in the same way as the previous example:

```
$ corebuild -pkg yojson parse_book.native
$ ./parse_book.native
Title: Real World OCaml (450)
Authors: Jason Hickey, Anil Madhavapeddy, Yaron Minsky
Tags: functional programming, ocaml, algorithms
Online: yes
Translated: <unknown>
```

This code introduces the Yojson.Basic.Util module, which contains *combinator* functions that let you easily map a JSON object into a more strongly typed OCaml value.

Functional Combinators

Combinators are a design pattern that crops up quite often in functional programming. John Hughes defines them as "a function which builds program fragments from program fragments." In a functional language, this generally means higher-order functions that combine other functions to apply useful transformations over values.

You've already run across several of these in the List module:

```
                                                                      OCaml
    val map  : 'a list -> f:('a -> 'b)   -> 'b list
    val fold : 'a list -> init:'accum -> f:('accum -> 'a -> 'accum) -> 'accum
```

map and fold are extremely common combinators that transform an input list by applying a function to each value of the list. The map combinator is simplest, with the
resulting list being output directly. fold applies each value in the input list to a function
that accumulates a single result, and returns that instead:

                                                                  OCaml (part 1)
```
    val iter : 'a list -> f:('a -> unit) -> unit
```

iter is a more specialized combinator that is only useful when writing imperative code.
The input function is applied to every value, but no result is supplied. The function must
instead apply some side effect such as changing a mutable record field or printing to the
standard output.

Yojson provides several combinators in the Yojson.Basic.Util module, some of which
are listed in Table 15-1.

Table 15-1. Yojson combinators

Function	Type	Purpose
member	string -> json -> json	Select a named field from a JSON record.
to_string	json -> string	Convert a JSON value into an OCaml string. Raises an exception if this is impossible.
to_int	json -> int	Convert a JSON value into an OCaml int. Raises an exception if this is impossible.
filter_string	json list -> string list	Filter valid strings from a list of JSON fields, and return them as an OCaml list of strings.

We'll go through each of these uses one by one now. The following examples also use
the |> pipe-forward operator that we explained in Chapter 2. This lets us chain together
multiple JSON selection functions and feed the output from one into the next one,
without having to create separate let bindings for each one.

Let's start with selecting a single title field from the record:

                                                                  OCaml utop (part 1)
```
    # open Yojson.Basic.Util ;;
    # let title = json |> member "title" |> to_string ;;
    val title : string = "Real World OCaml"
```

The member function accepts a JSON object and named key and returns the JSON field
associated with that key, or Null. Since we know that the title value is always a string
in our example schema, we want to convert it to an OCaml string. The to_string
function performs this conversion and raises an exception if there is an unexpected

JSON type. The |> operator provides a convenient way to chain these operations together:

OCaml utop (part 2)

```
# let tags = json |> member "tags" |> to_list |> filter_string ;;
val tags : string list = ["functional programming"; "ocaml"; "algorithms"]
# let pages = json |> member "pages" |> to_int ;;
val pages : int = 450
```

The tags field is similar to title, but the field is a list of strings instead of a single one. Converting this to an OCaml string list is a two-stage process. First, we convert the JSON List to an OCaml list of JSON values and then filter out the String values as an OCaml string list. Remember that OCaml lists must contain values of the same type, so any JSON values that cannot be converted to a string will be skipped from the output of filter_string:

OCaml utop (part 3)

```
# let is_online = json |> member "is_online" |> to_bool_option ;;
val is_online : bool option = Some true
# let is_translated = json |> member "is_translated" |> to_bool_option ;;
val is_translated : bool option = None
```

The is_online and is_translated fields are optional in our JSON schema, so no error should be raised if they are not present. The OCaml type is a bool option to reflect this and can be extracted via to_bool_option. In our example JSON, only is_online is present and is_translated will be None:

OCaml utop (part 4)

```
# let authors = json |> member "authors" |> to_list ;;
val authors : Yojson.Basic.json list =
  [`Assoc
    [("name", `String "Jason Hickey"); ("affiliation", `String "Google")];
   `Assoc
    [("name", `String "Anil Madhavapeddy");
     ("affiliation", `String "Cambridge")];
   `Assoc
    [("name", `String "Yaron Minsky");
     ("affiliation", `String "Jane Street")]]
```

The final use of JSON combinators is to extract all the name fields from the list of authors. We first construct the author list, and then map it into a string list. Notice that the example explicitly binds authors to a variable name. It can also be written more succinctly using the pipe-forward operator:

OCaml utop (part 5)

```
# let names =
  json |> member "authors" |> to_list
  |> List.map ~f:(fun json -> member "name" json |> to_string) ;;
val names : string list =
  ["Jason Hickey"; "Anil Madhavapeddy"; "Yaron Minsky"]
```

This style of programming, which omits variable names and chains functions together, is known as *point-free programming*. It's a succinct style but shouldn't be overused due to the increased difficulty of debugging intermediate values. If an explicit name is assigned to each stage of the transformations, debuggers in particular have an easier time making the program flow simpler to represent to the programmer.

This technique of using statically typed parsing functions is very powerful in combination with the OCaml type system. Many errors that don't make sense at runtime (for example, mixing up lists and objects) will be caught statically via a type error.

Constructing JSON Values

Building and printing JSON values is pretty straightforward given the Yojson.Ba sic.json type. You can just construct values of type json and call the to_string function on them. Let's remind ourselves of the Yojson.Basic.json type again:

OCaml

```
type json = [
  | `Assoc of (string * json) list
  | `Bool of bool
  | `Float of float
  | `Int of int
  | `List of json list
  | `Null
  | `String of string
]
```

We can directly build a JSON value against this type and use the pretty-printing functions in the Yojson.Basic module to display JSON output:

OCaml utop (part 1)

```
# let person = `Assoc [ ("name", `String "Anil") ] ;;
val person : [> `Assoc of (string * [> `String of string ]) list ] =
  `Assoc [("name", `String "Anil")]
```

In the preceding example, we've constructed a simple JSON object that represents a single person. We haven't actually defined the type of person explicitly, as we're relying on the magic of polymorphic variants to make this all work.

The OCaml type system infers a type for person based on how you construct its value. In this case, only the Assoc and String variants are used to define the record, and so the inferred type only contains these fields without knowledge of the other possible allowed variants in JSON records that you haven't used yet (e.g. Int or Null):

OCaml utop (part 2)

```
# Yojson.Basic.pretty_to_string ;;
- : ?std:bool -> Yojson.Basic.json -> string = <fun>
```

The pretty_to_string function has a more explicit signature that requires an argument of type Yojson.Basic.json. When person is applied to pretty_to_string, the inferred type of person is statically checked against the structure of the json type to ensure that they're compatible:

OCaml utop (part 3)

```
# Yojson.Basic.pretty_to_string person ;;
- : string = "{ \"name\": \"Anil\" }"
# Yojson.Basic.pretty_to_channel stdout person ;;
{ "name": "Anil" }
- : unit = ()
```

In this case, there are no problems. Our person value has an inferred type that is a valid subtype of json, and so the conversion to a string just works without us ever having to explicitly specify a type for person. Type inference lets you write more succinct code without sacrificing runtime reliability, as all the uses of polymorphic variants are still checked at compile time.

Polymorphic Variants and Easier Type Checking

One difficulty you will encounter is that type errors involving polymorphic variants can be quite verbose. For example, suppose you build an Assoc and mistakenly include a single value instead of a list of keys:

OCaml utop (part 4)

```
# let person = `Assoc ("name", `String "Anil");;
val person : [> `Assoc of string * [> `String of string ] ] =
  `Assoc ("name", `String "Anil")
# Yojson.Basic.pretty_to_string person ;;
Characters 30-36:
Error: This expression has type
         [> `Assoc of string * [> `String of string ] ]
       but an expression was expected of type Yojson.Basic.json
       Types for tag `Assoc are incompatible
```

The type error is more verbose than it needs to be, which can be inconvenient to wade through for larger values. You can help the compiler to narrow down this error to a shorter form by adding explicit type annotations as a hint about your intentions:

OCaml utop (part 5)

```
# let (person : Yojson.Basic.json) =
  `Assoc ("name", `String "Anil");;
Characters 37-68:
Error: This expression has type 'a * 'b
       but an expression was expected of type
         (string * Yojson.Basic.json) list
```

We've annotated person as being of type Yojson.Basic.json, and as a result, the compiler spots that the argument to the Assoc variant has the incorrect type. This illustrates the strengths and weaknesses of polymorphic variants: they're lightweight and flexible, but the error messages can be quite confusing. However, a bit of careful manual type annotation makes tracking down such issues much easier.

We'll discuss more techniques like this that help you interpret type errors more easily in Chapter 22.

Using Nonstandard JSON Extensions

The standard JSON types are *really* basic, and OCaml types are far more expressive. Yojson supports an extended JSON format for those times when you're not interoperating with external systems and just want a convenient human-readable, local format. The `Yojson.Safe.json` type is a superset of the `Basic` polymorphic variant and looks like this:

OCaml

```
type json = [
  | `Assoc of (string * json) list
  | `Bool of bool
  | `Float of float
  | `Floatlit of string
  | `Int of int
  | `Intlit of string
  | `List of json list
  | `Null
  | `String of string
  | `Stringlit of string
  | `Tuple of json list
  | `Variant of string * json option
]
```

The `Safe.json` type includes all of the variants from `Basic.json` and extends it with a few more useful ones. A standard JSON type such as a `String` will type-check against both the `Basic` module and also the nonstandard `Safe` module. If you use the extended values with the `Basic` module, however, the compiler will reject your code until you make it compliant with the portable subset of JSON.

Yojson supports the following JSON extensions:

The `lit` *suffix*
> Denotes that the value is stored as a JSON string. For example, a `Floatlit` will be stored as `"1.234"` instead of `1.234`.

The `Tuple` *type*
> Stored as `("abc", 123)` instead of a list.

The `Variant` *type*
> Encodes OCaml variants more explicitly, as `<"Foo">` or `<"Bar":123>` for a variant with parameters.

The only purpose of these extensions is to have greater control over how OCaml values are represented in JSON (for instance, storing a floating-point number as a JSON string).

The output still obeys the same standard format that can be easily exchanged with other languages.

You can convert a `Safe.json` to a `Basic.json` type by using the `to_basic` function as follows:

OCaml (part 1)

```
val to_basic : json -> Yojson.Basic.json
(** Tuples are converted to JSON arrays, Variants are converted to
    JSON strings or arrays of a string (constructor) and a json value
    (argument). Long integers are converted to JSON strings.
    Examples:

    `Tuple [ `Int 1; `Float 2.3 ]   ->    `List [ `Int 1; `Float 2.3 ]
    `Variant ("A", None)            ->    `String "A"
    `Variant ("B", Some x)          ->    `List [ `String "B", x ]
    `Intlit "12345678901234567890"  ->    `String "12345678901234567890"
*)
```

Automatically Mapping JSON to OCaml Types

The combinators described previously make it easy to write functions that extract fields from JSON records, but the process is still pretty manual. When you implement larger specifications, it's much easier to generate the mappings from JSON schemas to OCaml values more mechanically than writing conversion functions individually.

We'll cover an alternative JSON processing method that is better for larger-scale JSON handling now, using the OCaml (*http://mjambon.com/atd-biniou-intro.html*) tool. This will introduce our first *Domain Specific Language* that compiles JSON specifications into OCaml modules, which are then used throughout your application.

Installing the ATDgen Library and Tool

ATDgen installs some OCaml libraries that interface with Yojson, and also a command-line tool that generates code. It can all be installed via OPAM:

Terminal

```
$ opam install atdgen
$ atdgen -version
1.2.3
```

The command-line tool will be installed within your *~/.opam* directory and should already be on your PATH from running *opam config env*. See this Real World OCaml page (*http://realworldocaml.org/install*) if this isn't working.

ATD Basics

The idea behind ATD is to specify the format of the JSON in a separate file and then run a compiler (*atdgen*) that outputs OCaml code to construct and parse JSON values. This means that you don't need to write any OCaml parsing code at all, as it will all be autogenerated for you.

Let's go straight into looking at an example of how this works, by using a small portion of the GitHub API. GitHub is a popular code hosting and sharing website that provides a JSON-based web API (*http://developer.github.com*). The following ATD code fragment describes the GitHub authorization API (which is based on a pseudostandard web protocol known as OAuth):

OCaml

```
type scope = [
    User <json name="user">
  | Public_repo <json name="public_repo">
  | Repo <json name="repo">
  | Repo_status <json name="repo_status">
  | Delete_repo <json name="delete_repo">
  | Gist <json name="gist">
]

type app = {
  name: string;
  url: string;
}   <ocaml field_prefix="app_">

type authorization_request = {
  scopes: scope list;
  note: string;
} <ocaml field_prefix="auth_req_">

type authorization_response = {
  scopes: scope list;
  token: string;
  app: app;
  url: string;
  id: int;
  ?note: string option;
  ?note_url: string option;
}
```

The ATD specification syntax is deliberately quite similar to OCaml type definitions. Every JSON record is assigned a type name (e.g., app in the preceding example). You can also define variants that are similar to OCaml's variant types (e.g., scope in the example).

ATD Annotations

ATD does deviate from OCaml syntax due to its support for annotations within the specification. The annotations can customize the code that is generated for a particular target (of which the OCaml backend is of most interest to us).

For example, the preceding GitHub `scope` field is defined as a variant type, with each option starting with an uppercase letter as is conventional for OCaml variants. However, the JSON values that come back from GitHub are actually lowercase and so aren't exactly the same as the option name.

The annotation `<json name="user">` signals that the JSON value of the field is `user`, but that the variable name of the parsed variant in OCaml should be `User`. These annotations are often useful to map JSON values to reserved keywords in OCaml (e.g., `type`).

Compiling ATD Specifications to OCaml

The ATD specification we defined can be compiled to OCaml code using the *atdgen* command-line tool. Let's run the compiler twice to generate some OCaml type definitions and a JSON serializing module that converts between input data and those type definitions.

The *atdgen* command will generate some new files in your current directory. `git hub_t.ml` and `github_t.mli` will contain an OCaml module with types defined that correspond to the ATD file:

Terminal

```
$ atdgen -t github.atd
$ atdgen -j github.atd
$ ocamlfind ocamlc -package atd -i github_t.mli
type scope =
    [ `Delete_repo | `Gist | `Public_repo | `Repo | `Repo_status | `User ]
type app = { app_name : string; app_url : string; }
type authorization_request = {
  auth_req_scopes : scope list;
  auth_req_note : string;
}
type authorization_response = {
  scopes : scope list;
  token : string;
  app : app;
  url : string;
  id : int;
  note : string option;
  note_url : string option;
}
```

There is an obvious correspondence to the ATD definition. Note that field names in OCaml records in the same module cannot shadow one another, and so we instruct ATDgen to prefix every field with a name that distinguishes it from other records in the same module. For example, `<ocaml field_prefix="auth_req_">` in the ATD spec prefixes every field name in the generated `authorization_request` record with `auth_req`.

The `Github_t` module only contains the type definitions, while `Github_j` provides serialization functions to and from JSON. You can read the `github_j.mli` to see the full interface, but the important functions for most uses are the conversion functions to and from a string. For our preceding example, this looks like:

OCaml

```
val string_of_authorization_request :
  ?len:int -> authorization_request -> string
  (** Serialize a value of type {!authorization_request}
      into a JSON string.
      @param len specifies the initial length
                  of the buffer used internally.
                  Default: 1024. *)

val string_of_authorization_response :
  ?len:int -> authorization_response -> string
  (** Serialize a value of type {!authorization_response}
      into a JSON string.
      @param len specifies the initial length
                  of the buffer used internally.
                  Default: 1024. *)
```

This is pretty convenient! We've now written a single ATD file, and all the OCaml boilerplate to convert between JSON and a strongly typed record has been generated for us. You can control various aspects of the serializer by passing flags to *atdgen*. The important ones for JSON are:

`-j-std`
Converts tuples and variants into standard JSON and refuse to print NaN and infinities. You should specify this if you intend to interoperate with services that aren't using ATD.

`-j-custom-fields FUNCTION`
Calls a custom function for every unknown field encountered, instead of raising a parsing exception.

`-j-defaults`
Always explicitly outputs a JSON value if possible. This requires the default value for that field to be defined in the ATD specification.

The full ATD specification (*http://mjambon.com/atdgen/atdgen-manual.html*) is quite sophisticated and documented online. The ATD compiler can also target formats other than JSON and outputs code for other languages (such as Java) if you need more interoperability.

There are also several similar projects that automate the code generation process. Piqi (*http://piqi.org*) supports conversions between XML, JSON, and the Google protobuf format; and Thrift (*http://thrift.apache.org*) supports many other programming languages and includes OCaml bindings.

Example: Querying GitHub Organization Information

Let's finish up with an example of some live JSON parsing from GitHub and build a tool to query organization information via their API. Start by looking at the online API documentation (*http://developer.github.com/v3/orgs/*) for GitHub to see what the JSON schema for retrieving the organization information looks like.

Now create an ATD file that covers the fields we need. Any extra fields present in the response will be ignored by the ATD parser, so we don't need a completely exhaustive specification of every field that GitHub might send back:

OCaml

```
type org = {
  login: string;
  id: int;
  url: string;
  ?name: string option;
  ?blog: string option;
  ?email: string option;
  public_repos: int
}
```

Let's build the OCaml type declaration first by calling `atdgen -t` on the specification file:

Terminal

```
$ atdgen -t github_org.atd
$ cat github_org_t.mli
(* Auto-generated from "github_org.atd" *)


type org = {
  login: string;
  id: int;
  url: string;
  name: string option;
  blog: string option;
  email: string option;
  public_repos: int
}
```

The OCaml type has an obvious mapping to the ATD spec, but we still need the logic to convert JSON buffers to and from this type. Calling `atdgen -j` will generate this serialization code for us in a new file called `github_org_j.ml`:

```
$ atdgen -j github_org.atd
$ cat github_org_j.mli
(* Auto-generated from "github_org.atd" *)


type org = Github_org_t.org = {
  login: string;
  id: int;
  url: string;
  name: string option;
  blog: string option;
  email: string option;
  public_repos: int
}

val write_org :
  Bi_outbuf.t -> org -> unit
  (** Output a JSON value of type {!org}. *)

val string_of_org :
  ?len:int -> org -> string
  (** Serialize a value of type {!org}
      into a JSON string.
      @param len specifies the initial length
                 of the buffer used internally.
                 Default: 1024. *)

val read_org :
  Yojson.Safe.lexer_state -> Lexing.lexbuf -> org
  (** Input JSON data of type {!org}. *)

val org_of_string :
  string -> org
  (** Deserialize JSON data of type {!org}. *)
```

The `Github_org_j` serializer interface contains everything we need to map to and from the OCaml types and JSON. The easiest way to use this interface is by using the `string_of_org` and `org_of_string` functions, but there are also more advanced low-level buffer functions available if you need higher performance (but we won't go into that in this tutorial).

All we need to complete our example is an OCaml program that fetches the JSON and uses these modules to output a one-line summary. Our following example does just that.

The following code calls the cURL command-line utility by using the `Core_exten ded.Shell` interface to run an external command and capture its output. You'll need to ensure that you have cURL installed on your system before running the example. You might also need to `opam install core_extended` if you haven't installed it previously:

OCaml

```
open Core.Std

let print_org file () =
  let url = sprintf "https://api.github.com/orgs/%s" file in
  Core_extended.Shell.run_full "curl" [url]
  |> Github_org_j.org_of_string
  |> fun org ->
  let open Github_org_t in
  let name = Option.value ~default:"???" org.name in
  printf "%s (%d) with %d public repos\n"
    name org.id org.public_repos

let () =
  Command.basic ~summary:"Print Github organization information"
    Command.Spec.(empty +> anon ("organization" %: string))
    print_org
  |> Command.run
```

The following is a short shell script that generates all of the OCaml code and also builds the final executable:

Terminal

```
$ atdgen -t github_org.atd
$ atdgen -j github_org.atd
$ corebuild -pkg core_extended,yojson,atdgen github_org_info.native
```

You can now run the command-line tool with a single argument to specify the name of the organization, and it will dynamically fetch the JSON from the web, parse it, and render the summary to your console:

Terminal

```
$ ./github_org_info.native mirage
Mirage account (131943) with 37 public repos
$ ./github_org_info.native janestreet
??? (3384712) with 34 public repos
```

The JSON returned from the `janestreet` query is missing an organization name, but this is explicitly reflected in the OCaml type, since the ATD spec marked `name` as an optional field. Our OCaml code explicitly handles this case and doesn't have to worry about null-pointer exceptions. Similarly, the JSON integer for the `id` is mapped into a native OCaml integer via the ATD conversion.

While this tool is obviously quite simple, the ability to specify optional and default fields is very powerful. Take a look at the full ATD specification for the GitHub API in the `ocaml-github` (*http://github.com/avsm/ocaml-github*) repository online, which has lots of quirks typical in real-world web APIs.

Our example shells out to `curl` on the command line to obtain the JSON, which is rather inefficient. We'll explain how to integrate the HTTP fetch directly into your OCaml application in Chapter 18.

## CHAPTER 16

Parsing with OCamllex and Menhir

Many programming tasks start with the interpretion of some form of structured textual data. *Parsing* is the process of converting such data into data structures that are easy to program against. For simple formats, it's often enough to parse the data in an ad hoc way, say, by breaking up the data into lines, and then using regular expressions for breaking those lines down into their component pieces.

But this simplistic approach tends to fall down when parsing more complicated data, particularly data with the kind of recursive structure you find in full-blown programming languages or flexible data formats like JSON and XML. Parsing such formats accurately and efficiently while providing useful error messages is a complex task.

Often, you can find an existing parsing library that handles these issues for you. But there are tools to simplify the task when you do need to write a parser, in the form of *parser generators*. A parser generator creates a parser from a specification of the data format that you want to parse, and uses that to generate a parser.

Parser generators have a long history, including tools like *lex* and *yacc* that date back to the early 1970s. OCaml has its own alternatives, including *ocamllex*, which replaces *lex*, and *ocamlyacc* and *menhir*, which replace *yacc*. We'll explore these tools in the course of walking through the implementation of a parser for the JSON serialization format that we discussed in Chapter 15.

Parsing is a broad and often intricate topic, and our purpose here is not to teach all of the theoretical issues, but to provide a pragmatic introduction of how to build a parser in OCaml.

Menhir Versus ocamlyacc

Menhir is an alternative parser generator that is generally superior to the venerable *ocamlyacc*, which dates back quite a few years. Menhir is mostly compatible with *ocamlyacc* grammars, and so you can usually just switch to Menhir and expect older code to work (with some minor differences described in the Menhir manual).

The biggest advantage of Menhir is that its error messages are generally more human-comprehensible, and the parsers that it generates are fully reentrant and can be parameterized in OCaml modules more easily. We recommend that any new code you develop should use Menhir instead of *ocamlyacc*.

Menhir isn't distributed directly with OCaml but is available through OPAM by running `opam install menhir`.

Lexing and Parsing

Parsing is traditionally broken down into two parts: *lexical analysis*, which is a kind of simplified parsing phase that converts a stream of characters into a stream of logical tokens; and full-on parsing, which involves converting a stream of tokens into the final representation, which is often in the form of a tree-like data structure called an *abstract syntax tree*, or AST.

It's confusing that the term parsing is applied to both the overall process of converting textual data to structured data, and also more specifically to the second phase of converting a stream of tokens to an AST; so from here on out, we'll use the term parsing to refer only to this second phase.

Let's consider lexing and parsing in the context of the JSON format. Here's a snippet of text that represents a JSON object containing a string labeled `title` and an array containing two objects, each with a name and array of zip codes:

JSON

```
{
  "title": "Cities",
  "cities": [
    { "name": "Chicago",  "zips": [60601] },
    { "name": "New York", "zips": [10004] }
  ]
}
```

At a syntactic level, we can think of a JSON file as a series of simple logical units, like curly braces, square brackets, commas, colons, identifiers, numbers, and quoted strings. Thus, we could represent our JSON text as a sequence of tokens of the following type:

```ocaml
type token =
  | NULL
  | TRUE
  | FALSE
  | STRING of string
  | INT of int
  | FLOAT of float
  | ID of string
  | LEFT_BRACK
  | RIGHT_BRACK
  | LEFT_BRACE
  | RIGHT_BRACE
  | COMMA
  | COLON
  | EOF
```

Note that this representation loses some information about the original text. For example, whitespace is not represented. It's common, and indeed useful, for the token stream to forget some details of the original text that are not required for understanding its meaning.

If we converted the preceding example into a list of these tokens, it would look something like this:

```ocaml
[ LEFT_BRACE; ID("title"); COLON; STRING("Cities"); COMMA; ID("cities"); ...
```

This kind of representation is easier to work with than the original text, since it gets rid of some unimportant syntactic details and adds useful structure. But it's still a good deal more low-level than the simple AST we used for representing JSON data in Chapter 15:

```ocaml
type value = [
  | `Assoc of (string * value) list
  | `Bool of bool
  | `Float of float
  | `Int of int
  | `List of value list
  | `Null
  | `String of string
]
```

This representation is much richer than our token stream, capturing the fact that JSON values can be nested inside each other and that JSON has a variety of value types, including numbers, strings, arrays, and objects. The parser we'll write will convert a token stream into a value of this AST type, as shown below for our earlier JSON example:

```ocaml
`Assoc
  ["title", `String "Cities";
   "cities", `List
```

```
[`Assoc ["name", `String "Chicago"; "zips", `List [`Int 60601]];
 `Assoc ["name", `String "New York"; "zips", `List [`Int 10004]]]]
```

Defining a Parser

A parser-specification file has suffix .mly and contains two sections that are broken up by separator lines consisting of the characters %% on a line by themselves. The first section of the file is for declarations, including token and type specifications, precedence directives, and other output directives; and the second section is for specifying the grammar of the language to be parsed.

We'll start by declaring the list of tokens. A token is declared using the syntax %token `<type> uid`, where the `<type>` is optional and *uid* is a capitalized identifier. For JSON, we need tokens for numbers, strings, identifiers, and punctuation:

OCaml

```
%token <int> INT
%token <float> FLOAT
%token <string> ID
%token <string> STRING
%token TRUE
%token FALSE
%token NULL
%token LEFT_BRACE
%token RIGHT_BRACE
%token LEFT_BRACK
%token RIGHT_BRACK
%token COLON
%token COMMA
%token EOF
```

The `<type>` specifications mean that a token carries a value. The INT token carries an integer value with it, FLOAT has a float value, and STRING carries a string value. The remaining tokens, such as TRUE, FALSE, or the punctuation, aren't associated with any value, and so we can omit the `<type>` specification.

Describing the Grammar

The next thing we need to do is to specify the grammar of a JSON expression. *menhir*, like many parser generators, expresses grammars as *context-free grammars*. (More precisely, *menhir* supports LR(1) grammars, but we will ignore that technical distinction here.) You can think of a context-free grammar as a set of abstract names, called *nonterminal symbols*, along with a collection of rules for transforming a nonterminal symbol into a sequence of tokens and nonterminal symbols. A sequence of tokens is parsable by a grammar if you can apply the grammar's rules to produce a series of transformations, starting at a distinguished *start symbol* that produces the token sequence in question.

We'll start describing the JSON grammar by declaring the start symbol to be the non-terminal symbol `prog`, and by declaring that when parsed, a `prog` value should be converted into an OCaml value of type `Json.value option`. We then end the declaration section of the parser with a `%%`:

OCaml (part 1)

```
%start <Json.value option> prog
%%
```

Once that's in place, we can start specifying the productions. In *menhir*, productions are organized into *rules*, where each rule lists all the possible productions for a given nonterminal symbols. Here, for example, is the rule for `prog`:

OCaml (part 2)

```
prog:
  | EOF       { None }
  | v = value { Some v }
  ;
```

The syntax for this is reminiscent of an OCaml `match` statement. The pipes separate the individual productions, and the curly braces contain a *semantic action*: OCaml code that generates the OCaml value corresponding to the production in question. Semantic actions are arbitrary OCaml expressions that are evaluated during parsing to produce values that are attached to the non-terminal in the rule.

We have two cases for `prog`: either there's an `EOF`, which means the text is empty, and so there's no JSON value to read, we return the OCaml value `None`; or we have an instance of the `value` nonterminal, which corresponds to a well-formed JSON value, and we wrap the corresponding `Json.value` in a `Some` tag. Note that in the `value` case, we wrote `v = value` to bind the OCaml value that corresponds to the variable `v`, which we can then use within the curly braces for that production.

Now let's consider a more complex example, the rule for the `value` symbol:

OCaml (part 3)

```
value:
  | LEFT_BRACE; obj = object_fields; RIGHT_BRACE
    { `Assoc obj }
  | LEFT_BRACK; vl = array_values; RIGHT_BRACK
    { `List vl }
  | s = STRING
    { `String s }
  | i = INT
    { `Int i }
  | x = FLOAT
    { `Float x }
  | TRUE
    { `Bool true }
  | FALSE
    { `Bool false }
  | NULL
```

```
  { `Null }
;
```

According to these rules, a JSON `value` is either:

- An object bracketed by curly braces
- An array bracketed by square braces
- A string, integer, float, bool, or null value

In each of the productions, the OCaml code in curly braces shows what to transform the object in question to. Note that we still have two nonterminals whose definitions we depend on here but have not yet defined: `object_fields` and `array_values`. We'll look at how these are parsed next.

Parsing Sequences

The rule for `object_fields` follows, and is really just a thin wrapper that reverses the list returned by the following rule for `rev_object_fields`. Note that the first production in `rev_object_fields` has an empty lefthand side, because what we're matching on in this case is an empty sequence of tokens. The comment `(* empty *)` is used to make this clear:

OCaml (part 4)

```
object_fields: obj = rev_object_fields { List.rev obj };

rev_object_fields:
  | (* empty *) { [] }
  | obj = rev_object_fields; COMMA; k = ID; COLON; v = value
    { (k, v) :: obj }
  ;
```

The rules are structured as they are because *menhir* generates left-recursive parsers, which means that the constructed pushdown automaton uses less stack space with left-recursive definitions. The following right-recursive rule accepts the same input, but during parsing, it requires linear stack space to read object field definitions:

OCaml (part 4)

```
(* Inefficient right-recursive rule *)
object_fields:
  | (* empty *) { [] }
  | k = ID; COLON; v = value; COMMA; obj = object_fields
    { (k, v) :: obj }
```

Alternatively, we could keep the left-recursive definition and simply construct the returned value in left-to-right order. This is even less efficient, since the complexity of building the list incrementally in this way is quadratic in the length of the list:

OCaml (part 4)

```
(* Quadratic left-recursive rule *)
object_fields:
  | (* empty *) { [] }
  | obj = object_fields; COMMA; k = ID; COLON; v = value
    { obj @ [k, v] }
  ;
```

Assembling lists like this is a pretty common requirement in most realistic grammars, and the preceding rules (while useful for illustrating how parsing works) are rather verbose. Menhir features an extended standard library of built-in rules to simplify this handling. These rules are detailed in the Menhir manual and include optional values, pairs of values with optional separators, and lists of elements (also with optional separators).

A version of the JSON grammar using these more succinct Menhir rules follows. Notice the use of `separated_list` to parse both JSON objects and lists with one rule:

OCaml (part 1)

```
prog:
  | v = value { Some v }
  | EOF       { None   } ;

value:
  | LEFT_BRACE; obj = obj_fields; RIGHT_BRACE { `Assoc obj  }
  | LEFT_BRACK; vl = list_fields; RIGHT_BRACK { `List vl    }
  | s = STRING                                { `String s   }
  | i = INT                                   { `Int i      }
  | x = FLOAT                                 { `Float x    }
  | TRUE                                      { `Bool true  }
  | FALSE                                     { `Bool false }
  | NULL                                      { `Null       } ;

obj_fields:
    obj = separated_list(COMMA, obj_field)   { obj } ;

obj_field:
    k = STRING; COLON; v = value             { (k, v) } ;

list_fields:
    vl = separated_list(COMMA, value)        { vl } ;
```

We can invoke *menhir* by using *corebuild* with the `-use-menhir` flag. This tells the build system to switch to using *menhir* instead of *ocamlyacc* to handle files with the `.mly` suffix:

Terminal

```
$ corebuild -use-menhir short_parser.mli
```

Defining a Lexer

Now we can define a lexer, using *ocamllex*, to convert our input text into a stream of tokens. The specification of the lexer is placed in a file with an .mll suffix.

OCaml Prelude

Let's walk through the definition of a lexer section by section. The first section is on optional chunk of OCaml code that is bounded by a pair of curly braces:

OCaml

```
{
open Lexing
open Parser

exception SyntaxError of string

let next_line lexbuf =
  let pos = lexbuf.lex_curr_p in
  lexbuf.lex_curr_p <-
    { pos with pos_bol = lexbuf.lex_curr_pos;
               pos_lnum = pos.pos_lnum + 1
    }
}
```

This code is there to define utility functions used by later snippets of OCaml code and to set up the environment by opening useful modules and define an exception, Syntax Error.

We also define a utility function next_line for tracking the location of tokens across line breaks. The Lexing module defines a lexbuf structure that holds the state of the lexer, including the current location within the source file. The next_line function simply accesses the lex_curr_p field that holds the current location and updates its line number.

Regular Expressions

The next section of the lexing file is a collection of named regular expressions. These look syntactically like ordinary OCaml let bindings, but really this is a specialized syntax for declaring regular expressions. Here's an example:

OCaml (part 1)

```
let int = '-'? ['0'-'9'] ['0'-'9']*
```

The syntax here is something of a hybrid between OCaml syntax and traditional regular expression syntax. The int regular expression specifies an optional leading -, followed by a digit from 0 to 9, followed by some number of digits from 0 to 9. The question mark is used to indicate an optional component of a regular expression; the square brackets are used to specify ranges; and the * operator is used to indicate a (possibly empty) repetition.

Floating-point numbers are specified similarly, but we deal with decimal points and exponents. We make the expression easier to read by building up a sequence of named regular expressions, rather than creating one big and impenetrable expression:

OCaml (part 2)

```
let digit = ['0'-'9']
let frac = '.' digit*
let exp = ['e' 'E'] ['-' '+']? digit+
let float = digit* frac? exp?
```

Finally, we define whitespace, newlines, and identifiers:

OCaml (part 3)

```
let white = [' ' '\t']+
let newline = '\r' | '\n' | "\r\n"
let id = ['a'-'z' 'A'-'Z' '_'] ['a'-'z' 'A'-'Z' '0'-'9' '_']*
```

The newline introduces the | operator, which lets one of several alternative regular expressions match (in this case, the various carriage-return combinations of CR, LF, or CRLF).

Lexing Rules

The lexing rules are essentially functions that consume the data, producing OCaml expressions that evaluate to tokens. These OCaml expressions can be quite complicated, using side effects and invoking other rules as part of the body of the rule. Let's look at the read rule for parsing a JSON expression:

OCaml (part 4)

```
rule read =
  parse
  | white     { read lexbuf }
  | newline   { next_line lexbuf; read lexbuf }
  | int       { INT (int_of_string (Lexing.lexeme lexbuf)) }
  | float     { FLOAT (float_of_string (Lexing.lexeme lexbuf)) }
  | "true"    { TRUE }
  | "false"   { FALSE }
  | "null"    { NULL }
  | '"'       { read_string (Buffer.create 17) lexbuf }
  | '{'       { LEFT_BRACE }
  | '}'       { RIGHT_BRACE }
  | '['       { LEFT_BRACK }
  | ']'       { RIGHT_BRACK }
  | ':'       { COLON }
  | ','       { COMMA }
  | _ { raise (SyntaxError ("Unexpected char: " ^ Lexing.lexeme lexbuf)) }
  | eof       { EOF }
```

The rules are structured very similarly to pattern matches, except that the variants are replaced by regular expressions on the lefthand side. The righthand-side clause is the parsed OCaml return value of that rule. The OCaml code for the rules has a parameter called `lexbuf` that defines the input, including the position in the input file, as well as the text that was matched by the regular expression.

The first `white { read lexbuf }` calls the lexer recursively. That is, it skips the input whitespace and returns the following token. The action `newline { next_line lexbuf; read lexbuf }` is similar, but we use it to advance the line number for the lexer using the utility function that we defined at the top of the file. Let's skip to the third action:

```OCaml
| int { INT (int_of_string (Lexing.lexeme lexbuf)) }
```

This action specifies that when the input matches the `int` regular expression, then the lexer should return the expression `INT (int_of_string (Lexing.lexeme lexbuf))`. The expression `Lexing.lexeme lexbuf` returns the complete string matched by the regular expression. In this case, the string represents a number, so we use the `int_of_string` function to convert it to a number.

There are actions for each different kind of token. The string expressions like `"true" { TRUE }` are used for keywords, and the special characters have actions, too, like `'{' { LEFT_BRACE }`.

Some of these patterns overlap. For example, the regular expression `"true"` is also matched by the `id` pattern. *ocamllex* used the following disambiguation when a prefix of the input is matched by more than one pattern:

- The longest match always wins. For example, the first input `trueX: 167` matches the regular expression `"true"` for four characters, and it matches `id` for five characters. The longer match wins, and the return value is `ID "trueX"`.

- If all matches have the same length, then the first action wins. If the input were `true: 167`, then both `"true"` and `id` match the first four characters; `"true"` is first, so the return value is `TRUE`.

Recursive Rules

Unlike many other lexer generators, *ocamllex* allows the definition of multiple lexers in the same file, and the definitions can be recursive. In this case, we use recursion to match string literals using the following rule definition:

```OCaml
and read_string buf =
  parse
  | '"'     { STRING (Buffer.contents buf) }
  | '\\' '/' { Buffer.add_char buf '/'; read_string buf lexbuf }
```

```
  | '\\' '\\' { Buffer.add_char buf '\\'; read_string buf lexbuf }
  | '\\' 'b'  { Buffer.add_char buf '\b'; read_string buf lexbuf }
  | '\\' 'f'  { Buffer.add_char buf '\012'; read_string buf lexbuf }
  | '\\' 'n'  { Buffer.add_char buf '\n'; read_string buf lexbuf }
  | '\\' 'r'  { Buffer.add_char buf '\r'; read_string buf lexbuf }
  | '\\' 't'  { Buffer.add_char buf '\t'; read_string buf lexbuf }
  | [^ '"' '\\']+
    { Buffer.add_string buf (Lexing.lexeme lexbuf);
      read_string buf lexbuf
    }
  | _ { raise (SyntaxError ("Illegal string character: " ^ Lexing.lexeme lexbuf)) }
  | eof { raise (SyntaxError ("String is not terminated")) }
```

This rule takes a buf : Buffer.t as an argument. If we reach the terminating double quote ", then we return the contents of the buffer as a STRING.

The other cases are for handling the string contents. The action [^ '"' '\\']+ { ... } matches normal input that does not contain a double quote or backslash. The actions beginning with a backslash \ define what to do for escape sequences. In each of these cases, the final step includes a recursive call to the lexer.

That covers the lexer. Next, we need to combine the lexer with the parser to bring it all together.

Handling Unicode

We've glossed over an important detail here: parsing Unicode characters to handle the full spectrum of the world's writing systems. OCaml has several third-party solutions to handling Unicode, with varying degrees of flexibility and complexity:

- Camomile (*http://camomile.sourceforge.net*) supports the full spectrum of Unicode character types, conversion from around 200 encodings, and collation and locale-sensitive case mappings.

- Ulex (*http://www.cduce.org/ulex*) is a lexer generator for Unicode that can serve as a Unicode-aware replacement for *ocamllex*.

- Uutf (*http://erratique.ch/software/uutf*) is a nonblocking streaming Unicode codec for OCaml, available as a standalone library. It is accompanied by the Uunf (*http://erratique.ch/software/uunf*) text normalization and Uucd (*http://erratique.ch/software/uucd*) Unicode character database libraries. There is also a robust parser for JSON (*http://erratique.ch/software/jsonm*) available that illustrates the use of Uutf in your own libraries.

All of these libraries are available via OPAM under their respective names.

Bringing It All Together

For the final part, we need to compose the lexer and parser. As we saw in the type definition in `parser.mli`, the parsing function expects a lexer of type `Lexing.lexbuf -> token`, and a lexbuf:

OCaml

```
val prog:(Lexing.lexbuf -> token) -> Lexing.lexbuf -> Json.value option
```

Before we start with the lexing, let's first define some functions to handle parsing errors. There are currently two errors: `Parser.Error` and `Lexer.SyntaxError`. A simple solution when encountering an error is to print the error and give up:

OCaml

```
open Core.Std
open Lexer
open Lexing

let print_position outx lexbuf =
  let pos = lexbuf.lex_curr_p in
  fprintf outx "%s:%d:%d" pos.pos_fname
    pos.pos_lnum (pos.pos_cnum - pos.pos_bol + 1)

let parse_with_error lexbuf =
  try Parser.prog Lexer.read lexbuf with
  | SyntaxError msg ->
    fprintf stderr "%a: %s\n" print_position lexbuf msg;
    None
  | Parser.Error ->
    fprintf stderr "%a: syntax error\n" print_position lexbuf;
    exit (-1)
```

The "give up on the first error" approach is easy to implement but isn't very friendly. In general, error handling can be pretty intricate, and we won't discuss it here. However, the Menhir parser defines additional mechanisms you can use to try and recover from errors. These are described in detail in its reference manual (*http://gallium.inria.fr/~fpottier/menhir/*).

The standard lexing library `Lexing` provides a function `from_channel` to read the input from a channel. The following function describes the structure, where the `Lexing.from_channel` function is used to construct a lexbuf, which is passed with the lexing function `Lexer.read` to the `Parser.prog` function. `Parsing.prog` returns `None` when it reaches end of file. We define a function `Json.output_value`, not shown here, to print a `Json.value`:

OCaml (part 1)

```
let rec parse_and_print lexbuf =
  match parse_with_error lexbuf with
  | Some value ->
    printf "%a\n" Json.output_value value;
```

```
        parse_and_print lexbuf
  | None -> ()

let loop filename () =
  let inx = In_channel.create filename in
  let lexbuf = Lexing.from_channel inx in
  lexbuf.lex_curr_p <- { lexbuf.lex_curr_p with pos_fname = filename };
  parse_and_print lexbuf;
  In_channel.close inx
```

Here's a test input file we can use to test the code we just wrote:

JSON

```
true
false
null
[1, 2, 3., 4.0, .5, 5.5e5, 6.3]
"Hello World"
{ "field1": "Hello",
  "field2": 17e13,
  "field3": [1, 2, 3],
  "field4": { "fieldA": 1, "fieldB": "Hello" }
}
```

Now build and run the example using this file, and you can see the full parser in action:

Terminal

```
$ ocamlbuild -use-menhir -tag thread -use-ocamlfind -quiet -pkg core test.native
$ ./test.native test1.json
true
false
null
[1, 2, 3.000000, 4.000000, 0.500000, 550000.000000, 6.300000]
"Hello World"
{ "field1": "Hello",
  "field2": 170000000000000.000000,
  "field3": [1, 2, 3],
  "field4": { "fieldA": 1,
  "fieldB": "Hello" } }
```

With our simple error handling scheme, errors are fatal and cause the program to terminate with a nonzero exit code:

Terminal

```
$ cat test2.json
{ "name": "Chicago",
  "zips": [12345,
}
{ "name": "New York",
  "zips": [10004]
}
$ ./test.native test2.json
test2.json:3:2: syntax error
```

That wraps up our parsing tutorial. As an aside, notice that the JSON polymorphic variant type that we defined in this chapter is actually structurally compatible with the Yojson representation explained in Chapter 15. That means that you can take this parser and use it with the helper functions in Yojson to build more sophisticated applications.

CHAPTER 17

Data Serialization with S-Expressions

S-expressions are nested parenthetical expressions whose atomic values are strings. They were first popularized by the Lisp programming language in the 1960s. They have remained one of the simplest and most effective ways to encode structured data in a human-readable and editable form.

There's a full definition of s-expressions available online (*http://people.csail.mit.edu/ rivest/Sexp.txt*). An example s-expression might look like this:

```
(this (is an) (s expression))
```

S-expressions play a major role in Core, effectively acting as the default serialization format. Indeed, we've encountered s-expressions multiple times already, including in Chapter 7, Chapter 9, and Chapter 10.

This chapter will go into s-expressions in more depth. In particular, we'll discuss:

- The details of the s-expression format, including how to parse it while generating good error messages for debugging malformed inputs
- How to generate s-expressions from arbitrary OCaml types
- How to use custom type annotations to control the exact printing behavior for s-expression converters
- How to integrate s-expressions into your interfaces, in particular how to add s-expression converters to a module without breaking abstraction boundaries

We'll tie this together at the end of the chapter with a simple s-expression formatted configuration file for a web server

Basic Usage

The type used to represent an s-expression is quite simple:

OCaml

```
module Sexp : sig
  type t =
  | Atom of string
  | List of t list
end
```

An s-expression can be thought of as a tree where each node contains a list of its children, and where the leaves of the tree are strings. Core provides good support for s-expressions in its Sexp module, including functions for converting s-expressions to and from strings. Let's rewrite our example s-expression in terms of this type:

OCaml utop

```
# Sexp.List [
    Sexp.Atom "this";
    Sexp.List [ Sexp.Atom "is"; Sexp.Atom "an"];
    Sexp.List [ Sexp.Atom "s"; Sexp.Atom "expression" ];
  ];;
- : Sexp.t = (this (is an) (s expression))
```

This prints out nicely because Core registers a pretty printer with the toplevel. This pretty printer is based on the functions in Sexp for converting s-expressions to and from strings:

OCaml utop

```
# Sexp.to_string (Sexp.List [Sexp.Atom "1"; Sexp.Atom "2"]) ;;
- : string = "(1 2)"
# Sexp.of_string ("(1 2 (3 4))") ;;
- : Sexp.t = (1 2 (3 4))
```

In addition to providing the Sexp module, most of the base types in Core support conversion to and from s-expressions. For example, we can use the conversion functions defined in the respective modules for integers, strings, and exceptions:

OCaml utop

```
# Int.sexp_of_t 3;;
- : Sexp.t = 3
# String.sexp_of_t "hello";;
- : Sexp.t = hello
# Exn.sexp_of_t (Invalid_argument "foo");;
- : Sexp.t = (Invalid_argument foo)
```

It's also possible to convert more complex types such as lists or arrays that are polymorphic across the types that they can contain:

OCaml utop (part 1)

```
# List.sexp_of_t;;
- : ('a -> Sexp.t) -> 'a list -> Sexp.t = <fun>
```

```
# List.sexp_of_t Int.sexp_of_t [1; 2; 3];;
- : Sexp.t = (1 2 3)
```

Notice that `List.sexp_of_t` is polymorphic and takes as its first argument another conversion function to handle the elements of the list to be converted. Core uses this scheme more generally for defining sexp converters for polymorphic types.

The functions that go in the other direction, *i.e.*, reconstruct an OCaml value from an s-expression, use essentially the same trick for handling polymorphic types, as shown in the following example. Note that these functions will fail with an exception when presented with an s-expression that doesn't match the structure of the OCaml type in question.

OCaml utop (part 2)

```
# List.t_of_sexp;;
- : (Sexp.t -> 'a) -> Sexp.t -> 'a list = <fun>
# List.t_of_sexp Int.t_of_sexp (Sexp.of_string "(1 2 3)");;
- : int list = [1; 2; 3]
# List.t_of_sexp Int.t_of_sexp (Sexp.of_string "(1 2 three)");;
Exception:
(Sexplib.Conv.Of_sexp_error (Failure "int_of_sexp: (Failure int_of_string)")
 three).
```

More on Top-Level Printing

The values of the s-expressions that we created were printed properly as s-expressions in the toplevel, instead of as the tree of Atom and List variants that they're actually made of.

This is due to OCaml's facility for installing custom *top-level printers* that can rewrite some values into more top-level-friendly equivalents. They are generally installed as *ocamlfind* packages ending in top:

Terminal

```
$ ocamlfind list | grep top
compiler-libs.toplevel (version: [distributed with Ocaml])
core_top           (version: 109.37.00)
ctypes.top         (version: 0.1)
lwt.simple-top     (version: 2.4.3)
num-top            (version: 1.3.3)
sexplib.top        (version: 109.20.00)
uri.top            (version: 1.3.8)
```

The `core.top` package (which you should have loaded by default in your `.ocamlinit` file) loads in printers for the Core extensions already, so you don't need to do anything special to use the s-expression printer.

Generating S-Expressions from OCaml Types

But what if you want a function to convert a brand new type to an s-expression? You can of course write it yourself manually. Here's an example:

OCaml utop

```
# type t = { foo: int; bar: float } ;;
type t = { foo : int; bar : float; }
# let sexp_of_t t =
    let a x = Sexp.Atom x and l x = Sexp.List x in
    l [ l [a "foo"; Int.sexp_of_t t.foo  ];
        l [a "bar"; Float.sexp_of_t t.bar]; ] ;;
val sexp_of_t : t -> Sexp.t = <fun>
# sexp_of_t { foo = 3; bar = -5.5 } ;;
- : Sexp.t = ((foo 3) (bar -5.5))
```

This is somewhat tiresome to write, and it gets more so when you consider the parser, i.e., t_of_sexp, which is considerably more complex. Writing this kind of parsing and printing code by hand is mechanical and error prone, not to mention a drag.

Given how mechanical the code is, you could imagine writing a program that inspected the type definition and autogenerated the conversion code for you. As it turns out, Sexplib does just that. Sexplib, which is included with Core, provides both a library for manipulating s-expressions and a *syntax extension* for generating such conversion functions. With that syntax extension enabled, any type that has with sexp as an annotation will trigger the generation of the functions we want:

OCaml utop

```
# type t = { foo: int; bar: float } with sexp ;;
type t = { foo : int; bar : float; }
val t_of_sexp : Sexp.t -> t = <fun>
val sexp_of_t : t -> Sexp.t = <fun>
# t_of_sexp (Sexp.of_string "((bar 35) (foo 3))") ;;
- : t = {foo = 3; bar = 35.}
```

The syntax extension can be used outside of type declarations as well. As discussed in Chapter 7, with sexp can be attached to the declaration of an exception, which will improve the ability of Core to generate a useful string representation:

OCaml utop (part 1)

```
# exception Bad_message of string list ;;
exception Bad_message of string list
# Exn.to_string (Bad_message ["1";"2";"3"]) ;;
- : string = "(\"Bad_message(_)\")"
# exception Good_message of string list with sexp;;
exception Good_message of string list
# Exn.to_string (Good_message ["1";"2";"3"]) ;;
- : string = "(//toplevel//.Good_message (1 2 3))"
```

You don't always have to declare a named type to create an s-expression converter. The following syntax lets you create one inline, as part of a larger expression:

OCaml utop

```
# let l = [(1,"one"); (2,"two")] ;;
val l : (int * string) list = [(1, "one"); (2, "two")]
# List.iter l ~f:(fun x ->
    <:sexp_of<int * string>> x
    |> Sexp.to_string
    |> print_endline) ;;
(1 one)
(2 two)
- : unit = ()
```

The declaration `<:sexp_of<int * string>>` simply gets expanded to the sexp converter for the type `int * string`. This is useful whenever you need a sexp converter for an anonymous type.

The syntax extensions bundled with Core almost all have the same basic structure: they autogenerate code based on type definitions, implementing functionality that you could in theory have implemented by hand, but with far less programmer effort.

Syntax Extensions, Camlp4, and Type_conv

OCaml doesn't directly support generating code from type definitions. Instead, it supplies a powerful syntax extension mechanism known as Camlp4, which lets you extend the grammar of the language. Camlp4 is well integrated into the OCaml toolchain and can be activated within the toplevel and also included in compilation using the `-pp` compiler flag.

Sexplib is part of a family of syntax extensions, including Comparelib, described in Chapter 13, and Fieldslib, described in Chapter 5, that generate code based on type declarations and are all based on a common library called Type_conv. This library provides a common language for annotating types (e.g., using the `with` notation) and utilities for working with type definitions. If you want to build your own type-driven syntax extension, you should consider basing it on Type_conv.

The Sexp Format

The textual representation of s-expressions is pretty straightforward. An s-expression is written down as a nested parenthetical expression, with whitespace-separated strings as the atoms. Quotes are used for atoms that contain parentheses or spaces themselves; backslash is the escape character; and semicolons are used to introduce single-line comments. Thus, the following file, *example.scm*:

```
;; example.scm

((foo 3.3) ;; This is a comment
 (bar "this is () an \" atom"))
```

can be loaded using Sexplib. As you can see, the commented data is not part of the resulting s-expression:

```
# Sexp.load_sexp "example.scm" ;;
- : Sexp.t = ((foo 3.3) (bar "this is () an \" atom"))
```

All in, the s-expression format supports three comment syntaxes:

;

> Comments out everything to the end of line

#|
|#

> Delimiters for commenting out a block

#;

> Comments out the first complete s-expression that follows

The following example shows all of these in action:

```
;; comment_heavy_example.scm
((this is included)
 ; (this is commented out
 (this stays)
#; (all of this is commented
    out (even though it crosses lines.))
  (and #| block delimiters #| which can be nested |#
    will comment out
    an arbitrary multi-line block))) |#
  now we're done
  ))
```

Again, loading the file as an s-expression drops the comments:

```
# Sexp.load_sexp "comment_heavy.scm" ;;
- : Sexp.t = ((this is included) (this stays) (and now we're done))
```

If we introduce an error into our s-expression, by, say, creating a file broken_exam ple.scm which is example.scm, without open-paren in front of bar, we'll get a parse error:

```
# Exn.handle_uncaught ~exit:false (fun () ->
    ignore (Sexp.load_sexp "example_broken.scm")) ;;
Uncaught exception:
```

```
(Sexplib.Sexp.Parse_error
 ((location parse) (err_msg "unexpected character: ')'") (text_line 4)
  (text_char 29) (global_offset 78) (buf_pos 78)))
- : unit = ()
```

In the preceding example, we use Exn.handle_uncaught to make sure that the exception gets printed out in full detail. You should generally wrap every Core program in this handler to get good error messages for any unexpected exceptions.

Preserving Invariants

The most important functionality provided by Sexplib is the autogeneration of converters for new types. We've seen a bit of how this works already, but let's walk through a complete example. Here's the source for a simple library for representing integer intervals, very similar to the one described in Chapter 9:

OCaml

```
(* Module for representing closed integer intervals *)
open Core.Std

(* Invariant: For any Range (x,y), y >= x *)
type t =
  | Range of int * int
  | Empty
with sexp

let is_empty =
  function
  | Empty -> true
  | Range _ -> false

let create x y =
  if x > y then
    Empty
  else
    Range (x,y)

let contains i x =
  match i with
  | Empty -> false
  | Range (low,high) -> x >= low && x <= high
```

We can now use this module as follows:

OCaml

```
open Core.Std

let intervals =
  let module I = Int_interval in
  [ I.create 3 4;
```

```
      I.create 5 4; (* should be empty *)
      I.create 2 3;
      I.create 1 6;
    ]

let () =
  intervals
  |> List.sexp_of_t Int_interval.sexp_of_t
  |> Sexp.to_string_hum
  |> print_endline
```

But we're still missing something: we haven't created an mli signature for Int_inter
val yet. Note that we need to explicitly export the s-expression converters that were
created within the ml file. For example, here's an interface that doesn't export the s-
expression functions:

OCaml

```
type t

val is_empty : t -> bool
val create : int -> int -> t
val contains : t -> int -> bool
```

Building this will give us the following error:

Terminal

```
$ corebuild test_interval_nosexp.native
File "test_interval_nosexp.ml", line 14, characters 20-42:
Error: Unbound value Int_interval.sexp_of_t
Command exited with code 2.
```

We could export the types by hand in the signature, by writing the signatures for the
extra functions generated by Sexplib:

OCaml

```
open Core.Std

type t
val t_of_sexp : Sexp.t -> t
val sexp_of_t : t -> Sexp.t

val is_empty : t -> bool
val create : int -> int -> t
val contains : t -> int -> bool
```

This isn't an ideal solution, as it makes you repeatedly expose these extra functions in
every signature you create where you want to serialize values. Sexplib solves this by
exposing the same syntax extension in signature definitions so that we can just use the
same with shorthand in the mli file. Here's the final version of the signature that does
just this:

```
type t with sexp

val is_empty : t -> bool
val create : int -> int -> t
val contains : t -> int -> bool
```

At this point, `test_interval.ml` will compile again, and if we run it, we'll get the following output:

```
$ corebuild test_interval.native
$ ./test_interval.native
((Range 3 4) Empty (Range 2 3) (Range 1 6))
```

One easy mistake to make when dealing with sexp converters is to ignore the fact that those converters can violate the invariants of your code. For example, the `Int_inter val` module depends for the correctness of the `is_empty` check on the fact that for any value `Range (x,y)`, `y` is greater than or equal to `x`. The `create` function preserves this invariant, but the `t_of_sexp` function does not.

We can fix this problem by overriding the autogenerated function and writing a custom sexp converter that wraps the autogenerated converter with whatever invariant checks are necessary:

```
type t =
  | Range of int * int
  | Empty
with sexp

let create x y =
  if x > y then Empty else Range (x,y)

let t_of_sexp sexp =
  let t = t_of_sexp sexp in
  begin match t with
    | Empty -> ()
    | Range (x,y) ->
      if y < x then of_sexp_error "Upper and lower bound of Range swapped" sexp
  end;
  t
```

This trick of overriding an existing function definition with a new one is perfectly acceptable in OCaml. Since `t_of_sexp` is defined with an ordinary `let` rather than a `let rec`, the call to the `t_of_sexp` goes to the Sexplib-generated version of the function, rather than being a recursive call.

Another important aspect of our definition is that we call the function `of_sexp_er ror` to raise an exception when the parsing process fails. This improves the error reporting that Sexplib can provide when a conversion fails, as we'll see in the next section.

Getting Good Error Messages

There are two steps to deserializing a type from an s-expression: first, converting the bytes in a file to an s-expression; and the second, converting that s-expression into the type in question. One problem with this is that it can be hard to localize errors to the right place using this scheme. Consider the following example:

OCaml

```
open Core.Std

type t = {
  a: string;
  b: int;
  c: float option
} with sexp

let run () =
  let t =
    Sexp.load_sexp "foo_broken_example.scm"
    |> t_of_sexp
  in
  printf "b is: %d\n%!" t.b

let () =
  Exn.handle_uncaught ~exit:true run
```

If you were to run this on a malformatted file, say, this one:

Scheme

```
((a "not-an-integer")
 (b "not-an-integer")
 (c 1.0))
```

you'll get the following error:

Terminal

```
$ corebuild read_foo.native
$ ./read_foo.native foo_example_broken.scm
Uncaught exception:

  (Sexplib.Conv.Of_sexp_error
   (Failure "int_of_sexp: (Failure int_of_string)") not-an-integer)

Raised at file "lib/conv.ml", line 281, characters 36-72
Called from file "lib/core_int.ml", line 6, characters 7-14
Called from file "lib/std_internal.ml", line 115, characters 7-33
Called from file "read_foo.ml", line 5, characters 2-8
Called from file "read_foo.ml", line 4, characters 2-40
Called from file "read_foo.ml", line 11, characters 4-60
Called from file "lib/exn.ml", line 87, characters 6-10
```

If all you have is the error message and the string, it's not terribly informative. In particular, you know that the parsing errored out on the atom "not-an-integer," but you don't know which one! In a large file, this kind of bad error message can be pure misery.

But there's hope! We can make a small change to the code to improve the error message greatly:

OCaml

```ocaml
open Core.Std

type t = {
  a: string;
  b: int;
  c: float option
} with sexp

let run () =
  let t = Sexp.load_sexp_conv_exn "foo_broken_example.scm" t_of_sexp in
  printf "b is: %d\n%!" t.b

let () =
  Exn.handle_uncaught ~exit:true run
```

If we run it again, we'll see a much more specific error:

Terminal

```
$ corebuild read_foo_better_errors.native
$ ./read_foo_better_errors.native foo_example_broken.scm
Uncaught exception:

  (Sexplib.Conv.Of_sexp_error
   (Sexplib.Sexp.Annotated.Conv_exn foo_broken_example.scm:2:5
    (Failure "int_of_sexp: (Failure int_of_string)"))
   not-an-integer)

Raised at file "lib/pre_sexp.ml", line 1145, characters 12-58
Called from file "read_foo_better_errors.ml", line 10, characters 10-68
Called from file "lib/exn.ml", line 87, characters 6-10
```

In the preceding error, `foo_broken_example.scm:2:5` tells us that the error occurred in the file `"foo_broken_example.scm"` on line 2, character 5. This is a much better start for figuring out what went wrong. The ability to find the precise location of the error depends on the sexp converter reporting errors using the function `of_sexp_error`. This is already done by converters generated by Sexplib, but you should make sure to do the same when you write custom converters.

Sexp-Conversion Directives

Sexplib supports a collection of directives for modifying the default behavior of the autogenerated sexp converters. These directives allow you to customize the way in which types are represented as s-expressions without having to write a custom converter.

Note that the extra directives aren't part of the standard OCaml syntax, but are added via the Sexplib syntax extension. However, since Sexplib is used throughout Core and is part of the standard bundle activated by *corebuild*, you can use these in your own Core code without any special effort.

sexp_opaque

The most commonly used directive is `sexp_opaque`, whose purpose is to mark a given component of a type as being unconvertible. Anything marked with `sexp_opaque` will be presented as the atom <opaque> by the to-sexp converter, and will trigger an exception from the from-sexp converter.

Note that the type of a component marked as opaque doesn't need to have a sexp converter defined. Here, if we define a type without a sexp converter and then try to use another type with a sexp converter, we'll error out:

OCaml utop

```
# type no_converter = int * int ;;
type no_converter = int * int
# type t = { a: no_converter; b: string } with sexp ;;
Characters 14-26:
Error: Unbound value no_converter_of_sexp
```

But with `sexp_opaque`, we can embed our opaque `no_converter` type within the other data structure without an error.

OCaml utop (part 1)

```
# type t = { a: no_converter sexp_opaque; b: string } with sexp ;;
type t = { a : no_converter; b : string; }
val t_of_sexp : Sexp.t -> t = <fun>
val sexp_of_t : t -> Sexp.t = <fun>
```

And if we now convert a value of this type to an s-expression, we'll see the contents of field a marked as opaque:

OCaml utop (part 2)

```
# sexp_of_t { a = (3,4); b = "foo" } ;;
- : Sexp.t = ((a <opaque>) (b foo))
```

Note that the `t_of_sexp` function for an opaque type is generated, but will fail at runtime if it is used:

OCaml utop (part 3)

```
# t_of_sexp (Sexp.of_string "((a whatever) (b foo))") ;;
Exception:
```

```
(Sexplib.Conv.Of_sexp_error
 (Failure "opaque_of_sexp: cannot convert opaque values") whatever).
```

This is there to allow for s-expression converters to be created for types containing sexp_opaque values. This is useful because the resulting converters won't necessarily fail on all inputs. For example, if you have a record containing a no_converter list, the t_of_sexp function would still succeed when the list is empty:

OCaml utop (part 4)

```
# type t = { a: no_converter sexp_opaque list; b: string } with sexp ;;
type t = { a : no_converter list; b : string; }
val t_of_sexp : Sexp.t -> t = <fun>
val sexp_of_t : t -> Sexp.t = <fun>
# t_of_sexp (Sexp.of_string "((a ()) (b foo))") ;;
- : t = {a = []; b = "foo"}
```

If you really only want to generate one direction of converter, one can do this by annotating the type with with sexp_of or with of_sexp instead of with sexp:

OCaml utop (part 5)

```
# type t = { a: no_converter sexp_opaque; b: string } with sexp_of ;;
type t = { a : no_converter; b : string; }
val sexp_of_t : t -> Sexp.t = <fun>
# type t = { a: no_converter sexp_opaque; b: string } with of_sexp ;;
type t = { a : no_converter; b : string; }
val t_of_sexp : Sexp.t -> t = <fun>
```

sexp_list

Sometimes, sexp converters have more parentheses than one would ideally like. Consider, for example, the following variant type:

OCaml utop

```
# type compatible_versions =
  | Specific of string list
  | All with sexp ;;
type compatible_versions = Specific of string list | All
val compatible_versions_of_sexp : Sexp.t -> compatible_versions = <fun>
val sexp_of_compatible_versions : compatible_versions -> Sexp.t = <fun>
# sexp_of_compatible_versions
  (Specific ["3.12.0"; "3.12.1"; "3.13.0"]) ;;
- : Sexp.t = (Specific (3.12.0 3.12.1 3.13.0))
```

You might prefer to make the syntax a bit less parenthesis-laden by dropping the parentheses around the list. We can replace the string list in the type declaration with string sexp_list to give us this alternate syntax:

OCaml utop (part 1)

```
# type compatible_versions =
  | Specific of string sexp_list
  | All with sexp ;;
type compatible_versions = Specific of string list | All
```

```
val compatible_versions_of_sexp : Sexp.t -> compatible_versions = <fun>
val sexp_of_compatible_versions : compatible_versions -> Sexp.t = <fun>
# sexp_of_compatible_versions
  (Specific ["3.12.0"; "3.12.1"; "3.13.0"]) ;;
- : Sexp.t = (Specific 3.12.0 3.12.1 3.13.0)
```

sexp_option

Another common directive is `sexp_option`, which is used to make a record field optional in the s-expression. Normally, optional values are represented either as `()` for `None`, or as `(x)` for `Some x`, and a record field containing an option would be rendered accordingly. For example:

OCaml utop

```
# type t = { a: int option; b: string } with sexp ;;
type t = { a : int option; b : string; }
val t_of_sexp : Sexp.t -> t = <fun>
val sexp_of_t : t -> Sexp.t = <fun>
# sexp_of_t { a = None; b = "hello" } ;;
- : Sexp.t = ((a ()) (b hello))
# sexp_of_t { a = Some 3; b = "hello" } ;;
- : Sexp.t = ((a (3)) (b hello))
```

But what if we want a field to be optional, i.e., we want to allow it to be omitted from the record entirely? In that case, we can mark it with `sexp_option`:

OCaml utop (part 1)

```
# type t = { a: int sexp_option; b: string } with sexp ;;
type t = { a : int option; b : string; }
val t_of_sexp : Sexp.t -> t = <fun>
val sexp_of_t : t -> Sexp.t = <fun>
# sexp_of_t { a = Some 3; b = "hello" } ;;
- : Sexp.t = ((a 3) (b hello))
# sexp_of_t { a = None; b = "hello" } ;;
- : Sexp.t = ((b hello))
```

Specifying Defaults

The `sexp_option` declaration is really just an example of specifying a default behavior for dealing with an unspecified field. In particular, `sexp_option` fills in absent fields with `None`. But you might want to allow other ways of filling in default values.

Consider the following type, which represents the configuration of a very simple web server:

OCaml utop

```
# type http_server_config = {
    web_root: string;
    port: int;
    addr: string;
  } with sexp ;;
```

```
type http_server_config = { web_root : string; port : int; addr : string; }
val http_server_config_of_sexp : Sexp.t -> http_server_config = <fun>
val sexp_of_http_server_config : http_server_config -> Sexp.t = <fun>
```

One could imagine making some of these parameters optional; in particular, by default, we might want the web server to bind to port 80, and to listen as localhost. We can do this as follows:

OCaml utop (part 1)

```
# type http_server_config = {
    web_root: string;
    port: int with default(80);
    addr: string with default("localhost");
  } with sexp ;;
type http_server_config = { web_root : string; port : int; addr : string; }
val http_server_config_of_sexp : Sexp.t -> http_server_config = <fun>
val sexp_of_http_server_config : http_server_config -> Sexp.t = <fun>
```

Now, if we try to convert an s-expression that specifies only the web_root, we'll see that the other values are filled in with the desired defaults:

OCaml utop (part 2)

```
# let cfg = http_server_config_of_sexp
  (Sexp.of_string "((web_root /var/www/html))") ;;
val cfg : http_server_config =
  {web_root = "/var/www/html"; port = 80; addr = "localhost"}
```

If we convert the configuration back out to an s-expression, you'll notice that all of the fields are present, even though they're not strictly necessary:

OCaml utop (part 3)

```
# sexp_of_http_server_config cfg ;;
- : Sexp.t = ((web_root /var/www/html) (port 80) (addr localhost))
```

We could make the generated s-expression also drop exported values, by using the sexp_drop_default directive:

OCaml utop (part 4)

```
# type http_server_config = {
    web_root: string;
    port: int with default(80), sexp_drop_default;
    addr: string with default("localhost"), sexp_drop_default;
  } with sexp ;;
type http_server_config = { web_root : string; port : int; addr : string; }
val http_server_config_of_sexp : Sexp.t -> http_server_config = <fun>
val sexp_of_http_server_config : http_server_config -> Sexp.t = <fun>
# let cfg = http_server_config_of_sexp
  (Sexp.of_string "((web_root /var/www/html))") ;;
val cfg : http_server_config =
  {web_root = "/var/www/html"; port = 80; addr = "localhost"}
# sexp_of_http_server_config cfg ;;
- : Sexp.t = ((web_root /var/www/html))
```

As you can see, the fields that are at their default values are simply omitted from the s-expression. On the other hand, if we convert a config with other values, then those values will be included in the s-expression:

OCaml utop (part 5)

```
# sexp_of_http_server_config { cfg with port = 8080 } ;;
- : Sexp.t = ((web_root /var/www/html) (port 8080))
# sexp_of_http_server_config
  { cfg with port = 8080; addr = "192.168.0.1" } ;;
- : Sexp.t = ((web_root /var/www/html) (port 8080) (addr 192.168.0.1))
```

This can be very useful in designing config file formats that are both reasonably terse and easy to generate and maintain. It can also be useful for backwards compatibility: if you add a new field to your config record, but you make that field optional, then you should still be able to parse older version of your config.

## CHAPTER 18

Concurrent Programming with Async

The logic of building programs that interact with the outside world is often dominated by waiting: waiting for the click of a mouse, or for data to be fetched from disk, or for space to be available on an outgoing network buffer. Even mildly sophisticated interactive applications are typically *concurrent*: needing to wait for multiple different events at the same time, responding immediately to whatever event happens first.

One approach to concurrency is to use preemptive system threads, which is the dominant approach in languages like Java or C#. In this model, each task that may require simultaneous waiting is given an operating system thread of its own so it can block without stopping the entire program.

Another approach is to have a single-threaded program, where that single thread runs an *event loop* whose job is to react to external events like timeouts or mouse clicks by invoking a callback function that has been registered for that purpose. This approach shows up in languages like JavaScript that have single-threaded runtimes, as well as in many GUI toolkits.

Each of these mechanisms has its own trade-offs. System threads require significant memory and other resources per thread. Also, the operating system can arbitrarily interleave the execution of system threads, requiring the programmer to carefully protect shared resources with locks and condition variables, which is exceedingly error-prone.

Single-threaded event-driven systems, on the other hand, execute a single task at a time and do not require the same kind of complex synchronization that preemptive threads do. However, the inverted control structure of an event-driven program often means that your own control flow has to be threaded awkwardly through the system's event loop, leading to a maze of event callbacks.

This chapter covers the Async library, which offers a hybrid model that aims to provide the best of both worlds, avoiding the performance compromises and synchronization woes of preemptive threads without the confusing inversion of control that usually comes with event-driven systems.

Async Basics

Recall how I/O is typically done in Core. Here's a simple example:

OCaml utop (part 1)

```
# In_channel.read_all;;
- : string -> string = <fun>
# Out_channel.write_all "test.txt" ~data:"This is only a test.";;
- : unit = ()
# In_channel.read_all "test.txt";;
- : string = "This is only a test."
```

From the type of In_channel.read_all, you can see that it must be a blocking operation. In particular, the fact that it returns a concrete string means it can't return until the read has completed. The blocking nature of the call means that no progress can be made on anything else until the read is completed.

In Async, well-behaved functions never block. Instead, they return a value of type Deferred.t that acts as a placeholder that will eventually be filled in with the result. As an example, consider the signature of the Async equivalent of In_channel.read_all:

OCaml utop (part 3)

```
# #require "async";;
# open Async.Std;;
# Reader.file_contents;;
- : string -> string Deferred.t = <fun>
```

We first load the Async package in the toplevel using #require, and then open Async.Std, which adds a number of new identifiers and modules into our environment that make using Async more convenient. Opening Async.Std is standard practice for writing programs using Async, much like opening Core.Std is for using Core.

A deferred is essentially a handle to a value that may be computed in the future. As such, if we call Reader.file_contents, the resulting deferred will initially be empty, as you can see by calling Deferred.peek on the resulting deferred:

OCaml utop (part 4)

```
# let contents = Reader.file_contents "test.txt";;
val contents : string Deferred.t = <abstr>
# Deferred.peek contents;;
- : string option = None
```

The value in contents isn't yet determined partly because nothing running could do the necessary I/O. When using Async, processing of I/O and other events is handled by the Async scheduler. When writing a standalone program, you need to start the scheduler explicitly, but *utop* knows about Async and can start the scheduler automatically. More than that, *utop* knows about deferred values, and when you type in an expression of type `Deferred.t`, it will make sure the scheduler is running and block until the deferred is determined. Thus, we can write:

OCaml utop (part 5)

```
# contents;;
- : string = "This is only a test."
```

If we peek again, we'll see that the value of `contents` has been determined:

OCaml utop (part 6)

```
# Deferred.peek contents;;
- : string option = Some "This is only a test."
```

In order to do real work with deferreds, we need a way of waiting for a deferred computation to finish, which we do using `Deferred.bind`. First, let's consider the type-signature of `bind`:

OCaml utop (part 7)

```
# Deferred.bind ;;
- : 'a Deferred.t -> ('a -> 'b Deferred.t) -> 'b Deferred.t = <fun>
```

`Deferred.bind d f` takes a deferred value `d` and a function `f` that is to be run with the value of `d` once it's determined. You can think of `Deferred.bind` as a kind of sequencing operator, and what we're doing is essentially taking an asynchronous computation `d` and tacking on another stage comprised by the actions of the function `f`.

At a more concrete level, the call to `Deferred.bind` returns a new deferred that becomes determined when the deferred returned by `f` is determined. It also implicitly registers with the scheduler an *Async job* that is responsible for running `f` once `d` is determined.

Here's a simple use of `bind` for a function that replaces a file with an uppercase version of its contents:

OCaml utop (part 8)

```
# let uppercase_file filename =
    Deferred.bind (Reader.file_contents filename)
    (fun text ->
        Writer.save filename ~contents:(String.uppercase text))
  ;;
val uppercase_file : string -> unit Deferred.t = <fun>
# uppercase_file "test.txt";;
- : unit = ()
# Reader.file_contents "test.txt";;
- : string = "THIS IS ONLY A TEST."
```

Writing out `Deferred.bind` explicitly can be rather verbose, and so `Async.Std` includes an infix operator for it: `>>=`. Using this operator, we can rewrite `uppercase_file` as follows:

OCaml utop (part 9)

```
# let uppercase_file filename =
    Reader.file_contents filename
    >>= fun text ->
```

```
    Writer.save filename ~contents:(String.uppercase text)
  ;;
val uppercase_file : string -> unit Deferred.t = <fun>
```

In the preceding code, we've dropped the parentheses around the function on the right-hand side of the bind, and we didn't add a level of indentation for the contents of that function. This is standard practice for using the bind operator.

Now let's look at another potential use of bind. In this case, we'll write a function that counts the number of lines in a file:

OCaml utop (part 10)

```
# let count_lines filename =
    Reader.file_contents filename
    >>= fun text ->
    List.length (String.split text ~on:'\n')
  ;;
Characters 85-125:
Error: This expression has type int but an expression was expected of type
         'a Deferred.t
```

This looks reasonable enough, but as you can see, the compiler is unhappy. The issue here is that bind expects a function that returns a deferred, but we've provided it a function that returns the nondeferred result directly. To make these signatures match, we need a function for taking an ordinary value and wrapping it in a deferred. This function is a standard part of Async and is called return:

OCaml utop (part 11)

```
# return;;
- : 'a -> 'a Deferred.t = <fun>
# let three = return 3;;
val three : int Deferred.t = <abstr>
# three;;
- : int = 3
```

Using return, we can make count_lines compile:

OCaml utop (part 12)

```
# let count_lines filename =
    Reader.file_contents filename
    >>= fun text ->
    return (List.length (String.split text ~on:'\n'))
  ;;
val count_lines : string -> int Deferred.t = <fun>
```

Together, bind and return form a design pattern in functional programming known as a *monad*. You'll run across this signature in many applications beyond just threads. Indeed, we already ran across monads in "bind and Other Error Handling Idioms" on page 127.

Calling bind and return together is a fairly common pattern, and as such there is a standard shortcut for it called Deferred.map, which has the following signature:

```
# Deferred.map;;
- : 'a Deferred.t -> f:('a -> 'b) -> 'b Deferred.t = <fun>
```

and comes with its own infix equivalent, `>>|`. Using it, we can rewrite `count_lines` again a bit more succinctly:

```
# let count_lines filename =
    Reader.file_contents filename
    >>| fun text ->
    List.length (String.split text ~on:'\n')
  ;;
val count_lines : string -> int Deferred.t = <fun>
# count_lines "/etc/hosts";;
- : int = 12
```

Note that `count_lines` returns a deferred, but *utop* waits for that deferred to become determined, and shows us the contents of the deferred instead.

Ivars and Upon

Deferreds are usually built using combinations of `bind`, `map` and `return`, but sometimes you want to construct a deferred that you can determine explicitly with usercode. This is done using an *ivar*. (The term ivar dates back to a language called Concurrent ML that was developed by John Reppy in the early '90s. The "i" in ivar stands for incremental.)

There are three fundamental operations for working with an ivar: you can create one, using `Ivar.create`; you can read off the deferred that corresponds to the ivar in question, using `Ivar.read`; and you can fill an ivar, thus causing the corresponding deferred to become determined, using `Ivar.fill`. These operations are illustrated below:

```
# let ivar = Ivar.create ();;
val ivar : '_a Ivar.t = <abstr>
# let def = Ivar.read ivar;;
val def : '_a Deferred.t = <abstr>
# Deferred.peek def;;
- : '_a option = None
# Ivar.fill ivar "Hello";;
- : unit = ()
# Deferred.peek def;;
- : string option = Some "Hello"
```

Ivars are something of a low-level feature; operators like `map`, `bind` and `return` are typically easier to use and think about. But ivars can be useful when you want to build a synchronization pattern that isn't already well supported.

As an example, imagine we wanted a way of scheduling a sequence of actions that would run after a fixed delay. In addition, we'd like to guarantee that these delayed actions are executed in the same order they were scheduled in. Here's a reasonable signature that captures this idea:

```
# module type Delayer_intf = sig
    type t
    val create : Time.Span.t -> t
    val schedule : t -> (unit -> 'a Deferred.t) -> 'a Deferred.t
  end;;
module type Delayer_intf =
  sig
    type t
    val create : Core.Span.t -> t
    val schedule : t -> (unit -> 'a Deferred.t) -> 'a Deferred.t
  end
```

An action is handed to schedule in the form of a deferred-returning thunk (a thunk is a function whose argument is of type unit). A deferred is handed back to the caller of schedule that will eventually be filled with the contents of the deferred value returned by the thunk. To implement this, we'll use an operator called upon, which has the following signature:

```
# upon;;
- : 'a Deferred.t -> ('a -> unit) -> unit = <fun>
```

Like bind and return, upon schedules a callback to be executed when the deferred it is passed is determined; but unlike those calls, it doesn't create a new deferred for this callback to fill.

Our delayer implementation is organized around a queue of thunks, where every call to schedule adds a thunk to the queue and also schedules a job in the future to grab a thunk off the queue and run it. The waiting will be done using the function after, which takes a time span and returns a deferred which becomes determined after that time span elapses:

```
# module Delayer : Delayer_intf = struct
    type t = { delay: Time.Span.t;
               jobs: (unit -> unit) Queue.t;
             }

    let create delay =
      { delay; jobs = Queue.create () }

    let schedule t thunk =
      let ivar = Ivar.create () in
      Queue.enqueue t.jobs (fun () ->
        upon (thunk ()) (fun x -> Ivar.fill ivar x));
      upon (after t.delay) (fun () ->
        let job = Queue.dequeue_exn t.jobs in
```

```
        job ());
      Ivar.read ivar
   end;;
module Delayer : Delayer_intf
```

This code isn't particularly long, but it is subtle. In particular, note how the queue of thunks is used to ensure that the enqueued actions are run in order, even if the thunks scheduled by upon are run out of order. This kind of subtlety is typical of code that involves ivars and upon, and because of this, you should stick to the simpler map/bind/ return style of working with deferreds when you can.

Examples: An Echo Server

Now that we have the basics of Async under our belt, let's look at a small standalone Async program. In particular, we'll write an echo server, i.e., a program that accepts connections from clients and spits back whatever is sent to it.

The first step is to create a function that can copy data from an input to an output. Here, we'll use Async's Reader and Writer modules, which provide a convenient abstraction for working with input and output channels:

OCaml

```
open Core.Std
open Async.Std

(* Copy data from the reader to the writer, using the provided buffer
   as scratch space *)
let rec copy_blocks buffer r w =
  Reader.read r buffer
  >>= function
  | `Eof -> return ()
  | `Ok bytes_read ->
    Writer.write w buffer ~len:bytes_read;
    Writer.flushed w
    >>= fun () ->
    copy_blocks buffer r w
```

Bind is used in the code to sequence the operations: first, we call Reader.read to get a block of input. Then, when that's complete and if a new block was returned, we write that block to the writer. Finally, we wait until the writer's buffers are flushed, waiting on the deferred returned by Writer.flushed, at which point we recurse. If we hit an end-of-file condition, the loop is ended. The deferred returned by a call to copy_blocks becomes determined only once the end-of-file condition is hit.

One important aspect of how this is written is that it uses *pushback*, which is to say that if the writer can't make progress writing, the reader will stop reading. If you don't implement pushback in your servers, then a stopped client can cause your program to leak memory, since you'll need to allocate space for the data that's been read in but not yet written out.

You might also be concerned that the chain of deferreds that is built up as you go through the loop would lead to a memory leak. After all, this code constructs an ever-growing chain of binds, each of which creates a deferred. In this case, however, all of the deferreds should become determined precisely when the final deferred in the chain is determined, in this case, when the Eof condition is hit. Because of this, we could safely replace all of these deferreds with a single deferred. Async has logic to do just this, and so there's no memory leak after all. This is essentially a form of tail-call optimization, lifted to the Async monad.

copy_blocks provides the logic for handling a client connection, but we still need to set up a server to receive such connections and dispatch to copy_blocks. For this, we'll use Async's Tcp module, which has a collection of utilities for creating TCP clients and servers:

OCaml (part 1)

```
(** Starts a TCP server, which listens on the specified port, invoking
    copy_blocks every time a client connects. *)
let run () =
  let host_and_port =
    Tcp.Server.create
      ~on_handler_error:`Raise
      (Tcp.on_port 8765)
      (fun _addr r w ->
         let buffer = String.create (16 * 1024) in
         copy_blocks buffer r w)
  in
  ignore (host_and_port : (Socket.Address.Inet.t, int) Tcp.Server.t Deferred.t)
```

The result of calling Tcp.Server.create is a Tcp.Server.t, which is a handle to the server that lets you shut the server down. We don't use that functionality here, so we explicitly ignore server to suppress the unused-variables error. We put in a type annotation around the ignored value to make the nature of the value we're ignoring explicit.

The most important argument to Tcp.Server.create is the final one, which is the client connection handler. Notably, the preceding code does nothing explicit to close down the client connections when the communication is done. That's because the server will automatically shut down the connection once the deferred returned by the handler becomes determined.

Finally, we need to initiate the server and start the Async scheduler:

OCaml (part 2)

```
(* Call [run], and then start the scheduler *)
let () =
```

```
run ();
never_returns (Scheduler.go ())
```

One of the most common newbie errors with Async is to forget to run the scheduler. It can be a bewildering mistake, because without the scheduler, your program won't do anything at all; even calls to printf won't reach the terminal.

It's worth noting that even though we didn't spend much explicit effort on thinking about multiple clients, this server is able to handle many concurrent clients without further modification.

Now that we have the echo server, we can connect to the echo server using the netcat tool, which is invoked as nc:

Terminal

```
$ ./echo.native &
$ nc 127.0.0.1 8765
This is an echo server
This is an echo server
It repeats whatever I write.
It repeats whatever I write.
```

Functions that Never Return

You might wonder what's going on with the call to never_returns. never_returns is an idiom that comes from Core that is used to mark functions that don't return. Typically, a function that doesn't return is inferred as having return type 'a:

OCaml utop (part 19)

```
# let rec loop_forever () = loop_forever ();;
val loop_forever : unit -> 'a = <fun>
# let always_fail () = assert false;;
val always_fail : unit -> 'a = <fun>
```

This can be surprising when you call a function like this expecting it to return unit. The type-checker won't necessarily complain in such a case:

OCaml utop (part 20)

```
# let do_stuff n =
    let x = 3 in
    if n > 0 then loop_forever ();
    x + n
  ;;
val do_stuff : int -> int = <fun>
```

With a name like loop_forever, the meaning is clear enough. But with something like Scheduler.go, the fact that it never returns is less clear, and so we use the type system to make it more explicit by giving it a return type of never_returns. Let's do the same trick with loop_forever:

```
# let rec loop_forever () : never_returns = loop_forever ();;
val loop_forever : unit -> never_returns = <fun>
```

The type never_returns is uninhabited, so a function can't return a value of type nev
er_returns, which means only a function that never returns can have never_returns
as its return type! Now, if we rewrite our do_stuff function, we'll get a helpful type
error:

```
# let do_stuff n =
    let x = 3 in
    if n > 0 then loop_forever ();
    x + n
  ;;
Characters 38-67:
Error: This expression has type unit but an expression was expected of type
          never_returns
```

We can resolve the error by calling the function never_returns:

```
# never_returns;;
- : never_returns -> 'a = <fun>
# let do_stuff n =
    let x = 3 in
    if n > 0 then never_returns (loop_forever ());
    x + n
  ;;
val do_stuff : int -> int = <fun>
```

Thus, we got the compilation to go through by explicitly marking in the source that the
call to loop_forever never returns.

Improving the Echo Server

Let's try to go a little bit farther with our echo server by walking through a few improvements. In particular, we will:

- Add a proper command-line interface with Command
- Add a flag to specify the port to listen on and a flag to make the server echo back
  the capitalized version of whatever was sent to it
- Simplify the code using Async's Pipe interface

The following code does all of this:

```
open Core.Std
open Async.Std
```

```
let run ~uppercase ~port =
  let host_and_port =
    Tcp.Server.create
      ~on_handler_error:`Raise
      (Tcp.on_port port)
      (fun _addr r w ->
        Pipe.transfer (Reader.pipe r) (Writer.pipe w)
          ~f:(if uppercase then String.uppercase else Fn.id))
  in
  ignore (host_and_port : (Socket.Address.Inet.t, int) Tcp.Server.t Deferred.t);
  Deferred.never ()

let () =
  Command.async_basic
    ~summary:"Start an echo server"
    Command.Spec.(
      empty
      +> flag "-uppercase" no_arg
        ~doc:" Convert to uppercase before echoing back"
      +> flag "-port" (optional_with_default 8765 int)
        ~doc:" Port to listen on (default 8765)"
    )
    (fun uppercase port () -> run ~uppercase ~port)
  |> Command.run
```

Note the use of Deferred.never in the run function. As you might guess from the name, Deferred.never returns a deferred that is never determined. In this case, that indicates that the echo server doesn't ever shut down.

The biggest change in the preceding code is the use of Async's Pipe. A Pipe is an asynchronous communication channel that's used for connecting different parts of your program. You can think of it as a consumer/producer queue that uses deferreds for communicating when the pipe is ready to be read from or written to. Our use of pipes is fairly minimal here, but they are an important part of Async, so it's worth discussing them in some detail.

Pipes are created in connected read/write pairs:

OCaml utop (part 24)

```
# let (r,w) = Pipe.create ();;
val r : '_a Pipe.Reader.t = <abstr>
val w : '_a Pipe.Writer.t = <abstr>
```

r and w are really just read and write handles to the same underlying object. Note that r and w have weakly polymorphic types, as discussed in "Imperative Programming" on page 20, and so can only contain values of a single, yet-to-be-determined type.

If we just try and write to the writer, we'll see that we block indefinitely in *utop*. You can break out of the wait by hitting **Control-C**:

```
# Pipe.write w "Hello World!";;
Interrupted.
```

The deferred returned by write completes on its own once the value written into the pipe has been read out:

```
# let (r,w) = Pipe.create ();;
val r : '_a Pipe.Reader.t = <abstr>
val w : '_a Pipe.Writer.t = <abstr>
# let write_complete = Pipe.write w "Hello World!";;
val write_complete : unit Deferred.t = <abstr>
# Pipe.read r;;
- : [ `Eof | `Ok of string ] = `Ok "Hello World!"
# write_complete;;
- : unit = ()
```

In the function run, we're taking advantage of one of the many utility functions provided for pipes in the Pipe module. In particular, we're using Pipe.transfer to set up a process that takes data from a reader-pipe and moves it to a writer-pipe. Here's the type of Pipe.transfer:

```
# Pipe.transfer;;
- : 'a Pipe.Reader.t -> 'b Pipe.Writer.t -> f:('a -> 'b) -> unit Deferred.t =
<fun>
```

The two pipes being connected are generated by the Reader.pipe and Writer.pipe call respectively. Note that pushback is preserved throughout the process, so that if the writer gets blocked, the writer's pipe will stop pulling data from the reader's pipe, which will prevent the reader from reading in more data.

Importantly, the deferred returned by Pipe.transfer becomes determined once the reader has been closed and the last element is transferred from the reader to the writer. Once that deferred becomes determined, the server will shut down that client connection. So, when a client disconnects, the rest of the shutdown happens transparently.

The command-line parsing for this program is based on the Command library that we introduced in Chapter 14. Opening Async.Std, shadows the Command module with an extended version that contains the async_basic call:

```
# Command.async_basic;;
- : summary:string ->
    ?readme:(unit -> string) ->
    ('a, unit -> unit Deferred.t) Command.Spec.t -> 'a -> Command.t
= <fun>
```

This differs from the ordinary `Command.basic` call in that the main function must return a `Deferred.t`, and that the running of the command (using `Command.run`) automatically starts the Async scheduler, without requiring an explicit call to `Scheduler.go`.

Example: Searching Definitions with DuckDuckGo

DuckDuckGo is a search engine with a freely available search interface. In this section, we'll use Async to write a small command-line utility for querying DuckDuckGo to extract definitions for a collection of terms.

Our code is going to rely on a number of other libraries, all of which can be installed using OPAM. Refer to this Real World OCaml page (*http://realworldocaml.org/ install*) if you need help on the installation. Here's the list of libraries we'll need:

textwrap
> A library for wrapping long lines. We'll use this for printing out our results.

uri
> A library for handling URIs, or "Uniform Resource Identifiers," of which HTTP URLs are an example.

yojson
> A JSON parsing library that was described in Chapter 15.

cohttp
> A library for creating HTTP clients and servers. We need Async support, which comes with the `cohttp.async` package.

Now let's dive into the implementation.

URI Handling

HTTP URLs, which identify endpoints across the Web, are actually part of a more general family known as Uniform Resource Identifiers (URIs). The full URI specification is defined in RFC3986 (*http://tools.ietf.org/html/rfc3986*) and is rather complicated. Luckily, the `uri` library provides a strongly typed interface that takes care of much of the hassle.

We'll need a function for generating the URIs that we're going to use to query the DuckDuckGo servers:

OCaml

```
open Core.Std
open Async.Std

(* Generate a DuckDuckGo search URI from a query string *)
let query_uri query =
```

```
let base_uri = Uri.of_string "http://api.duckduckgo.com/?format=json" in
Uri.add_query_param base_uri ("q", [query])
```

A `Uri.t` is constructed from the `Uri.of_string` function, and a query parameter q is added with the desired search query. The library takes care of encoding the URI correctly when outputting it in the network protocol.

Parsing JSON Strings

The HTTP response from DuckDuckGo is in JSON, a common (and thankfully simple) format that is specified in RFC4627 (*http://www.ietf.org/rfc/rfc4627.txt*). We'll parse the JSON data using the Yojson library, which was introduced in Chapter 15.

We expect the response from DuckDuckGo to come across as a JSON record, which is represented by the `Assoc` tag in Yojson's JSON variant. We expect the definition itself to come across under either the key "Abstract" or "Definition," and so the following code looks under both keys, returning the first one for which a nonempty value is defined:

OCaml (part 1)
```
(* Extract the "Definition" or "Abstract" field from the DuckDuckGo results *)
let get_definition_from_json json =
  match Yojson.Safe.from_string json with
  | `Assoc kv_list ->
    let find key =
      begin match List.Assoc.find kv_list key with
      | None | Some (`String "") -> None
      | Some s -> Some (Yojson.Safe.to_string s)
      end
    in
    begin match find "Abstract" with
    | Some _ as x -> x
    | None -> find "Definition"
    end
  | _ -> None
```

Executing an HTTP Client Query

Now let's look at the code for dispatching the search queries over HTTP, using the Cohttp library:

OCaml (part 2)
```
(* Execute the DuckDuckGo search *)
let get_definition word =
  Cohttp_async.Client.get (query_uri word)
  >>= fun (_, body) ->
  Pipe.to_list body
  >>| fun strings ->
  (word, get_definition_from_json (String.concat strings))
```

To better understand what's going on, it's useful to look at the type for `Cohttp_async.Client.get`, which we can do in *utop*:

```
# #require "cohttp.async";;
# Cohttp_async.Client.get;;
- : ?interrupt:unit Deferred.t ->
    ?headers:Cohttp.Header.t ->
    Uri.t -> (Cohttp.Response.t * string Pipe.Reader.t) Deferred.t
= <fun>
```

The get call takes as a required argument a URI and returns a deferred value containing a Cohttp.Response.t (which we ignore) and a pipe reader to which the body of the request will be written.

In this case, the HTTP body probably isn't very large, so we call Pipe.to_list to collect the strings from the pipe as a single deferred list of strings. We then join those strings using String.concat and pass the result through our parsing function.

Running a single search isn't that interesting from a concurrency perspective, so let's write code for dispatching multiple searches in parallel. First, we need code for formatting and printing out the search result:

```
(* Print out a word/definition pair *)
let print_result (word,definition) =
  printf "%s\n%s\n\n%s\n\n"
    word
    (String.init (String.length word) ~f:(fun _ -> '-'))
    (match definition with
    | None -> "No definition found"
    | Some def ->
      String.concat ~sep:"\n"
        (Wrapper.wrap (Wrapper.make 70) def))
```

We use the Wrapper module from the textwrap package to do the line wrapping. It may not be obvious that this routine is using Async, but it does: the version of printf that's called here is actually Async's specialized printf that goes through the Async scheduler rather than printing directly. The original definition of printf is shadowed by this new one when you open Async.Std. An important side effect of this is that if you write an Async program and forget to start the scheduler, calls like printf won't actually generate any output!

The next function dispatches the searches in parallel, waits for the results, and then prints:

```
(* Run many searches in parallel, printing out the results after they're all
   done. *)
let search_and_print words =
  Deferred.all (List.map words ~f:get_definition)
  >>| fun results ->
  List.iter results ~f:print_result
```

We used `List.map` to call `get_definition` on each word, and `Deferred.all` to wait for all the results. Here's the type of `Deferred.all`:

```
# Deferred.all;;
- : 'a Deferred.t list -> 'a list Deferred.t = <fun>
```

Note that the list returned by `Deferred.all` reflects the order of the deferreds passed to it. As such, the definitions will be printed out in the same order that the search words are passed in, no matter what order the queries return in. We could rewrite this code to print out the results as they're received (and thus potentially out of order) as follows:

```
(* Run many searches in parallel, printing out the results as you go *)
let search_and_print words =
  Deferred.all_unit (List.map words ~f:(fun word ->
    get_definition word >>| print_result))
```

The difference is that we both dispatch the query and print out the result in the closure passed to `map`, rather than wait for all of the results to get back and then print them out together. We use `Deferred.all_unit`, which takes a list of `unit` deferreds and returns a single `unit` deferred that becomes determined when every deferred on the input list is determined. We can see the type of this function in *utop*:

```
# Deferred.all_unit;;
- : unit Deferred.t list -> unit Deferred.t = <fun>
```

Finally, we create a command-line interface using `Command.async_basic`:

```
let () =
  Command.async_basic
    ~summary:"Retrieve definitions from duckduckgo search engine"
    Command.Spec.(
      empty
      +> anon (sequence ("word" %: string))
    )
    (fun words () -> search_and_print words)
  |> Command.run
```

And that's all we need for a simple but usable definition searcher:

```
$ corebuild -pkg cohttp.async,yojson,textwrap search.native
$ ./search.native "Concurrent Programming" "OCaml"
Concurrent Programming
----------------------

"Concurrent computing is a form of computing in which programs are
designed as collections of interacting computational processes that
may be executed in parallel."
```

```
OCaml
-----
```

"OCaml, originally known as Objective Caml, is the main implementation
of the Caml programming language, created by Xavier Leroy, Jérôme
Vouillon, Damien Doligez, Didier Rémy and others in 1996."

Exception Handling

When programming with external resources, errors are everywhere: everything from a
flaky server to a network outage to exhausting of local resources can lead to a runtime
error. When programming in OCaml, some of these errors will show up explicitly in a
function's return type, and some of them will show up as exceptions. We covered exception handling in OCaml in "Exceptions" on page 128, but as we'll see, exception
handling in a concurrent program presents some new challenges.

Let's get a better sense of how exceptions work in Async by creating an asynchronous
computation that (sometimes) fails with an exception. The function maybe_raise
blocks for half a second, and then either throws an exception or returns unit, alternating
between the two behaviors on subsequent calls:

OCaml utop (part 31)

```
# let maybe_raise =
    let should_fail = ref false in
    fun () ->
      let will_fail = !should_fail in
      should_fail := not will_fail;
      after (Time.Span.of_sec 0.5)
      >>= fun () ->
      if will_fail then raise Exit else return ()
  ;;
val maybe_raise : unit -> unit Deferred.t = <fun>
# maybe_raise ();;
- : unit = ()
# maybe_raise ();;
Exception:
(lib/monitor.ml.Error_
 ((exn Exit) (backtrace (""))
  (monitor
   (((name block_on_async) (here ()) (id 55) (has_seen_error true)
     (someone_is_listening true) (kill_index 0))
    ((name main) (here ()) (id 1) (has_seen_error false)
     (someone_is_listening false) (kill_index 0)))))).
```

In *utop*, the exception thrown by maybe_raise () terminates the evaluation of just that
expression, but in a standalone program, an uncaught exception would bring down the
entire process.

So, how could we capture and handle such an exception? You might try to do this using OCaml's built-in try/with statement, but as you can see that doesn't quite do the trick:

OCaml utop (part 32)

```
# let handle_error () =
    try
      maybe_raise ()
      >>| fun () -> "success"
    with _ -> return "failure"
  ;;
val handle_error : unit -> string Deferred.t = <fun>
# handle_error ();;
- : string = "success"
# handle_error ();;
Exception:
(lib/monitor.ml.Error_
 ((exn Exit) (backtrace (""))
  (monitor
   (((name block_on_async) (here ()) (id 59) (has_seen_error true)
     (someone_is_listening true) (kill_index 0))
    ((name main) (here ()) (id 1) (has_seen_error false)
     (someone_is_listening false) (kill_index 0)))))).
```

This didn't work because try/with only captures exceptions that are thrown in the code directly executed within it, while maybe_raise schedules an Async job to run in the future, and it's that job that throws an exception.

We can capture this kind of asynchronous error using the try_with function provided by Async:

OCaml utop (part 33)

```
# let handle_error () =
    try_with (fun () -> maybe_raise ())
    >>| function
    | Ok ()    -> "success"
    | Error _ -> "failure"
  ;;
val handle_error : unit -> string Deferred.t = <fun>
# handle_error ();;
- : string = "success"
# handle_error ();;
- : string = "failure"
```

try_with f takes as its argument a deferred-returning thunk f and returns a deferred that becomes determined either as Ok of whatever f returned, or Error exn if f threw an exception before its return value became determined.

Monitors

try_with is a great way of handling exceptions in Async, but it's not the whole story. All of Async's exception-handling mechanisms, try_with included, are built on top of

---

Async's system of *monitors*, which are inspired by the error-handling mechanism in Erlang of the same name. Monitors are fairly low-level and are only occasionally used directly, but it's nonetheless worth understanding how they work.

In Async, a monitor is a context that determines what to do when there is an unhandled exception. Every Async job runs within the context of some monitor, which, when the job is running, is referred to as the current monitor. When a new Async job is scheduled, say, using bind or map, it inherits the current monitor of the job that spawned it.

Monitors are arranged in a tree—when a new monitor is created (say, using Moni tor.create), it is a child of the current monitor. You can explicitly run jobs within a monitor using within, which takes a thunk that returns a nondeferred value, or with in', which takes a thunk that returns a deferred. Here's an example:

OCaml utop (part 34)

```
# let blow_up () =
    let monitor = Monitor.create ~name:"blow up monitor" () in
    within' ~monitor maybe_raise
  ;;
val blow_up : unit -> unit Deferred.t = <fun>
# blow_up ();;
- : unit = ()
# blow_up ();;
Exception:
(lib/monitor.ml.Error_
  ((exn Exit) (backtrace (""))
   (monitor
    (((name "blow up monitor") (here ()) (id 71) (has_seen_error true)
      (someone_is_listening false) (kill_index 0))
     ((name block_on_async) (here ()) (id 70) (has_seen_error false)
      (someone_is_listening true) (kill_index 0))
     ((name main) (here ()) (id 1) (has_seen_error false)
      (someone_is_listening false) (kill_index 0))))))).
```

In addition to the ordinary stack-trace, the exception displays the trace of monitors through which the exception traveled, starting at the one we created, called "blow up monitor." The other monitors you see come from *utop*'s special handling of deferreds.

Monitors can do more than just augment the error-trace of an exception. You can also use a monitor to explicitly handle errors delivered to that monitor. The Monitor.er rors call is a particularly important one. It detaches the monitor from its parent, handing back the stream of errors that would otherwise have been delivered to the parent monitor. This allows one to do custom handling of errors, which may include reraising errors to the parent. Here is a very simple example of a function that captures and ignores errors in the processes it spawns:

OCaml utop

```
# let swallow_error () =
    let monitor = Monitor.create () in
    Stream.iter (Monitor.errors monitor) ~f:(fun _exn ->
```

```
      printf "an error happened\n");
    within' ~monitor (fun () ->
      after (Time.Span.of_sec 0.5) >>= fun () -> failwith "Kaboom!")
  ;;
val swallow_error : unit -> 'a Deferred.t = <fun>
# swallow_error ();;
an error happened
```

The message "an error happened" is printed out, but the deferred returned by swal
low_error is never determined. This makes sense, since the calculation never actually
completes, so there's no value to return. You can break out of this in *utop* by hitting
Control+C.

Here's an example of a monitor that passes some exceptions through to the parent and
handles others. Exceptions are sent to the parent using Monitor.send_exn, with Moni
tor.current being called to find the current monitor, which is the parent of the newly
created monitor:

OCaml utop (part 36)

```
# exception Ignore_me;;
exception Ignore_me
# let swallow_some_errors exn_to_raise =
    let child_monitor  = Monitor.create  () in
    let parent_monitor = Monitor.current () in
    Stream.iter (Monitor.errors child_monitor) ~f:(fun error ->
      match Monitor.extract_exn error with
      | Ignore_me -> printf "ignoring exn\n"
      | _ -> Monitor.send_exn parent_monitor error);
    within' ~monitor:child_monitor (fun () ->
      after (Time.Span.of_sec 0.5)
      >>= fun () -> raise exn_to_raise)
  ;;
val swallow_some_errors : exn -> 'a Deferred.t = <fun>
```

Note that we use Monitor.extract_exn to grab the underlying exception that was
thrown. Async wraps exceptions it catches with extra information, including the monitor trace, so you need to grab the underlying exception to match on it.

If we pass in an exception other than Ignore_me, like, say, the built-in exception
Not_found, then the exception will be passed to the parent monitor and delivered as
usual:

OCaml utop (part 37)

```
# swallow_some_errors Not_found;;
Exception:
(lib/monitor.ml.Error_
 ((exn Not_found) (backtrace (""))
  (monitor
   (((name (id 75)) (here ()) (id 75) (has_seen_error true)
     (someone_is_listening true) (kill_index 0))
    ((name block_on_async) (here ()) (id 74) (has_seen_error true)
     (someone_is_listening true) (kill_index 0))
```

```
((name main) (here ()) (id 1) (has_seen_error false)
 (someone_is_listening false) (kill_index 0)))))).
```

If instead we use `Ignore_me`, the exception will be ignorred, and the deferred never becomes determined:

```
# swallow_some_errors Ignore_me;;
ignoring exn
```

In practice, you should rarely use monitors directly, and instead use functions like `try_with` and `Monitor.protect` that are built on top of monitors. One example of a library that uses monitors directly is `Tcp.Server.create`, which tracks both exceptions thrown by the logic that handles the network connection and by the callback for responding to an individual request, in either case responding to an exception by closing the connection. It is for building this kind of custom error handling that monitors can be helpful.

Example: Handling Exceptions with DuckDuckGo

Let's now go back and improve the exception handling of our DuckDuckGo client. In particular, we'll change it so that any query that fails is reported without preventing other queries from completing.

The search code as it is fails rarely, so let's make a change that allows us to trigger failures more predictably. We'll do this by making it possible to distribute the requests over multiple servers. Then, we'll handle the errors that occur when one of those servers is misspecified.

First we'll need to change `query_uri` to take an argument specifying the server to connect to:

```
(* Generate a DuckDuckGo search URI from a query string *)
let query_uri ~server query =
  let base_uri =
    Uri.of_string (String.concat ["http://";server;"/?format=json"])
  in
  Uri.add_query_param base_uri ("q", [query])
```

In addition, we'll make the necessary changes to get the list of servers on the command-line, and to distribute the search qeuries round-robin across the list of servers. Now, let's see what happens if we rebuild the application and run it giving it a list of servers, some of which won't respond to the query:

```
$ corebuild -pkg cohttp.async,yojson,textwrap \
    search_with_configurable_server.native
$ ./search_with_configurable_server.native \
    -servers localhost,api.duckduckgo.com \
```

```
        "Concurrent Programming" OCaml
 (("unhandled exception"
  ((lib/monitor.ml.Error_
    ((exn (Unix.Unix_error "Connection refused" connect 127.0.0.1:80))
     (backtrace
      ("Raised by primitive operation at file \"lib/unix_syscalls.ml\", line 797,
        characters 12-69"
       "Called from file \"lib/deferred.ml\", line 20, characters 62-65"
       "Called from file \"lib/scheduler.ml\", line 125, characters 6-17"
       "Called from file \"lib/jobs.ml\", line 65, characters 8-13" ""))
     (monitor
      (((name Tcp.close_sock_on_error) (here ()) (id 5) (has_seen_error true)
        (someone_is_listening true) (kill_index 0))
       ((name main) (here ()) (id 1) (has_seen_error true)
        (someone_is_listening false) (kill_index 0))))))
  (Pid 15971)))
```

As you can see, we got a "Connection refused" failure, which ends the entire program, even though one of the two queries would have gone through successfully on its own. We can handle the failures of individual connections separately by using the `try_with` function within each call to `get_definition`, as follows:

OCaml (part 1)

```
(* Execute the DuckDuckGo search *)
let get_definition ~server word =
  try_with (fun () ->
    Cohttp_async.Client.get (query_uri ~server word)
    >>= fun (_, body) ->
    Pipe.to_list body
    >>| fun strings ->
    (word, get_definition_from_json (String.concat strings)))
  >>| function
  | Ok (word,result) -> (word, Ok result)
  | Error _          -> (word, Error "Unexpected failure")
```

Here, we first use `try_with` to capture the exception, and then use map (the `>>|` operator) to convert the error into the form we want: a pair whose first element is the word being searched for, and the second element is the (possibly erroneous) result.

Now we just need to change the code for `print_result` so that it can handle the new type:

OCaml (part 2)

```
(* Print out a word/definition pair *)
let print_result (word,definition) =
  printf "%s\n%s\n\n%s\n\n"
    word
    (String.init (String.length word) ~f:(fun _ -> '-'))
    (match definition with
     | Error s -> "DuckDuckGo query failed: " ^ s
     | Ok None -> "No definition found"
     | Ok (Some def) ->
```

```
    String.concat ~sep:"\n"
      (Wrapper.wrap (Wrapper.make 70) def))
```

Now, if we run that same query, we'll get individualized handling of the connection failures:

```
$ corebuild -pkg cohttp.async,yojson,textwrap \
    search_with_error_handling.native
$ ./search_with_error_handling.native \
    -servers localhost,api.duckduckgo.com \
    "Concurrent Programming" OCaml
Concurrent Programming
---------------------

DuckDuckGo query failed: Unexpected failure

OCaml
-----

"OCaml, originally known as Objective Caml, is the main implementation
of the Caml programming language, created by Xavier Leroy, Jérôme
Vouillon, Damien Doligez, Didier Rémy and others in 1996."
```

Now, only the query that went to localhost failed.

Note that in this code, we're relying on the fact that Cohttp_async.Client.get will clean up after itself after an exception, in particular by closing its file descriptors. If you need to implement such functionality directly, you may want to use the Monitor.pro tect call, which is analogous to the protect call described in "Cleaning Up in the Presence of Exceptions" on page 132.

Timeouts, Cancellation, and Choices

In a concurrent program, one often needs to combine results from multiple, distinct concurrent subcomputations going on in the same program. We already saw this in our DuckDuckGo example, where we used Deferred.all and Deferred.all_unit to wait for a list of deferreds to become determined. Another useful primitive is De ferred.both, which lets you wait until two deferreds of different types have returned, returning both values as a tuple. Here, we use the function sec, which is shorthand for creating a time-span equal to a given number of seconds:

```
# let string_and_float = Deferred.both
    (after (sec 0.5)  >>| fun () -> "A")
    (after (sec 0.25) >>| fun () -> 32.33);;
val string_and_float : (string * float) Deferred.t = <abstr>
# string_and_float;;
- : string * float = ("A", 32.33)
```

Sometimes, however, we want to wait only for the first of multiple events to occur. This happens particularly when dealing with timeouts. In that case, we can use the call `Deferred.any`, which, given a list of deferreds, returns a single deferred that will become determined once any of the values on the list is determined:

OCaml utop (part 40)

```
# Deferred.any [ (after (sec 0.5) >>| fun () -> "half a second")
              ; (after (sec 10.) >>| fun () -> "ten seconds") ] ;;
- : string = "half a second"
```

Let's use this to add timeouts to our DuckDuckGo searches. The following code is a wrapper for `get_definition` that takes a timeout (in the form of a `Time.Span.t`) and returns either the definition, or, if that takes too long, an error:

OCaml (part 1)

```
let get_definition_with_timeout ~server ~timeout word =
  Deferred.any
    [ (after timeout >>| fun () -> (word,Error "Timed out"))
    ; (get_definition ~server word
       >>| fun (word,result) ->
       let result' = match result with
         | Ok _ as x -> x
         | Error _ -> Error "Unexpected failure"
       in
       (word,result')
      )
    ]
```

We use `>>|` above to transform the deferred values we're waiting for so that `Deferred.any` can choose between values of the same type.

A problem with this code is that the HTTP query kicked off by `get_definition` is not actually shut down when the timeout fires. As such, `get_definition_with_timeout` can leak an open connection. Happily, Cohttp does provide a way of shutting down a client. You can pass a deferred under the label `interrupt` to `Cohttp_async.Client.get`. Once `interrupt` is determined, the client connection will be shut down.

The following code shows how you can change `get_definition` and `get_definition_with_timeout` to cancel the get call if the timeout expires:

OCaml (part 1)

```
(* Execute the DuckDuckGo search *)
let get_definition ~server ~interrupt word =
  try_with (fun () ->
    Cohttp_async.Client.get ~interrupt (query_uri ~server word)
    >>= fun  (_, body) ->
    Pipe.to_list body
    >>| fun strings ->
    (word, get_definition_from_json (String.concat strings)))
  >>| function
  | Ok (word,result) -> (word, Ok result)
  | Error exn        -> (word, Error exn)
```

Next, we'll modify `get_definition_with_timeout` to create a deferred to pass in to `get_definition`, which will become determined when our timeout expires:

OCaml (part 2)

```
let get_definition_with_timeout ~server ~timeout word =
  get_definition ~server ~interrupt:(after timeout) word
>>| fun (word,result) ->
let result' = match result with
  | Ok _ as x -> x
  | Error _ -> Error "Unexpected failure"
in
(word,result')
```

This will work and will cause the connection to shutdown cleanly when we time out; but our code no longer explicitly knows whether or not the timeout has kicked in. In particular, the error message on a timeout will now be "Unexpected failure" rather than "Timed out", which it was in our previous implementation.

We can get more precise handling of timeouts using Async's choose function. choose lets you pick among a collection of different deferreds, reacting to exactly one of them. Each deferred is paired, using the function choice, with a function that is called if and only if that deferred is chosen. Here's the type signature of choice and choose:

OCaml utop (part 41)

```
# choice;;
- : 'a Deferred.t -> ('a -> 'b) -> 'b Deferred.choice = <fun>
# choose;;
- : 'a Deferred.choice list -> 'a Deferred.t = <fun>
```

Note that there's no guarantee that the winning deferred will be the one that becomes determined first. But choose does guarantee that only one choice will be chosen, and only the chosen choice will execute the attached function.

In the following example, we use choose to ensure that the interrupt deferred becomes determined if and only if the timeout deferred is chosen. Here's the code:

OCaml (part 2)

```
let get_definition_with_timeout ~server ~timeout word =
  let interrupt = Ivar.create () in
  choose
    [ choice (after timeout) (fun () ->
        Ivar.fill interrupt ();
        (word,Error "Timed out"))
    ; choice (get_definition ~server ~interrupt:(Ivar.read interrupt) word)
        (fun (word,result) ->
           let result' = match result with
             | Ok _ as x -> x
             | Error _ -> Error "Unexpected failure"
           in
           (word,result')
        )
    ]
```

Now, if we run this with a suitably small timeout, we'll see that one query succeeds and the other fails reporting a timeout:

```
$ corebuild -pkg cohttp.async,yojson,textwrap \
    search_with_timeout_no_leak.native
$ ./search_with_timeout_no_leak.native \
    "concurrent programming" ocaml -timeout 0.2s
concurrent programming
---------------------

DuckDuckGo query failed: Timed out

ocaml
-----

"OCaml or Objective Caml, is the main implementation of the Caml
programming language, created by Xavier Leroy, Jérôme Vouillon,
Damien Doligez, Didier Rémy and others in 1996."
```

Working with System Threads

Although we haven't worked with them yet, OCaml does have built-in support for true system threads, i.e., kernel-level threads whose interleaving is controlled by the operating system. We discussed in the beginning of the chapter why Async is generally a better choice than system threads, but even if you mostly use Async, OCaml's system threads are sometimes necessary, and it's worth understanding them.

The most surprising aspect of OCaml's system threads is that they don't afford you any access to physical parallelism. That's because OCaml's runtime has a single runtime lock that at most one thread can be holding at a time.

Given that threads don't provide physical parallelism, why are they useful at all?

The most common reason for using system threads is that there are some operating system calls that have no nonblocking alternative, which means that you can't run them directly in a system like Async without blocking your entire program. For this reason, Async maintains a thread pool for running such calls. Most of the time, as a user of Async you don't need to think about this, but it is happening under the covers.

Another reason to have multiple threads is to deal with non-OCaml libraries that have their own event loop or for another reason need their own threads. In that case, it's sometimes useful to run some OCaml code on the foreign thread as part of the communication to your main program. OCaml's foreign function interface is discussed in more detail in Chapter 19.

Another occasional use for system threads is to better interoperate with compute-intensive OCaml code. In Async, if you have a long-running computation that never calls `bind` or `map`, then that computation will block out the Async runtime until it completes.

One way of dealing with this is to explicitly break up the calculation into smaller pieces that are separated by binds. But sometimes this explicit yielding is impractical, since it may involve intrusive changes to an existing codebase. Another solution is to run the code in question in a separate thread. Async's `In_thread` module provides multiple facilities for doing just this, `In_thread.run` being the simplest. We can simply write:

OCaml utop (part 42)

```
# let def = In_thread.run (fun () -> List.range 1 10);;
val def : int list Deferred.t = <abstr>
# def;;
- : int list = [1; 2; 3; 4; 5; 6; 7; 8; 9]
```

to cause `List.range 1 10` to be run on one of Async's worker threads. When the computation is complete, the result is placed in the deferred, where it can be used in the ordinary way from Async.

Interoperability between Async and system threads can be quite tricky. Consider the following function for testing how responsive Async is. The function takes a deferred-returning thunk, and it first runs that thunk, and then uses `Clock.every` to wake up every 100 milliseconds and print out a timestamp, until the returned deferred becomes determined, at which point it prints out one last timestamp:

OCaml utop (part 43)

```
# let log_delays thunk =
    let start = Time.now () in
    let print_time () =
      let diff = Time.diff (Time.now ()) start in
      printf "%s, " (Time.Span.to_string diff)
    in
    let d = thunk () in
    Clock.every (sec 0.1) ~stop:d print_time;
    d >>| fun () -> print_time (); printf "\n"
  ;;
val log_delays : (unit -> unit Deferred.t) -> unit Deferred.t = <fun>
```

If we feed this function a simple timeout deferred, it works as you might expect, waking up roughly every 100 milliseconds:

OCaml utop

```
# log_delays (fun () -> after (sec 0.5));;
0.154972ms, 102.126ms, 203.658ms, 305.73ms, 407.903ms, 501.563ms,
- : unit = ()
```

Now see what happens if, instead of waiting on a clock event, we wait for a busy loop to finish running:

OCaml utop

```
# let busy_loop () =
    let x = ref None in
```

```
    for i = 1 to 100_000_000 do x := Some i done
  ;;
val busy_loop : unit -> unit = <fun>
# log_delays (fun () -> return (busy_loop ()));;
19.2185s,
- : unit = ()
```

As you can see, instead of waking up 10 times a second, log_delays is blocked out entirely while busy_loop churns away.

If, on the other hand, we use In_thread.run to offload this to a different system thread, the behavior will be different:

OCaml utop

```
# log_delays (fun () -> In_thread.run busy_loop);;
0.332117ms, 16.6319s, 18.8722s,
- : unit = ()
```

Now log_delays does get a chance to run, but not nearly as often as every 100 milliseconds. The reason is that now that we're using system threads, we are at the mercy of the operating system to decide when each thread gets scheduled. The behavior of threads is very much dependent on the operating system and how it is configured.

Another tricky aspect of dealing with OCaml threads has to do with allocation. When compiling to native code, OCaml's threads only get a chance to give up the runtime lock when they interact with the allocator, so if there's a piece of code that doesn't allocate at all, then it will never allow another OCaml thread to run. Bytecode doesn't have this behavior, so if we run a nonallocating loop in bytecode, our timer process will get to run:

OCaml utop

```
# let noalloc_busy_loop () =
    for i = 0 to 100_000_000 do () done
  ;;
val noalloc_busy_loop : unit -> unit = <fun>
# log_delays (fun () -> In_thread.run noalloc_busy_loop);;
0.169039ms, 4.58345s, 4.77866s, 4.87957s, 12.4723s, 15.0134s,
- : unit = ()
```

But if we compile this to a native-code executable, then the nonallocating busy loop will block anything else from running:

Terminal

```
$ corebuild -pkg async native_code_log_delays.native
$ ./native_code_log_delays.native
15.5686s,
$
```

The takeaway from these examples is that predicting thread interleavings is a subtle business. Staying within the bounds of Async has its limitations, but it leads to more predictable behavior.

Thread-Safety and Locking

Once you start working with system threads, you'll need to be careful about mutable data structures. Most mutable OCaml data structures do not have well-defined semantics when accessed concurrently by multiple threads. The issues you can run into range from runtime exceptions to corrupted data structures to, in some rare cases, segfaults. That means you should always use mutexes when sharing mutable data between different systems threads. Even data structures that seem like they should be safe but are mutable under the covers, like lazy values, can have undefined behavior when accessed from multiple threads.

There are two commonly available mutex packages for OCaml: the `Mutex` module that's part of the standard library, which is just a wrapper over OS-level mutexes and `Nano_mutex`, a more efficient alternative that takes advantage of some of the locking done by the OCaml runtime to avoid needing to create an OS-level mutex much of the time. As a result, creating a `Nano_mutex.t` is 20 times faster than creating a `Mutex.t`, and acquiring the mutex is about 40 percent faster.

Overall, combining Async and threads is quite tricky, but it can be done safely if the following hold:

- There is no shared mutable state between the various threads involved.
- The computations executed by `In_thread.run` do not make any calls to the Async library.

It is possible to safely use threads in ways that violate these constraints. In particular, foreign threads can acquire the Async lock using calls from the `Thread_safe` module in Async, and thereby run Async computations safely. This is a very flexible way of connecting threads to the Async world, but it's a complex use case that is beyond the scope of this chapter.

## PART III

The Runtime System

Writing good OCaml code is only one half of the typical software engineering workflow —you also need to understand how OCaml executes this code, and how to debug and profile your production applications. Part III is thus all about understanding the compiler toolchain and runtime system in OCaml. It is a remarkably simple system in comparison to other language runtimes such as Java or the .NET CLR, so this chapter should be accessible to even the casual OCaml programmer.

We open by a guided tour through the Ctypes library for binding your OCaml code to foreign C libraries. We use a terminal interface and POSIX functions of increasing complexity to show the more advanced features of the library.

OCaml has a very predictable memory representation of values, which we explain in the next chapter by walking through the various datatypes. We then illustrate how the memory regions in OCaml are automatically managed by a garbage collector to ensure no memory leaks occur.

The part closes with two bigger chapters that explain the tools that comprise the OCaml compiler, breaking it up into two logical pieces. The first part covers the parser and type checker and highlights various tips to help you solve common problems in your source code. The second part covers code generation into bytecode and native code, and also explains how to debug and profile production binaries.

CHAPTER 19
Foreign Function Interface

OCaml has several options available to interact with non-OCaml code. The compiler can link with external system libraries via C code and also can produce standalone native object files that can be embedded within other non-OCaml applications.

The mechanism by which code in one programming language can invoke routines in a different programming language is called a *foreign function interface*. This chapter will:

- Show how to call routines in C libraries directly from your OCaml code
- Teach you how to build higher-level abstractions in OCaml from the low-level C bindings
- Work through some full examples for binding a terminal interface and UNIX date/time functions

The simplest foreign function interface in OCaml doesn't even require you to write any C code at all! The Ctypes library lets you define the C interface in pure OCaml, and the library then takes care of loading the C symbols and invoking the foreign function call.

Let's dive straight into a realistic example to show you how the library looks. We'll create a binding to the Ncurses terminal toolkit, as it's widely available on most systems and doesn't have any complex dependencies.

Installing the Ctypes Library

You'll need to install the libffi (*https://github.com/atgreen/libffi*) library as a prerequisite to using Ctypes. It's a fairly popular library and should be available in your OS package manager.

A special note for Mac users: the version of libffi installed by default in Mac OS X 10.8 is too old for some of the features that Ctypes needs. Use Homebrew to brew install libffi to get the latest version before installing the OCaml library.

Once that's done, Ctypes is available via OPAM as usual:

Terminal

```
$ brew install libffi      # for MacOS X users
$ opam install ctypes
$ utop
# require "ctypes.foreign" ;;
```

You'll also need the Ncurses library for the first example. This comes preinstalled on many operating systems such as Mac OS X, and Debian Linux provides it as the libncurses5-dev package.

Example: A Terminal Interface

Ncurses is a library to help build terminal-independent text interfaces in a reasonably efficient way. It's used in console mail clients like Mutt and Pine, and console web browsers such as Lynx.

The full C interface is quite large and is explained in the online documentation (*http://www.gnu.org/software/ncurses/*). We'll just use the small excerpt, since we just want to demonstrate Ctypes in action:

C

```
typedef struct _win_st WINDOW;
typedef unsigned int chtype;

WINDOW *initscr   (void);
WINDOW *newwin    (int, int, int, int);
void    endwin    (void);
void    refresh   (void);
void    wrefresh  (WINDOW *);
void    addstr (const char *);
int     mvwaddch  (WINDOW *, int, int, const chtype);
void    mvwaddstr (WINDOW *, int, int, char *);
void    box (WINDOW *, chtype, chtype);
int     cbreak (void);
```

The Ncurses functions either operate on the current pseudoterminal or on a window that has been created via newwin. The WINDOW structure holds the internal library state and is considered abstract outside of Ncurses. Ncurses clients just need to store the pointer somewhere and pass it back to Ncurses library calls, which in turn dereference its contents.

Note that there are over 200 library calls in Ncurses, so we're only binding a select few for this example. The `initscr` and `newwin` create `WINDOW` pointers for the global and subwindows, respectively. The `mvwaddrstr` takes a window, x/y offsets, and a string and writes to the screen at that location. The terminal is only updated after `refresh` or `wrefresh` are called.

Ctypes provides an OCaml interface that lets you map these C functions to equivalent OCaml functions. The library takes care of converting OCaml function calls and arguments into the C calling convention, invoking the foreign call within the C library and finally returning the result as an OCaml value.

Let's begin by defining the basic values we need, starting with the `WINDOW` state pointer:

OCaml

```
open Ctypes

type window = unit ptr
let window : window typ = ptr void
```

We don't know the internal representation of the window pointer, so we treat it as a C void pointer. We'll improve on this later on in the chapter, but it's good enough for now. The second statement defines an OCaml value that represents the `WINDOW` C pointer. This value is used later in the Ctypes function definitions:

OCaml (part 1)

```
open Foreign

let initscr =
  foreign "initscr" (void @-> returning window)
```

That's all we need to invoke our first function call to `initscr` to initialize the terminal. The `foreign` function accepts two parameters:

- The C function call name, which is looked up using the `dlsym` POSIX function.
- A value that defines the complete set of C function arguments and its return type. The `@->` operator adds an argument to the C parameter list, and `returning` terminates the parameter list with the return type.

The remainder of the Ncurses binding simply expands on these definitions:

OCaml (part 2)

```
let newwin =
  foreign "newwin"
    (int @-> int @-> int @-> int @-> returning window)

let endwin =
  foreign "endwin" (void @-> returning void)
```

```
let refresh =
  foreign "refresh" (void @-> returning void)

let wrefresh =
  foreign "wrefresh" (window @-> returning void)

let addstr =
  foreign "addstr" (string @-> returning void)

let mvwaddch =
  foreign "mvwaddch"
    (window @-> int @-> int @-> char @-> returning void)

let mvwaddstr =
  foreign "mvwaddstr"
    (window @-> int @-> int @-> string @-> returning void)

let box =
  foreign "box" (window @-> char @-> char @-> returning void)

let cbreak =
  foreign "cbreak" (void @-> returning int)
```

These definitions are all straightforward mappings from the C declarations in the Ncurses header file. Note that the string and int values here are nothing to do with OCaml type declarations; instead, they are values that come from opening the Ctypes module at the top of the file.

Most of the parameters in the Ncurses example represent fairly simple scalar C types, except for window (a pointer to the library state) and string, which maps from OCaml strings that have a specific length onto C character buffers whose length is defined by a terminating null character that immediately follows the string data.

The module signature for ncurses.mli looks much like a normal OCaml signature. You can infer it directly from the ncurses.ml by running a special build target:

```
$ corebuild -pkg ctypes.foreign ncurses.inferred.mli
$ cp _build/ncurses.inferred.mli .
```

The inferred.mli target instructs the compiler to generate the default signature for a module file and places it in the _build directory as a normal output. You should normally copy it out into your source directory and customize it to improve its safety for external callers by making some of its internals more abstract.

Here's the customized interface that we can safely use from other libraries:

```
type window
val window : window Ctypes.typ
val initscr : unit -> window
```

```
val endwin : unit -> unit
val refresh : unit -> unit
val wrefresh : window -> unit
val newwin : int -> int -> int -> int -> window
val mvwaddch : window -> int -> int -> char -> unit
val addstr : string -> unit
val mvwaddstr : window -> int -> int -> string -> unit
val box : window -> char -> char -> unit
val cbreak : unit -> int
```

The window type is left abstract in the signature to ensure that window pointers can only be constructed via the Ncurses.initscr function. This prevents void pointers obtained from other sources from being mistakenly passed to an Ncurses library call.

Now compile a "hello world" terminal drawing program to tie this all together:

OCaml

```
open Ncurses

let () =
  let main_window = initscr () in
  ignore(cbreak ());
  let small_window = newwin 10 10 5 5 in
  mvwaddstr main_window 1 2 "Hello";
  mvwaddstr small_window 2 2 "World";
  box small_window '\000' '\000';
  refresh ();
  Unix.sleep 1;
  wrefresh small_window;
  Unix.sleep 5;
  endwin ()
```

The hello executable is compiled by linking with the ctypes.foreign OCamlfind package:

Terminal

```
$ corebuild -pkg ctypes.foreign -lflags -cclib,-lncurses hello.native
```

Running ./hello.native should now display a Hello World in your terminal!

On Build Directives for Ctypes

The preceding command line includes some important extra link directives. The -lflags instructs *ocamlbuild* to pass the next comma-separated set of arguments through to the *ocaml* command when linking a binary. OCaml in turn uses -cclib to pass directives through to the system compiler (normally *gcc* or *clang*). We first need to link to the ncurses C library to make the symbols available to Ctypes, and -cclib,-lncurses does that.

On some distributions such as Ubuntu 11.10 upwards, you'll also need to add -cclib,-Xlinker,-cclib, and --no-as-needed to the -lflags directive. -Xlinker is interpreted by the compiler as a directive for the system linker *ld*, to which it passes --no-as-needed. Several modern OS distributions (such as Ubuntu 11.10 onwards) configure the system linker to only link in libraries that directly contain symbols used by the program. However, when we use Ctypes, those symbols are not referenced until runtime, which results an exception due to the library not being available.

The --no-as-needed flag disables this behavior and ensures all the specified libraries are linked despite not being directly used. The flag unfortunately doesn't work everywhere (notably, Mac OS X should *not* have this passed to it).

Ctypes wouldn't be very useful if it were limited to only defining simple C types, of course. It provides full support for C pointer arithmetic, pointer conversions, and reading and writing through pointers, using OCaml functions as function pointers to C code, as well as struct and union definitions.

We'll go over some of these features in more detail for the remainder of the chapter by using some POSIX date functions as running examples.

Basic Scalar C Types

First, let's look at how to define basic scalar C types. Every C type is represented by an OCaml equivalent via the single type definition:

OCaml

```
type 'a typ
```

Ctypes.typ is the type of values that represents C types to OCaml. There are two types associated with each instance of typ:

- The C type used to store and pass values to the foreign library.

- The corresponding OCaml type. The 'a type parameter contains the OCaml type such that a value of type t typ is used to read and write OCaml values of type t.

There are various other uses of typ values within Ctypes, such as:

- Constructing function types for binding native functions
- Constructing pointers for reading and writing locations in C-managed storage
- Describing component fields of structures, unions, and arrays

Here are the definitions for most of the standard C99 scalar types, including some platform-dependent ones:

OCaml (part 1)

```
val void      : unit typ
val char      : char typ
val schar     : int typ
val short     : int typ
val int       : int typ
val long      : long typ
val llong     : llong typ
val nativeint : nativeint typ

val int8_t    : int typ
val int16_t   : int typ
val int32_t   : int32 typ
val int64_t   : int64 typ
val uchar     : uchar typ
val uchar     : uchar typ
val uint8_t   : uint8 typ
val uint16_t  : uint16 typ
val uint32_t  : uint32 typ
val uint64_t  : uint64 typ
val size_t    : size_t typ
val ushort    : ushort typ
val uint      : uint typ
val ulong     : ulong typ
val ullong    : ullong typ

val float     : float typ
val double    : float typ

val complex32 : Complex.t typ
val complex64 : Complex.t typ
```

These values are all of type 'a typ, where the value name (e.g., void) tells you the C type and the 'a component (e.g., unit) is the OCaml representation of that C type. Most of the mappings are straightforward, but some of them need a bit more explanation:

- Void values appear in OCaml as the unit type. Using void in an argument or result type specification produces an OCaml function that accepts or returns unit. Dereferencing a pointer to void is an error, as in C, and will raise the IncompleteType exception.

- The C size_t type is an alias for one of the unsigned integer types. The actual size and alignment requirements for size_t varies between platforms. Ctypes provides an OCaml size_t type that is aliased to the appropriate integer type.

- OCaml only supports double-precision floating-point numbers, and so the C float and double types both map onto the OCaml float type, and the C float com plex and double complex types both map onto the OCaml double-precision Com plex.t type.

Pointers and Arrays

Pointers are at the heart of C, so they are necessarily part of Ctypes, which provides support for pointer arithmetic, pointer conversions, reading and writing through pointers, and passing and returning pointers to and from functions.

We've already seen a simple use of pointers in the Ncurses example. Let's start a new example by binding the following POSIX functions:

C

```
time_t time(time_t *);
double difftime(time_t, time_t);
char *ctime(const time_t *timep);
```

The time function returns the current calendar time and is a simple start. The first step is to open some of the Ctypes modules:

Ctypes
    The Ctypes module provides functions for describing C types in OCaml.

PosixTypes
    The PosixTypes module includes some extra POSIX-specific types (such as time_t).

Foreign
    The Foreign module exposes the foreign function that makes it possible to invoke C functions.

We can now create a binding to time directly from the toplevel.

OCaml utop

```
# #require "ctypes.foreign" ;;
# #require "ctypes.top" ;;
# open Ctypes ;;
# open PosixTypes ;;
```

```
# open Foreign ;;
# let time = foreign "time" (ptr time_t @-> returning time_t) ;;
val time : time_t ptr -> time_t = <fun>
```

The foreign function is the main link between OCaml and C. It takes two arguments: the name of the C function to bind, and a value describing the type of the bound function. In the time binding, the function type specifies one argument of type ptr time_t and a return type of time_t.

We can now call time immediately in the same toplevel. The argument is actually optional, so we'll just pass a null pointer that has been coerced into becoming a null pointer to time_t:

OCaml utop (part 1)

```
# let cur_time = time (from_voidp time_t null) ;;
val cur_time : time_t = 1376834134
```

Since we're going to call time a few times, let's create a wrapper function that passes the null pointer through:

OCaml utop (part 2)

```
# let time' () = time (from_voidp time_t null) ;;
val time' : unit -> time_t = <fun>
```

Since time_t is an abstract type, we can't actually do anything useful with it directly. We need to bind a second function to do anything useful with the return values from time. We'll move on to difftime; the second C function in our prototype list:

OCaml utop (part 3)

```
# let difftime =
    foreign "difftime" (time_t @-> time_t @-> returning double) ;;
val difftime : time_t -> time_t -> float = <fun>
# let t1 =
    time' () in
    Unix.sleep 2;
    let t2 = time' () in
    difftime t2 t1 ;;
- : float = 2.
```

The binding to difftime above is sufficient to compare two time_t values.

Allocating Typed Memory for Pointers

Let's look at a slightly less trivial example where we pass a nonnull pointer to a function. Continuing with the theme from earlier, we'll bind to the ctime function, which converts a time_t value to a human-readable string:

OCaml utop (part 4)

```
# let ctime = foreign "ctime" (ptr time_t @-> returning string) ;;
val ctime : time_t ptr -> string = <fun>
```

The binding is continued in the toplevel to add to our growing collection. However, we can't just pass the result of time to ctime:

OCaml utop (part 5)

```
# ctime (time' ()) ;;
Characters 7-15:
Error: This expression has type time_t but an expression was expected of type
       time_t ptr
```

This is because ctime needs a pointer to the time_t rather than passing it by value. We thus need to allocate some memory for the time_t and obtain its memory address:

OCaml utop (part 6)

```
# let t_ptr = allocate time_t (time' ()) ;;
val t_ptr : time_t ptr = (int64_t*) 0x238ac30
```

The allocate function takes the type of the memory to be allocated and the initial value and it returns a suitably typed pointer. We can now call ctime passing the pointer as an argument:

OCaml utop (part 7)

```
# ctime t_ptr ;;
- : string = "Sun Aug 18 14:55:36 2013\n"
```

Using Views to Map Complex Values

While scalar types typically have a 1:1 representation, other C types require extra work to convert them into OCaml. Views create new C type descriptions that have special behavior when used to read or write C values.

We've already used one view in the definition of ctime earlier. The string view wraps the C type char * (written in OCaml as ptr char) and converts between the C and OCaml string representations each time the value is written or read.

Here is the type signature of the Ctypes.view function:

OCaml (part 2)

```
val view :
  read:('a -> 'b) ->
  write:('b -> 'a) ->
  'a typ -> 'b typ
```

Ctypes has some internal low-level conversion functions that map between an OCaml string and a C character buffer by copying the contents into the respective data structure. They have the following type signature:

OCaml (part 3)

```
val string_of_char_ptr : char ptr -> string
val char_ptr_of_string : string -> char ptr
```

Given these functions, the definition of the Ctypes.string value that uses views is quite simple:

```
let string =
  view (char ptr)
    ~read:string_of_char_ptr
    ~write:char_ptr_of_string
```

The type of this `string` function is a normal `typ` with no external sign of the use of the view function:

```
val string    : string.typ
```

OCaml Strings Versus C Character Buffers

Although OCaml strings may look like C character buffers from an interface perspective, they're very different in terms of their memory representations.

OCaml strings are stored in the OCaml heap with a header that explicitly defines their length. C buffers are also fixed-length, but by convention, a C string is terminated by a null (a \0 byte) character. The C string functions calculate their length by scanning the buffer until the first null character is encountered.

This means that you need to be careful that OCaml strings that you pass to C functions don't contain any null values, since the first occurrence of a null character will be treated as the end of the C string. Ctypes also defaults to a *copying* interface for strings, which means that you shouldn't use them when you want the library to mutate the buffer in-place. In that situation, use the Ctypes `Bigarray` support to pass memory by reference instead.

Structs and Unions

The C constructs `struct` and `union` make it possible to build new types from existing types. Ctypes contains counterparts that work similarly.

Defining a Structure

Let's improve the timer function that we wrote earlier. The POSIX function `gettimeof day` retrieves the time with microsecond resolution. The signature of `gettimeofday` is as follows, including the structure definitions:

```
struct timeval {
  long tv_sec;
  long tv_usec;
};
```

```
      int gettimeofday(struct timeval *, struct timezone *tv);
```

Using Ctypes, we can describe this type as follows in our toplevel, continuing on from the previous definitions:

OCaml utop (part 8)

```
# type timeval ;;
type timeval
# let timeval : timeval structure typ = structure "timeval" ;;
val timeval : timeval structure typ = struct timeval
```

The first command defines a new OCaml type `timeval` that we'll use to instantiate the OCaml version of the struct. This is a *phantom type* that exists only to distinguish the underlying C type from other pointer types. The particular `timeval` structure now has a distinct type from other structures we define elsewhere, which helps to avoid getting them mixed up.

The second command calls `structure` to create a fresh structure type. At this point, the structure type is incomplete: we can add fields but cannot yet use it in `foreign` calls or use it to create values.

Adding Fields to Structures

The `timeval` structure definition still doesn't have any fields, so we need to add those next:

OCaml utop (part 9)

```
# let tv_sec  = field timeval "tv_sec" long ;;
val tv_sec : (Signed.long, (timeval, [ `Struct ]) structured) field = <abstr>
# let tv_usec = field timeval "tv_usec" long ;;
val tv_usec : (Signed.long, (timeval, [ `Struct ]) structured) field =
  <abstr>
# seal timeval ;;
- : unit = ()
```

The `field` function appends a field to the structure, as shown with `tv_sec` and `tv_usec`. Structure fields are typed accessors that are associated with a particular structure, and they correspond to the labels in C.

Every field addition mutates the structure variable and records a new size (the exact value of which depends on the type of the field that was just added). Once we `seal` the structure, we will be able to create values using it, but adding fields to a sealed structure is an error.

Incomplete Structure Definitions

Since `gettimeofday` needs a `struct timezone` pointer for its second argument, we also need to define a second structure type:

```
# type timezone ;;
type timezone
# let timezone : timezone structure typ = structure "timezone" ;;
val timezone : timezone structure typ = struct timezone
```

We don't ever need to create `struct timezone` values, so we can leave this struct as incomplete without adding any fields or sealing it. If you ever try to use it in a situation where its concrete size needs to be known, the library will raise an `IncompleteType` exception.

We're finally ready to bind to `gettimeofday` now:

```
# let gettimeofday = foreign "gettimeofday"
    (ptr timeval @-> ptr timezone @-> returning_checking_errno int) ;;
val gettimeofday : timeval structure ptr -> timezone structure ptr -> int =
    <fun>
```

There's one other new feature here: the `returning_checking_errno` function behaves like `returning`, except that it checks whether the bound C function modifies the C error flag. Changes to `errno` are mapped into OCaml exceptions and raise a `Unix.Unix_er ror` exception just as the standard library functions do.

As before, we can create a wrapper to make `gettimeofday` easier to use. The functions `make`, `addr`, and `getf` create a structure value, retrieve the address of a structure value, and retrieve the value of a field from a structure:

```
# let gettimeofday' () =
  let tv = make timeval in
  ignore(gettimeofday (addr tv) (from_voidp timezone null));
  let secs = Signed.Long.(to_int (getf tv tv_sec)) in
  let usecs = Signed.Long.(to_int (getf tv tv_usec)) in
  Pervasives.(float secs +. float usecs /. 1000000.0) ;;
val gettimeofday' : unit -> float = <fun>
# gettimeofday' () ;;
- : float = 1376834137.14
```

You need to be a little careful not to get all the open modules mixed up here. Both `Pervasives` and `Ctypes` define different `float` functions. The `Ctypes` module we opened up earlier overrides the `Pervasives` definition. As seen previously though, you just need to locally open `Pervasives` again to bring the usual `float` function back in scope.

Recap: A time-printing command

We built up a lot of bindings in the previous section, so let's recap them with a complete example that ties it together with a command-line frontend:

```
open Core.Std
open Ctypes
open PosixTypes
open Foreign

let time     = foreign "time" (ptr time_t @-> returning time_t)
let difftime = foreign "difftime" (time_t @-> time_t @-> returning double)
let ctime    = foreign "ctime" (ptr time_t @-> returning string)

type timeval
let timeval : timeval structure typ = structure "timeval"
let tv_sec   = field timeval "tv_sec" long
let tv_usec  = field timeval "tv_usec" long
let ()       = seal timeval

type timezone
let timezone : timezone structure typ = structure "timezone"

let gettimeofday = foreign "gettimeofday"
    (ptr timeval @-> ptr timezone @-> returning_checking_errno int)

let time' () = time (from_voidp time_t null)

let gettimeofday' () =
  let tv = make timeval in
  ignore(gettimeofday (addr tv) (from_voidp timezone null));
  let secs = Signed.Long.(to_int (getf tv tv_sec)) in
  let usecs = Signed.Long.(to_int (getf tv tv_usec)) in
  Pervasives.(float secs +. float usecs /. 1_000_000.)

let float_time () = printf "%f%!\n" (gettimeofday' ())

let ascii_time () =
  let t_ptr = allocate time_t (time' ()) in
  printf "%s%!" (ctime t_ptr)

let () =
  let open Command in
  basic ~summary:"Display the current time in various formats"
    Spec.(empty +> flag "-a" no_arg ~doc:" Human-readable output format")
    (fun human -> if human then ascii_time else float_time)
  |> Command.run
```

This can be compiled and run in the usual way:

```
$ corebuild -pkg ctypes.foreign datetime.native
$ ./datetime.native
1376833554.984496
$ ./datetime.native -a
Sun Aug 18 14:45:55 2013
```

Why Do We Need to Use returning?

The alert reader may be curious about why all these function definitions have to be terminated by returning:

OCaml

```
(* correct types *)
val time: ptr time_t @-> returning time_t
val difftime: time_t @-> time_t @-> returning double
```

The returning function may appear superfluous here. Why couldn't we simply give the types as follows?

OCaml (part 1)

```
(* incorrect types *)
val time: ptr time_t @-> time_t
val difftime: time_t @-> time_t @-> double
```

The reason involves higher types and two differences between the way that functions are treated in OCaml and C. Functions are first-class values in OCaml, but not in C. For example, in C it is possible to return a function pointer from a function, but not to return an actual function.

Secondly, OCaml functions are typically defined in a curried style. The signature of a two-argument function is written as follows:

OCaml (part 2)

```
val curried : int -> int -> int
```

but this really means:

OCaml (part 3)

```
val curried : int -> (int -> int)
```

and the arguments can be supplied one at a time to create a closure. In contrast, C functions receive their arguments all at once. The equivalent C function type is the following:

C

```
int uncurried_C(int, int);
```

and the arguments must always be supplied together:

C

```
uncurried_C(3, 4);
```

A C function that's written in curried style looks very different:

C

```
/* A function that accepts an int, and returns a function
   pointer that accepts a second int and returns an int. */
typedef int (function_t)(int);
function_t *curried_C(int);
```

```
/* supply both arguments */
curried_C(3)(4);

/* supply one argument at a time */
function_t *f = curried_C(3); f(4);
```

The OCaml type of `uncurried_C` when bound by Ctypes is `int -> int -> int`: a two-argument function. The OCaml type of `curried_C` when bound by ctypes is `int -> (int -> int)`: a one-argument function that returns a one-argument function.

In OCaml, of course, these types are absolutely equivalent. Since the OCaml types are the same but the C semantics are quite different, we need some kind of marker to distinguish the cases. This is the purpose of `returning` in function definitions.

Defining Arrays

Arrays in C are contiguous blocks of the same type of value. Any of the basic types defined previously can be allocated as blocks via the `Array` module:

OCaml (part 5)

```
module Array : sig
  type 'a t = 'a array

  val get : 'a t -> int -> 'a
  val set : 'a t -> int -> 'a -> unit
  val of_list : 'a typ -> 'a list -> 'a t
  val to_list : 'a t -> 'a list
  val length : 'a t -> int
  val start : 'a t -> 'a ptr
  val from_ptr : 'a ptr -> int -> 'a t
  val make : 'a typ -> ?initial:'a -> int -> 'a t
end
```

The array functions are similar to those in the standard library `Array` module except that they operate on arrays stored using the flat C representation rather than the OCaml representation described in Chapter 20.

As with standard OCaml arrays, the conversion between arrays and lists requires copying the values, which can be expensive for large data structures. Notice that you can also convert an array into a `ptr` pointer to the head of the underlying buffer, which can be useful if you need to pass the pointer and size arguments separately to a C function.

Unions in C are named structures that can be mapped onto the same underlying memory. They are also fully supported in Ctypes, but we won't go into more detail here.

Passing Functions to C

It's also straightforward to pass OCaml function values to C. The C standard library function `qsort` sorts arrays of elements using a comparison function passed in as a function pointer. The signature for `qsort` is:

C

```
void qsort(void *base, size_t nmemb, size_t size,
           int(*compar)(const void *, const void *));
```

C programmers often use `typedef` to make type definitions involving function pointers easier to read. Using a typedef, the type of `qsort` looks a little more palatable:

C:

```
typedef int(compare_t)(const void *, const void *);

void qsort(void *base, size_t nmemb, size_t size, compare_t *);
```

This also happens to be a close mapping to the corresponding Ctypes definition. Since type descriptions are regular values, we can just use `let` in place of `typedef` and end up with working OCaml bindings to `qsort`:

OCaml utop

```
# #require "ctypes.foreign" ;;
# open Ctypes ;;
# open PosixTypes ;;
# open Foreign ;;
# let compare_t = ptr void @-> ptr void @-> returning int ;;
val compare_t : (unit ptr -> unit ptr -> int) fn = <abstr>
```

```
# let qsort = foreign "qsort"
  (ptr void @-> size_t @-> size_t @->
   funptr compare_t @-> returning void) ;;
val qsort :
  unit ptr -> size_t -> size_t -> (unit ptr -> unit ptr -> int) -> unit =
  <fun>
```

We only use compare_t once (in the qsort definition), so you can choose to inline it in
the OCaml code if you prefer. As the type shows, the resulting qsort value is a higher-
order function, since the fourth argument is itself a function. As before, let's define a
wrapper function to make qsort easier to use. The second and third arguments to qsort
specify the length (number of elements) of the array and the element size.

Arrays created using Ctypes have a richer runtime structure than C arrays, so we don't
need to pass size information around. Furthermore, we can use OCaml polymorphism
in place of the unsafe void ptr type.

Example: A Command-Line Quicksort

The following is a command-line tool that uses the qsort binding to sort all of the
integers supplied on the standard input:

OCaml

```
open Core.Std
open Ctypes
open PosixTypes
open Foreign

let compare_t = ptr void @-> ptr void @-> returning int

let qsort = foreign "qsort"
    (ptr void @-> size_t @-> size_t @-> funptr compare_t @->
       returning void)

let qsort' cmp arr =
  let open Unsigned.Size_t in
  let ty = Array.element_type arr in
  let len = of_int (Array.length arr) in
  let elsize = of_int (sizeof ty) in
  let start = to_voidp (Array.start arr) in
  let compare l r = cmp (!@ (from_voidp ty l)) (!@ (from_voidp ty r)) in
  qsort start len elsize compare;
  arr

let sort_stdin () =
  In_channel.input_lines stdin
  |> List.map ~f:int_of_string
  |> Array.of_list int
  |> qsort' Int.compare
  |> Array.to_list
  |> List.iter ~f:(fun a -> printf "%d\n" a)
```

```
let () =
  Command.basic ~summary:"Sort integers on standard input"
    Command.Spec.empty sort_stdin
  |> Command.run
```

Compile it in the usual way with *corebuild* and test it against some input data, and also build the inferred interface so we can examine it more closely:

```
$ corebuild -pkg ctypes.foreign qsort.native
$ cat input.txt
5
3
2
1
4
$ ./qsort.native < input.txt
1
2
3
4
5
$ corebuild -pkg ctypes.foreign qsort.inferred.mli
$ cp _build/qsort.inferred.mli qsort.mli
```

The inferred interface shows us the types of the raw qsort binding and also the qsort' wrapper function:

```
val compare_t : (unit Ctypes.ptr -> unit Ctypes.ptr -> int) Ctypes.fn
val qsort :
  unit Ctypes.ptr ->
  PosixTypes.size_t ->
  PosixTypes.size_t -> (unit Ctypes.ptr -> unit Ctypes.ptr -> int) -> unit
val qsort' : ('a -> 'a -> int) -> 'a Ctypes.array -> 'a Ctypes.array
val sort_stdin : unit -> unit
```

The qsort' wrapper function has a much more canonical OCaml interface than the raw binding. It accepts a comparator function and a Ctypes array, and returns the same Ctypes array. It's not strictly required that it returns the array, since it modifies it in-place, but it makes it easier to chain the function using the |> operator (as sort_stdin does in the example).

Using qsort' to sort arrays is straightforward. Our example code reads the standard input as a list, converts it to a C array, passes it through qsort, and outputs the result to the standard output. Again, remember to not confuse the Ctypes.Array module with the Core.Std.Array module: the former is in scope since we opened Ctypes at the start of the file.

Lifetime of Allocated Ctypes

Values allocated via Ctypes (i.e., using allocate, Array.make, and so on) will not be garbage-collected as long as they are reachable from OCaml values. The system memory they occupy is freed when they do become unreachable, via a finalizer function registered with the garbage collector (GC).

The definition of reachability for Ctypes values is a little different from conventional OCaml values, though. The allocation functions return an OCaml-managed pointer to the value, and as long as some derivative pointer is still reachable by the GC, the value won't be collected.

"Derivative" means a pointer that's computed from the original pointer via arithmetic, so a reachable reference to an array element or a structure field protects the whole object from collection.

A corollary of the preceding rule is that pointers written into the C heap don't have any effect on reachability. For example, if you have a C-managed array of pointers to structs, then you'll need some additional way of keeping the structs themselves around to protect them from collection. You could achieve this via a global array of values on the OCaml side that would keep them live until they're no longer needed.

Functions passed to C have similar considerations regarding lifetime. On the OCaml side, functions created at runtime may be collected when they become unreachable. As we've seen, OCaml functions passed to C are converted to function pointers, and function pointers written into the C heap have no effect on the reachability of the OCaml functions they reference. With qsort things are straightforward, since the comparison function is only used during the call to qsort itself. However, other C libraries may store function pointers in global variables or elsewhere, in which case you'll need to take care that the OCaml functions you pass to them aren't prematurely garbage-collected.

Learning More About C Bindings

The Ctypes distribution (*http://github.com/ocamllabs/ocaml-ctypes*) contains a number of larger-scale examples, including:

- Bindings to the POSIX fts API, which demonstrates C callbacks more comprehensively
- A more complete Ncurses binding than the example we opened the chapter with

- A comprehensive test suite that covers the complete library, and can provide useful snippets for your own bindings

This chapter hasn't really needed you to understand the innards of OCaml at all. Ctypes does its best to make function bindings easy, but the rest of this part will also fill you in about interactions with OCaml memory layout in Chapter 20 and automatic memory management in Chapter 21.

Ctypes gives OCaml programs access to the C representation of values, shielding you from the details of the OCaml value representation, and introduces an abstraction layer that hides the details of foreign calls. While this covers a wide variety of situations, it's sometimes necessary to look behind the abstraction to obtain finer control over the details of the interaction between the two languages.

You can find more information about the C interface in several places:

- The standard OCaml foreign function interface allows you to glue OCaml and C together from the other side of the boundary, by writing C functions that operate on the OCaml representation of values. You can find details of the standard interface in the OCaml manual (*http://caml.inria.fr/pub/docs/manual-ocaml-4.00/manual033.html*) and in the book *Developing Applications with Objective Caml* (*http://caml.inria.fr/pub/docs/oreilly-book/ocaml-ora-book.pdf*).

- Florent Monnier maintains an excellent online OCaml (*http://www.linux-nantes.org/~fmonnier/ocaml/ocaml-wrapping-c.html*) that provides examples of how to call OCaml functions from C. This covers a wide variety of OCaml data types and also more complex callbacks between C and OCaml.

- SWIG (*http://www.swig.org*) is a tool that connects programs written in C/C++ to a variety of higher-level programming languages, including OCaml. The SWIG manual has examples of converting library specifications into OCaml bindings.

Struct Memory Layout

The C language gives implementations a certain amount of freedom in choosing how to lay out structs in memory. There may be padding between members and at the end of the struct, in order to satisfy the memory alignment requirements of the host platform. Ctypes uses platform-appropriate size and alignment information to replicate the struct layout process. OCaml and C will have consistent views about the layout of the struct as long as you declare the fields of a struct in the same order and with the same types as the C library you're binding to.

However, this approach can lead to difficulties when the fields of a struct aren't fully specified in the interface of a library. The interface may list the fields of a structure without specifying their order, or make certain fields available only on certain platforms, or insert undocumented fields into struct definitions for performance reasons. For example, the `struct timeval` definition used in this chapter accurately describes the layout of the struct on common platforms, but implementations on some more unusual architectures include additional padding members that will lead to strange behavior in the examples.

The Cstubs subpackage of Ctypes addresses this issue. Rather than simply assuming that struct definitions given by the user accurately reflect the actual definitions of structs used in C libraries, Cstubs generates code that uses the C library headers to discover the layout of the struct. The good news is that the code that you write doesn't need to change much. Cstubs provides alternative implementations of the `field` and `seal` functions that you've already used to describe `struct timeval`; instead of computing member offsets and sizes appropriate for the platform, these implementations obtain them directly from C.

The details of using Cstubs are available in the online documentation (*https://ocaml labs.github.io/ocaml-ctypes*), along with instructions on integration with *autoconf* platform portability instructions.

## CHAPTER 20

Memory Representation of Values

The FFI interface we described in Chapter 19 hides the precise details of how values are exchanged across C libraries and the OCaml runtime. There is a simple reason for this: using this interface directly is a delicate operation that requires understanding a few different moving parts before you can get it right. You first need to know the mapping between OCaml types and their runtime memory representation. You also need to ensure that your code is interfacing correctly with OCaml runtime's memory management.

However, knowledge of the OCaml internals is useful beyond just writing foreign function interfaces. As you build and maintain more complex OCaml applications, you'll need to interface with various external system tools that operate on compiled OCaml binaries. For example, profiling tools report output based on the runtime memory layout, and debuggers execute binaries without any knowledge of the static OCaml types. To use these tools effectively, you'll need to do some translation between the OCaml and C worlds.

Luckily, the OCaml toolchain is very predictable. The compiler minimizes the amount of optimization magic that it performs, and relies instead on its straightforward execution model for good performance. With some experience, you can know rather precisely where a block of performance-critical OCaml code is spending its time.

This chapter covers the precise mapping from OCaml types to runtime values and walks you through them via the toplevel. We'll cover how these values are managed by the runtime later on in Chapter 21.

OCaml Blocks and Values

A running OCaml program uses blocks of memory (i.e., contiguous sequences of words in RAM) to represent values such as tuples, records, closures, or arrays. An OCaml program implicitly allocates a block of memory when such a value is created:

OCaml utop

```
# type t = { foo: int; bar: int } ;;
type t = { foo : int; bar : int; }
# let x = { foo = 13; bar = 14 } ;;
val x : t = {foo = 13; bar = 14}
```

The type declaration t doesn't take up any memory at runtime, but the subsequent let binding allocates a new block of memory with two words of available space. One word holds the foo field, and the other word holds the bar field. The OCaml compiler translates such an expression into an explicit allocation for the block from OCaml's runtime system.

OCaml uses a uniform memory representation in which every OCaml variable is stored as a *value*. An OCaml value is a single memory word that is either an immediate integer

---

or a pointer to some other memory. The OCaml runtime tracks all values so that it can free them when they are no longer needed. It thus needs to be able to distinguish between integer and pointer values, since it scans pointers to find further values but doesn't follow integers that don't point to anything meaningful beyond their immediate value.

Distinguishing Integers and Pointers at Runtime

Wrapping primitives types (such as integers) inside another data structure that records extra metadata about the value is known as *boxing*. Values are boxed in order to make it easier for the garbage collector (GC) to do its job, but at the expense of an extra level of indirection to access the data within the boxed value.

OCaml values don't all have to be boxed at runtime. Instead, values use a single tag bit per word to distinguish integers and pointers at runtime. The value is an integer if the lowest bit of the block word is nonzero, and a pointer if the lowest bit of the block word is zero. Several OCaml types map onto this integer representation, including `bool`, `int`, the empty list, `unit`, and variants without constructors.

This representation means that integers are unboxed runtime values in OCaml so that they can be stored directly without having to allocate a wrapper block. They can be passed directly to other function calls in registers and are generally the cheapest and fastest values to use in OCaml.

A value is treated as a memory pointer if its lowest bit is zero. A pointer value can still be stored unmodified despite this, since pointers are guaranteed to be word-aligned (with the bottom bits always being zero).

The only problem that remains with this memory representation is distinguishing between pointers to OCaml values (which should be followed by the GC) and pointers into the system heap to C values (which shouldn't be followed).

The mechanism for this is simple, since the runtime system keeps track of the heap blocks it has allocated for OCaml values. If the pointer is inside a heap chunk that is marked as being managed by the OCaml runtime, it is assumed to point to an OCaml value. If it points outside the OCaml runtime area, it is treated as an opaque C pointer to some other system resource.

Some History About OCaml's Word-Aligned Pointers

The alert reader may be wondering how OCaml can guarantee that all of its pointers are word-aligned. In the old days, when RISC chips such as Sparc, MIPS, and Alpha were commonplace, unaligned memory accesses were forbidden by the instruction set architecture and would result in a CPU exception that terminated the program. Thus, all pointers were historically rounded off to the architecture word size (usually 32 or 64 bits).

Modern CISC processors such as the Intel x86 do support unaligned memory accesses, but the chip still runs faster if accesses are word-aligned. OCaml therefore simply mandates that all pointers be word-aligned, which guarantees that the bottom few bits of any valid pointer will be zero. Setting the bottom bit to a nonzero value is a simple way to mark an integer, at the cost of losing that single bit of precision.

An even more alert reader will be wondering about the performance implications are for integer arithmetic using this tagged representation. Since the bottom bit is set, any operation on the integer has to shift the bottom bit right to recover the "native" value. The native code OCaml compiler generates efficient x86 assembly code in this case, taking advantage of modern processor instructions to hide the extra shifts where possible. Addition is a single LEA x86 instruction, subtraction can be two instructions, and multiplication is only a few more.

Blocks and Values

An OCaml *block* is the basic unit of allocation on the heap. A block consists of a one-word header (either 32 or 64 bits depending on the CPU architecture) followed by variable-length data that is either opaque bytes or an array of *fields*. The header has a multipurpose tag byte that defines whether to interpret the subsequent data as opaque bytes or OCaml fields.

The GC never inspects opaque bytes. If the tag indicates an array of OCaml fields are present, their contents are all treated as more valid OCaml values. The GC always inspects fields and follows them as part of the collection process described earlier.

Diagram

size of block in words	color	tag byte	value[0]	value[1]	...
either 22 or 54 bits	2 bit	8 bit			

The `size` field records the length of the block in memory words. This is 22 bits on 32-bit platforms, which is the reason OCaml strings are limited to 16 MB on that architecture. If you need bigger strings, either switch to a 64-bit host, or use the `Bigarray` module.

The 2-bit color field is used by the GC to keep track of its state during mark-and-sweep collection. We'll come back to this field in Chapter 21. This tag isn't exposed to OCaml source code in any case.

A block's tag byte is multipurpose, and indicates whether the data array represents opaque bytes or fields. If a block's tag is greater than or equal to No_scan_tag (251), then the block's data are all opaque bytes, and are not scanned by the collector. The most common such block is the string type, which we describe in more detail later in this chapter.

The exact representation of values inside a block depends on their static OCaml type. All OCaml types are distilled down into values, and summarized in Table 20-1.

Table 20-1. OCaml values

OCaml value	Representation
int or char	Directly as a value, shifted left by 1 bit, with the least significant bit set to 1.
unit, [], false	As OCaml int 0.
true	As OCaml int 1.
Foo | Bar	As ascending OCaml ints, starting from 0.
Foo | Bar of int	Variants with parameters are boxed, while variants with no parameters are unboxed.
Polymorphic variants	Variable space usage depending on the number of parameters.
Floating-point number	As a block with a single field containing the double-precision float.
String	Word-aligned byte arrays with an explicit length.
[1; 2; 3]	As 1::2::3::[] where [] is an int, and h::t a block with tag 0 and two parameters.
Tuples, records, and arrays	An array of values. Arrays can be variable size, but tuples and records are fixed-size.
Records or arrays, all float	Special tag for unboxed arrays of floats, or records that only have float fields.

Integers, Characters, and Other Basic Types

Many basic types are efficiently stored as unboxed integers at runtime. The native int type is the most obvious, although it drops a single bit of precision due to the tag bit. Other atomic types such as unit and the empty list [] value are stored as constant integers. Boolean values have a value of 1 and 0 for true and false, respectively.

These basic types such as empty lists and unit are very efficient to use, since integers are never allocated on the heap. They can be passed directly in registers and not appear on the stack if you don't have too many parameters to your functions. Modern architectures such as x86_64 have a lot of spare registers to further improve the efficiency of using unboxed integers.

Tuples, Records, and Arrays

Diagram

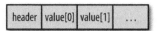

Tuples, records, and arrays are all represented identically at runtime as a block with tag 0. Tuples and records have constant sizes determined at compile time, whereas arrays can be of variable length. While arrays are restricted to containing a single type of element in the OCaml type system, this is not required by the memory representation.

You can check the difference between a block and a direct integer yourself using the `Obj` module, which exposes the internal representation of values to OCaml code:

OCaml utop

```
# Obj.is_block (Obj.repr (1,2,3)) ;;
- : bool = true
# Obj.is_block (Obj.repr 1) ;;
- : bool = false
```

The `Obj.repr` function retrieves the runtime representation of any OCaml value. `Obj.is_block` checks the bottom bit to determine if the value is a block header or an unboxed integer.

Floating-Point Numbers and Arrays

Floating-point numbers in OCaml are always stored as full, double-precision values. Individual floating-point values are stored as a block with a single field that contains the number. This block has the `Double_tag` set, which signals to the collector that the floating-point value is not to be scanned:

OCaml utop (part 1)

```
# Obj.tag (Obj.repr 1.0) ;;
- : int = 253
# Obj.double_tag ;;
- : int = 253
```

Since each floating-point value is boxed in a separate memory block, it can be inefficient to handle large arrays of floats in comparison to unboxed integers. OCaml therefore special-cases records or arrays that contain *only* `float` types. These are stored in a block that contains the floats packed directly in the data section, with `Double_array_tag` set to signal to the collector that the contents are not OCaml values.

Diagram

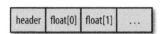

First, let's check that float arrays do in fact have a different tag number from normal floating-point values:

OCaml utop (part 2)

```
# Obj.double_tag ;;
- : int = 253
# Obj.double_array_tag ;;
- : int = 254
```

This tells us that float arrays have a tag value of 254. Now let's test some sample values using the `Obj.tag` function to check that the allocated block has the expected runtime tag, and also use `Obj.double_field` to retrieve a float from within the block:

OCaml utop (part 3)

```
# Obj.tag (Obj.repr [| 1.0; 2.0; 3.0 |]) ;;
- : int = 254
# Obj.tag (Obj.repr (1.0, 2.0, 3.0) ) ;;
- : int = 0
# Obj.double_field (Obj.repr [| 1.1; 2.2; 3.3 |]) 1 ;;
- : float = 2.2
# Obj.double_field (Obj.repr 1.234) 0 ;;
- : float = 1.234
```

The first thing we tested was that a float array has the correct unboxed float array tag value (254). However, the next line tests a tuple of floating-point values instead, which are *not* optimized in the same way and have the normal tuple tag value (0).

Only records and arrays can have the float array optimization, and for records, every single field must be a float.

Variants and Lists

Basic variant types with no extra parameters for any of their branches are simply stored as an OCaml integer, starting with 0 for the first option and in ascending order:

OCaml utop (part 4)

```
# type t - Apple | Orange | Pear ;;
type t = Apple | Orange | Pear
# ((Obj.magic (Obj.repr Apple)) : int) ;;
- : int = 0
# ((Obj.magic (Obj.repr Pear)) : int) ;;
- : int = 2
# Obj.is_block (Obj.repr Apple) ;;
- : bool = false
```

`Obj.magic` unsafely forces a type cast between any two OCaml types; in this example, the `int` type hint retrieves the runtime integer value. The `Obj.is_block` confirms that the value isn't a more complex block, but just an OCaml `int`.

Variants that have parameters arguments are a little more complex. They are stored as blocks, with the value *tags* ascending from 0 (counting from leftmost variants with parameters). The parameters are stored as words in the block:

OCaml utop (part 5)

```
# type t = Apple | Orange of int | Pear of string | Kiwi ;;
type t = Apple | Orange of int | Pear of string | Kiwi
# Obj.is_block (Obj.repr (Orange 1234)) ;;
- : bool = true
# Obj.tag (Obj.repr (Orange 1234)) ;;
- : int = 0
# Obj.tag (Obj.repr (Pear "xyz")) ;;
- : int = 1
# (Obj.magic (Obj.field (Obj.repr (Orange 1234)) 0) : int) ;;
- : int = 1234
# (Obj.magic (Obj.field (Obj.repr (Pear "xyz")) 0) : string) ;;
- : string = "xyz"
```

In the preceding example, the Apple and Kiwi values are still stored as normal OCaml integers with values 0 and 1, respectively. The Orange and Pear values both have parameters and are stored as blocks whose tags ascend from 0 (and so Pear has a tag of 1, as the use of Obj.tag verifies). Finally, the parameters are fields that contain OCaml values within the block, and Obj.field can be used to retrieve them.

Lists are stored with a representation that is exactly the same as if the list was written as a variant type with Nil and Cons. The empty list [ ] is an integer 0, and subsequent blocks have tag 0 and two parameters: a block with the current value, and a pointer to the rest of the list.

Obj Module Considered Harmful

Obj is an undocumented module that exposes the internals of the OCaml compiler and runtime. It is very useful for examining and understanding how your code will behave at runtime but should *never* be used for production code unless you understand the implications. The module bypasses the OCaml type system, making memory corruption and segmentation faults possible.

Some theorem provers such as Coq do output code that uses Obj internally, but the external module signatures never expose it. Unless you too have a machine proof of correctness to accompany your use of Obj, stay away from it except for debugging!

Due to this encoding, there is a limit around 240 variants with parameters that applies to each type definition, but the only limit on the number of variants without parameters is the size of the native integer (either 31 or 63 bits). This limit arises because of the size of the tag byte, and that some of the high-numbered tags are reserved.

Polymorphic Variants

Polymorphic variants are more flexible than normal variants when writing code but are slightly less efficient at runtime. This is because there isn't as much static compile-time information available to optimize their memory layout.

A polymorphic variant without any parameters is stored as an unboxed integer and so only takes up one word of memory, just like a normal variant. This integer value is determined by applying a hash function to the *name* of the variant. The hash function isn't exposed directly by the compiler, but the type_conv library from Core provides an alternative implementation:

OCaml utop (part 6)

```
# Pa_type_conv.hash_variant "Foo" ;;
- : int = 3505894
# (Obj.magic (Obj.repr `Foo) : int) ;;
- : int = 3505894
```

The hash function is designed to give the same results on 32-bit and 64-bit architectures, so the memory representation is stable across different CPUs and host types.

Polymorphic variants use more memory space than normal variants when parameters are included in the data type constructors. Normal variants use the tag byte to encode the variant value and save the fields for the contents, but this single byte is insufficient to encode the hashed value for polymorphic variants. They must allocate a new block (with tag 0) and store the value in there instead. Polymorphic variants with constructors thus use one word of memory more than normal variant constructors.

Another inefficiency over normal variants is when a polymorphic variant constructor has more than one parameter. Normal variants hold parameters as a single flat block with multiple fields for each entry, but polymorphic variants must adopt a more flexible uniform memory representation, since they may be reused in a different context across compilation units. They allocate a tuple block for the parameters that is pointed to from the argument field of the variant. There are thus three additional words for such variants, along with an extra memory indirection due to the tuple.

The extra space usage is generally not significant in a typical application, and polymorphic variants offer a great deal more flexibility than normal variants. However, if you're writing code that demands high performance or must run within tight memory bounds, the runtime layout is at least very predictable. The OCaml compiler never switches memory representation due to optimization passes. This lets you predict the precise runtime layout by referring to these guidelines and your source code.

String Values

Strings are standard OCaml blocks with the header size defining the size of the string in machine words. The String_tag (252) is higher than the No_scan_tag, indicating that the contents of the block are opaque to the collector. The block contents are the contents of the string, with padding bytes to align the block on a word boundary.

Diagram

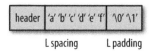

On a 32-bit machine, the padding is calculated based on the modulo of the string length and word size to ensure the result is word-aligned. A 64-bit machine extends the potential padding up to 7 bytes instead of 3 (see Table 20-2).

Table 20-2. String length and padding

String length mod 4	Padding
0	00 00 00 03
1	00 00 02
2	00 01
3	00

This string representation is a clever way to ensure that the contents are always zero-terminated by the padding word and to still compute its length efficiently without scanning the whole string. The following formula is used:

Diagram

number_of_words_in_block * sizeof(word) - last_byte_of_block - 1

The guaranteed NULL termination comes in handy when passing a string to C, but is not relied upon to compute the length from OCaml code. OCaml strings can thus contain NULL bytes at any point within the string.

Care should be taken that any C library functions that receive these buffers can also cope with arbitrary bytes within the buffer contents and are not expecting C strings. For instance, the C memcopy or memmove standard library functions can operate on arbitrary data, but strlen or strcpy both require a NULL-terminated buffer, and neither has a mechanism for encoding a NULL value within its contents.

Custom Heap Blocks

OCaml supports *custom* heap blocks via a `Custom_tag` that lets the runtime perform user-defined operations over OCaml values. A custom block lives in the OCaml heap like an ordinary block and can be of whatever size the user desires. The `Custom_tag` (255) is higher than `No_scan_tag` and so isn't scanned by the GC.

The first word of the data within the custom block is a C pointer to a `struct` of custom operations. The custom block cannot have pointers to OCaml blocks and is opaque to the GC:

C

```
struct custom_operations {
  char *identifier;
  void (*finalize)(value v);
  int (*compare)(value v1, value v2);
  intnat (*hash)(value v);
  void (*serialize)(value v,
                    /*out*/ uintnat * wsize_32 /*size in bytes*/,
                    /*out*/ uintnat * wsize_64 /*size in bytes*/);
  uintnat (*deserialize)(void * dst);
  int (*compare_ext)(value v1, value v2);
};
```

The custom operations specify how the runtime should perform polymorphic comparison, hashing and binary marshaling. They also optionally contain a *finalizer* that the runtime calls just before the block is garbage-collected. This finalizer has nothing to do with ordinary OCaml finalizers (as created by `Gc.finalize` and explained in Chapter 21). They are instead used to call C cleanup functions such as `free`.

Managing External Memory with Bigarray

A common use of custom blocks is to manage external system memory directly from within OCaml. The Bigarray interface was originally intended to exchange data with Fortran code, and maps a block of system memory as a multidimensional array that can be accessed from OCaml. Bigarray operations work directly on the external memory without requiring it to be copied into the OCaml heap (which is a potentially expensive operation for large arrays).

Bigarray sees a lot of use beyond just scientific computing, and several Core libraries use it for general-purpose I/O:

Iobuf

> The Iobuf module maps I/O buffers as a one-dimensional array of bytes. It provides a sliding window interface that lets consumer processes read from the buffer while it's being filled by producers. This lets OCaml use I/O buffers that have been externally allocated by the operating system without any extra data copying.

Bigstring

The `Bigstring` module provides a `String`-like interface that uses `Bigarray` internally. The `Bigbuffer` collects these into extensible string buffers that can operate entirely on external system memory.

The OCaml (*https://bitbucket.org/mmottl/lacaml*) library isn't part of Core but provides the recommended interfaces to the widely used BLAS and LAPACK mathematical Fortran libraries. These allow developers to write high-performance numerical code for applications that require linear algebra. It supports large vectors and matrices, but with static typing safety of OCaml to make it easier to write safe algorithms.

## CHAPTER 21

Understanding the Garbage Collector

We've described the runtime format of individual OCaml variables earlier, in Chapter 20. When you execute your program, OCaml manages the lifecycle of these variables by regularly scanning allocated values and freeing them when they're no longer needed. This in turn means that your applications don't need to manually implement memory management, and it greatly reduces the likelihood of memory leaks creeping into your code.

The OCaml runtime is a C library that provides routines that can be called from running OCaml programs. The runtime manages a *heap*, which is a collection of memory regions that it obtains from the operating system. The runtime uses this memory to hold *heap blocks* that it fills up with OCaml values in response to allocation requests by the OCaml program.

Mark and Sweep Garbage Collection

When there isn't enough memory available to satisfy an allocation request from the pool of allocated heap blocks, the runtime system invokes the garbage collector (GC). An OCaml program can't explicitly free a value when it is done with it. Instead, the GC regularly determines which values are *live* and which values are *dead*, i.e., no longer in use. Dead values are collected and their memory made available for reuse by the application.

The GC doesn't keep constant track of values as they are allocated and used. Instead, it regularly scans them by starting from a set of *root* values that the application always has access to (such as the stack). The GC maintains a directed graph in which heap blocks are nodes, and there is an edge from heap block b1 to heap block b2 if some field of b1 is a pointer to b2.

All blocks reachable from the roots by following edges in the graph must be retained, and unreachable blocks can be reused by the application. The algorithm used by OCaml to perform this heap traversal is commonly known as *mark and sweep* garbage collection, and we'll explain it further now.

Generational Garbage Collection

The usual OCaml programming style involves allocating many small variables that are used for a short period of time and then never accessed again. OCaml takes advantage of this fact to improve performance by using a *generational* GC.

A generational GC maintains separate memory regions to hold blocks based on how long the blocks have been live. OCaml's heap is split into two such regions:

- A small, fixed-size *minor heap* where most blocks are initially allocated
- A larger, variable-size *major heap* for blocks that have been live longer

A typical functional programming style means that young blocks tend to die young and old blocks tend to stay around for longer than young ones. This is often referred to as the *generational hypothesis*.

OCaml uses different memory layouts and garbage-collection algorithms for the major and minor heaps to account for this generational difference. We'll explain how they differ in more detail next.

The Gc Module and OCAMLRUNPARAM

OCaml provides several mechanisms to query and alter the behavior of the runtime system. The Gc module provides this functionality from within OCaml code, and we'll frequently refer to it in the rest of the chapter. As with several other standard library modules, Core alters the Gc interface from the standard OCaml library. We'll assume that you've opened Core.Std in our explanations.

You can also control the behavior of OCaml programs by setting the OCAMLRUNPARAM environment variable before launching your application. This lets you set GC parameters without recompiling, for example to benchmark the effects of different settings. The format of OCAMLRUNPARAM is documented in the OCaml manual (*http:// caml.inria.fr/pub/docs/manual-ocaml/manual024.html*).

The Fast Minor Heap

The minor heap is where most of your short-lived values are held. It consists of one contiguous chunk of virtual memory containing a sequence of OCaml blocks. If there is space, allocating a new block is a fast, constant-time operation that requires just a couple of CPU instructions.

To garbage-collect the minor heap, OCaml uses *copying collection* to move all live blocks in the minor heap to the major heap. This takes work proportional to the number of live blocks in the minor heap, which is typically small according to the generational hypothesis. The minor collection *stops the world* (that it, halts the application) while it runs, which is why it's so important that it complete quickly to let the application resume running with minimal interruption.

Allocating on the Minor Heap

The minor heap is a contiguous chunk of virtual memory that is usually a few megabytes in size so that it can be scanned quickly.

Diagram

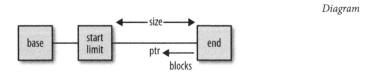

The runtime stores the boundaries of the minor heap in two pointers that delimit the start and end of the heap region (`caml_young_start` and `caml_young_end`, but we will drop the `caml_young` prefix for brevity). The `base` is the memory address returned by the system `malloc`, and `start` is aligned against the next nearest word boundary from `base` to make it easier to store OCaml values.

In a fresh minor heap, the `limit` equals the `start`, and the current `ptr` will equal the `end`. `ptr` decreases as blocks are allocated until it reaches `limit`, at which point a minor garbage collection is triggered.

Allocating a block in the minor heap just requires `ptr` to be decremented by the size of the block (including the header) and a check that it's not less than `limit`. If there isn't enough space left for the block without decrementing past `limit`, a minor garbage collection is triggered. This is a very fast check (with no branching) on most CPU architectures.

You may wonder why `limit` is required at all, since it always seems to equal `start`. It's because the easiest way for the runtime to schedule a minor heap collection is by setting `limit` to equal `end`. The next allocation will never have enough space after this is done and will always trigger a garbage collection. There are various internal reasons for such early collections, such as handling pending UNIX signals, and they don't ordinarily matter for application code.

Setting the Size of the Minor Heap

The default minor heap size in OCaml is normally 2 MB on 64-bit platforms, but this is increased to 8 MB if you use Core (which generally prefers default settings that improve performance, but at the cost of a bigger memory profile). This setting can be overridden via the s=<words> argument to OCAMLRUNPARAM. You can change it after the program has started by calling the Gc.set function:

OCaml utop

```
# let c = Gc.get () ;;
val c : Gc.control =
  {Core.Std.Gc.Control.minor_heap_size = 1000000;
   major_heap_increment = 1000448; space_overhead = 100; verbose = 0;
   max_overhead = 500; stack_limit = 1048576; allocation_policy = 0}
# Gc.tune ~minor_heap_size:(262144 * 2) () ;;
- : unit = ()
```

Changing the GC size dynamically will trigger an immediate minor heap collection. Note that Core increases the default minor heap size from the standard OCaml installation quite significantly, and you'll want to reduce this if running in very memory-constrained environments.

The Long-Lived Major Heap

The major heap is where the bulk of the longer-lived and larger values in your program are stored. It consists of any number of noncontiguous chunks of virtual memory, each containing live blocks interspersed with regions of free memory. The runtime system maintains a free-list data structure that indexes all the free memory that it has allocated, and uses it to satisfy allocation requests for OCaml blocks.

The major heap is typically much larger than the minor heap and can scale to gigabytes in size. It is cleaned via a mark-and-sweep garbage collection algorithm that operates in several phases:

- The *mark* phase scans the block graph and marks all live blocks by setting a bit in the tag of the block header (known as the *color* tag).

- The *sweep* phase sequentially scans the heap chunks and identifies dead blocks that weren't marked earlier.

- The *compact* phase relocates live blocks into a freshly allocated heap to eliminate gaps in the free list. This prevents the fragmentation of heap blocks in long-running programs and normally occurs much less frequently than the mark and sweep phases.

A major garbage collection must also stop the world to ensure that blocks can be moved around without this being observed by the live application. The mark-and-sweep phases run incrementally over slices of the heap to avoid pausing the application for long periods of time, and also precede each slice with a fast minor collection. Only the compaction phase touches all the memory in one go, and is a relatively rare operation.

Allocating on the Major Heap

The major heap consists of a singly linked list of contiguous memory chunks sorted in increasing order of virtual address. Each chunk is a single memory region allocated via *malloc(3)* and consists of a header and data area which contains OCaml heap chunks. A heap chunk header contains:

- The *malloc*ed virtual address of the memory region containing the chunk
- The size in bytes of the data area
- An allocation size in bytes used during heap compaction to merge small blocks to defragment the heap
- A link to the next heap chunk in the list

Each chunk's data area starts on a page boundary, and its size is a multiple of the page size (4 KB). It contains a contiguous sequence of heap blocks that can be as small as one or two 4 KB pages, but are usually allocated in 1 MB chunks (or 512 KB on 32-bit architectures).

Controlling Major Heap Growth

The Gc module uses the `major_heap_increment` value to control the major heap growth. This defines the number of words to add to the major heap per expansion and is the only memory allocation operation that the operating system observes from the OCaml runtime after initial startup (since the minor is fixed in size).

If you anticipate allocating some large OCaml values or many small values in one go, then setting the heap increment to a larger value will improve performance by reducing the amount of heap resizing required in order to satisfy the allocation requests. A small increment may result in lots of smaller heap chunks spread across different regions of virtual memory that require more housekeeping in the OCaml runtime to keep track of them:

OCaml utop (part 1)
```
# Gc.tune ~major_heap_increment:(1000448 * 4) () ;;
- : unit = ()
```

Allocating an OCaml value on the major heap first checks the free list of blocks for a suitable region to place it. If there isn't enough room on the free list, the runtime expands the major heap by allocating a fresh heap chunk that will be large enough. That chunk is then added to the free list, and the free list is checked again (and this time will definitely succeed).

Remember that most allocations to the major heap will go via the minor heap and only be promoted if they are still used by the program after a minor collection. The one exception to this is for values larger than 256 words (that is, 2 KB on 64-bit platforms). These will be allocated directly on the major heap, since an allocation on the minor heap would likely trigger an immediate collection and copy it to the major heap anyway.

Memory Allocation Strategies

The major heap does its best to manage memory allocation as efficiently as possible and relies on heap compaction to ensure that memory stays contiguous and unfragmented. The default allocation policy normally works fine for most applications, but it's worth bearing in mind that there are other options, too.

The free list of blocks is always checked first when allocating a new block in the major heap. The default free list search is called *next-fit allocation*, with an alternative *first-fit* algorithm also available.

Next-fit allocation

Next-fit allocation keeps a pointer to the block in the free list that was most recently used to satisfy a request. When a new request comes in, the allocator searches from the next block to the end of the free list, and then from the beginning of the free list up to that block.

Next-fit allocation is the default allocation strategy. It's quite a cheap allocation mechanism, since the same heap chunk can be reused across allocation requests until it runs out. This in turn means that there is good memory locality to use CPU caches better.

First-fit allocation

If your program allocates values of many varied sizes, you may sometimes find that your free list becomes fragmented. In this situation, the GC is forced to perform an expensive compaction despite there being free chunks, since none of the chunks alone are big enough to satisfy the request.

First-fit allocation focuses on reducing memory fragmentation (and hence the number of compactions), but at the expense of slower memory allocation. Every allocation scans the free list from the beginning for a suitable free chunk, instead of reusing the most recent heap chunk as the next-fit allocator does.

For some workloads that need more real-time behavior under load, the reduction in the frequency of heap compaction will outweigh the extra allocation cost.

Controlling the Heap Allocation Policy

You can set the heap allocation policy via the `Gc.allocation_policy` field. A value of `0` (the default) sets it to next-fit, and `1` to the first-fit allocator.

The same behavior can be controlled at runtime by setting `a=0` or `a=1` in `OCAMLRUNPARAM`.

Marking and Scanning the Heap

The marking process can take a long time to run over the complete major heap and has to pause the main application while it's active. It therefore runs incrementally by marking the heap in *slices*. Each value in the heap has a 2-bit *color* field in its header that is used to store information about whether the value has been marked so that the GC can resume easily between slices.

Table 21-1. Tag color statuses

Tag color	Block status
Blue	On the free list and not currently in use
White (during marking)	Not reached yet, but possibly reachable
White (during sweeping)	Unreachable and can be freed
Gray	Reachable, but its fields have not been scanned
Black	Reachable, and its fields have been scanned

The color tags in the value headers store most of the state of the marking process, allowing it to be paused and resumed later. The GC and application alternate between marking a slice of the major heap and actually getting on with executing the program logic. The OCaml runtime calculates a sensible value for the size of each major heap slice based on the rate of allocation and available memory.

The marking process starts with a set of *root* values that are always live (such as the application stack). All values on the heap are initially marked as white values that are possibly reachable but haven't been scanned yet. It recursively follows all the fields in the roots via a depth-first search, and pushes newly encountered white blocks onto an intermediate stack of *gray values* while it follows their fields. When a gray value's fields have all been followed, it is popped off the stack and colored black.

This process is repeated until the gray value stack is empty and there are no further values to mark. There's one important edge case in this process, though. The gray value stack can only grow to a certain size, after which the GC can no longer recurse into intermediate values since it has nowhere to store them while it follows their fields. If this happens, the heap is marked as *impure* and a more expensive check is initiated once the existing gray values have been processed.

To mark an impure heap, the GC first marks it as pure and walks through the entire heap block-by-block in increasing order of memory address. If it finds a gray block, it adds it to the gray list and recursively marks it using the usual strategy for a pure heap. Once the scan of the complete heap is finished, the mark phase checks again whether the heap has again become impure and repeats the scan until it is pure again. These full-heap scans will continue until a successful scan completes without overflowing the gray list.

Controlling Major Heap Collections

You can trigger a single slice of the major GC via the major_slice call. This performs a minor collection first, and then a single slice. The size of the slice is normally automatically computed by the GC to an appropriate value and returns this value so that you can modify it in future calls if necessary:

OCaml utop (part 2)

```
# Gc.major_slice 0 ;;
- : int = 260440
# Gc.full_major () ;;
- : unit = ()
```

The space_overhead setting controls how aggressive the GC is about setting the slice size to a large size. This represents the proportion of memory used for live data that will be "wasted" because the GC doesn't immediately collect unreachable blocks. Core defaults this to 100 to reflect a typical system that isn't overly memory-constrained. Set this even higher if you have lots of memory, or lower to cause the GC to work harder and collect blocks faster at the expense of using more CPU time.

Heap Compaction

After a certain number of major GC cycles have completed, the heap may begin to be fragmented due to values being deallocated out of order from how they were allocated. This makes it harder for the GC to find a contiguous block of memory for fresh allocations, which in turn would require the heap to be grown unnecessarily.

The heap compaction cycle avoids this by relocating all the values in the major heap into a fresh heap that places them all contiguously in memory again. A naive implementation of the algorithm would require extra memory to store the new heap, but OCaml performs the compaction in place within the existing heap.

Controlling Frequency of Compactions

The `max_overhead` setting in the `Gc` module defines the connection between free memory and allocated memory after which compaction is activated.

A value of `0` triggers a compaction after every major garbage collection cycle, whereas the maximum value of `1000000` disables heap compaction completely. The default settings should be fine unless you have unusual allocation patterns that are causing a higher-than-usual rate of compactions:

OCaml utop (part 3)

```
# Gc.tune ~max_overhead:0 () ;;
- : unit = ()
```

Intergenerational Pointers

One complexity of generational collection arises from the fact that minor heap sweeps are much more frequent than major heap collections. In order to know which blocks in the minor heap are live, the collector must track which minor-heap blocks are directly pointed to by major-heap blocks. Without this information, each minor collection would also require scanning the much larger major heap.

OCaml maintains a set of such *intergenerational pointers* to avoid this dependency between a major and minor heap collection. The compiler introduces a write barrier to update this so-called *remembered set* whenever a major-heap block is modified to point at a minor-heap block.

The mutable write barrier

The write barrier can have profound implications for the structure of your code. It's one of the reasons using immutable data structures and allocating a fresh copy with changes can sometimes be faster than mutating a record in place.

The OCaml compiler keeps track of any mutable types and adds a call to the runtime `caml_modify` function before making the change. This checks the location of the target write and the value it's being changed to, and ensures that the remembered set is consistent. Although the write barrier is reasonably efficient, it can sometimes be slower than simply allocating a fresh value on the fast minor heap and doing some extra minor collections.

Let's see this for ourselves with a simple test program. You'll need to install the Core benchmarking suite via `opam install core_bench` before you compile this code:

OCaml

```
open Core.Std
open Core_bench.Std

type t1 = { mutable iters1: int; mutable count1: float }
```

```
type t2 = { iters2: int; count2: float }

let rec test_mutable t1 =
  match t1.iters1 with
  |0 -> ()
  |_ ->
    t1.iters1 <- t1.iters1 - 1;
    t1.count1 <- t1.count1 +. 1.0;
    test_mutable t1

let rec test_immutable t2 =
  match t2.iters2 with
  |0 -> ()
  |n ->
    let iters2 = n - 1 in
    let count2 = t2.count2 +. 1.0 in
    test_immutable { iters2; count2 }

let () =
  let iters = 1000000 in
  let tests = [
    Bench.Test.create ~name:"mutable"
      (fun () -> test_mutable { iters1=iters; count1=0.0 });
    Bench.Test.create ~name:"immutable"
      (fun () -> test_immutable { iters2=iters; count2=0.0 })
  ] in
  Bench.make_command tests |> Command.run
```

This program defines a type t1 that is mutable and t2 that is immutable. The benchmark
loop iterates over both fields and increments a counter. Compile and execute this with
some extra options to show the amount of garbage collection occurring:

Terminal

```
$ corebuild -pkg core_bench barrier_bench.native
$ ./barrier_bench.native -ascii name alloc
Estimated testing time 20s (change using -quota SECS).
```

Name	Time (ns)	Minor	Major	Promoted	% of max
mutable	6_304_612	2_000_004	9.05	9.05	100.00
immutable	4_775_718	5_000_005	0.03	0.03	75.75

There is a stark space/time trade-off here. The mutable version takes significantly longer
to complete than the immutable one but allocates many fewer minor-heap words than
the immutable version. Minor allocation in OCaml is very fast, and so it is often better
to use immutable data structures in preference to the more conventional mutable versions. On the other hand, if you only rarely mutate a value, it can be faster to take the
write-barrier hit and not allocate at all.

The only way to know for sure is to benchmark your program under real-world scenarios using Core_bench and experiment with the trade-offs. The command-line benchmark binaries have a number of useful options that affect garbage collection behavior:

```
$ ./barrier_bench.native -help
Benchmark for mutable, immutable

  barrier_bench.native [COLUMN ...]

Columns that can be specified are:
        name       - Name of the test.
        cycles     - Number of CPU cycles (RDTSC) taken.
        cycles-err - 95% confidence interval and R^2 error for cycles.
        ~cycles    - Cycles taken excluding major GC costs.
        time       - Number of nano secs taken.
        time-err   - 95% confidence interval and R^2 error for time.
        ~time      - Time (ns) taken excluding major GC costs.
        alloc      - Allocation of major, minor and promoted words.
        gc         - Show major and minor collections per 1000 runs.
        percentage - Relative execution time as a percentage.
        speedup    - Relative execution cost as a speedup.
        samples    - Number of samples collected for profiling.

R^2 error indicates how noisy the benchmark data is. A value of
1.0 means the amortized cost of benchmark is almost exactly predicated
and 0.0 means the reported values are not reliable at all.
Also see: http://en.wikipedia.org/wiki/Coefficient_of_determination

Major and Minor GC stats indicate how many collections happen per 1000
runs of the benchmarked function.

The following columns will be displayed by default:
        +name time percentage

To specify that a column should be displayed only if it has a non-trivial value,
prefix the column name with a '+'.

=== flags ===

  [-ascii]              Display data in simple ascii based tables.
  [-clear-columns]      Don't display default columns. Only show user specified
                        ones.
  [-display STYLE]      Table style (short, tall, line, blank or column). Default
                        short.
  [-geometric SCALE]    Use geometric sampling. (default 1.01)
  [-linear INCREMENT]   Use linear sampling to explore number of runs, example 1.
  [-no-compactions]     Disable GC compactions.
  [-quota SECS]         Time quota allowed per test (default 10s).
  [-save]               Save benchmark data to <test name>.txt files.
  [-stabilize-gc]       Stabilize GC between each sample capture.
```

```
[-v]                 High verbosity level.
[-width WIDTH]       width limit on column display (default 150).
[-build-info]        print info about this build and exit
[-version]           print the version of this build and exit
[-help]              print this help text and exit
                     (alias: -?)
```

The -no-compactions and -stabilize-gc options can help force a situation where your application has fragmented memory. This can simulate the behavior of a long-running application without you having to actually wait that long to re-create the behavior in a performance unit test.

Attaching Finalizer Functions to Values

OCaml's automatic memory management guarantees that a value will eventually be freed when it's no longer in use, either via the GC sweeping it or the program terminating. It's sometimes useful to run extra code just before a value is freed by the GC, for example, to check that a file descriptor has been closed, or that a log message is recorded.

What Values Can Be Finalized?

Various values cannot have finalizers attached since they aren't heap-allocated. Some examples of values that are not heap-allocated are integers, constant constructors, Booleans, the empty array, the empty list, and the unit value. The exact list of what is heap-allocated or not is implementation-dependent, which is why Core provides the Heap_block module to explicitly check before attaching the finalizer.

Some constant values can be heap-allocated but never deallocated during the lifetime of the program, for example, a list of integer constants. Heap_block explicitly checks to see if the value is in the major or minor heap, and rejects most constant values. Compiler optimizations may also duplicate some immutable values such as floating-point values in arrays. These may be finalized while another duplicate copy is being used by the program.

For this reason, attach finalizers only to values that you are explicitly sure are heap-allocated and aren't immutable. A common use is to attach them to file descriptors to ensure they are closed. However, the finalizer normally shouldn't be the primary way of closing the file descriptor, since it depends on the GC running in order to collect the value. For a busy system, you can easily run out of a scarce resource such as file descriptors before the GC catches up.

Core provides a `Heap_block` module that dynamically checks if a given value is suitable for finalizing. This block is then passed to Async's `Gc.add_finalizer` function that schedules the finalizer safely with respect to all the other concurrent program threads.

Let's explore this with a small example that finalizes values of different types, some of which are heap-allocated and others which are compile-time constants:

OCaml

```
open Core.Std
open Async.Std

let attach_finalizer n v =
  match Heap_block.create v with
  | None -> printf "%20s: FAIL\n%!" n
  | Some hb ->
    let final _ = printf "%20s: OK\n%!" n in
    Gc.add_finalizer hb final

type t = { foo: bool }

let main () =
  let alloced_float = Unix.gettimeofday () in
  let alloced_bool = alloced_float > 0.0 in
  let alloced_string = String.create 4 in
  attach_finalizer "immediate int" 1;
  attach_finalizer "immediate float" 1.0;
  attach_finalizer "immediate variant" (`Foo "hello");
  attach_finalizer "immediate string" "hello world";
  attach_finalizer "immediate record" { foo=false };
  attach_finalizer "allocated float" alloced_float;
  attach_finalizer "allocated bool" alloced_bool;
  attach_finalizer "allocated variant" (`Foo alloced_bool);
  attach_finalizer "allocated string" alloced_string;
  attach_finalizer "allocated record" { foo=alloced_bool };
  Gc.compact ();
  return ()

let () =
  Command.async_basic ~summary:"Testing finalizers"
    Command.Spec.empty main
  |> Command.run
```

Building and running this should show the following output:

Terminal

```
$ corebuild -pkg async finalizer.native
$ ./finalizer.native
       immediate int: FAIL
     immediate float: FAIL
   immediate variant: FAIL
    immediate string: FAIL
    immediate record: FAIL
      allocated bool: FAIL
```

```
allocated record: OK
allocated string: OK
allocated variant: OK
   allocated float: OK
```

The GC calls the finalization functions in the order of the deallocation. If several values become unreachable during the same GC cycle, the finalization functions will be called in the reverse order of the corresponding calls to `add_finalizer`. Each call to `add_fi nalizer` adds to the set of functions, which are run when the value becomes unreachable. You can have many finalizers all pointing to the same heap block if you wish.

After a garbage collection determines that a heap block b is unreachable, it removes from the set of finalizers all the functions associated with b, and serially applies each of those functions to b. Thus, every finalizer function attached to b will run at most once. However, program termination will not cause all the finalizers to be run before the runtime exits.

The finalizer can use all features of OCaml, including assignments that make the value reachable again and thus prevent it from being garbage-collected. It can also loop forever, which will cause other finalizers to be interleaved with it.

## CHAPTER 22

The Compiler Frontend: Parsing and Type Checking

Compiling source code into executable programs is a fairly complex libraries, linkers, and assemblers. It's important to understand how these fit together to help with your day-to-day workflow of developing, debugging, and deploying applications.

OCaml has a strong emphasis on static type safety and rejects source code that doesn't meet its requirements as early as possible. The compiler does this by running the source code through a series of checks and transformations. Each stage performs its job (e.g., type checking, optimization, or code generation) and discards some information from the previous stage. The final native code output is low-level assembly code that doesn't know anything about the OCaml modules or objects that the compiler started with.

You don't have to do all of this manually, of course. The compiler frontends (`ocamlc` and `ocamlopt`) are invoked via the command line and chain the stages together for you. Sometimes though, you'll need to dive into the toolchain to hunt down a bug or investigate a performance problem. This chapter explains the compiler pipeline in more depth so you understand how to harness the command-line tools effectively.

In this chapter, we'll cover the following topics:

- The compilation pipeline and what each stage represents
- Source preprocessing via Camlp4 and the intermediate forms
- The type-checking process, including module resolution

The details of the compilation process into executable code can be found next, in Chapter 23.

An Overview of the Toolchain

The OCaml tools accept textual source code as input, using the filename extensions `.ml` and `.mli` for modules and signatures, respectively. We explained the basics of the build process in Chapter 4, so we'll assume you've built a few OCaml programs already by this point.

Each source file represents a *compilation unit* that is built separately. The compiler generates intermediate files with different filename extensions to use as it advances through the compilation stages. The linker takes a collection of compiled units and produces a standalone executable or library archive that can be reused by other applications.

The overall compilation pipeline looks like this:

Diagram

Notice that the pipeline branches toward the end. OCaml has multiple compiler backends that reuse the early stages of compilation but produce very different final outputs. The *bytecode* can be run by a portable interpreter and can even be transformed into JavaScript (via js_of_ocaml (*http://ocsigen.org/js_of_ocaml*)) or C source code (via OCamlCC (*https://github.com/ocaml-bytes/ocamlcc*)). The *native code* compiler generates specialized executable binaries suitable for high-performance applications.

Obtaining the Compiler Source Code

Although it's not necessary to understand the examples, you may find it useful to have a copy of the OCaml source tree checked out while you read through this chapter. The source code is available from multiple places:

- Stable releases as *zip* and *tar* archives from the OCaml download site (*http://caml.inria.fr/download.en.html*)
- A Subversion anonymous mirror of the main development sources available on the development resources (*http://caml.inria.fr/ocaml/anonsvn.en.html*) page online
- A Git mirror of the Subversion repository with all the history and development branches included, browsable online at GitHub (*https://github.com/ocaml/ocaml*)

The source tree is split up into subdirectories. The core compiler consists of:

config/
: Configuration directives to tailor OCaml for your operating system and architecture.

bytecomp/ *and* byterun/
: Bytecode compiler and runtime, including the garbage collector (GC).

asmcomp/ *and* asmrun/
: Native-code compiler and runtime. The native runtime symlinks many modules from the byterun directory to share code, most notably the GC.

parsing/
: The OCaml lexer, parser, and libraries for manipulating them.

typing/
: The static type checking implementation and type definitions.

camlp4/
: The source code macro preprocessor.

driver/
: Command-line interfaces for the compiler tools.

A number of tools and scripts are also built alongside the core compiler:

debugger/
: The interactive bytecode debugger.

toplevel/
: Interactive top-level console.

emacs/
: A *caml-mode* for the Emacs editor.

stdlib/
: The compiler standard library, including the `Pervasives` module.

ocamlbuild/
: Build system that automates common OCaml compilation modes.

otherlibs/
: Optional libraries such as the Unix and graphics modules.

tools/
: Command-line utilities such as `ocamldep` that are installed with the compiler.

testsuite/
: Regression tests for the core compiler.

We'll go through each of the compilation stages now and explain how they will be useful to you during day-to-day OCaml development.

Parsing Source Code

When a source file is passed to the OCaml compiler, its first task is to parse the text into a more structured abstract syntax tree (AST). The parsing logic is implemented in OCaml itself using the techniques described earlier in Chapter 16. The lexer and parser rules can be found in the `parsing` directory in the source distribution.

Syntax Errors

The OCaml parser's goal is to output a well-formed AST data structure to the next phase of compilation, and so it any source code that doesn't match basic syntactic requirements. The compiler emits a *syntax error* in this situation, with a pointer to the filename and line and character number that's as close to the error as possible.

Here's an example syntax error that we obtain by performing a module assignment as a statement instead of as a `let` binding:

OCaml

```
let () =
  module MyString = String;
  ()
```

The code results in a syntax error when compiled:

Terminal

```
$ ocamlc -c broken_module.ml
File "broken_module.ml", line 2, characters 2-8:
Error: Syntax error
```

The correct version of this source code creates the `MyString` module correctly via a local open, and compiles successfully:

OCaml

```
let () =
  let module MyString = String in
  ()
```

The syntax error points to the line and character number of the first token that couldn't be parsed. In the broken example, the `module` keyword isn't a valid token at that point in parsing, so the error location information is correct.

Automatically Indenting Source Code

Sadly, syntax errors do get more inaccurate sometimes, depending on the nature of your mistake. Try to spot the deliberate error in the following function definitions:

OCaml

```
let concat_and_print x y =
  let v = x ^ y in
  print_endline v;
  v;

let add_and_print x y =
  let v = x + y in
  print_endline (string_of_int v);
  v

let () =
  let _x = add_and_print 1 2 in
  let _y = concat_and_print "a" "b" in
  ()
```

When you compile this file, you'll get a syntax error again:

Terminal

```
$ ocamlc -c follow_on_function.ml
File "follow_on_function.ml", line 11, characters 0-3:
Error: Syntax error
```

The line number in the error points to the end of the `add_and_print` function, but the actual error is at the end of the *first* function definition. There's an extra semicolon at the end of the first definition that causes the second definition to become part of the first `let` binding. This eventually results in a parsing error at the very end of the second function.

This class of bug (due to a single errant character) can be hard to spot in a large body of code. Luckily, there's a great tool available via OPAM called *ocp-indent* that applies structured indenting rules to your source code on a line-by-line basis. This not only beautifies your code layout, but it also makes this syntax error much easier to locate.

Let's run our erroneous file through *ocp-indent* and see how it processes it:

Terminal

```
$ ocp-indent follow_on_function.ml
let concat_and_print x y =
  let v = x ^ y in
  print_endline v;
  v;

  let add_and_print x y =
    let v = x + y in
    print_endline (string_of_int v);
    v

let () =
  let _x = add_and_print 1 2 in
  let _y = concat_and_print "a" "b" in
  ()
```

The add_and_print definition has been indented as if it were part of the first con
cat_and_print definition, and the errant semicolon is now much easier to spot. We
just need to remove that semicolon and rerun *ocp-indent* to verify that the syntax is
correct:

Terminal

```
$ ocp-indent follow_on_function_fixed.ml
let concat_and_print x y =
  let v = x ^ y in
  print_endline v;
  v

let add_and_print x y =
  let v = x + y in
  print_endline (string_of_int v);
  v

let () =
  let _x = add_and_print 1 2 in
  let _y = concat_and_print "a" "b" in
  ()
```

The *ocp-indent* home page (*https://github.com/OCamlPro/ocp-indent*) documents how
to integrate it with your favorite editor. All the Core libraries are formatted using it to
ensure consistency, and it's a good idea to do this before publishing your own source
code online.

Generating Documentation from Interfaces

Whitespace and source code comments are removed during parsing and aren't significant in determining the semantics of the program. However, other tools in the OCaml
distribution can interpret comments for their own ends.

The *ocamldoc* tool uses specially formatted comments in the source code to generate documentation bundles. These comments are combined with the function definitions and signatures, and output as structured documentation in a variety of formats. It can generate HTML pages, LaTeX and PDF documents, UNIX manual pages, and even module dependency graphs that can be viewed using Graphviz (*http://www.graph viz.org*).

Here's a sample of some source code that's been annotated with *ocamldoc* comments:

OCaml

```
(** example.ml: The first special comment of the file is the comment
    associated with the whole module. *)

(** Comment for exception My_exception. *)
exception My_exception of (int -> int) * int

(** Comment for type [weather]  *)
type weather =
  | Rain of int (** The comment for construtor Rain *)
  | Sun         (** The comment for constructor Sun *)

(** Find the current weather for a country
    @author Anil Madhavapeddy
    @param location The country to get the weather for.
*)
let what_is_the_weather_in location =
  match location with
  | `Cambridge  -> Rain 100
  | `New_york   -> Rain 20
  | `California -> Sun
```

The *ocamldoc* comments are distinguished by beginning with the double asterisk. There are formatting conventions for the contents of the comment to mark metadata. For instance, the @tag fields mark specific properties such as the author of that section of code.

Try compiling the HTML documentation and UNIX man pages by running *ocamldoc* over the source file:

Terminal

```
$ mkdir -p html man/man3
$ ocamldoc -html -d html doc.ml
$ ocamldoc -man -d man/man3 doc.ml
$ man -M man Doc
```

You should now have HTML files inside the *html/* directory and also be able to view the UNIX manual pages held in *man/man3*. There are quite a few comment formats and options to control the output for the various backends. Refer to the OCaml manual (*http://caml.inria.fr/pub/docs/manual-ocaml/manual029.html*) for the complete list.

Using Custom ocamldoc Generators

The default HTML output stylesheets from *ocamldoc* are pretty spartan and distinctly Web 1.0. The tool supports plugging in custom documentation generators, and there are several available that provide prettier or more detailed output:

- Argot (*http://argot.x9c.fr/*) is an enhanced HTML generator that supports code folding and searching by name or type definition.

- ocamldoc generators (*https://gitorious.org/ocamldoc-generators/ocamldoc-generators*) add support for Bibtex references within comments and generating literate documentation that embeds the code alongside the comments.

- JSON output is available via a custom generator (*https://github.com/xen-org/ocamldoc-json*) in Xen.

Preprocessing Source Code

One powerful feature in OCaml is a facility to extend the standard-language grammar without having to modify the compiler. You can roughly think of it as a type-safe version of the cpp preprocessor used in C/C++ to control conditional compilation directives.

The OCaml distribution includes a system called Camlp4 for writing extensible parsers. This provides some OCaml libraries that are used to define grammars, as well as dynamically loadable syntax extensions of such grammars. Camlp4 modules register new language keywords and later transform these keywords (or indeed, any portion of the input program) into conventional OCaml code that can be understood by the rest of the compiler.

We've already seen several Core libraries that use Camlp4:

Fieldslib
    Generates first-class values that represent fields of a record

Sexplib
    To convert types to textual s-expressions

Bin_prot
    For efficient binary conversion and parsing

These libraries all extend the language in quite a minimal way by adding a with keyword to type declarations to signify that extra code should be generated from that declaration. For example, here's a trivial use of Sexplib and Fieldslib:

OCaml

```
open Sexplib.Std
```

```
type t = {
  foo: int;
  bar: string
} with sexp, fields
```

Compiling this code will normally give you a syntax error if you do so without Camlp4, since the `with` keyword isn't normally allowed after a type definition:

```
$ ocamlfind ocamlc -c type_conv_example.ml
File "type_conv_example.ml", line 6, characters 2-6:
Error: Syntax error
```

Now add in the syntax extension packages for Fieldslib and Sexplib, and everything will compile again:

```
$ ocamlfind ocamlc -c -syntax camlp4o -package sexplib.syntax \
    -package fieldslib.syntax type_conv_example.ml
```

We've specified a couple of additional flags here. The `-syntax` flag directs *ocamlfind* to add the `-pp` flag to the compiler command line. This flag instructs the compiler to run the preprocessor during its parsing phase.

The `-package` flag imports other OCaml libraries. The `.syntax` suffix in the package name is a convention that indicates these libraries are preprocessors that should be run during parsing. The syntax extension modules are dynamically loaded into the *camlp4o* command, which rewrites the input source code into conventional OCaml code that has no trace of the new keywords. The compiler then compiles this transformed code with no knowledge of the preprocessor's actions.

Both Fieldslib and Sexplib need this new `with` keyword, but they both can't register the same extension. Instead, a library called Type_conv provides the common extension framework for them to use. Type_conv registers the `with` grammar extension to Camlp4, and the OCamlfind packaging ensures that it's loaded before Fieldslib or Sexplib.

The two extensions generate boilerplate OCaml code based on the type definition at compilation time. This avoids the performance hit of doing the code generation dynamically and also doesn't require a just-in-time (JIT) runtime that can be a source of unpredictable dynamic behavior. Instead, all the extra code is simply generated at compilation time via Camlp4, and type information can be discarded from the runtime image.

The syntax extensions accept an input AST and output a modified one. If you're not familiar with the Camlp4 module in question, how do you figure out what changes it's made to your code? The obvious way is to read the documentation that accompanies the extension. Another approach is to use the toplevel to explore the extension's behavior or run Camlp4 manually yourself to see the transformation in action. We'll show you how to do both of these now.

Using Camlp4 Interactively

The *utop* toplevel can run the phrases that you type through *camlp4* automatically. You should have at least these lines in your ~/.ocamlinit file in your home directory (see this Real World OCaml page (*http://realworldocaml.org/install*) for more information):

OCaml utop

```
# #use "topfind" ;;
- : unit = ()
Findlib has been successfully loaded. Additional directives:
  #require "package";;      to load a package
  #list;;                   to list the available packages
  #camlp4o;;                to load camlp4 (standard syntax)
  #camlp4r;;                to load camlp4 (revised syntax)
  #predicates "p,q,...";;   to set these predicates
  Topfind.reset();;         to force that packages will be reloaded
  #thread;;                 to enable threads

- : unit = ()
# #camlp4o ;;
```

The first directive loads the *ocamlfind* top-level interface that lets you require *ocamlfind* packages (including all their dependent packages). The second directive instructs the toplevel to filter all phrases via Camlp4. You can now run *utop* and load the syntax extensions in. We'll use the comparelib syntax extension for our experiments.

OCaml provides a built-in polymorphic comparison operator that inspects the runtime representation of two values to see if they're equal. As we noted in Chapter 13, the polymorphic comparison is less efficient than defining explicit comparison functions between values. However, it quickly becomes tedious to manually define comparison functions for complex type definitions.

Let's see how comparelib solves this problem by running it in *utop*:

OCaml utop (part 1)

```
# #require "comparelib.syntax" ;;
# type t = { foo: string; bar: t } ;;
type t = { foo : string; bar : t; }
# type t = { foo: string; bar: t } with compare ;;
type t = { foo : string; bar : t; }
val compare : t -> t -> int = <fun>
val compare_t : t -> t -> int = <fun>
```

The first definition of t is a standard OCaml phrase and results in the expected output. The second one includes the with compare directive. This is intercepted by compare lib and transformed into the original type definition with two new functions also included.

Running Camlp4 from the Command Line

The toplevel is a quick way to examine the signatures generated from the extensions, but how can we see what these new functions actually do? We can't do this from *utop* directly, since it embeds the Camlp4 invocation as an automated part of its operation.

Let's turn to the command line to obtain the result of the `comparelib` transformation instead. Create a file that contains the type declaration from earlier:

OCaml

```
type t = {
  foo: string;
  bar: t
} with compare
```

We need to run the Camlp4 binary with the library paths to Comparelib and Type_conv. Let's use a small shell script to wrap this invocation:

Shell script

```
#!/bin/sh

OCAMLFIND="ocamlfind query -predicates syntax,preprocessor -r"
INCLUDE=`$OCAMLFIND -i-format comparelib.syntax`
ARCHIVES=`$OCAMLFIND -a-format comparelib.syntax`
camlp4o -printer o $INCLUDE $ARCHIVES $1
```

The script uses the *ocamlfind* package manager to list the include and library paths needed by `comparelib`. It then invokes the *camlp4o* preprocessor with these paths and outputs the resulting AST to the standard output:

Terminal

```
$ sh camlp4_dump.cmd comparelib_test.ml
type t = { foo : string; bar : t }

let _ = fun (_ : t) -> ()

let rec compare : t -> t -> int =
  fun a__001_ b__002_ ->
    if Pervasives.( == ) a__001_ b__002_
    then 0
    else
      (let ret =
         (Pervasives.compare : string -> string -> int) a__001_.foo
           b__002_.foo
       in
         if Pervasives.( <> ) ret 0
         then ret
         else compare a__001_.bar b__002_.bar)

let _ = compare

let compare_t = compare
```

```
let _ = compare_t
```

The output contains the original type definition accompanied by some automatically generated code that implements an explicit comparison function for each field in the record. If you're using the extension in your compiler command line, this generated code is then compiled as if you had typed it in yourself.

Note that although the generated code uses `Pervasives.compare`, it is also annotated with a `string` type. This lets the compiler use a specialized string comparison function and not actually call the runtime polymorphic comparison function. This has implications for correctness, too: recall from Chapter 13 that `comparelib` provides reliable comparison functions that work for values that are logically the same but that have differing internal representations (e.g., `Int.Set.t`).

A Style Note: Wildcards in let Bindings

You may have noticed the `let _ = fun` construct in the autogenerated code above. The underscore in a `let` binding is just the same as a wildcard underscore in a pattern match, and tells the compiler to accept any return value and discard it immediately.

This is fine for mechanically generated code from Type_conv but should be avoided in code that you write by hand. If it's a unit-returning expression, then write a `unit` binding explicitly instead. This will cause a type error if the expression changes type in the future (e.g., due to code refactoring):

Syntax

```
let () = <expr>
```

If the expression has a different type, then write it explicitly:

OCaml

```
let (_:some_type) = <expr>
let () = ignore (<expr> : some_type)
)(* if the expression returns a unit Deferred.t *)
let () = don't_wait_for (<expr>
```

The last one is used to ignore Async expressions that should run in the background rather than blocking in the current thread.

One other important reason for using wildcard matches is to bind a variable name to something that you want to use in future code but don't want to use right away. This would normally generate an "unused value" compiler warning. These warnings are suppressed for any variable name that's prepended with an underscore:

OCaml

```
let fn x y =
  let _z = x + y in
  ()
```

Although you don't use _z in your code, this will never generate an unused variable warning.

Preprocessing Module Signatures

Another useful feature of type_conv is that it can generate module signatures, too. Copy the earlier type definition into a comparelib_test.mli that's got exactly the same content:

OCaml

```
type t = {
  foo: string;
  bar: t
} with compare
```

If you rerun the Camlp4 dumper script now, you'll see that different code is produced for signature files:

Terminal

```
$ sh camlp4_dump.cmd comparelib_test.mli
type t = { foo : string; bar : t }

val compare : t -> t -> int
```

The external signature generated by comparelib is much simpler than the actual code. Running Camlp4 directly on the original source code lets you see these all these transformations precisely.

Don't Overdo the Syntax Extensions

Syntax extensions are a powerful extension mechanism that can completely alter your source code's layout and style. Core includes a very conservative set of extensions that take care to minimize the syntax changes. There are a number of third-party libraries that are much more ambitious—some introduce whitespace-sensitive indentation, while others build entirely new embedded languages using OCaml as a host language, and yet others introduce conditional compilation for macros or optional logging.

While it's tempting to compress all your boilerplate code into Camlp4 extensions, it can make your source code much harder for other people to quickly read and understand. Core mainly focuses on type-driven code generation using the type_conv extension and doesn't fundamentally change the OCaml syntax.

Another thing to consider before deploying your own syntax extension is compatibility with other extensions. Two separate extensions can create a grammar clash that leads to odd syntax errors and hard-to-reproduce bugs. That's why most of Core's syntax extensions go through `type_conv`, which acts as a single point for extending the grammar via the `with` keyword.

Further Reading on Camlp4

We've deliberately only shown you how to use Camlp4 extensions here, and not how to build your own. The full details of building new extensions are fairly daunting and could be the subject of an entirely new book.

The best resources to get started are:

- A series of blog posts (*http://ambassadortothecomputers.blogspot.co.uk/p/reading-camlp4.html*) by Jake Donham describe the internals of Camlp4 and its syntax extension mechanism
- The online Camlp4 wiki (*http://brion.inria.fr/gallium/index.php/Camlp4*)
- Using OPAM to install existing Camlp4 extensions and inspecting their source code

Static Type Checking

After obtaining a valid abstract syntax tree, the compiler has to verify that the code obeys the rules of the OCaml type system. Code that is syntactically correct but misuses values is rejected with an explanation of the problem.

Although type checking is done in a single pass in OCaml, it actually consists of three distinct steps that happen simultaneously:

automatic type inference
> An algorithm that calculates types for a module without requiring manual type annotations

module system
> Combines software components with explicit knowledge of their type signatures

explicit subtyping
> Checks for objects and polymorphic variants

Automatic type inference lets you write succinct code for a particular task and have the compiler ensure that your use of variables is locally consistent.

Type inference doesn't scale to very large codebases that depend on separate compilation of files. A small change in one module may ripple through thousands of other files and libraries and require all of them to be recompiled. The module system solves this by providing the facility to combine and manipulate explicit type signatures for modules within a large project, and also to reuse them via functors and first-class modules.

Subtyping in OCaml objects is always an explicit operation (via the `:>` operator). This means that it doesn't complicate the core type inference engine and can be tested as a separate concern.

Displaying Inferred Types from the Compiler

We've already seen how you can explore type inference directly from the toplevel. It's also possible to generate type signatures for an entire file by asking the compiler to do the work for you. Create a file with a single type definition and value:

OCaml

```
type t = Foo | Bar
let v = Foo
```

Now run the compiler with the `-i` flag to infer the type signature for that file. This runs the type checker but doesn't compile the code any further after displaying the interface to the standard output:

Terminal

```
$ ocamlc -i typedef.ml
type t = Foo | Bar
val v : t
```

The output is the default signature for the module that represents the input file. It's often useful to redirect this output to an `mli` file to give you a starting signature to edit the external interface without having to type it all in by hand.

The compiler stores a compiled version of the interface as a `cmi` file. This interface is either obtained from compiling an `mli` signature file for a module, or by the inferred type if there is only an `ml` implementation present.

The compiler makes sure that your `ml` and `mli` files have compatible signatures. The type checker throws an immediate error if this isn't the case:

Terminal

```
$ echo type t = Foo > test.ml
$ echo type t = Bar > test.mli
$ ocamlc -c test.mli test.ml
File "test.ml", line 1:
Error: The implementation test.ml does not match the interface test.cmi:
       Type declarations do not match:
         type t = Foo
       is not included in
         type t = Bar
       File "test.ml", line 1, characters 5-12: Actual declaration
       Fields number 1 have different names, Foo and Bar.
```

Which Comes First: The ml or the mli?

There are two schools of thought on which order OCaml code should be written in. It's very easy to begin writing code by starting with an ml file and using the type inference to guide you as you build up your functions. The mli file can then be generated as described, and the exported functions documented.

If you're writing code that spans multiple files, it's sometimes easier to start by writing all the mli signatures and checking that they type-check against one another. Once the signatures are in place, you can write the implementations with the confidence that they'll all glue together correctly, with no cyclic dependencies among the modules.

As with any such stylistic debate, you should experiment with which system works best for you. Everyone agrees on one thing though: no matter in what order you write them, production code should always explicitly define an mli file for every ml file in the project. It's also perfectly fine to have an mli file without a corresponding ml file if you're only declaring signatures (such as module types).

Signature files provide a place to write succinct documentation and to abstract internal details that shouldn't be exported. Maintaining separate signature files also speeds up incremental compilation in larger code bases, since recompiling a mli signature is much faster than a full compilation of the implementation to native code.

Type Inference

Type inference is the process of determining the appropriate types for expressions based on their use. It's a feature that's partially present in many other languages such as Haskell and Scala, but OCaml embeds it as a fundamental feature throughout the core language.

OCaml type inference is based on the Hindley-Milner algorithm, which is notable for its ability to infer the most general type for an expression without requiring any explicit type annotations. The algorithm can deduce multiple types for an expression and has the notion of a *principal type* that is the most general choice from the possible inferences. Manual type annotations can specialize the type explicitly, but the automatic inference selects the most general type unless told otherwise.

OCaml does have some language extensions that strain the limits of principal type inference, but by and large, most programs you write will never *require* annotations (although they sometimes help the compiler produce better error messages).

Adding type annotations to find errors

It's often said that the hardest part of writing OCaml code is getting past the type checker —but once the code does compile, it works correctly the first time! This is an exaggeration of course, but it can certainly feel true when moving from a dynamically typed language. The OCaml static type system protects you from certain classes of bugs such as memory errors and abstraction violations by rejecting your program at compilation time rather than by generating an error at runtime. Learning how to navigate the type checker's compile-time feedback is key to building robust libraries and applications that take full advantage of these static checks.

There are a couple of tricks to make it easier to quickly locate type errors in your code. The first is to introduce manual type annotations to narrow down the source of your error more accurately. These annotations shouldn't actually change your types and can be removed once your code is correct. However, they act as anchors to locate errors while you're still writing your code.

Manual type annotations are particularly useful if you use lots of polymorphic variants or objects. Type inference with row polymorphism can generate some very large signatures, and errors tend to propagate more widely than if you are using more explicitly typed variants or classes.

For instance, consider this broken example that expresses some simple algebraic operations over integers:

OCaml

```
let rec algebra =
  function
  | `Add (x,y) -> (algebra x) + (algebra y)
  | `Sub (x,y) -> (algebra x) - (algebra y)
  | `Mul (x,y) -> (algebra x) * (algebra y)
  | `Num x     -> x

let _ =
  algebra (
    `Add (
      (`Num 0),
      (`Sub (
          (`Num 1),
          (`Mul (
              (`Nu 3),(`Num 2)
            ))
        ))
    ))
```

There's a single character typo in the code so that it uses Nu instead of Num. The resulting type error is impressive:

Terminal

```
$ ocamlc -c broken_poly.ml
File "broken_poly.ml", line 9, characters 10-154:
Error: This expression has type
         [> `Add of
             ([< `Add of 'a * 'a
              | `Mul of 'a * 'a
              | `Num of int
```

```
          | `Sub of 'a * 'a
          > `Num ]
        as 'a) *
          [> `Sub of 'a * [> `Mul of [> `Nu of int ] * [> `Num of int ] ] ] ]
 but an expression was expected of type 'a
 The second variant type does not allow tag(s) `Nu
```

The type error is perfectly accurate, but rather verbose and with a line number that doesn't point to the exact location of the incorrect variant name. The best the compiler can do is to point you in the general direction of the `algebra` function application.

This is because the type checker doesn't have enough information to match the inferred type of the `algebra` definition to its application a few lines down. It calculates types for both expressions separately, and when they don't match up, outputs the difference as best it can.

Let's see what happens with an explicit type annotation to help the compiler out:

OCaml

```
type t = [
  | `Add of t * t
  | `Sub of t * t
  | `Mul of t * t
  | `Num of int
]

let rec algebra (x:t) =
  match x with
  | `Add (x,y) -> (algebra x) + (algebra y)
  | `Sub (x,y) -> (algebra x) - (algebra y)
  | `Mul (x,y) -> (algebra x) * (algebra y)
  | `Num x     -> x

let _ =
  algebra (
    `Add (
      (`Num 0),
      (`Sub (
          (`Num 1),
          (`Mul (
              (`Nu 3),(`Num 2)
          ))
      ))
    ))
```

This code contains exactly the same error as before, but we've added a closed type definition of the polymorphic variants, and a type annotation to the `algebra` definition. The compiler error we get is much more useful now:

Terminal

```
$ ocamlc -i broken_poly_with_annot.ml
File "broken_poly_with_annot.ml", line 22, characters 14-21:
```

```
Error: This expression has type [> `Nu of int ]
       but an expression was expected of type t
       The second variant type does not allow tag(s) `Nu
```

This error points directly to the correct line number that contains the typo. Once you fix the problem, you can remove the manual annotations if you prefer more succinct code. You can also leave the annotations there, of course, to help with future refactoring and debugging.

Enforcing principal typing

The compiler also has a stricter *principal type checking* mode that is activated via the -principal flag. This warns about risky uses of type information to ensure that the type inference has one principal result. A type is considered risky if the success or failure of type inference depends on the order in which subexpressions are typed.

The principality check only affects a few language features:

- Polymorphic methods for objects
- Permuting the order of labeled arguments in a function from their type definition
- Discarding optional labeled arguments
- Generalized algebraic data types (GADTs) present from OCaml 4.0 onward
- Automatic disambiguation of record field and constructor names (since OCaml 4.1)

Here's an example of principality warnings when used with record disambiguation.

OCaml

```
type s = { foo: int; bar: unit }
type t = { foo: int }

let f x =
  x.bar;
  x.foo
```

Inferring the signature with -principal will show you a new warning:

Terminal

```
$ ocamlc -i -principal non_principal.ml
File "non_principal.ml", line 6, characters 4-7:
Warning 18: this type-based field disambiguation is not principal.
type s = { foo : int; bar : unit; }
type t = { foo : int; }
val f : s -> int
```

This example isn't principal, since the inferred type for x.foo is guided by the inferred type of x.bar, whereas principal typing requires that each subexpression's type can be calculated independently. If the x.bar use is removed from the definition of f, its argument would be of type t and not type s.

You can fix this either by permuting the order of the type declarations, or by adding an explicit type annotation:

OCaml

```
type s = { foo: int; bar: unit }
type t = { foo: int }

let f (x:s) =
  x.bar;
  x.foo
```

There is now no ambiguity about the inferred types, since we've explicitly given the argument a type, and the order of inference of the subexpressions no longer matters.

Terminal

```
$ ocamlc -i -principal principal.ml
type s = { foo : int; bar : unit; }
type t = { foo : int; }
val f : s -> int
```

The *ocamlbuild* equivalent is to add the tag `principal` to your build. The *corebuild* wrapper script actually adds this by default, but it does no harm to explicitly repeat it:

Terminal

```
$ corebuild -tag principal principal.cmi non_principal.cmi
File "non_principal.ml", line 6, characters 4-7:
Warning 18: this type-based field disambiguation is not principal.
```

Ideally, all code should systematically use `-principal`. It reduces variance in type inference and enforces the notion of a single known type. However, there are drawbacks to this mode: type inference is slower, and the `cmi` files become larger. This is generally only a problem if you extensively use objects, which usually have larger type signatures to cover all their methods.

If compiling in principal mode works, it is guaranteed that the program will pass type checking in nonprincipal mode, too. For this reason, the *corebuild* wrapper script activates principal mode by default, preferring stricter type inference over a small loss in compilation speed and extra disk space usage.

Bear in mind that the `cmi` files generated in principal mode differ from the default mode. Try to ensure that you compile your whole project with it activated. Getting the files mixed up won't let you violate type safety, but it can result in the type checker failing unexpectedly very occasionally. In this case, just recompile with a clean source tree.

Modules and Separate Compilation

The OCaml module system enables smaller components to be reused effectively in large projects while still retaining all the benefits of static type safety. We covered the basics of using modules earlier in Chapter 4. The module language that operates over these signatures also extends to functors and first-class modules, described in Chapter 9 and Chapter 10, respectively.

This section discusses how the compiler implements them in more detail. Modules are essential for larger projects that consist of many source files (also known as *compilation units*). It's impractical to recompile every single source file when changing just one or two files, and the module system minimizes such recompilation while still encouraging code reuse.

The mapping between files and modules

Individual compilation units provide a convenient way to break up a big module hierarchy into a collection of files. The relationship between files and modules can be explained directly in terms of the module system.

Create a file called `alice.ml` with the following contents:

OCaml

```
let friends = [ Bob.name ]
```

and a corresponding signature file:

OCaml

```
val friends : Bob.t list
```

These two files are exactly analogous to including the following code directly in another module that references `Alice`:

OCaml

```
module Alice : sig
  val friends : Bob.t list
end = struct
  let friends = [ Bob.name ]
end
```

Defining a module search path

In the preceding example, `Alice` also has a reference to another module `Bob`. For the overall type of `Alice` to be valid, the compiler also needs to check that the `Bob` module contains at least a `Bob.name` value and defines a `Bob.t` type.

The type checker resolves such module references into concrete structures and signatures in order to unify types across module boundaries. It does this by searching a list of directories for a compiled interface file matching that module's name. For example, it will look for `alice.cmi` and `bob.cmi` on the search path and use the first ones it encounters as the interfaces for `Alice` and `Bob`.

The module search path is set by adding `-I` flags to the compiler command line with the directory containing the cmi files as the argument. Manually specifying these flags gets complex when you have lots of libraries, and is the reason why the OCamlfind frontend to the compiler exists. OCamlfind automates the process of turning third-party package names and build descriptions into command-line flags that are passed to the compiler command line.

By default, only the current directory and the OCaml standard library will be searched for cmi files. The Pervasives module from the standard library will also be opened by default in every compilation unit. The standard library location is obtained by running ocamlc -where and can be overridden by setting the CAMLLIB environment variable. Needless to say, don't override the default path unless you have a good reason to (such as setting up a cross-compilation environment).

Inspecting Compilation Units with ocamlobjinfo

For separate compilation to be sound, we need to ensure that all the cmi files used to type-check a module are the same across compilation runs. If they vary, this raises the possibility of two modules checking different type signatures for a common module with the same name. This in turn lets the program completely violate the static type system and can lead to memory corruption and crashes.

OCaml guards against this by recording a MD5 checksum in every cmi. Let's examine our earlier typedef.ml more closely:

Terminal

```
$ ocamlc -c typedef.ml
$ ocamlobjinfo typedef.cmi
File typedef.cmi
Unit name: Typedef
Interfaces imported:
        bd274dc132ce5c3d8b6774d19cd373a6 Typedef
        36b5bc8227dc9914c6d9fd9bdcfadb45 Pervasives
```

ocamlobjinfo examines the compiled interface and displays what other compilation units it depends on. In this case, we don't use any external modules other than Perva sives. Every module depends on Pervasives by default, unless you use the - nopervasives flag (this is an advanced use case, and you shouldn't normally need it).

The long alphanumeric identifier beside each module name is a hash calculated from all the types and values exported from that compilation unit. It's used during type-checking and linking to ensure that all of the compilation units have been compiled consistently against one another. A difference in the hashes means that a compilation unit with the same module name may have conflicting type signatures in different modules. The compiler will reject such programs with an error similar to this:

Terminal

```
$ ocamlc -c foo.ml
File "foo.ml", line 1, characters 0-1:
Error: The files /home/build/bar.cmi
        and /usr/lib/ocaml/map.cmi make inconsistent assumptions
        over interface Map
```

This hash check is very conservative, but ensures that separate compilation remains type-safe all the way up to the final link phase. Your build system should ensure that you never see the preceding error messages, but if you do run into it, just clean out your intermediate files and recompile from scratch.

Packing Modules Together

The module-to-file mapping described so far rigidly enforces a 1:1 mapping between a top-level module and a file. It's often convenient to split larger modules into separate files to make editing easier, but still compile them all into a single OCaml module.

The `-pack` compiler option accepts a list of compiled object files (`.cmo` in bytecode and `.cmx` for native code) and their associated `.cmi` compiled interfaces, and combines them into a single module that contains them as submodules of the output. Packing thus generates an entirely new `.cmo` (or `.cmx` file) and `.cmi` that includes the input modules.

Packing for native code introduces an additional requirement: the modules that are intended to be packed must be compiled with the `-for-pack` argument that specifies the eventual name of the pack. The easiest way to handle packing is to let *ocamlbuild* figure out the command-line arguments for you, so let's try that out next with a simple example.

First, create a couple of toy modules called A.ml and B.ml that contain a single value. You will also need a _tags file that adds the `-for-pack` option for the cmx files (but careful to exclude the pack target itself). Finally, the X.mlpack file contains the list of modules that are intended to be packed under module X. There are special rules in *ocamlbuild* that tell it how to map %.mlpack files to the packed %.cmx or %.cmo equivalent:

Terminal

```
$ cat A.ml
let v - "hello"
$ cat B.ml
let w = 42
$ cat _tags
<*.cmx> and not "X.cmx": for-pack(X)
$ cat X.mlpack
A
B
```

You can now run *corebuild* to build the X.cmx file directly, but let's create a new module to link against X to complete the example:

OCaml

```
let v = X.A.v
let w = X.B.w
```

You can now compile this test module and see that its inferred interface is the result of using the packed contents of X. We further verify this by examining the imported interfaces in Test and confirming that neither A nor B are mentioned in there and that only the packed X module is used:

Terminal

```
$ corebuild test.inferred.mli test.cmi
$ cat _build/test.inferred.mli
val v : string
val w : int
$ ocamlobjinfo _build/test.cmi
File _build/test.cmi
Unit name: Test
Interfaces imported:
        906fc1b74451f0c24ceaa085e0f26e5f Test
        36b5bc8227dc9914c6d9fd9bdcfadb45 Pervasives
        25f4b4e10ec64c56b2987f5900045fec X
```

Packing and Search Paths

One very common build error that happens with packing is confusion resulting from building the packed cmi in the same directory as the submodules. When you add this directory to your module search path, the submodules are also visible. If you forget to include the top-level prefix (e.g., X.A) and instead use a submodule directly (A), then this will compile and link fine.

However, the types of A and X.A are *not* automatically equivalent so the type checker will complain if you attempt to mix and match the packed and unpacked versions of the library.

This mostly only happens with unit tests, since they are built at the same time as the library. You can avoid it by being aware of the need to open the packed module from the test, or only using the library after it has been installed (and hence not exposing the intermediate compiled modules).

Shorter Module Paths in Type Errors

Core uses the OCaml module system quite extensively to provide a complete replacement standard library. It collects these modules into a single Std module, which provides a single module that needs to be opened to import the replacement modules and functions.

There's one downside to this approach: type errors suddenly get much more verbose. We can see this if you run the vanilla OCaml toplevel (not *utop*).

Terminal

```
$ ocaml
# List.map print_endline "" ;;
```

```
Error: This expression has type string but an expression was expected of type
        string list
```

This type error without `Core.Std` has a straightforward type error. When we switch to Core, though, it gets more verbose:

```
$ ocaml
# open Core.Std ;;
# List.map ~f:print_endline "" ;;
Error: This expression has type string but an expression was expected of type
        'a Core.Std.List.t = 'a list
```

The default `List` module in OCaml is overridden by `Core.Std.List`. The compiler does its best to show the type equivalence, but at the cost of a more verbose error message.

The compiler can remedy this via a so-called short paths heuristic. This causes the compiler to search all the type aliases for the shortest module path and use that as the preferred output type. The option is activated by passing `-short-paths` to the compiler, and works on the toplevel, too.

```
$ ocaml -short-paths
# open Core.Std;;
# List.map ~f:print_endline "foo";;
Error: This expression has type string but an expression was expected of type
        'a list
```

The *utop* enhanced toplevel activates short paths by default, which is why we have not had to do this before in our interactive examples. However, the compiler doesn't default to the short path heuristic, since there are some situations where the type aliasing information is useful to know, and it would be lost in the error if the shortest module path is always picked.

You'll need to choose for yourself if you prefer short paths or the default behavior in your own projects, and pass the `-short-paths` flag to the compiler if you need it.

The Typed Syntax Tree

When the type checking process has successfully completed, it is combined with the AST to form a *typed abstract syntax tree*. This contains precise location information for every token in the input file, and decorates each token with concrete type information.

The compiler can output this as compiled `cmt` and `cmti` files that contain the typed AST for the implementation and signatures of a compilation unit. This is activated by passing the `-bin-annot` flag to the compiler.

The `cmt` files are particularly useful for IDE tools to match up OCaml source code at a specific location to the inferred or external types.

Using ocp-index for Autocompletion

One such command-line tool to display autocompletion information in your editor is *ocp-index*. Install it via OPAM as follows:

Terminal

```
$ opam install ocp-index
$ ocp-index
```

Let's refer back to our Ncurses binding example from the beginning of Chapter 19. This module defined bindings for the Ncurses library. First, compile the interfaces with -bin-annot so that we can obtain the cmt and cmti files, and then run *ocp-index* in completion mode:

Terminal

```
$ corebuild -pkg ctypes.foreign -tag bin_annot ncurses.cmi
$ ocp-index complete -I . Ncur
Ncurses module
$ ocp-index complete -I . Ncurses.a
Ncurses.addstr val string -> unit
$ ocp-index complete -I . Ncurses.
Ncurses.window val Ncurses.window Ctypes.typ
Ncurses.wrefresh val Ncurses.window -> unit
Ncurses.initscr val unit -> Ncurses.window
Ncurses.endwin val unit -> unit
Ncurses.refresh val unit -> unit
Ncurses.newwin val int -> int -> int -> int -> Ncurses.window
Ncurses.mvwaddch val Ncurses.window -> int -> int -> char -> unit
Ncurses.mvwaddstr val Ncurses.window -> int -> int -> string -> unit
Ncurses.addstr val string -> unit
Ncurses.box val Ncurses.window -> char -> char -> unit
Ncurses.cbreak val unit -> int
```

You need to pass *ocp-index* a set of directories to search for cmt files in, and a fragment of text to autocomplete. As you can imagine, autocompletion is invaluable on larger codebases. See the *ocp-index* (*https://github.com/ocamlpro/ocp-index*) home page for more information on how to integrate it with your favorite editor.

Examining the Typed Syntax Tree Directly

The compiler has a couple of advanced flags that can dump the raw output of the internal AST representation. You can't depend on these flags to give the same output across compiler revisions, but they are a useful learning tool.

We'll use our toy typedef.ml again:

OCaml

```
type t = Foo | Bar
let v = Foo
```

Let's first look at the untyped syntax tree that's generated from the parsing phase:

```
$ ocamlc -dparsetree typedef.ml 2>&1
[
  structure_item (typedef.ml[1,0+0]..[1,0+18])
    Pstr_type
    [
      "t" (typedef.ml[1,0+5]..[1,0+6])
        type_declaration (typedef.ml[1,0+5]..[1,0+18])
          ptype_params =
            []
          ptype_cstrs =
            []
          ptype_kind =
            Ptype_variant
              [
                (typedef.ml[1,0+9]..[1,0+12])
                  "Foo" (typedef.ml[1,0+9]..[1,0+12])
                  []
                  None
                (typedef.ml[1,0+15]..[1,0+18])
                  "Bar" (typedef.ml[1,0+15]..[1,0+18])
                  []
                  None
              ]
          ptype_private = Public
          ptype_manifest =
            None
    ]
  structure_item (typedef.ml[2,19+0]..[2,19+11])
    Pstr_value Nonrec
    [
      <def>
        pattern (typedef.ml[2,19+4]..[2,19+5])
          Ppat_var "v" (typedef.ml[2,19+4]..[2,19+5])
        expression (typedef.ml[2,19+8]..[2,19+11])
          Pexp_construct "Foo" (typedef.ml[2,19+8]..[2,19+11])
          None
          false
    ]
]
```

This is rather a lot of output for a simple two-line program, but it shows just how much structure the OCaml parser generates even from a small source file.

Each portion of the AST is decorated with the precise location information (including the filename and character location of the token). This code hasn't been type checked yet, so the raw tokens are all included.

The typed AST that is normally output as a compiled cmt file can be displayed in a more developer-readable form via the -dtypedtree option:

```
$ ocamlc -dtypedtree typedef.ml 2>&1
[
  structure_item (typedef.ml[1,0+0]..typedef.ml[1,0+18])
    Pstr_type
    [
      t/1008
        type_declaration (typedef.ml[1,0+5]..typedef.ml[1,0+18])
          ptype_params =
            []
          ptype_cstrs =
            []
          ptype_kind =
            Ptype_variant
              [
                "Foo/1009"
                []
                "Bar/1010"
                []
              ]
          ptype_private = Public
          ptype_manifest =
            None
    ]
  structure_item (typedef.ml[2,19+0]..typedef.ml[2,19+11])
    Pstr_value Nonrec
    [
      <def>
        pattern (typedef.ml[2,19+4]..typedef.ml[2,19+5])
          Ppat_var "v/1011"
        expression (typedef.ml[2,19+8]..typedef.ml[2,19+11])
          Pexp_construct "Foo"
          []
          false
    ]
]
```

The typed AST is more explicit than the untyped syntax tree. For instance, the type declaration has been given a unique name (t/1008), as has the v value (v/1011).

You'll rarely need to look at this raw output from the compiler unless you're building IDE tools such as *ocp-index*, or are hacking on extensions to the core compiler itself. However, it's useful to know that this intermediate form exists before we delve further into the code generation process next, in Chapter 23.

There are several new integrated tools emerging that combine these typed AST files with common editors such as Emacs or Vim. The best of these is Merlin (*https://github.com/def-lkb/merlin*), which adds value and module autocompletion, displays inferred types and can build and display errors directly from within your editor. There are instructions available on its homepage for configuring Merlin with your favorite editor.

## CHAPTER 23

The Compiler Backend: Bytecode and Native code

Once OCaml has passed the type checking stage, it can stop emitting syntax and type errors and begin the process of compiling the well-formed modules into executable code.

In this chapter, we'll cover the following topics:

- The untyped intermediate lambda code where pattern matching is optimized
- The bytecode *ocamlc* compiler and *ocamlrun* interpreter
- The native code *ocamlopt* code generator, and debugging and profiling native code

The Untyped Lambda Form

The first code generation phase eliminates all the static type information into a simpler intermediate *lambda form*. The lambda form discards higher-level constructs such as modules and objects and replaces them with simpler values such as records and function pointers. Pattern matches are also analyzed and compiled into highly optimized automata.

The lambda form is the key stage that discards the OCaml type information and maps the source code to the runtime memory model described in Chapter 20. This stage also performs some optimizations, most notably converting pattern-match statements into more optimized but low-level statements.

Pattern Matching Optimization

The compiler dumps the lambda form in an s-expression syntax if you add the -dlambda directive to the command line. Let's use this to learn more about how the OCaml pattern-matching engine works by building three different pattern matches and comparing their lambda forms.

Let's start by creating a straightforward exhaustive pattern match using four normal variants:

OCaml

```
type t = | Alice | Bob | Charlie | David

let test v =
  match v with
  | Alice   -> 100
  | Bob     -> 101
  | Charlie -> 102
  | David   -> 103
```

The lambda output for this code looks like this:

Terminal

```
$ ocamlc -dlambda -c pattern_monomorphic_large.ml 2>&1
(setglobal Pattern_monomorphic_large!
  (let
    (test/1013
      (function v/1014
        (switch* v/1014
          case int 0: 100
          case int 1: 101
          case int 2: 102
          case int 3: 103)))
  (makeblock 0 test/1013)))
```

It's not important to understand every detail of this internal form, and it is explicitly undocumented since it can change across compiler revisions. Despite these caveats, some interesting points emerge from reading it:

- There are no mention of modules or types any more. Global values are created via setglobal, and OCaml values are constructed by makeblock. The blocks are the runtime values you should remember from Chapter 20.

- The pattern match has turned into a switch case that jumps to the right case depending on the header tag of v. Recall that variants without parameters are stored in memory as integers in the order which they appear. The pattern-matching engine knows this and has transformed the pattern into an efficient jump table.

- Values are addressed by a unique name that distinguishes shadowed values by appending a number (e.g., v/1014). The type safety checks in the earlier phase ensure that these low-level accesses never violate runtime memory safety, so this layer doesn't do any dynamic checks. Unwise use of unsafe features such as the `Obj.mag ic` module can still easily induce crashes at this level.

The compiler computes a jump table in order to handle all four cases. If we drop the number of variants to just two, then there's no need for the complexity of computing this table:

OCaml

```ocaml
type t = | Alice | Bob

let test v =
  match v with
  | Alice   -> 100
  | Bob     -> 101
```

The lambda output for this code is now quite different:

Terminal

```
$ ocamlc -dlambda -c pattern_monomorphic_small.ml 2>&1
(setglobal Pattern_monomorphic_small!
  (let (test/1011 (function v/1012 (if (!= v/1012 0) 101 100)))
    (makeblock 0 test/1011)))
```

The compiler emits simpler conditional jumps rather than setting up a jump table, since it statically determines that the range of possible variants is small enough. Finally, let's look at the same code, but with polymorphic variants instead of normal variants:

OCaml

```ocaml
let test v =
  match v with
  | `Alice   -> 100
  | `Bob     -> 101
  | `Charlie -> 102
  | `David   -> 103
  | `Eve     -> 104
```

The lambda form for this also shows up the runtime representation of polymorphic variants:

Terminal

```
$ ocamlc -dlambda -c pattern_polymorphic.ml 2>&1
(setglobal Pattern_polymorphic!
  (let
    (test/1008
      (function v/1009
        (if (!= v/1009 3306965)
          (if (>= v/1009 482771474) (if (>= v/1009 884917024) 100 102)
          (if (>= v/1009 3457716) 104 103))
        101)))
    (makeblock 0 test/1008)))
```

We mentioned in Chapter 6 that pattern matching over polymorphic variants is slightly less efficient, and it should be clearer why this is the case now. Polymorphic variants have a runtime value that's calculated by hashing the variant name, and so the compiler can't use a jump table as it does for normal variants. Instead, it creates a decision tree that compares the hash values against the input variable in as few comparisons as possible.

Learning More About Pattern Matching Compilation

Pattern matching is an important part of OCaml programming. You'll often encounter deeply nested pattern matches over complex data structures in real code. A good paper that describes the fundamental algorithms implemented in OCaml is "Optimizing pattern matching" (*http://dl.acm.org/citation.cfm?id=507641*) by Fabrice Le Fessant and Luc Maranget.

The paper describes the backtracking algorithm used in classical pattern matching compilation, and also several OCaml-specific optimizations, such as the use of exhaustiveness information and control flow optimizations via static exceptions.

It's not essential that you understand all of this just to use pattern matching, of course, but it'll give you insight as to why pattern matching is such a lightweight language construct to use in OCaml code.

Benchmarking Pattern Matching

Let's benchmark these three pattern-matching techniques to quantify their runtime costs more accurately. The Core_bench module runs the tests thousands of times and also calculates statistical variance of the results. You'll need to opam install core_bench to get the library:

OCaml

```
open Core.Std
open Core_bench.Std

type t = | Alice | Bob
type s = | A | B | C | D | E

let polymorphic_pattern () =
  let test v =
    match v with
    | `Alice    -> 100
    | `Bob      -> 101
    | `Charlie -> 102
    | `David    -> 103
    | `Eve      -> 104
  in
  List.iter ~f:(fun v -> ignore(test v))
    [`Alice; `Bob; `Charlie; `David]
```

```
let monomorphic_pattern_small () =
  let test v =
    match v with
    | Alice    -> 100
    | Bob      -> 101 in
  List.iter ~f:(fun v -> ignore(test v))
    [ Alice; Bob ]

let monomorphic_pattern_large () =
  let test v =
    match v with
    | A        -> 100
    | B        -> 101
    | C        -> 102
    | D        -> 103
    | E        -> 104
  in
  List.iter ~f:(fun v -> ignore(test v))
    [ A; B; C; D ]

let tests = [
  "Polymorphic pattern", polymorphic_pattern;
  "Monomorphic larger pattern", monomorphic_pattern_large;
  "Monomorphic small pattern", monomorphic_pattern_small;
]

let () =
  List.map tests ~f:(fun (name,test) -> Bench.Test.create ~name test)
  |> Bench.make_command
  |> Command.run
```

Building and executing this example will run for around 30 seconds by default, and
you'll see the results summarized in a neat table:

Terminal

```
$ corebuild -pkg core_bench bench_patterns.native
$ ./bench_patterns.native -ascii
Estimated testing time 30s (change using -quota SECS).

  Name                        Time (ns)   % of max
  --------------------------- ----------- ----------
  Polymorphic pattern            31.51     100.00
  Monomorphic larger pattern     29.19      92.62
  Monomorphic small pattern      16.25      51.57
```

These results confirm the performance hypothesis that we obtained earlier by inspecting
the lambda code. The shortest running time comes from the small conditional pattern
match, and polymorphic variant pattern matching is the slowest. There isn't a hugely
significant difference in these examples, but you can use the same techniques to peer
into the innards of your own source code and narrow down any performance hotspots.

The lambda form is primarily a stepping stone to the bytecode executable format that we'll cover next. It's often easier to look at the textual output from this stage than to wade through the native assembly code from compiled executables.

Generating Portable Bytecode

After the lambda form has been generated, we are very close to having executable code. The OCaml toolchain branches into two separate compilers at this point. We'll describe the bytecode compiler first, which consists of two pieces:

ocamlc
> Compiles files into a bytecode that is a close mapping to the lambda form

ocamlrun
> A portable interpreter that executes the bytecode

The big advantage of using bytecode is simplicity, portability, and compilation speed. The mapping from the lambda form to bytecode is straightforward, and this results in predictable (but slow) execution speed.

The bytecode interpreter implements a stack-based virtual machine. The OCaml stack and an associated accumulator store values that consist of:

long
> Values that correspond to an OCaml int type

block
> Values that contain the block header and a memory address with the data fields that contain further OCaml values indexed by an integer

code offset
> Values that are relative to the starting code address

The interpreter virtual machine only has seven registers in total: the program counter, stack pointer, accumulator, exception and argument pointers, and environment and global data. You can display the bytecode instructions in textual form via -dinstr. Try this on one of our earlier pattern-matching examples:

Terminal

```
$ ocamlc -dinstr pattern_monomorphic_small.ml 2>&1
        branch L2
L1: acc 0
        push
        const 0
        neqint
        branchifnot L3
        const 101
        return 1
L3: const 100
        return 1
```

```
L2: closure L1, 0
      push
      acc 0
      makeblock 1, 0
      pop 1
      setglobal Pattern_monomorphic_small!
```

The preceding bytecode has been simplified from the lambda form into a set of simple instructions that are executed serially by the interpreter.

There are around 140 instructions in total, but most are just minor variants of commonly encountered operations (e.g., function application at a specific arity). You can find full details online (*http://cadmium.x9c.fr/distrib/caml-instructions.pdf*).

Where Did the Bytecode Instruction Set Come From?

The bytecode interpreter is much slower than compiled native code, but is still remarkably performant for an interpreter without a JIT compiler. Its efficiency can be traced back to Xavier Leroy's ground-breaking work in 1990, "The ZINC experiment: An Economical Implementation of the ML Language". (*http://hal.inria.fr/docs/00/07/00/49/PS/RT-0117.ps*)

This paper laid the theoretical basis for the implementation of an instruction set for a strictly evaluated functional language such as OCaml. The bytecode interpreter in modern OCaml is still based on the ZINC model. The native code compiler uses a different model since it uses CPU registers for function calls instead of always passing arguments on the stack, as the bytecode interpreter does.

Understanding the reasoning behind the different implementations of the bytecode interpreter and the native compiler is a very useful exercise for any budding language hacker.

Compiling and Linking Bytecode

The *ocamlc* command compiles individual ml files into bytecode files that have a cmo extension. The compiled bytecode files are matched with the associated cmi interface, which contains the type signature exported to other compilation units.

A typical OCaml library consists of multiple source files, and hence multiple cmo files that all need to be passed as command-line arguments to use the library from other code. The compiler can combine these multiple files into a more convenient single archive file by using the -a flag. Bytecode archives are denoted by the cma extension.

The individual objects in the library are linked as regular cmo files in the order specified when the library file was built. If an object file within the library isn't referenced elsewhere in the program, then it isn't included in the final binary unless the `-linkall` flag forces its inclusion. This behavior is analogous to how C handles object files and archives (`.o` and `.a`, respectively).

The bytecode files are then linked together with the OCaml standard library to produce an executable program. The order in which `.cmo` arguments are presented on the command line defines the order in which compilation units are initialized at runtime. Remember that OCaml has no single `main` function like C, so this link order is more important than in C programs.

Executing Bytecode

The bytecode runtime comprises three parts: the bytecode interpreter, GC, and a set of C functions that implement the primitive operations. The bytecode contains instructions to call these C functions when required.

The OCaml linker produces bytecode that targets the standard OCaml runtime by default, and so needs to know about any C functions that are referenced from other libraries that aren't loaded by default.

Information about these extra libraries can be specified while linking a bytecode archive:

Terminal

```
$ ocamlc -a -o mylib.cma a.cmo b.cmo -dllib -lmylib
```

The `dllib` flag embeds the arguments in the archive file. Any subsequent packages linking this archive will also include the extra C linking directive. This in turn lets the interpreter dynamically load the external library symbols when it executes the bytecode.

You can also generate a complete standalone executable that bundles the *ocamlrun* interpreter with the bytecode in a single binary. This is known as a *custom runtime* mode and is built as follows:

Terminal

```
$ ocamlc -a -o mylib.cma -custom a.cmo b.cmo -cclib -lmylib
```

OCamlbuild takes care of many of these details with its built-in rules. The `%.byte` rule that you've been using throughout the book builds a bytecode executable, and adding the `custom` tag will bundle the interpreter with it, too.

The custom mode is the most similar mode to native code compilation, as both generate standalone executables. There are quite a few other options available for compiling bytecode (notably with shared libraries or building custom runtimes). Full details can be found in the OCaml (*http://caml.inria.fr/pub/docs/manual-ocaml/manual022.html*).

Embedding OCaml Bytecode in C

A consequence of using the bytecode compiler is that the final link phase must be performed by *ocamlc*. However, you might sometimes want to embed your OCaml code inside an existing C application. OCaml also supports this mode of operation via the `-output-obj` directive.

This mode causes *ocamlc* to output an object file containing the bytecode for the OCaml part of the program, as well as a `caml_startup` function. All of the OCaml modules are linked into this object file as bytecode, just as they would be for an executable.

This object file can then be linked with C code using the standard C compiler, needing only the bytecode runtime library (which is installed as `libcamlrun.a`). Creating an executable just requires you to link the runtime library with the bytecode object file. Here's an example to show how it all fits together.

Create two OCaml source files that contain a single print line:

OCaml

```
let () = print_endline "hello embedded world 1"
```

OCaml

```
let () = print_endline "hello embedded world 2"
```

Next, create a C file to be your main entry point:

C

```
#include <stdio.h>
#include <caml/alloc.h>
#include <caml/mlvalues.h>
#include <caml/memory.h>
#include <caml/callback.h>

int
main (int argc, char **argv)
{
  printf("Before calling OCaml\n");
  fflush(stdout);
  caml_startup (argv);
  printf("After calling OCaml\n");
  return 0;
}
```

Now compile the OCaml files into a standalone object file:

Terminal

```
$ rm -f embed_out.c
$ ocamlc -output-obj -o embed_out.o embed_me1.ml embed_me2.ml
```

After this point, you no longer need the OCaml compiler, as `embed_out.o` has all of the OCaml code compiled and linked into a single object file. Compile an output binary using *gcc* to test this out:

```
$ gcc -fPIC -Wall -I`ocamlc -where` -L`ocamlc -where` -ltermcap -lm -ldl \
  -o finalbc.native main.c embed_out.o -lcamlrun
$ ./finalbc.native
Before calling OCaml
hello embedded world 1
hello embedded world 2
After calling OCaml
```

You can inspect the commands that *ocamlc* is invoking by adding -verbose to the command line to help figure out the GCC command line if you get stuck. You can even obtain the C source code to the -output-obj result by specifying a .c output file extension instead of the .o we used earlier:

```
$ ocamlc -output-obj -o embed_out.c embed_me1.ml embed_me2.ml
```

Embedding OCaml code like this lets you write OCaml that interfaces with any environment that works with a C compiler. You can even cross back from the C code into OCaml by using the Callback module to register named entry points in the OCaml code. This is explained in detail in the interfacing with C (*http://caml.inria.fr/pub/docs/manual-ocaml/manual033.html#toc149*) section of the OCaml manual.

Compiling Fast Native Code

The native code compiler is ultimately the tool that most production OCaml code goes through. It compiles the lambda form into fast native code executables, with cross-module inlining and additional optimization passes that the bytecode interpreter doesn't perform. Care is taken to ensure compatibility with the bytecode runtime, so the same code should run identically when compiled with either toolchain.

The *ocamlopt* command is the frontend to the native code compiler and has a very similar interface to *ocamlc*. It also accepts ml and mli files, but compiles them to:

- A .o file containing native object code
- A .cmx file containing extra information for linking and cross-module optimization
- A .cmi compiled interface file that is the same as the bytecode compiler

When the compiler links modules together into an executable, it uses the contents of the cmx files to perform cross-module inlining across compilation units. This can be a significant speedup for standard library functions that are frequently used outside of their module.

Collections of .cmx and .o files can also be be linked into a .cmxa archive by passing the -a flag to the compiler. However, unlike the bytecode version, you must keep the individual cmx files in the compiler search path so that they are available for cross-

---

module inlining. If you don't do this, the compilation will still succeed, but you will have missed out on an important optimization and have slower binaries.

Inspecting Assembly Output

The native code compiler generates assembly language that is then passed to the system assembler for compiling into object files. You can get *ocamlopt* to output the assembly by passing the -S flag to the compiler command line.

The assembly code is highly architecture-specific, so the following discussion assumes an Intel or AMD 64-bit platform. We've generated the example code using -inline 20 and -nodynlink since it's best to generate assembly code with the full optimizations that the compiler supports. Even though these optimizations make the code a bit harder to read, it will give you a more accurate picture of what executes on the CPU. Don't forget that you can use the lambda code from earlier to get a slightly higher-level picture of the code if you get lost in the more verbose assembly.

The impact of polymorphic comparison

We warned you in Chapter 13 that using polymorphic comparison is both convenient and perilous. Let's look at precisely what the difference is at the assembly language level now.

First let's create a comparison function where we've explicitly annotated the types, so the compiler knows that only integers are being compared:

OCaml

```
let cmp (a:int) (b:int) =
  if a > b then a else b
```

Now compile this into assembly and read the resulting compare_mono.S file. This file extension may be lowercase on some platforms such as Linux:

Terminal

```
$ ocamlopt -inline 20 -nodynlink -S compare_mono.ml
```

If you've never seen assembly language before, then the contents may be rather scary. While you'll need to learn x86 assembly to fully understand it, we'll try to give you some basic instructions to spot patterns in this section. The excerpt of the implementation of the cmp function can be found below:

Assembly

```
_camlCompare_mono__cmp_1008:
        .cfi_startproc
.L101:
        cmpq    %rbx, %rax
        jle     .L100
        ret
        .align  2
.L100:
```

```
        movq    %rbx, %rax
        ret
        .cfi_endproc
```

The _camlCompare_mono__cmp_1008 is an assembly label that has been computed from
the module name (Compare_mono) and the function name (cmp_1008). The numeric
suffix for the function name comes straight from the lambda form (which you can
inspect using -dlambda, but in this case isn't necessary).

The arguments to cmp are passed in the %rbx and %rax registers, and compared using
the jle "jump if less than or equal" instruction. This requires both the arguments to be
immediate integers to work. Now let's see what happens if our OCaml code omits the
type annotations and is a polymorphic comparison instead:

OCaml

```
let cmp a b =
  if a > b then a else b
```

Compiling this code with -S results in a significantly more complex assembly output
for the same function:

Assembly

```
_camlCompare_poly__cmp_1008:
        .cfi_startproc
        subq    $24, %rsp
        .cfi_adjust_cfa_offset   24
.L101:
        movq    %rax, 8(%rsp)
        movq    %rbx, 0(%rsp)
        movq    %rax, %rdi
        movq    %rbx, %rsi
        leaq    _caml_greaterthan(%rip), %rax
        call    _caml_c_call
.L102:
        leaq    _caml_young_ptr(%rip), %r11
        movq    (%r11), %r15
        cmpq    $1, %rax
        je      .L100
        movq    8(%rsp), %rax
        addq    $24, %rsp
        .cfi_adjust_cfa_offset   -24
        ret
        .cfi_adjust_cfa_offset   24
        .align  2
.L100:
        movq    0(%rsp), %rax
        addq    $24, %rsp
        .cfi_adjust_cfa_offset   -24
        ret
        .cfi_adjust_cfa_offset   24
        .cfi_endproc
```

The .cfi directives are assembler hints that contain Call Frame Information that lets the debugger provide more sensible backtraces, and they have no effect on runtime performance. Notice that the rest of the implementation is no longer a simple register comparison. Instead, the arguments are pushed on the stack (the %rsp register), and a C function call is invoked by placing a pointer to caml_greaterthan in %rax and jumping to caml_c_call.

OCaml on x86_64 architectures caches the location of the minor heap in the %r15 register since it's so frequently referenced in OCaml functions. The minor heap pointer can also be changed by the C code that's being called (e.g., when it allocates OCaml values), and so %r15 is restored after returning from the caml_greaterthan call. Finally, the return value of the comparison is popped from the stack and returned.

Benchmarking polymorphic comparison

You don't have to fully understand the intricacies of assembly language to see that this polymorphic comparison is much heavier than the simple monomorphic integer comparison from earlier. Let's confirm this hypothesis again by writing a quick Core_bench test with both functions:

OCaml

```
open Core.Std
open Core_bench.Std

let polymorphic_compare () =
  let cmp a b = if a > b then a else b in
  for i = 0 to 1000 do
    ignore(cmp 0 i)
  done

let monomorphic_compare () =
  let cmp (a:int) (b:int) =
    if a > b then a else b in
  for i = 0 to 1000 do
    ignore(cmp 0 i)
  done

let tests =
  [ "Polymorphic comparison", polymorphic_compare;
    "Monomorphic comparison", monomorphic_compare ]

let () =
  List.map tests ~f:(fun (name,test) -> Bench.Test.create ~name test)
  |> Bench.make_command
  |> Command.run
```

Running this shows quite a significant runtime difference between the two:

Terminal

```
$ corebuild -pkg core_bench bench_poly_and_mono.native
$ ./bench_poly_and_mono.native -ascii
```

```
Estimated testing time 20s (change using -quota SECS).

Name                        Time (ns)   % of max
-----------------------     ----------  ----------
Polymorphic comparison         13_919      100.00
Monomorphic comparison            815        5.86
```

We see that the polymorphic comparison is close to 20 times slower! These results shouldn't be taken too seriously, as this is a very narrow test that, like all such microbenchmarks, isn't representative of more complex codebases. However, if you're building numerical code that runs many iterations in a tight inner loop, it's worth manually peering at the produced assembly code to see if you can hand-optimize it.

Debugging Native Code Binaries

The native code compiler builds executables that can be debugged using conventional system debuggers such as GNU *gdb*. You need to compile your libraries with the -g option to add the debug information to the output, just as you need to with C compilers.

Extra debugging information is inserted into the output assembly when the library is compiled in debug mode. These include the CFI stubs you will have noticed in the profiling output earlier (.cfi_start_proc and .cfi_end_proc to delimit an OCaml function call, for example).

Understanding name mangling

So how do you refer to OCaml functions in an interactive debugger like *gdb*? The first thing you need to know is how OCaml function names compile down to symbol names in the compiled object files, a procedure generally called *name mangling*.

Each OCaml source file is compiled into a native object file that must export a unique set of symbols to comply with the C binary interface. This means that any OCaml values that may be used by another compilation unit need to be mapped onto a symbol name. This mapping has to account for OCaml language features such as nested modules, anonymous functions, and variable names that shadow one another.

The conversion follows some straightforward rules for named variables and functions:

- The symbol is prefixed by caml and the local module name, with dots replaced by underscores.
- This is followed by a double __ suffix and the variable name.
- The variable name is also suffixed by a _ and a number. This is the result of the lambda compilation, which replaces each variable name with a unique value within the module. You can determine this number by examining the -dlambda output from *ocamlopt*.

Anonymous functions are hard to predict without inspecting intermediate compiler output. If you need to debug them, it's usually easier to modify the source code to let-bind the anonymous function to a variable name.

Interactive breakpoints with the GNU debugger

Let's see name mangling in action with some interactive debugging using GNU *gdb*.

Beware gdb on Mac OS X

The examples here assume that you are running *gdb* on either Linux or FreeBSD. Mac OS X 10.8 does have *gdb* installed, but it's a rather quirky experience that doesn't reliably interpret the debugging information contained in the native binaries. This can result in function names showing up as raw symbols such as .L101 instead of their more human-readable form.

For OCaml 4.1, we'd recommend you do native code debugging on an alternate platform such as Linux, or manually look at the assembly code output to map the symbol names onto their precise OCaml functions.

MacOS 10.9 removes *gdb* entirely and uses the lldb debugger from the LLVM project by default. Many of the guidelines here still apply since the debug information embedded in the binary output can be interpreted by lldb (or any other DWARF-aware debugger), but the command-line interfaces to lldb is different from *gdb*. Refer to the lldb manual for more information.

Let's write a mutually recursive function that selects alternating values from a list. This isn't tail-recursive, so our stack size will grow as we single-step through the execution:

OCaml

```
open Core.Std

let rec take =
  function
  |[] -> []
  |hd::tl -> hd :: (skip tl)
and skip =
  function
  |[] -> []
  |_::tl -> take tl

let () =
  take [1;2;3;4;5;6;7;8;9]
  |> List.map ~f:string_of_int
  |> String.concat ~sep:","
  |> print_endline
```

Compile and run this with debugging symbols. You should see the following output:

```
$ corebuild -tag debug alternate_list.native
$ ./alternate_list.native -ascii
1,3,5,7,9
```

Now we can run this interactively within *gdb*:

```
$ gdb ./alternate_list.native
GNU gdb (GDB) 7.4.1-debian
Copyright (C) 2012 Free Software Foundation, Inc.
License GPLv3+: GNU GPL version 3 or later <http://gnu.org/licenses/gpl.html>
This is free software: you are free to change and redistribute it.
There is NO WARRANTY, to the extent permitted by law.  Type "show copying"
and "show warranty" for details.
This GDB was configured as "x86_64-linux-gnu".
For bug reporting instructions, please see:
<http://www.gnu.org/software/gdb/bugs/>...
Reading symbols from /home/avsm/alternate_list.native...done.
(gdb)
```

The *gdb* prompt lets you enter debug directives. Let's set the program to break just before the first call to take:

```
(gdb) break camlAlternate_list__take_69242
Breakpoint 1 at 0x5658d0: file alternate_list.ml, line 5.
```

We used the C symbol name by following the name mangling rules defined earlier. A convenient way to figure out the full name is by tab completion. Just type in a portion of the name and press the <tab> key to see a list of possible completions.

Once you've set the breakpoint, start the program executing:

```
(gdb) run
Starting program: /home/avsm/alternate_list.native
[Thread debugging using libthread_db enabled]
Using host libthread_db library "/lib/x86_64-linux-gnu/libthread_db.so.1".

Breakpoint 1, camlAlternate_list__take_69242 () at alternate_list.ml:5
4           function
```

The binary has run until the first take invocation and stopped, waiting for further instructions. GDB has lots of features, so let's continue the program and check the stack-trace after a couple of recursions:

```
(gdb) cont
Continuing.

Breakpoint 1, camlAlternate_list__take_69242 () at alternate_list.ml:5
4           function
(gdb) cont
```

```
Continuing.

Breakpoint 1, camlAlternate_list__take_69242 () at alternate_list.ml:5
4          function
(gdb) bt
#0  camlAlternate_list__take_69242 () at alternate_list.ml:4
#1  0x00000000005658e7 in camlAlternate_list__take_69242 () at alternate_list.ml:6
#2  0x00000000005658e7 in camlAlternate_list__take_69242 () at alternate_list.ml:6
#3  0x00000000005659f7 in camlAlternate_list__entry () at alternate_list.ml:14
#4  0x0000000000560029 in caml_program ()
#5  0x000000000080984a in caml_start_program ()
#6  0x00000000008099a0 in ?? ()
#7  0x0000000000000000 in ?? ()
(gdb) clear camlAlternate_list__take_69242
Deleted breakpoint 1
(gdb) cont
Continuing.
1,3,5,7,9
[Inferior 1 (process 3546) exited normally]
```

The cont command resumes execution after a breakpoint has paused it, bt displays a stack backtrace, and clear deletes the breakpoint so the application can execute until completion. GDB has a host of other features we won't cover here, but you can view more guidelines via Mark Shinwell's talk on "Real-world debugging in OCaml." (*http:// www.youtube.com/watch?v=NF2WpWnB-nk<*)

One very useful feature of OCaml native code is that C and OCaml share the same stack. This means that GDB backtraces can give you a combined view of what's going on in your program *and* runtime library. This includes any calls to C libraries or even callbacks into OCaml from the C layer if you're in an environment which embeds the OCaml runtime as a library.

Profiling Native Code

The recording and analysis of where your application spends its execution time is known as *performance profiling*. OCaml native code binaries can be profiled just like any other C binary, by using the name mangling described earlier to map between OCaml variable names and the profiler output.

Most profiling tools benefit from having some instrumentation included in the binary. OCaml supports two such tools:

- GNU *gprof*, to measure execution time and call graphs
- The Perf (*https://perf.wiki.kernel.org/*) profiling framework in modern versions of Linux

Note that many other tools that operate on native binaries, such as Valgrind, will work just fine with OCaml as long as the program is linked with the -g flag to embed debugging symbols.

Gprof

gprof produces an execution profile of an OCaml program by recording a call graph of which functions call one another, and recording the time these calls take during the program execution.

Getting precise information out of *gprof* requires passing the -p flag to the native code compiler when compiling *and* linking the binary. This generates extra code that records profile information to a file called gmon.out when the program is executed. This profile information can then be examined using *gprof*.

Perf

Perf is a more modern alternative to *gprof* that doesn't require you to instrument the binary. Instead, it uses hardware counters and debug information within the binary to record information accurately.

Run Perf on a compiled binary to record information first. We'll use our write barrier benchmark from earlier, which measures memory allocation versus in-place modification:

Terminal

```
$ perf record -g ./barrier_bench.native
Estimated testing time 20s (change using -quota SECS).

  Name       Time (ns)           Time 95ci    Percentage
  ----       ---------           ---------    ----------
  mutable    7_306_219    7_250_234-7_372_469      96.83
  immutable  7_545_126    7_537_837-7_551_193     100.00

[ perf record: Woken up 11 times to write data ]
[ perf record: Captured and wrote 2.722 MB perf.data (~118926 samples) ]
perf record -g ./barrier.native
Estimated testing time 20s (change using -quota SECS).

  Name       Time (ns)           Time 95ci    Percentage
  ----       ---------           ---------    ----------
  mutable    7_306_219    7_250_234-7_372_469      96.83
  immutable  7_545_126    7_537_837-7_551_193     100.00

[ perf record: Woken up 11 times to write data ]
[ perf record: Captured and wrote 2.722 MB perf.data (~118926 samples) ]
```

When this completes, you can interactively explore the results:

Terminal

```
$ perf report -g
+   48.86%  barrier.native  barrier.native  [.] camlBarrier__test_immutable_69282
```

```
+   30.22%   barrier.native   barrier.native   [.] camlBarrier__test_mutable_69279
+   20.22%   barrier.native   barrier.native   [.] caml_modify
```

This trace broadly reflects the results of the benchmark itself. The mutable benchmark consists of the combination of the call to `test_mutable` and the `caml_modify` write barrier function in the runtime. This adds up to slightly over half the execution time of the application.

Perf has a growing collection of other commands that let you archive these runs and compare them against each other. You can read more on the home page (*http://perf.wiki.kernel.org*).

Using the Frame Pointer to Get More Accurate Traces

Although Perf doesn't require adding in explicit probes to the binary, it does need to understand how to unwind function calls so that the kernel can accurately record the function backtrace for every event.

OCaml stack frames are too complex for Perf to understand directly, and so it needs the compiler to fall back to using the same conventions as C for function calls. On 64-bit Intel systems, this means that a special register known as the *frame pointer* is used to record function call history.

Using the frame pointer in this fashion means a slowdown (typically around 3-5%) since it's no longer available for general-purpose use. OCaml 4.1 thus makes the frame pointer an optional feature that can be used to improve the resolution of Perf traces.

OPAM provides a compiler switch that compiles OCaml with the frame pointer activated:

Terminal

```
$ opam switch 4.01.0+fp
```

Using the frame pointer changes the OCaml calling convention, but OPAM takes care of recompiling all your libraries with the new interface. You can read more about this on the OCamlPro blog (*http://www.ocamlpro.com/blog/2012/08/08/profile-native-code.html*).

Embedding Native Code in C

The native code compiler normally links a complete executable, but can also output a standalone native object file just as the bytecode compiler can. This object file has no further dependencies on OCaml except for the runtime library.

The native code runtime is a different library from the bytecode one, and is installed as `libasmrun.a` in the OCaml standard library directory.

Try this custom linking by using the same source files from the bytecode embedding example earlier in this chapter:

```
$ ocamlopt -output-obj -o embed_native.o embed_me1.ml embed_me2.ml
$ gcc -Wall -I `ocamlc -where` -o final.native embed_native.o main.c \
    -L `ocamlc -where` -lasmrun -ltermcap -lm -ldl
$ ./final.native
Before calling OCaml
hello embedded world 1
hello embedded world 2
After calling OCaml
```

The embed_native.o is a standalone object file that has no further references to OCaml code beyond the runtime library, just as with the bytecode runtime. Do remember that the link order of the libraries is significant in modern GNU toolchains (especially as used in Ubuntu 11.10 and later) that resolve symbols from left to right in a single pass.

Activating the Debug Runtime

Despite your best efforts, it is easy to introduce a bug into some components, such as C bindings, that causes heap invariants to be violated. OCaml includes a libasmrund.a variant of the runtime library which is compiled with extra debugging checks that perform extra memory integrity checks during every garbage collection cycle. Running these extra checks will abort the program nearer the point of corruption and help isolate the bug in the C code.

To use the debug library, just link your program with the -runtime-variant d flag:

```
$ ocamlopt -runtime-variant d -verbose -o hello.native hello.ml
$ ./hello.native
### OCaml runtime: debug mode ###
Initial minor heap size: 2048k bytes
Initial major heap size: 992k bytes
Initial space overhead: 80%
Initial max overhead: 500%
Initial heap increment: 992k bytes
Initial allocation policy: 0
Hello OCaml World!
```

If you get an error that libasmrund.a is not found, it's probably because you're using OCaml 4.00 and not 4.01. It's only installed by default in the very latest version, which you should be using via the 4.01.0 OPAM switch.

Summarizing the File Extensions

We've seen how the compiler uses intermediate files to store various stages of the compilation toolchain. Here's a cheat sheet of all them in one place.

Table 23-1 shows the intermediate files generated by *ocamlc*.

Table 23-1. Intermediate files generated by the OCaml compiler toolchain

Extension	Purpose
.ml	Source files for compilation unit module implementations.
.mli	Source files for compilation unit module interfaces. If missing, generated from the .ml file.
.cmi	Compiled module interface from a corresponding .mli source file.
.cmo	Compiled bytecode object file of the module implementation.
.cma	Library of bytecode object files packed into a single file.
.o	C source files are compiled into native object files by the system cc.
.cmt	Typed abstract syntax tree for module implementations.
.cmti	Typed abstract syntax tree for module interfaces.
.annot	Old-style annotation file for displaying typed, superseded by cmt files.

The native code compiler generates some additional files (see Table 23-2).

Table 23-2. Intermediate outputs produced by the native code OCaml toolchain

Extension	Purpose
.o	Compiled native object file of the module implementation.
.cmx	Contains extra information for linking and cross-module optimization of the object file.
.cmxa and .a	Library of cmx and o units, stored in the cmxa and a files respectively. These files are always needed together.
.S *or* .s	Assembly language output if -S is specified.

Index

Symbols

%.byte rule, 456

A

abstract types, 71, 76, 197
algebraic data types, 107
alignment, formatting with printf, 163
animation
    creating with mixins, 247
    displaying animated shapes, 249
annotations, for type checking, 437
anonymous arguments, 272
anonymous functions, 20, 31
Arg module, 292
Argot HTML generator, 427
arguments
    anonymous arguments, 272
    argument types, 275
    default arguments, 277
    defining custom types, 276
    inference of, 45
    labeled arguments, 11, 40, 289
    optional arguments, 43–48, 277
    sequences of, 279
    unit argument to callbacks, 273
Array module
    Array.blit, 144
    Array.set, 144

array-like data, 143
arrays
    definition of, 388
    imperative programming and, 20
    memory representation of, 400
    pointers and, 380
assert directive, 131
association lists, 253
AST (abstract syntax-tree), 312, 396, 424, 445
Async library
    basics of, 342–347
    benefits of, 342
    DuckDuckGo searching example, 353–356
    echo server example, 347–353
    exception handling in, 357–363
    ivars, 345
    system threads and, 366–369
    timeouts and cancellations, 363
ATDgen Library
    annotations in, 305
    basics of, 304
    compiling specifications to OCaml, 305
    example of, 307
    installation of, 303
autocompletion, 290, 446
automatic type inference, 434
    (see also type inference)

We'd like to hear your suggestions for improving our indexes. Send email to index@oreilly.com.

B

backtraces, 135, 461
bash autocompletion, 290
benign effects
    laziness, 151
    memoization, 153–159
Bibtex, 427
bigarrays, 144, 405
Bigstring module, 405
binary methods, 239
binary numbers, formatting with printf, 163
bind function, 127, 344
bindings
    scope of, 27
    top-level, 27
    wildcards in let bindings, 432
Bin_prot library, 428
BLAS mathematical library, 405
block values, 454
blocking, 342
blocks (of memory), 396–399
boxing (of values), 397
byte arrays, 144
bytecode compiler
    compiling and linking code, 455
    instruction set for, 455
    vs. native-code compiler, 69
    tools used, 454
    values stored by, 454

C

C object files, 457
C99 scalar types, 379
callback function, 273, 285, 289
Camlimages library, 217
Camlp4 syntax extension mechanism, 329, 428–434
Camomile unicode parser, 321
cancellations, 363
catch-all cases, 118
classes
    basic syntax for, 227
    benefits of, 217
    binary methods for, 239
    class parameters and polymorphism, 228
    class types, 234
    inheritance in, 233
    initializers for, 245

    multiple inheritance in, 245
    object types as interfaces, 230
    open recursion in, 236
    private methods for, 237
    virtual classes, 242
client queries, 354
Cmdliner, 292
cmi files, 442, 458
cmt files, 445
cmti files, 445
cmx files, 458
code compilers
    bytecode vs. native code, 69, 422
    order of code, 436
        (see also compilaton process)
    warning enable/disable, 89
code offset values, 454
cohttp library, 353
combinators
    functional combinators, 271, 297
    in Yojson library, 298
Command module, 285
command-line parsing
    advanced control over, 284–290
    alternatives to Command library, 292
    argument types, 275
    autocompletion with bash, 290
    basic approach to, 272
    Command library for, 271
    labeled flags and, 280
    subcommand grouping, 282
    with Camlp4, 431
Command.basic module, 273
Command.group, 282
commas vs. semicolons, 12
compaction, 414
Comparable module
    Comparable.Make, 192, 260
    Comparable.S, 260
Comparator.Poly module, 258
comparators, creating maps with, 255
compilation process
    compiler source code, 422
    diagram of, 422
    fast native code, 458–468
    file extensions, 469
    parsing source code, 424–427
    phases of, 396
    portable bytecode, 454–458

dynamic type checking, 223, 240, 396

E

echo servers, 347–353
edit distance, 154
elements
    combining with List.reduce, 58
    defining new, 149
    inserting in lists, 149
    partitioning with List.partition_tf, 60
    setting with Array.set, 144
    traversing with iterator objects, 230
ellipses (..), 215
end-of-file condition, 347
eprintf function, 163
equal (=) operator, 270
equal equal (= =) operator, 270
equality, tests of, 270
error handling
    combining exceptions and error-aware
        types, 137
    error-aware return types, 123–128
    exception backtracing, 135
    exception clean up, 132
    exception detection, 133
    exception handlers, 132
    exception helper functions, 131
    exceptions, 128
    and imperative data structures, 150
    strategy choice, 138
    (see also errors)
error-aware return types, 123–128, 137
Error.of_list, 126
Error.t type, 125
Error.tag, 126
errors
    catch-all cases and refactoring, 105
    compiler warnings, 89
    cyclic dependencies, 82
    detecting with match statements, 54
    detecting with type annotations, 437
    error messages with s-expressions, 334
    "give up on first error" approach, 322
    missing field warnings, 89
    missing module definitions, 81
    module type definition mismatches, 82
    module type mismatches, 81
    reducing verbosity in, 444
    runtime vs. compile time, 9

syntax errors, 424
timeouts and cancellations, 363
transformation of, 126
type errors, 301
    (see also error handling)
evaluation, order of, 166
event loops, 341
exceptions
    asynchronous errors, 358
    benefits and drawbacks of, 138
    catching specific, 133
    and error-aware types, 137
    exception clean up, 132
    exception handlers, 132
    helper functions for, 131
    in concurrent programming, 357
    search engine example, 361
    stack backtraces for, 135
    textual representation of, 130
    usefulness of, 128
    vs. type errors, 9
exhaustion checks, 107
Exn module
    Backtrace.Exn.set_recording false, 135
    Exn.backtrace, 135
exn type, 129
explicit subtyping, 434
    (see also subtyping)
expressions, order of evaluation, 166
extensible parsers, 428
extensions (see syntax extensions)
external libraries
    Camlimages, 217
    Cryptokit, 217
    for graphics, 250
    interfacing with, 146
external memory, 405

F

Field module
    Field.fset, 100
    Field.get, 100
    Field.name, 100
    Field.setter, 100
fields
    adding to structures, 384
    field punning, 18, 91
    first-class fields, 98–102
    mutability of, 140, 145

Gc module, 408
    (see also garbage collection)
gdb debugger, 462
generational garbage collection, 408
generational hypothesis, 408
geometric shapes, 217, 242
GitHub API, 304, 307
GNU debugger, 463
gprof code profiler, 466
grammars
    avoiding grammar clashes, 433
    context-free, 314
    extension of standard language, 428
graphics libraries, 250
gray values, 413

H

hash tables
    basics of, 254, 264
    vs. maps, 267
    polymorphic hash function, 266
    satisfying Hashable.S interface, 266
    time complexity of, 264
Hashable.Make, 192, 266
Hashable.S interface, 266
Hashtbl module, 264
heaps
    definition of, 407
    heap blocks, 407
    Heap_block module, 419
    major heaps, 410–418
    minor heaps, 408
    regions of, 408
hex numbers, formatting with printf, 163
higher-order functions, and labels, 42
Hindley-Milner algorithm, 436
HTML generators, 427
HTTP client queries, 354

I

I.Query_handler module, 203
I/O (input/output) operations
    copying data, 347
    file I/O, 163
    formatted output, 161
    terminal I/O, 159
identifiers
    adding to modules, 79

dealing with multiple, 75
    open modules and, 77
imperative programming
    arrays, 20
    benefits of, 139
    benign effects and, 151
    doubly-linked lists, 147–151
    drawbacks of, 150
    for and while loops, 23
    imperative dictionaries, 140–143
    input and output, 159–165
    mutable record fields, 21
    order of evaluation, 166
    overview of, 173
    primitive mutable data, 143
    ref type, 22
    side effects/weak polymorphism, 167–173
impure heaps, 413
infix operators, 35
inheritance, 233, 245
initializers, 245
install keyword, 282
installation instructions, xix
integers, 397, 399
interactive input
    with camlp4, 430
    concurrent programming for, 341
    prompts for, 287
interfaces
    Comparable.S, 260
    foreign function interface (FFI), 373–394
    generating documentation from, 426
    Hashable.S, 266
    hiding implementation details with, 71
    object types as, 230
    with OCaml binaries, 395
    synonyms for, 72
intergenerational pointers, 415
interval computation
    abstract functor for, 181
    comparison function for, 180
    destructive substitution, 184
    generic library for, 177
    multiple interfaces and, 185
    sharing constraints, 182
invariance, 219
invariant checks, 333
In_channel module, 160
In_thread module, 367

R

Random module, 23
Reader module, 347
rec keyword, 34
record field accessor functions, 98
records
    basic syntax for, 87
    construction of, 91
    field punning in, 91
    first-class fields in, 98–102
    functional updates to, 96
    label punning in, 91
    memory representation of, 400
    missing field warnings, 89
    mutable fields in, 97
    patterns and exhaustiveness in, 88
    record types, 18, 22
    reusing field names, 92–95
    and variant types, 107–111
recursion
    in lexers, 320
    in json types, 295
    open recursion, 217, 236
    tail recursion, 61
recursive data structures, 111
recursive functions
    definition of, 34
    list functions, 14
ref cells, 145
refactoring, 105, 287
regular expressions, 318
remembered sets, 415
remote keyword, 282
representation types, 240
Result.t option, 125
return function, 344
returning function, 386
rev_object_fields, 316
RFC3986, 353
RFC4627, 293, 354
risky type, 439
root values, 413
row polymorphism, 215, 224, 437
runtime exceptions vs. type errors, 9
runtime memory representation
    blocks and values, 398
    custom heap blocks, 405
    importance of, 395
    polymorphic variants, 403

    string values, 404
    tuples, records, and arrays, 400
    variants and lists, 401

S

s-expressions
    basic usage of, 326
    deserializing a type from, 334
    example of, 126, 185
    format of, 329
    generating from OCaml types, 328
    modifying default behavior of, 336
    preserving invariants in, 331
    in queries and responses, 199
    specifying defaults in, 338
    uses for, 325
scalar C types, 378
Scheduler.go, 349
scope, 27
search engines, 353
security issues
    denial-of-service attacks, 265
    Obj module warning, 402
segfaults, 369
semantic actions, 315
semicolons vs. commas, 12
serialization formats
    JSON, 293–310
    s-expressions, 325–340
set types, 260
sexp declaration, 130, 185, 199
Sexplib package
    sexp converter, 126, 256, 428
    sexp_list, 337
    sexp_opaque, 336
    sexp_option, 338
    syntax extension in, 328
    Type_conv library and, 329
shadowing, 28
sharing constraint, 182
short paths heuristic, 445
side effects, 151, 167
signatures
    abstract types, 71
    concrete types, 74
    preprocessing module signatures, 433
source code
    automatically indenting, 425
    parsing of, 424–427

About the Authors

Yaron Minsky heads the technology group at Jane Street, a proprietary trading firm that is the largest industrial user of OCaml. He was responsible for introducing OCaml to the company and for managing the company's transition to using OCaml for all of its core infrastructure. Today, billions of dollars worth of securities transactions flow each day through those systems. Yaron obtained his PhD in Computer Science from Cornell University, where he studied distributed systems. Yaron has lectured, blogged, and written about OCaml for years, with articles published in *Communications of the ACM* and the *Journal of Functional Programming*. He chairs the steering committee of the Commercial Users of Functional Programming, and is a member of the steering committee for the International Conference on Functional Programming.

Anil Madhavapeddy is a senior research fellow at the University of Cambridge, based in the Systems Research Group. He was on the original team that developed the Xen hypervisor, and he helped develop an industry-leading cloud management toolstack written entirely in OCaml. This XenServer product has been deployed on hundreds of thousands of physical hosts and drives critical infrastructure for many Fortune 500 companies. Prior to obtaining his PhD in 2006 from the University of Cambridge, Anil had a diverse background in industry at Network Appliance, NASA, and Internet Vision. In addition to professional and academic activities, he is an active member of the open source development community with the OpenBSD operating system, is co-chair of the Commercial Uses of Functional Programming workshop, and serves on the boards of startup companies such as Ashima Arts, where OCaml is extensively used.

Jason Hickey is a software engineer at Google Inc. in Mountain View, California. He is part of the team that designs and develops the global computing infrastructure used to support Google services, including the software systems for managing and scheduling massively distributed computing resources. Prior to joining Google, Jason was an assistant professor of computer science at Caltech, where his research was in reliable and fault-tolerant computing systems, including programming language design, formal methods, compilers, and new models of distributed computation. He obtained his PhD in computer science from Cornell University, where he studied programming languages. He is the author of the MetaPRL system, a logical framework for design and analysis of large software systems; and OMake, an advanced build system for large software projects. He is also the author of the textbook *An Introduction to Objective Caml* (unpublished).

Colophon

The animal on the cover of *Real World OCaml* is the Bactrian camel (*Camelus bactrianus*). The Bactrian camel, one of two species of camel, is native to Central Asia and has been used domestically in the area for thousands of years. Even though there are over two million domesticated Bactrian camels, only about a thousand are considered wild.

The Bactrian camel is a large animal at 6 to 7.5 feet in height and 7.4 to 11.5 feet in length. An adult will typically weigh between 660 and 2,200 pounds. The Bactrian camel is distinctive for its two large humps on their back, hefty wooly coat, and dark brown color. It is a herbivore that will eat all kinds of vegetation, though they have been known to feed on dead animals.

Humans have domesticated the Bactrian camel for travel purposes because of its great natural resiliency. For example, the Bactrian camel can thrive in habitats of both extreme cold and heat. It can also go without water for months and when water is available it can consume up to 55 litres.

The cover image is from *Meyers Kleines Lexicon*. The cover fonts are URW Typewriter and Guardian Sans. The text font is Adobe Minion Pro; the heading font is Adobe Myriad Condensed; and the code font is Dalton Maag's Ubuntu Mono.

Get even more for your money.

Join the O'Reilly Community, and register the O'Reilly books you own. It's free, and you'll get:

- $4.99 ebook upgrade offer
- 40% upgrade offer on O'Reilly print books
- Membership discounts on books and events
- Free lifetime updates to ebooks and videos
- Multiple ebook formats, DRM FREE
- Participation in the O'Reilly community
- Newsletters
- Account management
- 100% Satisfaction Guarantee

Signing up is easy:

1. **Go to: oreilly.com/go/register**
2. **Create an O'Reilly login.**
3. **Provide your address.**
4. **Register your books.**

Note: English-language books only

To order books online:
oreilly.com/store

For questions about products or an order:
orders@oreilly.com

To sign up to get topic-specific email announcements and/or news about upcoming books, conferences, special offers, and new technologies:
elists@oreilly.com

For technical questions about book content:
booktech@oreilly.com

To submit new book proposals to our editors:
proposals@oreilly.com

O'Reilly books are available in multiple DRM-free ebook formats. For more information:
oreilly.com/ebooks

Spreading the knowledge of innovators   oreilly.com

Have it your way.

Lightning Source UK Ltd.
Milton Keynes UK
UKOW07f1135290416

273222UK00002B/7/P